Archibald Hamilton Bryce, of Sicca Arnobius, Hugh Campbell

The Seven Books of Arnobius Adversus Gentes

Archibald Hamilton Bryce, of Sicca Arnobius, Hugh Campbell
The Seven Books of Arnobius Adversus Gentes
ISBN/EAN: 9783744660075
Printed in Europe, USA, Canada, Australia, Japan
Cover: Foto ©ninafisch / pixelio.de

More available books at **www.hansebooks.com**

CLARK'S
FOREIGN THEOLOGICAL LIBRARY.

ANNUAL SUBSCRIPTION:
One Guinea (payable in advance) for Four Volumes, Demy 8vo.
When not paid in advance, the Retail Bookseller is entitled to charge 24s.

N.B.—Any two Years in this Series can be had at Subscription Price. A single Year's Books (except in the case of the current Year) cannot be supplied separately. Non-subscribers, price 10s. 6d. each volume, with exceptions marked.

1 8 6 4—
    Lange on the Acts of the Apostles. Two Volumes.
    Keil and Delitzsch on the Pentateuch. Vols. I. and II.

1 8 6 5—
    Keil and Delitzsch on the Pentateuch. Volume III.
    Hengstenberg on the Gospel of John. Two Volumes.
    Keil and Delitzsch on Joshua, Judges, and Ruth. One Volume.

1 8 6 6—
    Keil and Delitzsch on Samuel. One Volume.
    Keil and Delitzsch on Job. Two Volumes.
    Martensen's System of Christian Doctrine. One Volume.

1 8 6 7—
    Delitzsch on Isaiah. Vol. I.
    Delitzsch on Biblical Psychology. 12s.
    Delitzsch on Isaiah. Vol. II.
    Auberlen on Divine Revelation.

1 8 6 8—
    Keil's Commentary on the Minor Prophets. Two Volumes.
    Delitzsch's Commentary on Epistle to the Hebrews. Vol. I.
    Harless' System of Christian Ethics. One Volume.

1 8 6 9—
    Hengstenberg on Ezekiel. One Volume.
    Stier on the Words of the Apostles. One Volume.
    Keil's Introduction to the Old Testament. Vol. I.
    Bleek's Introduction to the New Testament. Vol. I.

1 8 7 0—
    Keil's Introduction to the Old Testament. Vol. II.
    Bleek's Introduction to the New Testament. Vol. II.
    Schmid's New Testament Theology. One Volume.
    Delitzsch's Commentary on Epistle to the Hebrews. Vol. II.

The First Issue for 1871 will comprise—

    Delitzsch's Commentary on the Psalms. Vols. I. and II.

This Subscription includes other two volumes, the titles of which will be announced shortly.

MESSRS. CLARK have resolved to allow a SELECTION of TWENTY VOLUMES (or more at the same ratio) from the various Series previous to the Volumes issued in 1868 (see next page),

At the Subscription Price of Five Guineas.

They trust that this will still more largely extend the usefulness of the FOREIGN THEOLOGICAL LIBRARY, which has so long been recognised as holding an important place in modern Theological literature.

T. and T. Clark's Publications.

CLARK'S FOREIGN THEOLOGICAL LIBRARY—*Continued.*

The following are the works from which a Selection may be made (non-subscription prices within brackets):—

Dr. E. W. Hengstenberg.—Commentary on the Psalms. By E. W. HENGSTENBERG, D.D., Professor of Theology in Berlin. In Three Volumes 8vo. (33s.)

Dr. J. C. L. Gieseler.—Compendium of Ecclesiastical History. By J. C. L. GIESELER, D.D., Professor of Theology in Göttingen. Five Volumes 8vo. (£2, 12s. 6d.)

Dr. Hermann Olshausen.—Biblical Commentary on the Gospels and Acts, adapted especially for Preachers and Students. By HERMANN OLSHAUSEN, D.D., Professor of Theology in the University of Erlangen. In Four Volumes demy 8vo. (£2, 2s.)

Biblical Commentary on the Romans, adapted especially for Preachers and Students. By HERMANN OLSHAUSEN, D.D., Professor of Theology in the University of Erlangen. In One Volume 8vo. (10s. 6d.)

Biblical Commentary on St. Paul's First and Second Epistles to the Corinthians. By HERMANN OLSHAUSEN, D.D., Professor of Theology in the University of Erlangen. In One Volume 8vo. (9s.)

Biblical Commentary on St. Paul's Epistle to the Galatians, Ephesians, Colossians, and Thessalonians. By HERMANN OLSHAUSEN, D.D., Professor of Theology in the University of Erlangen. In One Volume 8vo. (10s. 6d.)

Biblical Commentary on St. Paul's Epistle to the Philippians, to Titus, and the First to Timothy; in continuation of the Work of Olshausen. By LIC. AUGUST WIESINGER. In One Volume 8vo. (10s. 6d.)

Biblical Commentary on the Hebrews. By Dr. EBRARD. In continuation of the Work of Olshausen. In One Volume 8vo. (10s. 6d.)

Dr. Augustus Neander.—General History of the Christian Religion and Church. By AUGUSTUS NEANDER, D.D. Translated from the Second and Improved Edition. In Nine Volumes 8vo. (£2, 11s. 6d.)
This is the only Edition in a Library size.

Prof. H. A. Ch. Havernick.—General Introduction to the Old Testament. By Professor HAVERNICK. One Volume 8vo. (10s. 6d.)

Dr. Julius Müller.—The Christian Doctrine of Sin. By Dr. JULIUS MÜLLER. Two Volumes 8vo. (21s.) New Edition.

Dr. E. W. Hengstenberg.—Christology of the Old Testament, and a Commentary on the Messianic Predictions. By E. W. HENGSTENBERG, D.D., Professor of Theology, Berlin. Four Volumes. (£2, 2s.)

Dr. M. Baumgarten.—The Acts of the Apostles; or the History of the Church in the Apostolic Age. By M. BAUMGARTEN, Ph.D., and Professor in the University of Rostock. Three Volumes. (£1, 7s.)

Dr. Rudolph Stier.—The Words of the Lord Jesus. By RUDOLPH STIER, D.D., Chief Pastor and Superintendent of Schkeuditz. In Eight Volumes 8vo. (£4, 4s.)

Dr. Carl Ullmann.—Reformers before the Reformation, principally in Germany and the Netherlands. Translated by the Rev. R. MENZIES. Two Volumes 8vo. (£1, 1s.)

Professor Kurtz.—History of the Old Covenant; or, Old Testament Dispensation. By Professor KURTZ of Dorpat. In Three Volumes. (£1, 11s. 6d.)

Dr. Rudolph Stier.—The Words of the Risen Saviour, and Commentary on the Epistle of St. James. By RUDOLPH STIER, D.D., Chief Pastor and Superintendent of Schkeuditz. One Volume. (10s. 6d.)

Professor Tholuck.—Commentary on the Gospel of St. John. By Professor THOLUCK of Halle. In One Volume. (9s.)

Professor Tholuck.—Commentary on the Sermon on the Mount. By Professor THOLUCK of Halle. In One Volume. (10s. 6d.)

Dr. E. W. Hengstenberg.—Commentary on the Book of Ecclesiastes. To which are appended: Treatises on the Song of Solomon; on the Book of Job; on the Prophet Isaiah; on the Sacrifices of Holy Scripture; and on the Jews and the Christian Church. By E. W. HENGSTENBERG, D.D. In One Volume 8vo. (9s.)

T. and T. Clark's Publications.

CLARK'S FOREIGN THEOLOGICAL LIBRARY—Continued.

Dr. John H. A. Ebrard.—**Commentary on the Epistles of St. John.** By Dr. JOHN H. A. EBRARD, Professor of Theology in the University of Erlangen. In One Volume. (10s. 6d.)

Dr. J. P. Lange.—**Theological and Homiletical Commentary on the Gospel of St. Matthew and Mark.** Specially Designed and Adapted for the Use of Ministers and Students. By J. P. LANGE, D.D., Professor of Divinity in the University of Bonn. Three Volumes. (10s. 6d. each.)

Dr. J. A. Dorner.—**History of the Development of the Doctrine of the Person of Christ.** By Dr. J. A. DORNER, Professor of Theology in the University of Berlin. Five Volumes. (£2, 12s. 6d.)

Dr. J. J. Van Oosterzee.—**Theological and Homiletical Commentary on the Gospel of St. Luke.** Specially Designed and Adapted for the Use of Ministers and Students. Edited by J. P. LANGE, D.D. Two Volumes. (18s.)

Professor Kurtz.—**The Sacrificial Worship of the Old Testament.** One Volume. (10s. 6d.)

Professor Ebrard.—**The Gospel History: A Compendium of Critical Investigations in support of the Historical Character of the Four Gospels.** One Volume. (10s. 6d.)

Lechler and Gerok.—**Theological and Homiletical Commentary on the Acts of the Apostles.** Edited by Dr. LANGE. (Lange Series.) Two Volumes. (21s.)

Dr. Hengstenberg.—**Commentary on the Gospel of St. John.** Two Volumes. (21s.)

Professor Keil.—**Biblical Commentary on the Pentateuch.** Three Volumes. (31s. 6d.)

Professor Keil.—**Commentary on Joshua, Judges, and Ruth.** One Volume. (10s. 6d.)

Professor Delitzsch.—**A System of Biblical Psychology.** One Volume. (12s.)

Professor Delitzsch.—**Commentary on the Prophecies of Isaiah.** Two Volumes. (21s.)

Professor Auberlen.—**The Divine Revelation: An Essay in Defence of the Faith.** One Volume. (10s. 6d.)

Professor Keil.—**Commentary on the Books of Samuel.** One Volume. (10s. 6d.)

Professor Delitzsch.—**Commentary on the Book of Job.** Two Volumes. (21s.)

Bishop Martensen.—**Christian Dogmatics. A Compendium of the Doctrines of Christianity.** One Volume. (10s. 6d.)

And, in connection with the Series,—

Shedd's History of Christian Doctrine. Two Volumes. (21s.)
Macdonald's Introduction to the Pentateuch. Two Volumes. (21s.)
Hengstenberg's Egypt and the Books of Moses. (7s. 6d.)
Ackerman on the Christian Element in Plato. (7s. 6d.)
Robinson's Greek Lexicon of the New Testament. 8vo. (9s.)
Gerlach's Commentary on the Pentateuch. Demy 8vo. (10s. 6d.)

The above, in 102 Volumes (including 1870), price £26, 15s. 6d., form an *Apparatus*, without which it may be truly said *no Theological Library can be complete*, and the Publishers take the liberty of suggesting that no more appropriate gift could be presented to a Clergyman than the Series, in whole or in part.

_{*} *In reference to the above, it must be noted that* NO DUPLICATES *can be included in the Selection of Twenty Volumes: and it will save trouble and correspondence if it be distinctly understood that* NO LESS *number than Twenty can be supplied, unless at non-subscription price.*

Subscribers' Names received by all Retail Booksellers.
CHEQUES on COUNTRY BANKS under £2, 2s. must have 6d. added for Bank charge.

LONDON: (*For Works at Non-subscription price only*) HAMILTON, ADAMS, & CO.

NOTICE TO SUBSCRIBERS.

MESSRS. CLARK have pleasure in forwarding to their Subscribers the second issue of Fifth Year (Vols. 19 and 20 of the Series), viz. The WRITINGS of ARNOBIUS, One Volume; and The WRITINGS of GREGORY THAUMATURGUS, The EXTANT FRAGMENTS of DIONYSIUS, and ANCIENT SYRIAC DOCUMENTS, One Volume.

The Series approaches completion; and the Publishers are thankful for the support they have received, which they trust will be continued to the Series of the WORKS of ST. AUGUSTINE, which will be commenced this year.

There remain to be published—

LACTANTIUS, two vols. ;
The Completion of ORIGEN CONTRA CELSUM ;
And a Volume of EARLY LITURGIES.

These are all in progress, and no endeavour will be spared to publish them as rapidly as possible. It is hoped the Series will be completed in the course of this year.

It is requested that the Subscription for Sixth Year may be remitted as soon as possible.

EDINBURGH, 38, GEORGE STREET,
April 1871.

ANTE-NICENE

CHRISTIAN LIBRARY:

TRANSLATIONS OF
THE WRITINGS OF THE FATHERS
DOWN TO A.D. 325.

EDITED BY THE
REV. ALEXANDER ROBERTS, D.D.,
AND
JAMES DONALDSON, LL.D.

VOL. XIX.
THE SEVEN BOOKS OF ARNOBIUS ADVERSUS GENTES.

EDINBURGH:
T. & T. CLARK, 38, GEORGE STREET.
MDCCCLXXI.

ARNOBIUS ADVERSUS GENTES.

Translated by

ARCH^{D.} HAMILTON BRYCE, LL.D. D.C.L.

AND

HUGH CAMPBELL, M.A.

EDINBURGH:
T. & T. CLARK, 38, GEORGE STREET.
MDCCCLXXI.

CONTENTS.

	PAGE
PREFACE,	vii
INTRODUCTION,	ix
§ 1. Account of Arnobius given by Jerome,	ix
§ 2. Facts derived from Arnobius himself,	x
§ 3. Result,	xii
§ 4. His Work: its Style and Character,	xiv
§ 5. Knowledge of Scriptures, and References to other Writings,	xv
§ 6. MS. and Editions of the Seven Books *adversus Gentes*,	xvii
§ 7. Title,	xviii
BOOK I.,	1
II.,	58
III.,	148
IV.,	183
V.,	221
VI.,	269
VII.,	304
APPENDIX,	365
INDEX OF AUTHORS QUOTED,	369
INDEX OF SUBJECTS,	370

PREFACE.

HE translation of Arnobius was begun in the hope that it would be possible to adhere throughout to the text of Orelli, and that very little attention to the various readings would be found necessary. This was, however, found to be impossible, not merely because Hildebrand's collation of the Paris MS. showed how frequently liberties had been taken with the text, but on account of the corrupt state of the text itself.

It has therefore been thought advisable to lay before the reader a close translation founded on the MS., so far as known. A conjectural reading has in no case been adopted without notice.

Throughout the Work use has been made of four editions, —Oehler's, Orelli's, Hildebrand's, and that of Leyden; other editions being consulted only for special reasons.

It is to be regretted that our knowledge of the single MS. of Arnobius is still incomplete; but it is hoped that this will soon be remedied, by the publication of a revised text, based upon a fresh collation of the MS., with a complete *apparatus* and a carefully digested body of notes.

INTRODUCTION.

§ 1. ARNOBIUS has been most unjustly neglected in modern times; but some excuse for this may be found in the fact that even less attention seems to have been paid to him in the ages immediately succeeding his own. We find no mention of him in any author except Jerome; and even Jerome has left only a few lines about him, which convey very little information.

In his list of ecclesiastical writers he says,[1] "During the reign of Diocletian, Arnobius taught rhetoric with the greatest success, at Sicca, in Africa, and wrote against the heathen the books extant;" and again speaks of this work more particularly when he says,[2] "Arnobius published seven books against the heathen." In his *Chronicon*, however, he writes under the year 2342 (*i.e.* A.D. 326), "Arnobius is considered a distinguished rhetorician in Africa, who, while engaged at Sicca in teaching young men rhetoric, was led by visions to the faith; and not being received by the bishop as hitherto a persistent enemy to Christ, composed very excellent books against his former belief." It must at once be seen that there is here a mistake, for Arnobius is put some twenty-three years later than in the former passage. Jerome himself shows us that the former date is the one he meant, for elsewhere[3] he speaks of Lactantius as the disciple of Arnobius. Lactantius, in extreme old age,[4] was appointed tutor of Con-

[1] *Cat. Script. Eccl.* lxxix. f. 121, Bened. ed. tom. iv.
[2] Ep. lxxxiii. f. 656.
[3] *Cat. Script. Eccl.* lxxx. f. 121, ep. lxxxiii.
[4] *Cat. Script. Eccl.* lxxx.

stantine's son Crispus; and this, we are told in the *Chronicon*,[1] was in the year 317. No one will suppose that if the disciple was a very old man in 317, his master could have been in his prime in 326. It is certain, therefore, that this date is not correct; and it seems very probable that Oehler's conjecture is true, who supposes that Jerome accidentally transposed his words from the year 303 to the place where we find them, misled by noticing the *vicenalia* of Constantine when he was looking for those of Diocletian.

It is with some difficulty that we can believe that Arnobius was led to embrace Christianity by dreams, as he speaks of these with little respect as "vain,"—which he could hardly have done if by them the whole course of his life had been changed; but in our utter ignorance we cannot say that this may not have been to some extent the case. The further statement, that his apology for Christianity was submitted as a proof of his sincerity to the bishop of Sicca, is even less credible,—for these two reasons, that it is evidently the fruit not of a few weeks' but of protracted labour, and that it is hardly likely that any bishop would have allowed some parts of it to pass into circulation. It is just possible that the first or third books may have been so presented; but it is not credible that any pledge would be required of a man seeking to cast in his lot with the persecuted and terrified Church referred to in the fourth.

§ 2. If we learn but little from external sources as to the life of Arnobius, we are not more fortunate when we turn to his own writings. One or two facts, however, are made clear; and these are of some importance. "But lately," he says, "O blindness, I worshipped images just brought from the furnaces, gods made on anvils and forged with hammers: now, led by so great a teacher into the ways of truth, I know what all these things are."[2] We have thus his own assurance of his conversion from heathenism. He speaks of himself, however, as actually a Christian,—not as a waverer, not as one purposing to forsake the ancient superstitions and

[1] Anno 2333.   [2] i. 39, p. 31.

embrace the new religion, but as a firm believer, whose faith is already established, and whose side has been taken and stedfastly maintained. In a word, he refers to himself as once lost in error, but now a true Christian.

Again, in different passages he marks pretty accurately the time or times at which he wrote. Thus, in the first book[1] he speaks of about three hundred years as the time during which Christianity had existed; and in the second,[2] of a thousand and fifty, or not many less, having elapsed since the foundation of Rome. There has been much discussion as to what era is here referred to; and it has been pretty generally assumed that the Fabian must be intended, —in which case 303 would be the year meant. If it is observed, however, that Arnobius shows an intimate acquaintance with Varro, and great admiration for him, it will probably be admitted that it is most likely that the Varronian, or common, era was adopted by him; and in this case the year referred to will be 297 A.D. This coincides sufficiently with the passage in the first book, and is in harmony with the idea which is there predominant,—the thought, that is, of the accusation so frequently on the lips of the heathen, that Christianity was the cause of the many and terrible afflictions with which the empire was visited. These accusations, ever becoming more bitter and threatening, would naturally be observed with care and attention by thoughtful Christians towards the close of the third century; and accordingly we find that the words with which Arnobius begins his apology, express the feeling of awakening anxiety with which he viewed the growth of this fear and hatred in the minds of the heathen. He declares, in effect, that one great object—indeed the main object—which he had proposed to himself, was to show that it was not because of the Christians that fresh evils and terrible calamities were continually assailing the state. And it must be remembered that we cannot refer such a proposal to a later period than that assigned. It would certainly not have occurred to a Christian in the midst of persecution, with death overhang-

[1] i. 13, p. 13. [2] ii. 71, p. 141.

ing him, and danger on every side, to come forward and attempt calmly to show the heathen that there was no reason for their complaints against the Christians. In the later books there is a change in tone, upon which we cannot now dwell, although it is marked. In one passage he asks indignantly,[1] " Why should our writings be given to the flames, our meetings be cruelly broken up, in which prayer is offered to the supreme God, peace and pardon are asked for all in authority, for soldiers, kings, friends, enemies?" In the calm tranquillity of the last half of the third century these words could hardly have been written, but they are a striking testimony to the terms of the imperial edict issued in the year 303 A.D. So, too, the expression of anger and disgust at the anti-pagan character of some of Cicero's works, noticed in iii. 7, belongs to the incipient stages of persecution.

Nor must it be supposed that the whole work may be referred to the era which ensued after the abdication of Diocletian, in 305. From this time an apology for Christianity with such a design would have been an anachronism, for it was no longer necessary to disarm the fears of the heathen by showing that the gods could not be enraged at the Christians. It has further to be noticed, that although it is perfectly clear that Arnobius spent much time on his apology, it has never been thoroughly revised, and does not seem to have been ever finished.[2]

We surely have in all this sufficient reason to assign the composition of these books *adversus Gentes* to the end of the third and beginning of the fourth centuries. Beyond this we cannot go, for we have no *data* from which to derive further inferences.

§ 3. We have seen that the facts transmitted to us are very few and scanty indeed; but, few as they are, they suggest an interesting picture. Arnobius comes before us in Sicca; we are made spectators of two scenes of his life there, and the rest—the beginning and the end—are shrouded in

[1] iv. 36, p. 218.   [2] Cf. pp. 347, n. 3, and 364, n. 3.

darkness. Sicca Veneria was an important town, lying on the Numidian border, to the south-west of Carthage. As its name signifies, it was a seat of that vile worship of the goddess of lust, which was dear to the Phœnician race. The same cultus was found there which disgraced Corinth; and in the temple of the goddess the maidens of the town were wont to procure for themselves, by the sacrifice of their chastity, the dowries which the poverty of their parents could not provide.

In the midst of traditions of such bestial foulness Arnobius found himself,—whether as a native, or as one who had been led to settle there. He has told us himself how true an idolater he was, how thoroughly he complied with the ceremonial demands of superstition; but the frequency and the vehemence of language with which his abhorrence of the sensuality of heathenism is expressed, tell us as plainly that practices so horrible had much to do in preparing his mind to receive another faith.

In strong contrast to the filthy indulgences with which paganism gratified its adherents, must have appeared the strict purity of life which was enjoined by Christianity and aimed at by its followers; and perhaps it was in such a place as Sicca that considerations of this nature would have most influence. There, too, the story of Cyprian's martyrdom must have been well known,—may indeed have been told in the nursery of the young Arnobius,—and many traditions must have been handed down about the persistency with which those of the new religion had held fast their faith, in spite of exile, torture, and death. However distorted such tales might be, there would always remain in them the evidence of so exalted nobility of spirit, that every disclosure of the meanness and baseness of the old superstition must have induced an uneasy feeling as to whether that could be impiety which ennobled men,—that piety which degraded them lower than the brutes.

For some time all went well with Arnobius. He was not too pure for the world, and his learning and eloquence won him fame and success in his profession. But in some way, we know not how, a higher learning was communicated to him, and the admired rhetorician became first a suspected, then a persecuted Christian. He has left us in no doubt as to the reason of the change. Upon his darkness, he says, there shone out a heavenly light, a great teacher appeared to him and pointed out the way of truth; and he who had been an earnest worshipper of images, of stones, of unknown gods, was now as earnest, as zealous in his service of the true God. Of the trials which he must have endured we know nothing. A terrible persecution swept over the world, and many a Christian perished in it. Such a man as Arnobius must have been among the first to be assailed, but we hear of him no more. With his learning and talents he could not have failed to make himself a name in the church, or outside its pale, if he had lived. The conclusion seems inevitable, that he was one of the victims of that last fiery trial to which Christians under the Roman empire were exposed.

§ 4. The vast range of learning shown in this apology has been admitted on all sides. Even Jerome says that it should at times be read on account of the learning displayed in it.[1] In another passage Jerome says,[2] "Arnobius is unequal and prolix, confused from want of arrangement." This may be admitted to a certain extent; but although such defects are to be found in his work, they are certainly not characteristic of Arnobius. So, too, many passages may be found strangely involved and mystical, and it is at times hard to understand what is really meant. Solecisms and barbarisms are also met with, as Nourry has objected, so that it cannot be said that Arnobius writes pure Latin. Still we must not be misled into supposing that by enumerating these defects we have a fair idea of his style.

If we remember that no man can wholly escape the influences of his age, and that Arnobius was so warm an admirer of Varro and Lucretius that he imitated their style and adopted their vocabulary, we shall be able to understand in what way he may be fairly spoken of as a good writer,

[1] Ep. lxii. *ad Tranquill.*   [2] Ep. xlix. *ad Paulinum.*

although not free from defects. His style is, in point of fact, clear and lucid, rising at times into genuine eloquence; and its obscurity and harshness are generally caused by an attempt to express a vague and indefinite idea. Indeed very considerable power of expression is manifested in the philosophical reasonings of the second book, the keen satire of the fourth and fifth, and the vigorous argument of the sixth and seventh.

Jerome's last stricture is scarcely applicable. Arnobius wrote *adversus Gentes*; he addressed himself to meet the taunts and accusations of the heathen, and in so doing he retorts upon them the charges which they preferred against the Christians. His work must therefore be criticised from this standpoint, not as a systematic exposition or vindication of Christianity. Christianity is indeed defended, but it is by attacking heathenism. We must consider, also, that evidently the work was not revised as a whole, and that the last book would have been considerably altered had Arnobius lived or found opportunity to correct it.[1] If we remember these things, we shall find little to object to in the arrangement.

After making all deductions, it may be said fairly that in Arnobius the African church found no unfitting champion. Living amidst impurity and corruption, and seeing on every side the effects of a superstitious and sensual faith, he stands forward to proclaim that man has a nobler ideal set before him than the worship of the foul imaginations of his depraved fancy, to call his fellows to a purer life, and to point out that the Leader who claims that men should follow Him is both worthy and able to guide. This he does with enthusiasm, vigour, and effect; and in doing this he accomplishes his end.

§ 5. Various opinions have been entertained as to the position which Arnobius occupied with regard to the Bible. We cannot here enter into a discussion of these, and shall merely present a brief statement of facts.

[1] Cf. pp. 347, n. 3, and 364, n. 3, with the Appendix.

It is evident that with regard to the Jews and the Old Testament Arnobius was in a state of perfect ignorance; for he confounds the Sadducees with the Pharisees,[1] makes no allusion to the history of the Israelites, and shows that he was not acquainted with their forms of sacrifice.[2]

He was evidently well acquainted with the life of Christ and the history of the church, and alludes at times to well-known Christian sayings; but how far in so doing he quotes the Gospels and Epistles, is not easily determined. Thus it has been supposed, and with some probability, that in referring to the miracles of Christ he must allude to the Gospels as recording them. But it must be observed that he ascribes to Christ a miracle of which the New Testament makes no mention,—of being understood by men of different nations, as though He spoke in several languages at the same moment.[3] So, too, his account[4] of the passion differs from that of the New Testament. On the other hand, we find that he speaks of Christ as having taught men "not to return evil for evil,"[5] as "the *way* of salvation, the door of life, by whom alone there is access to the light,"[6] and as having been seen by "countless numbers of men" after His resurrection.[7] Still further, he makes frequent references to accounts of Christ written by the apostles and handed down to their followers,[8] and asks why their writings should be burned.[9] In one place,[10] also, he asks, "Have the well-known words never rung in your ears, that the wisdom of man is foolishness with God?" where the reference seems to be very distinct;[11] but he nowhere says that he is quoting, or mentions any books.

This is, however, less remarkable when we take into account his mode of dealing with Clemens Alexandrinus and

[1] P. 158, n. 2.
[2] Cf. B. vii., on sacrifices generally.
[3] P. 37, n. 2.
[4] P. 45, n. 1.
[5] P. 9, n. 1.
[6] P. 135, n. 6.
[7] P. 37; cf. 1 Cor. xv. 6.
[8] i. 55, p. 45; 56, p. 46; 58, p. 47; 59, p. 48.
[9] iv. 36, p. 218.
[10] ii. 6, p. 68, n. 5.
[11] Cf. 1 Cor. iii. 19.

Cicero. The fourth, fifth, and sixth books are based on these two authors, and from Clement, in particular, whole sentences are taken unchanged. Yet the only reference made to either is the very general allusion in the third and fourth books.[1]

On the other hand, he quotes frequently and refers distinctly to many authors, and is especially careful to show that he has good authority for his statements, as will be seen by observing the number of books to which he refers on the mysteries and temples. If we bear this in mind, the principle which guided him seems to have been, that when he has occasion to quote an author once or twice, he does so by name, but that he takes it for granted that every one knows what are the great sources of information, and that it is therefore unnecessary to specify in each case what is the particular authority.

There are many interesting questions connected with this subject, but these we must for the present leave untouched.

§ 6. No other works by Arnobius have been preserved, and only two MSS. are known to exist. Of these, the one in Brussels is merely a transcript of that preserved in the public library at Paris, on which all editions have been based. This is a MS. of the ninth or tenth century, and contains the *Octavius* of Minucius Felix immediately after the seventh book *adversus Gentes*, in consequence of which that treatise was at first printed as the eighth book of Arnobius. Although it has been collated several times, we are still in doubt as to its true readings,—Hildebrand, who last examined it, having done so with too little care.

The first[2] edition was printed at Rome in 1542, and was followed by that of Gelenius,[3] in which much was done for the emendation of the text; but arbitrary conjectures were too frequently admitted. Next in order follow those of Canterus,[4] who did especial service by

---

[1] Pp. 154 and 195, n. 3.
[2] Arnobii *Disputationum adversus Gentes*, libri octo, nunc primum in lucem editi Romæ, apud Franc. Priscianum Florentinum.
[3] Basileæ 1546.   [4] Antverpiæ 1582.

xviii *INTRODUCTION.*

pointing out what use Arnobius has made of Clement, Ursinus,[1] Elmenhorst,[2] Stewechius,[3] Heraldus,[4] and the Leyden[5] *variorum* edition, based on a recension of the text by Salmasius.[6] The later editions are those of Oberthür,[7] whose text is adopted by Orelli,[8] Hildebrand,[9] and Oehler.[10] Oberthür's edition is of little importance, and that of Orelli is valuable solely as a collection of notes gathered from many sources into a crude and undigested mass. Hildebrand seems to have taken too little pains with his work; and Oehler, whose critical sagacity and industry might have given us a most satisfactory edition, was unfortunately hampered by want of space.

No edition of Arnobius has been published in England; and the one Englishman who has taken any pains with this author seems to be John Jones, who, under the pseudonym of Leander de St. Martino, prepared summaries, which were added to a reprint of Stewechius at Douay 1634. As this edition has not come into our hands, we are unable to speak of it more particularly.

§ 7. It will be observed that *adversus Gentes* is the title of this work in all editions except those of Hildebrand and Oehler, in which it is *adversus Nationes*. The difference is very slight, but it may be well to mention that neither can be said with certainty to be correct. The first is the form used by Jerome in two passages of his writings;[11] and as he

---

[1] Romæ 1583. This is the second Roman ed., and restores the *Octavius* to Minucius Felix.
[2] Hanoviæ 1603; dedicated to Joseph Scaliger.   [3] Antwerpiæ 1604.
[4] Paris 1605. This edition, which is of great value, and shows great learning and ability, was completed in two months, as Heraldus himself tells us.
[5] Lugduni Batavorum 1651, containing the notes of Canterus, Elmenhorst, Stewechius, and Heraldus.
[6] Salmasius purposed writing commentaries for this edition, but died without doing more than beginning them.
[7] Wirceburgi 1783, 8vo, preceded by a rambling introductory epistle.
[8] Lipsiæ 1816–17, 8vo.   [9] Halis Saxonum 1844, 8vo.
[10] Lipsiæ 1846, 8vo.   [11] Cf. § 1, notes 1 and 2.

must have seen earlier MSS. than that now extant, he is supposed to give the title which he found in them. In the Paris MS., however, at the end of the second book, the subscription is, "The second book of Arnobius *adversus Nationes* ends;" and it has been argued that, as the copyist would hardly have gone so far astray, while it is quite possible that Jerome did not attempt to do more than indicate generally the purpose of the book without quoting its title-page, this must be the true title. The first page of the existing MS. is torn away, and the question remains therefore undecided: fortunately its decision is not of the slightest importance.

ERRATA.

Page 7, n. 1, *for* Hist. Nat. xx. 24, *read* ii. 38.
    28, l. 5, *for* Opis, *read* Ops.
    141, l. 24, *for* 1500, *read* 1050.
    173, n. 2, *for* i. 7, *read* i. 5.

THE SEVEN BOOKS OF
ARNOBIUS ADVERSUS GENTES.

BOOK I.

ARGUMENT.

THE enemies of Christianity were wont to say that, since its appearance on earth, the gods had shown their hatred of it by sending upon men all manner of calamities, and that, owing to the neglect of sacred rites, the divine care no longer guarded the world. Arnobius begins by showing how baseless this opinion is (1), for the laws and course of nature remain unchanged (2); and though the heathen said that since Christianity came into the world there had been wars, famines, pestilences, and many other similar calamities, these were not new evils, for history tells of terrible misery and destruction resulting from such causes in past ages (3-5); while it should also be noticed, that through the gentle and peaceful spirit of Christianity, the world is already relieved in part, and that war would be unknown, and men live peacefully together, if it prevailed universally (6). If asked, What are, then, the causes of human misery? Arnobius answers that this is no part of his subject (7), but suggests that all evil results necessarily from the very nature of things, —is, indeed, perhaps not evil at all, but, however opposed to the pleasures or even interests of individuals, tends to general good (8-11); and that it is therefore somewhat presumptuous in man, a creature so ignorant of himself, to seek to impose conditions on the superior powers (12). He further shows the futility of blaming the Christians for all these ills, by reminding his opponents that there had been no unvarying series of calamities since Christianity came to earth, but that success had counterbalanced defeat, and abundance scarcity; so that arguments such as these would prove that the gods were angry at times, at times forgot their anger (13-16). But, Arnobius asks, if the gods can be enraged, does not this argue mortality and imperfection in them (17, 18), and even injustice (19), or weakness, if they need the aid of men in punishing their enemies (20)? As, however, all alike suffer, it is absurd to say that Christians are specially aimed at; and, indeed, this is a cry raised by those interested in upholding the superstitious rites of antiquity (21-24). But assuming that the gods could be enraged, why should they be angry at Christians more than others? Because, the heathen said, Christianity introduced new and impious forms of religion. In reply to this, Arnobius points out that Christians are nothing but worshippers of the supreme God, under Christ's teaching and guidance (25-27); and shows how absurd it is to accuse those of impiety who worship the Creator and supreme Ruler, while those who serve the lesser gods—even foul and loathsome deities—are called religious (28-30); and then turns to God Himself, beseeching pardon for these ignorant worshippers of His creatures, who had neglected Himself (31). He merely notices but refuses to discuss the position of those who deny that God exists, holding it impious even to reason about this, as though it were questionable, while there is an instinctive belief and reverence implanted in our breasts (31-33). But, his opponents said, we worship Jupiter as the supreme God. Jupiter, however, Arnobius points out, cannot claim this rank, for he is admittedly not self-existent (34); or if, as some said, Jupiter is only another name for the Supreme Being, then, as all alike worship Him, all must be regarded by Him alike (35). But, his opponents urged, you are guilty not in worshipping God, but in worshipping a mere man who died on the cross; to which Arnobius replies, in the first place, by retorting the charge as bearing much more forcibly on the heathen themselves (36, 37); and then argues that Christ has sufficiently vindicated his claims to divinity by leading the blind and erring and lost into the ways of truth and salvation, and by his revelation of things previously unknown (38, 39); while, again, his death on the cross does not affect his teaching and miracles, any more than the loss of life deprived of fame Pythagoras, Socrates, Aquilius, Trebonius, or Regulus (40), and contrasts favourably with the stories told about Bacchus, Æsculapius, Hercules, Attis, and Romulus (41); and, finally, asserts Christ's divinity as proved by his miracles (42), which are compared with those of the Magi both as to their end and the manner in which they were wrought (43, 44); and the chief features of the miracles of his life on earth and his resurrection, of the power of his name, and the spread of his church are summarily noticed (45-47). Arnobius next remarks that the heathen did not even pretend that their gods had healed the sick without using medicines, merely by a word or touch, as Christ did (48); and, recalling the thousands who had in vain sought divine aid at temple or shrine, says that Christ sent none away unhelped (49), and that he gave this same power to his followers also (50), which neither priest nor magian is found to possess (51, 52). His divinity was shown also by the wonders which attended his death (53). Eye-witnesses—and these most trustworthy—testified to Christ's miracles (54); and the acceptance by the whole world, in so short a time, of his religion attests its truth (55). It might be said, however, that the Christian writers were not trustworthy, and exaggerated the number and importance of Christ's miracles (56) : in reply to which, Arnobius shows that their writings rest on as good authority as those of the heathen (57), and that their greater novelty and literary rudeness are in their favour rather than otherwise, and are certainly of no weight against them (57-59). But, said the heathen, if Christ was God, why did he live and die as a man? Because, it is replied, God's own nature could not be made manifest to men (60), and His reasons for choosing so to manifest Himself, and not otherwise, though they may be within our reach, are certainly concealed in much obscurity (61) ; while as to Christ's death, that was but the dissolution of his human frame (62). Hurrying, it would seem, to conclude this part of the discussion, Arnobius hastily points out the great powers which Christ might have wielded in his own defence, if he had refused to submit to the violence offered him, which however were unused, because he rather chose to do for his disciples all that he had led them to look for (63). If, then, kings and tyrants and others who lived most wickedly, are honoured and deified, why should Christ, even if he asserted falsely that he was a heaven-sent Saviour, be so hated and assailed (64) ? If one came from distant and unknown regions, promising to deliver all from bodily sickness, how gladly would men flock to do him honour, and strive for his favour! How extraordinary, then, is the conduct of those who revile and abuse, and would destroy, if they could, him who has come to deliver us from spiritual evils, and work out our salvation (65)!

1. SINCE I have found some who deem themselves very wise in their opinions, acting as if they were inspired,[1] and announcing with all the authority of an oracle,[2] that from the time when the Christian people began to exist in the world the universe has gone to ruin, that the human race has been visited with ills of many kinds, that even the very gods, abandoning their accustomed charge, in virtue of which they

[1] The words *insanire, bacchari*, refer to the appearance of the ancient seers when under the influence of the deity. So Virgil says, *Insanam vatem aspicies* (*Æn.* iii. 443), and, *Bacchatur vates* (*Æn.* vi. 78). The meaning is, that they make their asseverations with all the confidence of a seer when filled, as he pretended, with the influence of the god.

[2] *Et velut quiddam promptum ex oraculo dicere, i.e.* to declare a matter with boldness and majesty, as if most certain and undoubted.

were wont in former days to regard with interest our affairs, have been driven from the regions of earth,—I have resolved, so far as my capacity and my humble power of language will allow, to oppose public prejudice, and to refute calumnious accusations; lest, on the one hand, those persons should imagine that they are declaring some weighty matter, when they are merely retailing vulgar rumours;[1] and on the other, lest, if we refrain from such a contest, they should suppose that they have gained a cause, lost by its own inherent demerits, not abandoned by the silence of its advocates. For I should not deny that that charge is a most serious one, and that we fully deserve the hatred attaching to public enemies,[2] if it should appear that to us are attributable causes by reason of which the universe has deviated from its laws, the gods have been driven far away, and such swarms of miseries have been inflicted on the generations of men.

2. Let us therefore examine carefully the real significance of that opinion, and what is the nature of the allegation; and laying aside all desire for wrangling,[3] by which the calm view of subjects is wont to be dimmed, and [even] intercepted, let us test, by fairly balancing the considerations on both sides, whether that which is alleged be true. For it will assuredly be proved by an array of convincing arguments, not that we are discovered to be more impious, but that they themselves are convicted of that charge who profess to be worshippers of the deities, and devotees of an antiquated superstition. And, in the first place, we ask this of them in friendly and calm language: Since the name of the Christian religion began to be used on the earth, what phenomenon, unseen before,[4] unheard of before, what event contrary to the laws established in the beginning, has the so-called "Nature of Things" felt or suffered? Have these first elements, from which it is agreed that all things were compacted, been

---

[1] *Popularia verba, i.e.* rumours arising from the ignorance of the common people.
[2] The Christians were regarded as " public enemies," and were so called.
[3] Or, " all party zeal."
[4] So Meursius,—the MS. reading is *inusitatum*, " extraordinary."

altered into elements of an opposite character? Has the fabric of this machine and mass [of the universe], by which we are all covered, and in which we are held enclosed, relaxed in any part, or broken up? Has the revolution of the globe, to which we are accustomed, departing from the rate of its primal motion, begun either to move too slowly, or to be hurried onward in headlong rotation? Have the stars begun to rise in the west, and the setting of the constellations to take place in the east? Has the sun himself, the chief of the heavenly bodies, with whose light all things are clothed, and by whose heat all things are vivified, blazed forth with increased vehemence? has he become less warm, and has he altered for the worse into opposite conditions that well-regulated temperature by which he is wont to act upon the earth? Has the moon ceased to shape herself anew, and to change into former phases by the constant recurrence of fresh ones? Has the cold of winter, has the heat of summer, has the moderate warmth of spring and autumn, been modified by reason of the intermixture of ill-assorted seasons? Has the winter begun to have long days? has the night begun to recall the very tardy twilights of summer? Have the winds at all exhausted their violence? Is the sky not collected[1] into clouds by reason of the blasts having lost their force, and do the fields when moistened by the showers not prosper? Does the earth refuse to receive the seed committed to it, or will not the trees assume their foliage? Has the flavour of excellent fruits altered, or has the vine changed in its juice? Is foul blood pressed forth from the olive berries, and is [oil] no longer supplied to the lamp, now extinguished? Have animals of the land and of the sea no sexual desires, and do they not conceive young? Do they not guard, according to their own habits and their own instinct, the offspring generated in their wombs? In fine, do men themselves, whom an active energy with its first impulses has scattered over habitable lands, not form marriages with due rites? Do they not beget dear children? do they not attend to public, to individual, and to family concerns? Do they not apply their talents, as

[1] So Gelenius; MS., *coartatur*, " pressed together."

each one pleases, to varied occupations, to different kinds of learning? and do they not reap the fruit of diligent application? Do those to whom it has been so allotted, not exercise kingly power or military authority? Are men not every day advanced in posts of honour, in offices of power? Do they not preside in the discussions of the law courts? Do they not explain the code of law? do they not expound the principles of equity? All other things with which the life of man is surrounded, in which it consists, do not all men in their own tribes practise, according to the established order of their country's manners?

3. Since this is so, and since no strange influence has suddenly manifested itself to break the continuous course of events by interrupting their succession, what is the ground of the allegation, that a plague was brought upon the earth after the Christian religion came into the world, and after it revealed the mysteries of hidden truth? But pestilences, say my opponents, and droughts, wars, famines, locusts, mice, and hailstones, and other hurtful things, by which the property of men is assailed, the gods bring upon us, incensed as they are by your wrong-doings and by your transgressions. If it were not a mark of stupidity to linger on matters which are already clear, and which require no defence, I should certainly show, by unfolding the history of past ages, that those ills which you speak of were not unknown, were not sudden in their visitation; and that the plagues did not burst upon us, and the affairs of men begin to be attacked by a variety of dangers, from the time that our sect[1] won the honour[2] of this appellation. For if we are to blame, and if these plagues have been devised against our sin, whence did antiquity know these names for misfortunes? Whence did she give a designation to wars? By what conception

---

[1] Or, "race," *gens*, *i.e.* the Christian people.
[2] The verb *mereri*, used in this passage, has in Roman writers the idea of merit or excellence of some kind in a person, in virtue of which he is deemed worthy of some favour or advantage; but in ecclesiastical Latin it means, as here, to gain something by the mere favour of God, without any merit of one's own.

could she indicate pestilence and hailstorms, or how could she introduce these terms among her words, by which speech was rendered plain? For if these ills are entirely new, and if they derive their origin from recent transgressions, how could it be that the ancients coined terms for these things, which, on the one hand, they knew that they themselves had never experienced, and which, on the other, they had not heard of as occurring in the time of their ancestors? Scarcity of produce, say my opponents, and short supplies of grain, press more heavily on us. For [I would ask] were the former generations, even the most ancient, at any period wholly free from such an inevitable calamity? Do not the very words by which these ills are characterized bear evidence and proclaim loudly that no mortal ever escaped from them with entire immunity? But if the matter were difficult of belief, we might urge, on the testimony of authors, how great nations, and what individual nations, and how often [such nations] experienced dreadful famine, and perished by accumulated devastation. Very many hailstorms fall upon and assail all things. For do we not find it contained and deliberately stated in ancient literature, that even showers of stones[1] often ruined entire districts? Violent rains cause the crops to perish, and proclaim barrenness to countries:—were the ancients, indeed, free from these ills, when we have known of[2] mighty rivers even being dried up, and the mud of their channels parched? The contagious influences of pestilence consume the human race:—ransack the records of history written in various languages, and you will find that all countries have often been desolated and deprived of their inhabitants. Every kind of crop is consumed, and devoured by locusts and by mice:—go through your own annals, and you will be taught by these plagues how often former ages were visited by them, and how often they were brought to the wretchedness of poverty. Cities shaken by powerful earthquakes totter to their destruction:—what! did not bygone days wit-

---

[1] See Livy, i. 31, etc.; and Pliny, *Nat. Hist.* xx. 24.
[2] The MS. reads, *flumina* cognoverimus ingentia *lim-*in-*is ingentia siccatis*, "that mighty rivers shrunk up, leaving the mud," etc.

ness cities with their populations engulphed by huge rents of the earth?[1] or did they enjoy a condition exempt from such disasters?

4. When was the human race destroyed by a flood? was it not before us? When was the world set on fire,[2] and reduced to coals and ashes? was it not before us? When were the greatest cities engulphed in the billows of the sea? was it not before us? When were wars waged with wild beasts, and battles fought with lions?[3] was it not before us? When was ruin brought on whole communities by poisonous serpents?[4] was it not before us? For, inasmuch as you are wont to lay to our blame the cause of frequent wars, the devastation of cities, the irruptions of the Germans and the Scythians, allow me, with your leave, to say,—In your eagerness to calumniate us, you do not perceive the real nature of that which is alleged.

5. Did we bring it about, that ten thousand years ago a vast number of men burst forth from the island which is called the Atlantis of Neptune,[5] as Plato tells us, and utterly ruined and blotted out countless tribes? Did this form a prejudice against us, that between the Assyrians and Bactrians, under the leadership of Ninus and Zoroaster of old, a struggle was maintained not only by the sword and by physical power, but also by magicians, and by the mysterious learning of the Chaldeans? Is it to be laid to the charge of our religion,

---

[1] So Tertullian, *Apologet.* 40, says,—" We have read that the islands Hiera, Anaphe, Delos, Rhodes, and Cos were destroyed, together with many human beings."

[2] Arnobius, no doubt, speaks of the story of Phaethon, as told by Ovid; on which, cf. Plato, *Tim.* st. p. 22.

[3] Nourry thinks that reference is here made to the contests of gladiators and athletes with lions and other beasts in the circus. But it is more likely that the author is thinking of African tribes who were harassed by lions. Thus Ælian (*de Nat. Anim.* xvii. 24) tells of a Libyan people, the Nomæi, who were entirely destroyed by lions.

[4] The city of Amyclæ in Italy is referred to, which was destroyed by serpents.

[5] In the *Timæus* of Plato, c. vi. st. p. 24, an old priest of Saïs, in Egypt, is represented as telling Solon that in times long gone by the Athenians were a very peaceful and very brave people, and that 9000

that Helen was carried off under the guidance and at the instigation of the gods, and that she became a direful destiny to her own and to after times? Was it because of our name, that that mad-cap Xerxes let the ocean in upon the land, and that he marched over the sea on foot? Did we produce and stir into action the causes, by reason of which one youth, starting from Macedonia, subjected the kingdoms and peoples of the East to captivity and to bondage? Did we, forsooth, urge the deities into frenzy, so that the Romans lately, like some swollen torrent, overthrew all nations, and swept them beneath the flood? But if there is no man who would dare to attribute to our times those things which took place long ago, how can we be the causes of the present misfortunes, when nothing new is occurring, but all things are old, and were unknown to none of the ancients?

6. Although you allege that those wars which you speak of were excited through hatred of our religion, it would not be difficult to prove, that after the name of Christ was heard in the world, not only were they not increased, but they were even in great measure diminished by the restraining of furious passions. For since we, a numerous band of men as we are, have learned from his teaching and his laws that evil ought not to be requited with evil,[1] that it is better to suffer wrong than to inflict it, that we should rather shed our own blood than stain our hands and our conscience with

years before that time they had overcome a mighty host which came rushing from the Atlantic Sea, and which threatened to subjugate all Europe and Asia. The sea was then navigable, and in front of the pillars of Hercules (Strait of Gibraltar) lay an island larger than Africa and Asia together: from it travellers could pass to other islands, and from these again to the opposite continent. In this island great kings arose, who made themselves masters of the whole island, as well as of other islands, and parts of the continent. Having already possessions in Libya and Europe, which they wished to increase, they gathered an immense host; but it was repelled by the Athenians. Great earthquakes and storms ensued, in which the island of Atlantis was submerged, and the sea ever after rendered impassable by shoals of mud produced by the sunken island. For other forms of this legend, and explanations of it, see Smith's *Dictionary of Geography*, under *Atlantis*.

[1] Cf. Matt. v. 39.

that of another, an ungrateful world is now for a long period enjoying a benefit from Christ, inasmuch as by his means the rage of savage ferocity has been softened, and has begun to withhold hostile hands from the blood of a fellow-creature. But if all without exception, who feel that they are men not in form of body but in power of reason, would lend an ear for a little to his salutary and peaceful rules, and would not, in the pride and arrogance of enlightenment, trust to their own senses rather than to his admonitions, the whole world, having turned the use of steel into more peaceful occupations, would now be living in the most placid tranquillity, and would unite in blessed harmony, maintaining inviolate the sanctity of treaties.

7. But if, say my opponents, no damage is done to human affairs by you, whence arise those evils by which wretched mortals are now oppressed and overwhelmed? You ask of me a decided statement,[1] which is by no means necessary to this cause. For no immediate and prepared discussion regarding it has been undertaken by me, for the purpose of showing or proving from what causes and for what reasons each event took place; but in order to demonstrate that the reproaches of so grave a charge are far removed from our door. And if I prove this, if by examples and[2] by powerful arguments the truth of the matter is made clear, I care not whence these evils come, or from what sources and first beginnings they flow.

8. And yet, that I may not seem to have no opinion on subjects of this kind; that I may not appear when asked to have nothing to offer, I may say, What if the primal matter which has been diffused through the four elements of the universe, contains the causes of all miseries inherent in its own constitution? What if the movements of the heavenly bodies produce these evils in certain signs, regions, seasons, and tracts, and impose upon things placed under them the necessity of various dangers? What if, at stated intervals,

---

[1] The MS. here inserts a mark of interrogation.

[2] So the MS., *si facto et*, corrected, however, by a later copyist, *si facio ut*, "if I cause that," etc.

changes take place in the universe, and, as in the tides of the sea, prosperity at one time flows, at another time ebbs, evils alternating with it? What if those impurities of matter which we tread under our feet have this condition imposed upon them, that they give forth the most noxious exhalations, by means of which this our atmosphere is corrupted, and brings pestilence on our bodies, and weakens the human race? What if—and this seems nearest the truth—whatever appears to us adverse, is in reality not an evil to the world itself? And what if, measuring by our own advantages all things which take place, we blame the results of nature through ill-formed judgments? Plato, that sublime head and pillar of philosophers, has declared in his writings, that those cruel floods and those conflagrations of the world are a purification of the earth; nor did that wise man dread to call the overthrow of the human race, its destruction, ruin, and death, a renewal of things, and to affirm that a youthfulness, as it were, was secured by this renewed strength.[1]

9. It rains not from heaven, my opponent says, and we are in distress from some extraordinary deficiency of grain crops. What then, do you demand that the elements should be the slaves of your wants? and that you may be able to live more softly and more delicately, ought the compliant seasons to minister to your convenience? What if, in this way, one who is intent on voyaging complains that now for a long time there are no winds, and that the blasts of heaven have for ever lulled? Is it therefore to be said that that peacefulness of the universe is pernicious, because it interferes with the wishes of traders? What if one, accustomed to bask himself in the sun, and thus to acquire dryness of body, similarly complains that by the clouds the pleasure of serene weather is taken away? Should the clouds, therefore, be said to hang over with an injurious veil, because idle lust is not permitted to scorch itself in the burning heat, and to devise excuses for drinking? All these events which are brought to pass, and which happen under this mass of the universe, are not to be regarded as sent for our petty advan-

[1] Plato, *Tim.* st. p. 22.

tages, but as consistent with the plans and arrangements of Nature herself.

10. And if anything happens which does not foster ourselves or our affairs with joyous success, it is not to be set down forthwith as an evil, and as a pernicious thing. The world rains or does not rain : for itself it rains or does not rain; and, though you perhaps are ignorant of it, it either diminishes excessive moisture by a burning drought, or by the outpouring of rain moderates the dryness extending over a very long period. It raises pestilences, diseases, famines, and other baneful forms of plagues : how can you tell whether it does not thus remove that which is in excess, and whether, through loss to themselves, it does not fix a limit to things prone to luxuriance?

11. Would you venture to say that, in this universe, this thing or the other thing is an evil, whose origin and cause you are unable to explain and to analyze?[1] And because it interferes with your lawful, perhaps even your unlawful pleasures, would you say that it is pernicious and adverse? What, then, because cold is disagreeable to your members, and is wont to chill[2] the warmth of your blood, ought not winter on that account to exist in the world? And because you are unable[3] to endure the hottest rays of the sun, is summer to be removed from the year, and a different course of nature to be instituted under different laws? Hellebore is poison to men; should it therefore not grow? The wolf lies in wait by the sheepfolds; is nature at all in fault, because she has produced a beast most dangerous to sheep? The serpent by his bite takes away life; a reproach, forsooth, to creation, because it has added to animals monsters so cruel.

12. It is rather presumptuous, when you are not your own master, even when you are the property of another, to dictate terms to those more powerful; to wish that that should happen which you desire, not that which you have found fixed

---

[1] "To analyze"—*dissolvere*—is in the MS. marked as spurious.
[2] In the MS. we find "to chill and numb"—*congelare, constringere;* but the last word, too, is marked as spurious.
[3] MS. *sustinere* (marked as a gloss), "to sustain;" *perferre,* "to endure."

in things by their original constitution. Wherefore, if you wish that your complaints should have a basis, you must first inform us whence you are, or who you are; whether the world was created and fashioned for you, or whether you came into it as sojourners from other regions. And since it is not in your power to say or to explain for what purpose you live beneath this vault of heaven, cease to believe that anything belongs to you; since those things which take place are not brought about in favour of a part, but have regard to the interest of the whole.

13. Because of the Christians, my opponents say, the gods inflict upon us all calamities, and ruin is brought on our crops by the heavenly deities. I ask, when you say these things, do you not see that you are accusing us with barefaced effrontery, with palpable and clearly proved falsehoods? It is almost three hundred years[1]—something less or more—since we Christians began to exist, and to be taken account of in the world. During all these years, have wars been incessant, has there been a yearly failure of the crops, has there been no peace on earth, has there been no season of cheapness and abundance of all things? For this must first be proved by him who accuses us, that these calamities have been endless and incessant, that men have never had a breathing time at all, and that without any relaxation[2] they have undergone dangers of many forms.

14. And yet do we not see that, in these years and seasons that have intervened, victories innumerable have been gained from the conquered enemy,—that the boundaries of the empire have been extended, and that nations whose names we had not previously heard, have been brought under our power,—that very often there have been the most plentiful yields of grain, seasons of cheapness, and such abundance of commodities, that all commerce was paralyzed, being prostrated by the standard of prices? For in what manner could affairs be carried on, and how could the human race have

[1] See Introduction.
[2] *Sine ullis feriis*, a proverbial expression, "without any holidays," *i.e.* without any intermixture of good.

existed¹ even to this time, had not the productiveness of nature continued to supply all things which use demanded?

15. Sometimes, however, there were seasons of scarcity; yet they were relieved by times of plenty. Again, certain wars were carried on contrary to our wishes.² But they were afterwards compensated by victories and successes. What shall we say, then?—that the gods at one time bore in mind our acts of wrong-doing, at another time again forgot them? If, when there is a famine, the gods are said to be enraged at us, it follows that in time of plenty they are not wroth, and ill-to-be-appeased; and so the matter comes to this, that they both lay aside and resume anger with sportive whim, and always renew their wrath afresh by the recollection of the causes of offence.

16. Yet one cannot discover by any rational process of reasoning, what is the meaning of these statements. If the gods willed that the Alemanni³ and the Persians should be overcome because Christians dwelt among their tribes, how did they grant victory to the Romans when Christians dwelt among their peoples also? If they willed that mice and locusts should swarm forth in prodigious numbers in Asia and in Syria because Christians dwelt among their tribes too, why was there at the same time no such phenomenon in Spain and in Gaul, although innumerable Christians lived in those provinces also? If among the Gætuli and the Tinguitani⁴ they sent dryness and aridity on the crops on account of this circumstance, why did they in that very year give the most bountiful harvest to the Moors and to the Nomads, when a similar religion had its abode in these regions as well? If in any one state whatever they have caused many

---

¹ For *qui durare* Ursinus would read *quiret durare;* but this seems to have no MS. authority, though giving better sense and an easier construction.

² That is, unsuccessfully.

³ *Alemanni, i.e.* the Germans; hence the French *Allemagne.* The MS. has *Alamanni.*

⁴ The *Gætuli* and *Tinguitani* were African tribes. For *Tinguitanos,* another reading is *tunc Aquitanos;* but *Tinguitanos* is much to be preferred on every ground.

to die with hunger, through disgust at our name, why have they in the same state made wealthier, ay, very rich, by the high price of corn, not only men not of our body, but even Christians themselves? Accordingly, either all should have had no blessing if we are the cause of the evils, for we are in all nations; or when you see blessings mixed with misfortunes, cease to attribute to us that which damages your interests, when we in no respect interfere with your blessings and prosperity. For if I cause it to be ill with you, why do I not prevent it from being well with you? If my name is the cause of a great dearth, why am I powerless to prevent the greatest productiveness? If I am said to bring the [ill] luck of a wound being received in war, why, when the enemy are slain, am I not an evil augury; and why am I not set forth against good hopes, through the ill luck of a bad omen?

17. And yet, O ye great worshippers and priests of the deities, why, as you assert that those most holy gods are enraged at Christian communities, do you not likewise perceive, do you not see what base feelings, what unseemly frenzies, you attribute to your deities? For, to be angry, what else is it than to be insane, to rave, to be urged to the lust of vengeance, and to revel in the troubles of another's grief, through the madness of a savage disposition? Your great gods, then, know, are subject to and feel that which wild beasts, which monstrous brutes experience, which the deadly plant natrix contains in its poisoned roots. That nature which is superior to others, and which is based on the firm foundation of unwavering virtue, experiences, as you allege, the instability which is in man, the faults which are in the animals of earth. And what therefore follows of necessity, but that from their eyes flashes dart, flames burst forth, a panting breast emits a hurried breathing from their mouth, and by reason of their burning words their parched lips become pale?

18. But if this that you say is true,—if it has been tested and thoroughly ascertained both that the gods boil with rage, and that an impulse of this kind agitates the divinities with excitement, on the one hand they are not immortal, and on the other they are not to be reckoned as at all partaking of

divinity. For wherever, as the philosophers hold, there is any agitation, there of necessity passion must exist. Where passion is situated, it is reasonable that mental excitement follow. Where there is mental excitement, there grief and sorrow exist. Where grief and sorrow exist, there is already room for weakening and decay; and if these two harass them, extinction is at hand, viz. death, which ends all things, and takes away life from every sentient being.

19. Moreover, in this way you represent them as not only unstable and excitable, but, what all agree is far removed from the character of deity, as unfair in their dealings, as wrong-doers, and, in fine, as possessing positively no amount of even moderate fairness. For what is a greater wrong than to be angry with some, and to injure others, to complain of human beings, and to ravage the harmless corn crops, to hate the Christian name, and to ruin the worshippers of Christ with every kind of loss?

20. [1]Do they on this account wreak their wrath on you too, in order that, roused by your own private wounds, you may rise up for their vengeance? It seems, then, that the gods seek the help of mortals; and were they not protected by your strenuous advocacy, they are not able of themselves to repel and to avenge[2] the insults offered them. Nay rather, if it be true that they burn with anger, give them an opportunity of defending themselves, and let them put forth and make trial of their innate powers, to take vengeance for their offended dignity. By heat, by hurtful cold, by noxious winds, by the most occult diseases, they can slay us, they can consume[3] us, and they can drive us entirely from all intercourse with men; or if it is impolitic to assail us by violence, let them give forth some token of their indignation,[4] by which it may be clear to all that we live under heaven subject to their strong displeasure.

21. To you let them give good health, to us bad, ay, the

[1] The MS. reads *at*, " but."
[2] *Defendere* is added in the MS., but marked as a gloss.
[3] *Consumere* is in like manner marked as a gloss.
[4] So Orelli, for the MS. *judicationis*, " judgment."

very worst. Let them water your farms with seasonable showers; from our little fields let them drive away all those rains which are gentle. Let them see to it that your sheep are multiplied by a numerous progeny; on our flocks let them bring luckless barrenness. From your olive-trees and vineyards let them bring the full harvest; but let them see to it that from not one shoot of ours one drop be expressed. Finally, and as their worst, let them give orders that in your mouth the products of the earth retain their natural qualities; but, on the contrary, that in ours the honey become bitter, the flowing oil grow rancid, and that the wine when sipped, be in the very lips suddenly changed into disappointing vinegar.

22. And since facts themselves testify that this result never occurs, and since it is plain that to us no less share of the bounties of life accrues, and to you no greater, what inordinate desire is there to assert that the gods are unfavourable, nay, inimical to the Christians, who, in the greatest adversity, just as in prosperity, differ from you in no respect? If you allow the truth to be told you, and that, too, without reserve, these allegations are but words,—words, I say; nay, matters believed on calumnious reports not proved by any certain evidence.

23. But the true[1] gods, and those who are worthy to have and to wear the dignity of this name, neither conceive anger nor indulge a grudge, nor do they contrive by insidious devices what may be hurtful to another party. For verily it is profane, and surpasses all acts of sacrilege, to believe that that wise and most blessed nature is uplifted in mind if one prostrates himself before it in humble adoration; and if this adoration be not paid, that it deems itself despised, and regards itself as fallen from the pinnacle of its glory. It is childish, weak, and petty, and scarcely becoming for those whom the experience of learned men has for a long time called demigods and heroes,[2] not to be versed in heavenly

---

[1] The carelessness of some copyist makes the MS. read *ve-st-ri*, "your," corrected as above by Ursinus.

[2] So Ursinus, followed by Heraldus, LB., and Orelli, for the MS.

things, and, divesting themselves of their own proper state, to be busied with the coarser matter of earth.

24. These are your ideas, these are your sentiments, impiously conceived, and more impiously believed. Nay, rather, to speak out more truly, the augurs, the dream interpreters, the soothsayers, the prophets, and the priestlings, ever vain, have devised these fables; for they, fearing that their own arts be brought to nought, and that they may extort but scanty contributions from the devotees, now few and infrequent, whenever they have found you to be willing[1] that their craft should come into disrepute, cry aloud, The gods are neglected, and in the temples there is now a very thin attendance. Former ceremonies are exposed to derision, and the time-honoured rites of institutions once sacred have sunk before the superstitions of new religions. Justly is the human race afflicted by so many pressing calamities, justly is it racked by the hardships of so many toils. And men—a senseless race —being unable, from their inborn blindness, to see even that which is placed in open light, dare to assert in their frenzy what you in your sane mind do not blush to believe.

25. And lest any one should suppose that we, through distrust in our reply, invest the gods with the gifts of serenity, that we assign to them minds free from resentment, and far removed from all excitement, let us allow, since it is pleasing to you, that they put forth their passion upon us, that they thirst for our blood, and that now for a long time they are eager to remove us from the generations of men. But if it is not troublesome to you, if it is not offensive, if it is a matter of common duty to discuss the points of this argument

---

errores, which Stewechius would change into *errones*—" vagrants "—referring to the spirits wandering over the earth: most other edd., following Gelenius, read, " called demigods, that these indeed "—*dæmonas appellat, et hos*, etc.

[1] So the MS., which is corrected in the first ed. " us to be willing "— *nos velle:* Stewechius reads, " us to be making good progress, are envious, enraged, and cry aloud," etc.—*nos belle provenire compererunt, invident, indignantur, declamitantque,* etc.; to both of which it is sufficient objection that they do not improve the passage by their departure from the MS.

not on grounds of partiality, but on those of truth, we demand to hear from you what is the explanation of this, what the cause, why, on the one hand, the gods exercise cruelty on us alone, and why, on the other, men burn against us with exasperation. You follow, our opponents say, profane religious systems, and you practise rites unheard of throughout the entire world. What do you, O men, endowed with reason, dare to assert? What do you dare to prate of? What do you try to bring forward in the recklessness of unguarded speech? To adore God as the highest existence, as the Lord of all things that be, as occupying the highest place among all exalted ones, to pray to Him with respectful submission in our distresses, to cling to Him with all our senses, so to speak, to love Him, to look up to Him with faith,—is this an execrable and unhallowed religion, full of impiety and of sacrilege, polluting by the superstition of its own novelty ceremonies instituted of old?

26. Is this, I pray, that daring and heinous iniquity on account of which the mighty powers of heaven whet against us the stings of passionate indignation, on account of which you yourselves, whenever the savage desire has seized you, spoil us of our goods, drive us from the homes of our fathers, inflict upon us capital punishment, torture, mangle, burn us, and at the last expose us to wild beasts, and give us to be torn by monsters? Whosoever condemns that in us, or considers that it should be laid against us as a charge, is he deserving either to be called by the name of man, though he seem so to himself? or is he to be believed a god, although he declare himself to be so by the mouth of a thousand[1] prophets? Does Trophonius,[2] or Jupiter of Dodona, pronounce us to be wicked? And will he himself be called god, and be reckoned among the number of the deities, who either fixes the charge of impiety on those who serve the King Supreme, or is racked with envy because His majesty and His worship are preferred to his own?

[1] So LB. and Orelli; but the MS. reads, "himself to be like [a god] by [his] prophets," etc.—*se esse similem profiteatur in vatibus.*

[2] So corrected by Pithœus for the MS. *profanus.*

Is Apollo, whether called Delian or Clarian, Didymean, Philesian, or Pythian, to be reckoned divine, who either knows not the Supreme Ruler, or who is not aware that He is entreated by us in daily prayers? And although he knew not the secrets of our hearts, and though he did not discover what we hold in our inmost thoughts, yet he might either know by his ear, or might perceive by the very tone of voice which we use in prayer, that we invoke God Supreme, and that we beg from Him what we require.

27. This is not the place to examine all our traducers, who they are, or whence they are, what is their power, what their knowledge, why they tremble at the mention of Christ, why they regard his disciples as enemies and as hateful persons; but [with regard to ourselves] to state expressly to those who will exercise common reason, in terms applicable to all of us alike,—We Christians are nothing else than worshippers of the Supreme King and Head, under our Master, Christ. If you examine carefully, you will find that nothing else is implied in that religion. This is the sum of all that we do; this is the proposed end and limit of sacred duties. Before Him we all prostrate ourselves, according to our custom; Him we adore in joint prayers; from Him we beg things just and honourable, and worthy of his ear. Not that He needs our supplications, or loves to see the homage of so many thousands laid at his feet. This is our benefit, and has a regard to our advantage. For since we are prone to err, and to yield to various lusts and appetites through the fault of our innate weakness, He allows Himself at all times to be comprehended in our thoughts, that whilst we entreat Him and strive to merit his bounties, we may receive a desire for purity, and may free ourselves from every stain by the removal of all our shortcomings.

28. What say ye, O interpreters of sacred and of divine law?[1] Are they attached to a better cause who adore

[1] So Gelenius, followed by Orelli and others, for the MS., reading *divini interpretes viri* (instead of *juris*)—" O men, interpreters of the sacred and divine," which is retained by the 1st ed., Hildebrand, and Oehler.

the Lares Grundules, the Aii Locutii,[1] and the Limentini,[2] than we who worship God the Father of all things, and demand of Him protection in danger and distress? They, too, seem to you wary, wise, most sagacious, and not worthy of any blame, who revere Fauni and Fatuæ, and the genii of states,[3] who worship Pausi and Bellonæ :—we are pronounced dull, doltish, fatuous, stupid, and senseless, who have given ourselves up to God, at whose nod and pleasure everything which exists has its being, and remains immoveable by his eternal decree. Do you put forth this opinion? Have you ordained this law? Do you publish this decree, that he be crowned with the highest honours who shall worship your slaves? that he merit the extreme penalty of the cross who shall offer prayers to you yourselves, his masters? In the greatest states, and in the most powerful nations, sacred rites are performed in the public name to harlots, who in old days earned the wages of impurity, and prostituted themselves to the lust of all ;[4] [and yet for this] there are no swellings of indignation on the part of the deities. Temples have been erected with lofty roofs to cats, to beetles, and to heifers :[5]— the powers of the deities thus insulted are silent; nor are they affected with any feeling of envy because they see the sacred attributes of vile animals put in rivalry with them. Are the deities inimical to us alone? To us are they most

[1] Aii Locutii. Shortly before the Gallic invasion, B.C. 390, a voice was heard at the dead of night announcing the approach of the Gauls, but the warning was unheeded. After the departure of the Gauls, the Romans dedicated an altar and sacred enclosure to Aius Locutius, or Loquens, *i.e.* "The Announcing Speaker," at a spot on the Via Nova, where the voice was heard. The MS. reads *aiaceos loctios*, which Gelenius emended Aios Locutios.

[2] So emended by Ursinus for the MS. *libentinos*, which is retained in the 1st ed., and by Gelenius, Canterus, and others. Cf. iv. 9, where Libentina is spoken of as presiding over lusts.

[3] As a soul was assigned to each individual at his birth, so a genius was attributed to a state. The genius of the Roman people was often represented on ancient coins.

[4] Thus the Athenians paid honours to Leæna, the Romans to Acca Laurentia and Flora.

[5] The superstitions of the Egyptians are here specially referred to.

unrelenting, because we worship their Author, by whom, if they do exist, they began to be, and to have the essence of their power and their majesty, from whom, having obtained their very divinity, so to speak, they feel that they exist, and realize that they are reckoned among things that be, at whose will and at whose behest they are able both to perish and be dissolved, and not to be dissolved and not to perish?[1] For if we all grant that there is only one great Being, whom in the long lapse of time nought else precedes, it necessarily follows that after Him all things were generated and put forth, and that they burst into an existence each of its kind. But if this is unchallenged and sure, you[2] will be compelled as a consequence to confess, on the one hand, that the deities are created,[3] and on the other, that they derive the spring of their existence from the great source of things. And if they are created and brought forth, they are also doubtless liable to annihilation and to dangers; but yet they are believed to be immortal, ever-existent, and subject to no extinction. This is also a gift from God their Author, that they have been privileged to remain the same through countless ages, though by nature they are fleeting, and liable to dissolution.

29. And would that it were allowed me to deliver this argument with the whole world formed, as it were, into one assembly, and to be placed in the hearing of all the human race! Are we therefore charged before you with an impious religion? and because we approach the Head and Pillar[4] of the universe with worshipful service, are we to be considered (to use the terms employed by you in reproaching us) as persons to be shunned, and as godless ones? And who would more properly bear the odium of these names than he

---

[1] That is, by whose pleasure and at whose command they are preserved from annihilation.

[2] So Orelli, adopting a conjecture of Meursius, for the MS. *nobis*.

[3] That is, not self-existent, but sprung from something previously in being.

[4] *Columen* is here regarded by some as equal to *culmen*; but the term "pillar" makes a good sense likewise.

who either knows, or inquires after, or believes any other god rather than this of ours? To Him do we not owe this first, that we exist, that we are said to be men, that, being either sent forth from Him, or having fallen from Him, we are confined in the darkness of this body?[1] Does it not come from Him that we walk, that we breathe and live? and by the very power of living, does He not cause us to exist and to move with the activity of animated being? From this do not causes emanate, through which our health is sustained by the bountiful supply of various pleasures? Whose is that world in which you live? or who hath authorized you to retain its produce and its possession? Who hath given that common light, enabling us to see distinctly all things lying beneath it, to handle them, and to examine them? Who has ordained that the fires of the sun should exist for the growth of things, lest elements pregnant with life should be numbed by settling down in the torpor of inactivity? When you believe that the sun is a deity, do you not ask who is his founder, who has fashioned him? Since the moon is a goddess in your estimation, do you in like manner care to know who is her author and framer?

30. Does it not occur to you to reflect and to examine in whose domain you live? on whose property you are? whose is that earth which you till?[2] whose is that air which you inhale, and return again in breathing? whose fountains do you abundantly enjoy? whose water? who has regulated the blasts of the wind? who has contrived the watery clouds? who has discriminated the productive powers of seeds by special characteristics? Does Apollo give you rain? Does Mercury send you water from heaven? Has Æsculapius, Hercules, or Diana devised the plan of showers and

---

[1] This is according to the doctrine of Pythagoras, Plato, Origen, and others, who taught that the souls of men first existed in heavenly beings, and that on account of sins of long standing they were transferred to earthly bodies to suffer punishment. Cf. Clem. Alex. *Strom.* iii. p. 433.

[2] The Peripatetics called God the *locus rerum*, τόπος πάντων, the "locality and the area of all things," that is, the being in whom all else was contained.

of storms? And how can this be, when you give forth that they were born on earth, and that at a fixed period they received vital perceptions? For if the world preceded them in the long lapse of time, and if before they were born nature already experienced rains and storms, those who were born later have no right of rain-giving, nor can they mix themselves up with those methods which they found to be in operation here, and to be derived from a greater Author.

31. O greatest, O supreme Creator of things invisible! O thou who art thyself unseen, and who art incomprehensible! Thou art worthy, thou art verily worthy—if only mortal tongue may speak of thee—that all breathing and intelligent nature should never cease to feel and to return thanks; that it should throughout the whole of life fall on bended knee, and offer supplication with never-ceasing prayers. For thou art the first cause; in thee created things exist, and thou art the space in which rest the foundations of all things, whatever they be. Thou art illimitable, unbegotten, immortal, enduring for aye, God thyself alone, whom no bodily shape may represent, no outline delineate; of virtues inexpressible, of greatness indefinable; unrestricted as to locality, movement, and condition, concerning whom nothing can be clearly expressed by the significance of man's words. That thou mayest be understood, we must be silent; and that erring conjecture may track thee through the shady cloud, no word must be uttered. Grant pardon, O King Supreme, to those who persecute thy servants; and in virtue of thy benign nature, forgive those who fly from the worship of thy name and the observance of thy religion. It is not to be wondered at if thou art unknown; it is a cause of greater astonishment if thou art clearly comprehended. But perchance some one dares—for this remains for frantic madness to do—to be uncertain, and to express doubt whether that God exists or not; whether He is believed in on the proved truth of reliable evidence, or on the imaginings of empty rumour. For of those who have given themselves to philosophizing, we have heard that some[1] deny the existence

---
[1] Diagoras of Melos and Theodorus of Cyrene, called the Atheists.

of any divine power, that others[1] inquire daily whether there be or not; that others[2] construct the whole fabric of the universe by chance accidents and by random collision, and fashion it by the concourse of atoms of different shapes; with whom we by no means intend to enter at this time on a discussion of such perverse convictions.[3] For those who think wisely say, that to argue against things palpably foolish, is a mark of greater folly.

32. Our discussion deals with those who, acknowledging that there is a divine race of beings, doubt about those of greater rank and power, whilst they admit that there are deities inferior and more humble. What then? Do we strive and toil to obtain such results by arguments? Far hence be such madness; and, as the phrase is, let the folly, say I, be averted from us. For it is as dangerous to attempt to prove by arguments that God is the highest being, as it is to wish to discover by reasoning of this kind that He exists. It is a matter of indifference whether you deny that He exists, or affirm it and admit it; since equally culpable are both the assertion of such a thing, and the denial of an unbelieving opponent.

33. Is there any human being who has not entered on the first day of his life with an idea of that Great Head? In whom has it not been implanted by nature, on whom has it not been impressed, aye, stamped almost in his mother's womb even, in whom is there not a native instinct, that He is King and Lord, the ruler of all things that be? In fine, if the dumb animals even could stammer forth their thoughts, if they were able to use our languages; nay, if trees, if the clods of the earth, if stones animated by vital perceptions were able to produce vocal sounds, and to utter articulate speech, would they not in that case, with nature as their guide and teacher,

---

The former flourished about B.C. 430, the latter about B.C. 310. See Cic. *Nat. Deor.* i. 2.

[1] Protagoras of Abdera, b. B.C. 480, d. 411.
[2] Democritus of Abdera, b. B.C. 460, and Epicurus, b. B.C. 342, d. 270.
[3] *Obstinatione*, literally "stubbornness;" Walker conjectures *opinatione*, "imaginings," which Orelli approves.

in the faith of uncorrupted innocence, both feel that there is a God, and proclaim that He alone is Lord of all?

34. But in vain, says one, do you assail us with a groundless and calumnious charge, as if we deny that there is a deity of a higher kind, since Jupiter is by us both called and esteemed the best and the greatest; and since we have dedicated to him the most sacred abodes, and have raised huge Capitols. You are endeavouring to connect together things which are dissimilar, and to force them into one class, [thereby] introducing confusion. For by the unanimous judgment of all, and by the common consent of the human race, the omnipotent God is regarded as having never been born, as having never been brought forth to new light, and as not having begun to exist at any time or century. For He Himself is the source of all things, the Father of ages and of seasons. For they do not exist of themselves, but from His everlasting perpetuity they move on in unbroken and ever endless flow. Yet Jupiter indeed, as you allege, has both father and mother, grandfathers, grandmothers, and brothers: now lately conceived in the womb of his mother, being completely formed and perfected in ten months, he burst with vital sensations into light unknown to him before. If, then, this is so, how can Jupiter be God [supreme], when it is evident that He is everlasting, and the former is represented by you as having had a natal day, and as having uttered a mournful cry, through terror at the strange scene?

35. But suppose they be one, as you wish, and not different in any power of deity and in majesty, do you therefore persecute us with undeserved hatred? Why do you shudder at the mention of our name as of the worst omen, if we too worship the deity whom you worship? or why do you contend that the gods are friendly to you, but inimical, aye, most hostile to us, though our relations to them are the same? For if one religion is common to us and to you, the anger of the gods is stayed;[1] but if they are hostile to us alone, it is

---

[1] So the MS.; for which Meursius would read, *nobis vobisque, communis esset* (for *cessat*)—"is to us and to you, the anger of the gods would be [shared in] common."

plain that both you and they have no knowledge of God. And that that God is not Jove, is evident by the very wrath of the deities.

36. But, says my opponent, the deities are not inimical to you, because you worship the omnipotent God; but because you both allege that one born as men are, and put to death on the cross, which is a disgraceful punishment even for worthless men, was God, and because you believe that he still lives, and because you worship him in daily supplications. If it is agreeable to you, my friends, state clearly what deities those are who believe that the worship of Christ by us has a tendency to injure them? Is it Janus, the founder of the Janiculum, and Saturn, the author of the Saturnian state? Is it Fauna Fatua,[1] the wife of Faunus, who is called the Good Goddess, but who is better and more deserving of praise in the drinking of wine? Is it those gods [Indigetes] who swim in the river, and live in the channels of the Numicius, in company with frogs and little fishes? Is it Æsculapius and father Bacchus, the former born of Coronis, and the other dashed by lightning from his mother's womb? Is it Mercury, son of Maia, and what is more divine, [Maia] the beautiful? Is it the bow-bearing deities Diana and Apollo, who were companions of their mother's wanderings, and who were scarcely safe in floating islands? Is it Venus, daughter of Dione, paramour of a man of Trojan family, and the prostituter of her secret charms? Is it Ceres, born in Sicilian territory, and Proserpine, surprised while gathering flowers? Is it the Theban or the Phœnician Hercules,—the latter buried in Spanish territory, the other burned by fire on Mount Œta? Is it the brothers Castor and Pollux, sons of Tyndareus,—the one accustomed to tame horses, the other an excellent boxer, and unconquerable with the untanned gauntlet? Is it the Titans and the Bocchores of the Moors, and the Syrian[2]

[1] So Ursinus, followed by most edd., for the reading of the MS. *Fenta Fatua*, cf. v. 18. A later writer has corrected the MS. *Fanda*, which, Rigaltius says, an old gloss renders " mother."

[2] So restored by Salmasius for *Dioscuri*, and understood by him as

deities, the offspring of eggs? Is it Apis, born in the Peloponnese, and in Egypt called Serapis? Is it Isis, tanned by Ethiopian suns, lamenting her lost son and husband torn limb from limb? Passing on, we omit the royal offspring of Opis, which your writers have in their books set forth for your instruction, telling you both who they are, and of what character. Do these, then, hear with offended ears that Christ is worshipped, and that he is accepted by us and regarded as a divine person? And being forgetful of the grade and state in which they recently were, are they unwilling to share with another that which has been granted to themselves? Is this the justice of the heavenly deities? Is this the righteous judgment of the gods? Is not this a kind of malice and of greed? is it not a species of base envy, to wish their own fortunes only to rise,—those of others to be lowered, and to be trodden down in despised lowliness?

37. We worship one who was born a man. What then? do you worship no one who was born a man? Do you not worship one and another, aye, deities innumerable? Nay, have you not taken from the number of mortals all those whom you now have in your temples; and have you not set them in heaven, and among the constellations? For if, perchance, it has escaped you that they once partook of human destiny, and of the state common to all men, search the most ancient literature, and range through the writings of those who, living nearest to the days of antiquity, set forth all things with undisguised truth and without flattery: you will learn in detail from what fathers, from what mothers they were each sprung, in what district they were

meaning Dea Syria, *i.e.* Venus, because it is said that a large egg having been found by the fish in the Euphrates, was pushed up by them to the dry land, when a dove came down, and sat upon it until the goddess came forth. Such was the form of the legend according to Nigidius; but Eratosthenes spoke of both Venus and Cupid as being produced in this manner. The Syrian deities were therefore Venus, Cupid, and perhaps Adonis. It should be remembered, however, that the Syrians paid reverence to pigeons and fish as gods (Xen. *Anab.* i. 4, 9), and that these may therefore be meant.

born, of what tribe; what they made, what they did, what they endured, how they employed themselves, what fortunes they experienced of an adverse or of a favourable kind in discharging their functions. But if, while you know that they were borne in the womb, and that they lived on the produce of the earth, you nevertheless upbraid us with the worship of one born like ourselves, you act with great injustice, in regarding that as worthy of condemnation in us which you yourselves habitually do; or what you allow to be lawful for you, you are unwilling to be in like manner lawful for others.

38. But in the meantime let us grant, in submission to your ideas, that Christ was one of us—similar in mind, soul, body, weakness, and condition; is he not worthy to be called and to be esteemed God by us, in consideration of his bounties, so numerous as they are? For if you have placed in the assembly[1] of the gods Liber, because he discovered the use of wine; Ceres, because she discovered the use of bread; Æsculapius, because he discovered the use of herbs; Minerva, because she produced the olive; Triptolemus, because he invented the plough; Hercules, because he overpowered and restrained wild beasts and robbers, and water-serpents of many heads,—with how great distinctions is he to be honoured by us, who, by instilling his truth into our hearts, has freed us from great errors; who, when we were straying everywhere, as if blind and without a guide, withdrew us from precipitous and devious paths, and set our feet on more smooth places; who has pointed out what is especially profitable and salutary for the human race; who has shown us what God is,[2] who he is, how great and how good; who has permitted and taught us to conceive and to understand, as far as our limited capacity can, his profound and inexpressible depths; who, in his great kindness, has caused it to be known by what founder, by what creator this world was established and made; who has explained the nature of

[1] So all edd., except those of Hildebrand and Oehler, for the MS. *censum*—" list."
[2] That is, that God is a Spirit.

its origin [1] and essential substance, never before imagined in the conceptions of any; whence generative warmth is added to the rays of the sun; why the moon, always uninjured [2] in her motions, is believed to alternate her light and her obscurity from intelligent causes; [3] what is the origin of animals, what rules regulate seeds; who designed man himself, who fashioned him, or from what kind of material did he compact the very build of bodies; what the perceptions are; what the soul, and whether it flew to us of its own accord, or whether it was generated and brought into existence with our bodies themselves; whether it sojourns with us, partaking of death, or whether it is gifted with an endless immortality; what condition awaits us when we shall have separated from our bodies relaxed in death; whether we shall retain our perceptions, [4] or have no recollection of our former sensations or of past memories; [5] who has restrained [6] our arrogance, and has caused our necks, uplifted with pride, to acknowledge the measure of their weakness; who hath shown that we are creatures imperfectly formed, that we trust in vain expectations, that we understand

[1] Orelli would refer these words to God; he thinks that with those immediately following they may be understood of God's spiritual nature, —an idea which he therefore supposes Arnobius to assert had never been grasped by the heathen.

[2] So Gelenius, followed by Orelli and others, for the corrupt reading of the MS., *idem ne quis;* but possibly both this and the preceding clause have crept into the text from the margin, as in construction they differ from the rest of the sentence, both that which precedes, and that which follows.

[3] The phrase *animalibus causis* is regarded by commentators as equal to *animatis causis*, and refers to the doctrine of the Stoics, that in the sun, moon, stars, etc., there was an intelligent nature, or a certain impulse of mind, which directed their movements.

[4] Lit. "shall see"—*visuri*, the reading of the MS.; changed in the first ed. and others to *victuri*—"shall live."

[5] Some have suggested a different construction of these words—*memoriam nullam nostri sensus et recordationis habituri*, thus—"have no memory of ourselves and senses of recollection;" but that adopted above is simpler, and does not force the words as this seems to do.

[6] The MS. and 1st and 2d Roman edd. read, *qui constringit*—"who restrains."

nothing thoroughly, that we know nothing, and that we do not see those things which are placed before our eyes; who has guided us from false superstitions to the true religion,—a blessing which exceeds and transcends all his other gifts; who has raised our thoughts to heaven from brutish statues formed of the vilest clay, and has caused us to hold converse in thanksgiving and prayer with the Lord of the universe.

39. But lately, O blindness, I worshipped images produced from the furnace, gods made on anvils and by hammers, the bones of elephants, paintings, wreaths on aged trees;[1] whenever I espied an anointed stone and one bedaubed with olive oil, as if some power resided in it I worshipped it, I addressed myself to it and begged blessings from a senseless stock. And these very gods of whose existence I had convinced myself, I treated with gross insults, when I believed them to be wood, stone, and bones, or imagined that they dwelt in the substance of such objects. Now, having been led into the paths of truth by so great a teacher, I know what all these things are, I entertain honourable thoughts concerning those which are worthy, I offer no insult to any divine name; and what is due to each, whether inferior[2] or superior, I assign with clearly-defined gradations, and on distinct authority. Is Christ, then, not to be regarded by us as God? and is he, who in other respects may be deemed the very greatest, not to be honoured with divine worship, from whom we have already received while alive so great gifts, and from whom, when the day comes, we expect greater ones?

40. But he died nailed to the cross. What is that to the argument? For neither does the kind and disgrace of the death change his words or deeds, nor will the weight of his

[1] It was a common practice with the Romans to hang the spoils of an enemy on a tree, which was thus consecrated to some deity. Hence such trees were sacred, and remained unhurt even to old age. Some have supposed that the epithet " old " is applied from the fact that the heathen used to offer to their gods objects no longer of use to themselves; thus it was only old trees, past bearing fruit, which were generally selected to hang the *spolia* upon.

[2] *Vel personæ vel capiti.*

teaching appear less; because he freed himself from the shackles of the body, not by a natural separation, but departed by reason of violence offered to him. Pythagoras of Samos was burned to death in a temple, under an unjust suspicion of aiming at sovereign power. Did his doctrines lose their peculiar influence, because he breathed forth his life not willingly, but in consequence of a savage assault? In like manner Socrates, condemned by the decision of his fellow-citizens, suffered capital punishment: have his discussions on morals, on virtues, and on duties been rendered vain, because he was unjustly hurried from life? Others without number, conspicuous by their renown, their merit, and their public character, have experienced the most cruel forms of death, as Aquilius, Trebonius, and Regulus: were they on that account adjudged base after death, because they perished not by the common law of the fates, but after being mangled and tortured in the most cruel kind of death? No innocent person foully slain is ever disgraced thereby; nor is he stained by the mark of any baseness, who suffers severe punishment, not from his own deserts, but by reason of the savage nature of his persecutor.[1]

41. And yet, O ye who laugh because we worship one who died an ignominious death, do not ye too, by consecrating shrines to him, honour father Liber, who was torn limb from limb by the Titans? Have you not, after his punishment and his death by lightning, named Æsculapius, the discoverer of medicines, as the guardian and protector of health, of strength, and of safety? Do you not invoke the great Hercules himself by offerings, by victims, and by kindled frankincense, whom you yourselves allege to have been burned alive after his punishment,[2] and to have been

---

[1] So all the later edd.; but in the MS., 1st and 2d Roman edd., and in those of Gelenius and Canterus, this clause reads, *cruciatoris perpetitur sævitatem*—" but suffers the cruelty of his persecutor."

[2] The words *post pœnas* in the text are regarded as spurious by Orelli, who supposes them to have crept in from the preceding sentence; but they may be defended as sufficiently expressing the agonies which Hercules suffered through the fatal shirt of Nessus.

consumed on the fatal pyres? Do you not, with the unanimous approbation of the Gauls, invoke as a propitious[1] and as a holy god, in the temples of the Great Mother,[2] that Phrygian Atys[3] who was mangled and deprived of his virility? Father Romulus himself, who was torn in pieces by the hands of a hundred senators, do you not call Quirinus Martius, and do you not honour him with priests and with gorgeous couches,[4] and do you not worship him in most spacious temples; and in addition to all this, do you not affirm that he has ascended into heaven? Either, therefore, you too are to be laughed at, who regard as gods men slain by the most cruel tortures; or if there is a sure ground for your thinking that you should do so, allow us too to feel assured for what causes and on what grounds we do this.

42. You worship one who was born a human being, [say my opponents]. Even if that were true, as has been already said in former passages, yet, in consideration of the many liberal gifts which he has bestowed on us, he ought to be called and be addressed as God. Since he is a God in reality and without any shadow of doubt, do you think that we will deny that he is worshipped by us with all the fervour we are capable of, and assumed as the guardian of our body? Is that Christ of yours a god, then? some raving, wrathful, and excited man will say. A god, we will reply, and a god of the inner powers;[5] and—what may still further torture unbelievers

[1] The words *deum propitium* are indeed found in the MS., but according to Rigaltius are not in the same handwriting as the rest of the work.
[2] Cybele, whose worship was conjoined with that of Atys.
[3] So Orelli, but the MS. *Attis*.
[4] This refers to the practice of placing the images of the gods on pillows at feasts. In the temples there were *pulvinaria*, or couches, specially for the purpose.
[5] The phrase *potentiarum interiorum* is not easily understood. Orelli is of opinion that it means those powers which in the Bible are called the "powers of heaven," the "army of heaven," *i.e.* the angels. The Jews and the early fathers of the church divided the heaven into circles or zones, each inhabited by its peculiar powers or intelligent natures, differing in dignity and in might. The central place was assigned to God himself, and to Christ, who sat on his right hand, and who is called by the fathers of the church the "Angel of the Church,"

with the most bitter pains—he was sent to us by the King Supreme for a purpose of the very highest moment. My opponent, becoming more mad and more frantic, will perhaps ask whether the matter can be proved, as we allege. There is no greater proof than the credibility of the acts done by him, than the unwonted excellence of the virtues [he exhibited], than the conquest and the abrogation of all those deadly ordinances which peoples and tribes saw executed in the light of day,[1] with no objecting voice; and even they whose ancient laws or whose country's laws he shows to be full of vanity and of the most senseless superstition, (even they) dare not allege these things to be false.

43. My opponent will perhaps meet me with many other slanderous and childish charges which are commonly urged. Jesus was a Magian;[2] he effected all these things by secret arts. From the shrines of the Egyptians he stole the names of angels of might,[3] and the religious system of a remote country. Why, O witlings, do you speak of things which you have not examined, and which are unknown to you, prating with the garrulity of a rash tongue? Were, then, those things which were done, the freaks of demons, and

---

and the "Angel of the New Covenant." Next in order came "Thrones," "Archangels," "Cherubim and Seraphim," and most remote from God's throne, the "Chorus of Angels," the tutelar genii of men. The system of zones and powers seems to have been derived from the Chaldeans, who made a similar division of the heavens. According to this idea, Arnobius speaks of Christ as nearest to the Father, and God of the "inner powers," who enjoyed God's immediate presence. Reference is perhaps made to some recondite doctrine of the Gnostics. It may mean, however, the more subtile powers of nature, as affecting both the souls of men and the physical universe.

[1] So Orelli with most edd., following Ursinus, for the MS. *suo ge-ne-ri-s sub limine*, which might, however, be retained, as if the sense were that these ordinances were coeval with man's origin, and translated, "tribes saw at the beginning of their race."

[2] *Magus*, almost equivalent to sorcerer.

[3] Arnobius uses *nomina*, "names," with special significance, because the Magi in their incantations used barbarous and fearful names of angels and of powers, by whose influence they thought strange and unusual things were brought to pass.

the tricks of magical arts? Can you specify and point out to me any one of all those magicians who have ever existed in past ages, that did anything similar, in the thousandth degree, to Christ? Who has done this without any power of incantations, without the juice of herbs and of grasses, without any anxious watching of sacrifices, of libations, or of seasons? For we do not press it, and inquire what they profess to do, nor in what kind of acts all their learning and experience are wont to be comprised. For who is not aware that these men either study to know beforehand things impending, which, whether they will or not, come of necessity as they have been ordained? or to inflict a deadly and wasting disease on whom they choose; or to sever the affections of relatives; or to open without keys places which are locked; or to seal the mouth in silence; or in the chariot race to weaken, urge on, or retard horses; or to inspire in wives, and in the children of strangers, whether they be males or females, the flames and mad desires of illicit love?[1] Or if they seem to attempt anything useful, to be able to do it not by their own power, but by the might of those deities whom they invoke.

44. And yet it is agreed on that Christ performed all those miracles which he wrought without any aid from external things, without the observance of any ceremonial, without any definite mode of procedure, [but solely] by the inherent might of his authority; and as was the proper duty of a true God, as was consistent with his nature, as was worthy of him, in the generosity of his bounteous power he bestowed nothing hurtful or injurious, but [only that which is] helpful, beneficial, and full of blessings good[2] for men.

---

[1] All these different effects the magicians of old attempted to produce: to break family ties by bringing plagues into houses, or by poisons; open doors and unbind chains by charms (Orig. contra Cels. ii.); affect horses in the race (of which Hieronymus in his *Life of Hilarion* gives an example); and use philters and love potions to kindle excessive and unlawful desires.

[2] So Orelli and most edd., following a marginal reading of Ursinus, *auxiliaribus plenum bonis* (for the MS. *nobis*).

45. What do you say again, oh you¹ ——? Is he then a man, is he one of us, at whose command, at whose voice, raised in the utterance of audible and intelligible words,² infirmities, diseases, fevers, and other ailments of the body fled away? Was he one of us, whose presence, whose very sight, that race of demons which took possession of men was unable to bear, and terrified by the strange power, fled away? Was he one of us, to whose order the foul leprosy, at once checked, was obedient, and left sameness of colour to bodies formerly spotted? Was he one of us, at whose light touch the issues of blood were stanched, and stopped their excessive flow?³ Was he one of us, whose hands the waters of the lethargic dropsy fled from, and that searching⁴ fluid avoided; and did the swelling body, assuming a healthy dryness, find relief? Was he one of us, who bade the lame run? Was it his work, too, that the maimed stretched forth their hands, and the joints relaxed the rigidity⁵ acquired even at birth; that the paralytic rose to their feet, and persons now carried home their beds who a little before were borne on the shoulders of others; the blind were restored to sight, and men born without eyes now looked on the heaven and the day?

46. Was he one of us, I say, who by one act of intervention at once healed a hundred or more afflicted with various infirmities and diseases; at whose word only the raging and maddened seas were still, the whirlwinds and tempests were lulled; who walked over the deepest pools

---

¹ In the height of his indignation and contempt, the writer stops short and does not apply to his opponents any new epithet.
² This is contrasted with the mutterings and strange words used by the magicians.
³ So the MS. according to Oehler, and seemingly Heraldus; but according to Orelli, the MS. reads *immoderati* (instead of —*os*) *cohibebant fluores*, which Meursius received as equivalent to " the excessive flow stayed itself."
⁴ *Penetrabilis*, " searching," *i.e.* finding its way to all parts of the body.
⁵ So Orelli, LB., Elmenhorst, and Stewechius, adopting a marginal reading of Ursinus, which prefixes *im*— to the MS. *mobilitates*—" looseness"—retained by the other edd.

with unwet foot; who trod the ridges of the deep, the very waves being astonished, and nature coming under bondage; who with five loaves satisfied five thousand of his followers; and who, lest it might appear to the unbelieving and hard of heart to be an illusion, filled twelve capacious baskets with the fragments that remained? Was he one of us, who ordered the breath that had departed to return to the body, persons buried to come forth from the tomb, and after three days to be loosed from the swathings of the undertaker? Was he one of us, who saw clearly in the hearts of the silent what each was pondering,[1] what each had in his secret thoughts? Was he one of us, who, when he uttered a single word, was thought by nations far removed from one another and of different speech to be using well-known sounds, and the peculiar language of each?[2] Was he one of us, who, when he was teaching his followers the duties of a religion that could not be gainsaid, suddenly filled the whole world, and showed how great he was and who he was, by unveiling the boundlessness of his authority? Was he one of us, who, after his body had been laid in the tomb, manifested himself in open day to countless numbers of men; who spoke to them, and listened to them; who taught them, reproved and admonished them; who, lest they should imagine that they were deceived by unsubstantial fancies, showed himself once, a second time, aye frequently, in familiar conversation; who appears even now to righteous men of unpolluted mind who love him, not in airy dreams, but in a form of pure simplicity;[3] whose name, when heard, puts to flight evil spirits, imposes silence on soothsayers, prevents men from consulting the augurs, causes the efforts of arrogant magicians to be frustrated, not by the dread of his name, as you allege, but by the free exercise of a greater power?

---

[1] Cf. John ii. 25.
[2] No such miracle is recorded of Christ, and Oehler suggests with some probability that Arnobius may have here fallen into confusion as to what is recorded of the apostles on the day of Pentecost.
[3] The Latin is, *per puræ speciem simplicitatis*, which is not easily understood, and is less easily expressed.

47. These facts set forth in summary we have put forward, not on the supposition that the greatness of the agent was to be seen in these virtues alone. For however great these things be, how excessively petty and trifling will they be found to be, if it shall be revealed from what realms he has come, of what God he is the minister! But with regard to the acts which were done by him, they were performed, indeed, not that he might boast himself in empty ostentation, but that hardened and unbelieving men might be assured that what was professed was not deceptive, and that they might now learn to imagine, from the beneficence of his works, what a true god was. At the same time we wish this also to be known,[1] when, as was said, an enumeration of his acts has been given in summary, that Christ was able to do not only those things which he did, but that he could even overcome the decrees of fate. For if, as is evident, and as is agreed by all, infirmities and bodily sufferings, if deafness, deformity, and dumbness, if shrivelling of the sinews and the loss of sight happen to us, and are brought on us by the decrees of fate, and if Christ alone has corrected this, has restored and cured man, it is clearer than the sun himself that he was more powerful than the fates are when he has loosened and overpowered those things which were bound with everlasting knots, and fixed by unalterable necessity.

48. But, says some one, you in vain claim so much for Christ, when we now know, and have in past times known, of other gods both giving remedies to many who were sick, and healing the diseases and the infirmities of many men. I do not inquire, I do not demand, what god did so, or at what time; whom he relieved, or what shattered frame he restored to sound health: this only I long to hear, whether, without the addition of any substance—that is, of any medical application—he ordered diseases to fly away from men at a touch; whether he commanded and compelled the cause of ill health to be eradicated, and the bodies of the weak to return to their natural strength. For it is known that Christ, either

[1] So almost all edd.; but the MS. and 1st and 2d Roman edd. read *scire*—" to know," etc.

by applying his hand to the parts affected, or by the command of his voice only, opened the ears of the deaf, drove away blindness from the eyes, gave speech to the dumb, loosened the rigidity of the joints, gave the power of walking to the shrivelled,—was wont to heal by a word and by an order, leprosies, agues, dropsies, and all other kinds of ailments, which some fell power[1] has willed that the bodies of men should endure. What act like these have all those gods done, by whom you allege that help has been brought to the sick and the imperilled? for if they have at any time ordered, as is reported, either that medicine or a special diet be given to some,[2] or that a draught be drunk off, or that the juices of plants and of blades be placed[3] on that which causes uneasiness, or [have ordered] that persons should walk, remain at rest, or abstain from something hurtful,—and that this is no great matter, and deserves no great admiration, is evident, if you will attentively examine it—a similar mode of treatment is followed by physicians also, a creature earth-born and not relying on true science, but founding on a system of conjecture, and wavering in estimating probabilities. Now there is no [special] merit in removing by remedies those ailments which affect men: the healing qualities belong to the drugs—not virtues inherent in him who applies them; and though it is praiseworthy to know by what medicine or by what method it may be suitable for persons to be treated, there is room for this credit being assigned to man, but not to the deity. For it is [at least] no discredit that he[4] should have improved the health of man by things taken from without: it is a disgrace to a god that he is not able to effect it of himself, but that he gives soundness and safety [only] by the aid of external objects.

49. And since you compare Christ and the other deities as

[1] See Bk. ii. chap. 36.
[2] The gods in whose temples the sick lay ordered remedies through the priests.
[3] So all edd. except LB., which reads with the MS. *superponere*—"that [one] place the juices," etc.
[4] That is, the physician.

to the blessings of health bestowed, how many thousands of infirm persons do you wish to be shown to you by us; how many persons affected with wasting diseases, whom no appliances whatever restored, although they went as suppliants through all the temples, although they prostrated themselves before the gods, and swept the very thresholds with their lips—though, as long as life remained, they wearied with prayers, and importuned with most piteous vows Æsculapius himself, the health-giver, as they call him? Do we not know that some died of their ailments? that others grew old by the torturing pain of their diseases? that others began to live a more abandoned life after they had wasted their days[1] and nights in incessant prayers, and in expectation of mercy?[2] Of what avail is it, then, to point to one or another who may have been healed, when so many thousands have been left unaided, and the shrines are full of all the wretched and the unfortunate? Unless, perchance, you say that the gods help the good, but that the miseries of the wicked are overlooked. And yet Christ assisted the good and the bad alike; nor was there any one rejected by him, who in adversity sought help against violence and the ills of fortune. For this is the mark of a true god and of kingly power, to deny his bounty to none, and not to consider who merits it or who does not; since natural infirmity and not the choice of his desire, or of his sober judgment, makes a sinner. To say, moreover, that aid is given by the gods to the deserving when in distress, is to leave undecided and render doubtful what you assert: so that both he who has been made whole may seem to have been preserved by chance, and he who is not may appear to have been unable to banish infirmity, not because of his demerit, but by reason of a heaven-sent weakness.[3]

---

[1] So the edd., reading *tri-v-erunt*, for the MS. *tri-bu-erunt*—" given up," which is retained in the first ed.

[2] *Pietatis*, " of mercy," in which sense the word is often used in late writers. Thus it was from his clemency that Antoninus, the Roman emperor, received the title of *Pius*.

[3] So most edd., following a marginal reading of Ursinus, which prefixes *in*— to the MS. *firmitate*.

50. Moreover, by his own power he not only performed those miraculous deeds which have been detailed by us in summary, and not as the importance of the matter demanded; but, what was more sublime, he has permitted many others to attempt them, and to perform them by the use of his name. For when he foresaw that you were to be the detractors of his deeds and of his divine work, in order that no lurking suspicion might remain of his having lavished these gifts and bounties by magic arts, from the immense multitude of people, which with admiring wonder strove to gain his favour, he chose fishermen, artisans, rustics, and unskilled persons of a similar kind, that they being sent through various nations should perform all those miracles without any deceit and without any material aids. By a word he assuaged the racking pains of the aching members; and by a word they checked the writhings of maddening sufferings. By one command he drove demons from the body, and restored their senses to the lifeless; they, too, by no different command, restored to health and to soundness of mind those labouring under the inflictions of these [demons].[1] By the application of his hand he removed the marks of leprosy; they, too, restored to the body its natural skin by a touch not dissimilar. He ordered the dropsical and swollen flesh to recover its natural dryness; and his servants in the same manner stayed the wandering waters, and ordered them to glide through their own channels, avoiding injury to the frame. Sores of immense size, refusing to admit of healing, he restrained from further feeding on the flesh, by the interposition of one word; and they in like manner, by restricting its ravages, compelled the obstinate and merciless cancer to confine itself to a scar. To the lame he gave the power of walking, to the dark eyes sight, the dead he recalled to

---

[1] "They, too, ... those labouring under the inflictions of these:" so LB., with the warm approval of Orelli (who, however, with previous edd., retains the MS. reading in his text) and others, reading *sub eorum t-ortantes* (for MS. *p—*) *et illi se casibus;* Heraldus having suggested *rotantes*. This simple and elegant emendation makes it unnecessary to notice the harsh and forced readings of earlier edd.

life; and not less surely did they, too, relax the tightened nerves, fill the eyes with light already lost, and order the dead to return from the tombs, reversing the ceremonies of the funeral rites. Nor was anything calling forth the bewildered admiration of all done by him, which he did not freely allow to be performed by those humble and rustic men, and which he did not put in their power.

51. What say ye, O minds incredulous, stubborn, hardened? Did that great Jupiter Capitolinus of yours give to any human being power of this kind? Did he endow with this right any priest of a curia, the Pontifex Maximus, nay, even the Dialis, in whose name he is [revealed as] the god of life?[1] I shall not say, [did he impart power] to raise the dead, to give light to the blind, restore the normal condition of their members to the weakened and the paralyzed, but [did he even enable any one] to check a pustule, a hangnail, a pimple, either by the word of his mouth or the touch of his hand? Was this, then, a power natural to man, or could such a right be granted, could such a licence be given by the mouth of one reared on the vulgar produce of earth; and was it not a divine and sacred gift? or if the matter admits of any hyperbole, was it not more than divine and sacred? For if you do that which you are able to do, and what is compatible with your strength and your ability, there is no ground for the expression of astonishment; for you will have done that which you were able, and which your power was bound to accomplish, in order that there should be a perfect correspondence[2] between the deed and the doer. To be able to transfer to a man your own power,

---

[1] So understood by Orelli, who reads *quo Dius est*, adopting the explanation of Dialis given by Festus. The MS., however, according to Crusius, reads, *Dialem, quod ejus est, flaminem isto jure donavit;* in which case, from the position of the *quod*, the meaning might be, "which [term] is his," or possibly, "because he (*i.e.* the priest) is his," only that in the latter case a pronoun would be expected: the commentators generally refer it to the succeeding *jure*, with this "right," which is his. Canterus reads, *quod majus est, i.e.* than the Pontifex Maximus.

[2] So the MS. reading *æqualitas*, which is retained by Hild. and Oehler; all other editions drop *æ*—"that the quality of deed and doer might be one."

share with the frailest being the ability to perform that which you alone are able to do, is a proof of power supreme over all, and holding in subjection the causes of all things, and the natural laws of methods and of means.

52. Come, then, let some Magian Zoroaster[1] arrive from a remote part of the globe, crossing over the fiery zone,[2] if we believe Hermippus as an authority. Let these join him too —that Bactrian, whose deeds Ctesias sets forth in the first book of his History; the Armenian, grandson of Hosthanes;[3] and Pamphilus, the intimate friend of Cyrus; Apollonius, Damigero, and Dardanus; Velus, Julianus, and Bæbulus; and if there be any other one who is supposed to have especial powers and reputation in such magic arts. Let them grant to one of the people to adapt the mouths of the dumb for the purposes of speech, to unseal the ears of the deaf, to give the natural powers of the eye to those born without sight, and to restore feeling and life to bodies long cold in death. Or if that is [too] difficult, and if they cannot impart to others

---

[1] This passage has furnished occasion for much discussion as to text and interpretation. In the text Orelli's punctuation has been followed, who regards Arnobius as mentioning four Zoroasters—the Assyrian or Chaldæan, the Bactrian (cf. c. 5 of this book), the Armenian, and finally the Pamphylian, or Pamphilos, who, according to Clem. Alex. (*Strom.* v. p. 598), is referred to in Plato's *Republic*, Bk. x., under the name Er; Meursius and Salmasius, however, regarding the whole as one sentence, consider that only three persons are so referred to, the first being either Libyan or Bactrian, and the others as with Orelli. To seek to determine which view is most plausible even, would be a fruitless task, as will be evident on considering what is said in the index under Zoroaster.

[2] So Orelli, reading *veniat qu-is su-per igneam zonam*. LB. reads for the second and third words, *quæ-so per*—"let there come, I pray you, through," etc., from the MS. *quæ super*; while Heraldus would change the last three words into Azonaces, the name of the supposed teacher of Zoroaster. By the "fiery zone" Salmasius would understand Libya; but the legends should be borne in mind which spoke of Zoroaster as having shown himself to a wondering multitude from a hill blazing with fire, that he might teach them new ceremonies of worship, or as being otherwise distinguished in connection with fire.

[3] So Stewechius, Orelli, and others, for the MS. *Zostriani*—"grandson of Zostrianus," retained in the 1st ed. and LB.

the power to do such acts, let themselves perform them, and with their own rites. Whatever noxious herbs the earth brings forth from its bosom, whatever powers those muttered words and accompanying spells contain—these let them add, we envy them not; [those] let them collect, we forbid them not. We wish to make trial and to discover whether they can effect, with the aid of their gods, what has often been accomplished by unlearned Christians with a word only.

53. Cease in your ignorance to receive such great deeds with abusive language, which will in no wise injure him who did them, but which will bring danger to yourselves—danger, I say, by no means small, but one dealing with matters of great,[1] aye, even the greatest importance, since beyond a doubt the soul is a precious thing, and nothing can be found dearer to a man than himself. There was nothing magical, as you suppose, nothing human, delusive, or crafty in Christ; no deceit lurked in him,[2] although you smile in derision, as your wont is, and though you split with roars of laughter. He was God on high, God in his inmost nature, God from unknown realms, and was sent by the Ruler of all as a Saviour God; whom neither the sun himself, nor any stars, if they have powers of perception, not the rulers and princes of the world, nor, in fine, the great gods, or those who, feigning themselves so, terrify the whole human race, were able to know or to guess whence and who he was—and naturally so. But[3] when, freed from the body, which he carried about as but a very small part of himself, he allowed himself to be seen, and [let it be known] how great he was, all the elements of the universe bewildered by the strange events were thrown into confusion. An earthquake shook

---

[1] So the edd., reading *in rebus eximiis* for the MS. *exi-gu-is*, which would, of course, give an opposite and wholly unsuitable meaning.

[2] So generally, Heraldus having restored *delitu-it in Christo* from the MS., which had omitted *-it*, for the reading of Gelenius, Canterus, and Ursinus, *delicti*—" no deceit, no sin [was]," etc.

[3] So emended by Salmasius, followed by most later edd. In the earlier edd. the reading is *et merito exutus a corpore* (Salm. reading *at* instead of *a*, and inserting a period after *mer.*)—" and when rightly freed from the body," etc.

the world, the sea was heaved up from its depths, the heaven was shrouded in darkness, the sun's fiery blaze was checked, and his heat became moderate;[1] for what else could occur when he was discovered to be God who heretofore was reckoned one of us?

54. But you do not believe these things; yet those who witnessed their occurrence, and who saw them done before their eyes—the very best vouchers and the most reliable authorities—both believed them themselves, and transmitted them to us who follow them to be believed with no scanty measure of confidence. Who are these? you perhaps ask. Tribes, peoples, nations, and that incredulous human race; but[2] if the matter were not plain, and, as the saying is, clearer than day itself, they would never grant their assent with so ready belief to events of such a kind. But shall we say that the men of that time were untrustworthy, false, stupid, and brutish to such a degree that they pretended to have seen what they never had seen, and that they put forth under false evidence, or alleged with childish asseveration things which never took place, and that when they were able to live in harmony and to maintain friendly relations with you, they wantonly incurred hatred, and were held in execration?

55. But if this record of events is false, as you say, how comes it that in so short a time the whole world has been filled with such a religion? or how could nations dwelling widely apart, and separated by climate and by the convexities of heaven,[3] unite in one conclusion? They have been prevailed upon [say my opponents] by mere assertions, been led into vain hopes; and in their reckless madness have chosen to incur voluntarily the risks of death, although they had hitherto seen nothing of such a kind as could by

---

[1] It may be instructive to notice how the simpler narrative of the Gospels is amplified. Matthew (xxvii. 51) says that the earth trembled, and Luke (xxiii. 45) that the sun was darkened; but they go no further.

[2] Or, "which if ... itself, would never," etc.

[3] That is, by the climate and the inclination of the earth's surface.

its wonderful and strange character induce them to adopt this manner of worship. Nay, because they saw all these things to be done by [Christ] himself and by his apostles, who being sent throughout the whole world carried with them the blessings of the Father, which they dispensed in benefiting[1] as well the minds as the bodies of men; overcome by the force of the very truth itself they both devoted themselves to God, and reckoned it as but a small sacrifice to surrender their bodies to you and to give their flesh to be mangled.

56. But our writers [we shall be told] have put forth these statements with false effrontery; they have extolled[2] small matters to an inordinate degree, and have magnified trivial affairs with most pretentious boastfulness. And[3] would that all things could have been reduced to writing,— both those which were done by himself, and those which were accomplished by his apostles with equal authority and power. Such an assemblage of miracles, however, would make you more incredulous; and perhaps you might be able to discover a passage from which[4] it would seem very probable, both that additions were made to facts, and that falsehoods were inserted in writings and commentaries. But in nations which were unknown to the writers, and which themselves knew not the use of letters, all that was done could not have been embraced in the records or even have reached the ears of all men; or, if any were committed to written and connected narrative, some insertions and additions would have been made by the malevolence of the demons and of men like to them, whose

---

[1] So the 1st ed., Ursinus, Elmenhorst, Orelli, and Hildebrand, reading *munerandis*, which is found in the MS. in a later handwriting, for the original reading of the MS. *munera dis*.

[2] According to Rigaltius the MS. reads *ista promiserunt in immensum*— "have put forth (*i.e.* exaggerated) these things to an immense degree falsely, small matters and trivial affairs have magnified," etc.; while by a later hand has been superscribed over *in immensum*, in ink of a different colour, *extulere*—"have extolled."

[3] So the MS., 1st ed., and Hildebrand, while all others read *atqu-i*— "but."

[4] So LB., reading *quo* for the MS. *quod*.

care and study it is to obstruct[1] the progress of this truth: there would have been some changes and mutilations of words and of syllables, at once to mar the faith of the cautious and to impair the moral effect of the deeds. But it will never avail them that it be gathered from written testimony [only] who and what Christ was; for his cause has been put on such a basis, that if what we say be admitted to be true, he is by the confession of all proved to have been God.

57. You do not believe our writings, and we do not believe yours. We devise falsehoods concerning Christ [you say]; and you put forth baseless and false statements concerning your gods: for no god has descended from heaven, or in his own person and life has sketched out your system, or in a similar way thrown discredit on our system and our ceremonies. These were written by men; those, too, were written by men—set forth in human speech; and whatever you seek to say concerning our writers, remember that about yours, too, you will find these things said with equal force. What is contained in your writings you wish to be treated as true; those things, also, which are attested in our books, you must of necessity confess to be true. You accuse our system of falsehood; we, too, accuse yours of falsehood. But ours is more ancient, say you, therefore most credible and trustworthy; as if, indeed, antiquity were not the most fertile source of errors, and did not herself put forth those things which in discreditable fables have attached the utmost infamy to the gods. For could not falsehoods have been both spoken and believed ten thousand years ago, or is it not most probable that that which is near to our own time should be more credible than that which is separated by a long term of years? For these of ours are brought forward on the faith of witnesses, those of yours on the ground of opinions; and it is much more natural that there should be less invention in matters of recent occurrence, than in those far removed in the darkness of antiquity.

58. But they were written by unlearned and ignorant

[1] So most edd., reading *intercip-ere* for the MS. *intercipi*—"it is that the progress be obstructed," etc.

men, and should not therefore be readily believed. See that this be not rather a stronger reason for believing that they have not been adulterated by any false statements, but were put forth by men of simple mind, who knew not how to trick out their tales with meretricious ornaments. But the language is mean and vulgar. For truth never seeks deceitful polish, nor in that which is well ascertained and certain does it allow itself to be led away into excessive prolixity. Syllogisms, enthymemes, definitions, and all those ornaments by which men seek to establish their statements, aid those groping for the truth, but do not clearly mark its great features. But he who really knows the subject under discussion, neither defines, nor deduces, nor seeks the other tricks of words by which an audience is wont to be taken in, and to be beguiled into a forced assent to a proposition.

59. Your narratives, my opponent says, are overrun with barbarisms and solecisms, and disfigured by monstrous blunders. A censure, truly, which shows a childish and petty spirit; for if we allow that it is reasonable, let us cease to use certain kinds of fruit because they grow with prickles on them, and other growths useless for food, which on the one hand cannot support us, and yet do not on the other hinder us from enjoying that which specially excels, and which nature has designed to be most wholesome for us. For how, I pray you, does it interfere with or retard the comprehension [of a statement], whether anything be pronounced smoothly[1] or with uncouth roughness? whether that have the grave accent which ought to have the acute, or that have the acute which ought to have the grave? Or how is the truth of a statement diminished, if an error is made in number or case, in preposition, participle, or conjunction? Let that pomposity of style and strictly regulated diction be reserved for public assemblies, for lawsuits, for the forum and the courts of justice, and by all means be handed over to those who, striving after the soothing influences of pleasant sensations, bestow all their care upon splendour of language.

[1] So Orelli and Hildebrand, reading *glabre* from a conjecture of Grotius, for the MS. *grave*.

[But] when we are discussing matters far removed from mere display, we should consider what is said, not with what charm it is said nor how it tickles the ears, but what benefits it confers on the hearers, especially since we know that some even who devoted themselves to philosophy, not only disregarded refinement of style, but also purposely adopted a vulgar meanness when they might have spoken with greater elegance and richness, lest forsooth they might impair the stern gravity of speech and revel rather in the pretentious show of the Sophists. For indeed it evidences a worthless heart to seek enjoyment in matters of importance; and when you have to deal with those who are sick and diseased, to pour into their ears dulcet sounds, not to apply a remedy to their wounds. Yet, if you consider the true state of the case, no language is naturally perfect, and in like manner none is faulty. For what natural reason is there, or what law written in the constitution of the world, that *paries* should be called *hic*[1] and *sella hæc*?—since neither have they sex distinguished by male and female, nor can the most learned man tell me what *hic* and *hæc* are, or why one of them denotes the male sex while the other is applied to the female. These conventionalities are man's, and certainly are not indispensable to all persons for the use of forming their language; for *paries* might perhaps have been called *hæc*, and *sella hic*, without any fault being found, if it had been agreed upon at first that they should be so called, and if this practice had been maintained by following generations in their daily conversation. And yet, O you who charge our writings with disgraceful blemishes, have you not these solecisms in those most perfect and wonderful books of yours? Does not one of you make the plur. of *uter*, *utria*? another *utres*?[2] [and do you not write] *cœlus* and *cœlum*, *filus* and *filum*, *crocus* and *crocum*, *fretus* and *fretum*? Do you not also say *hoc pane* and *hic panis*, *hic sanguis* and *hoc sanguen*? Are not *candelabrum* and *jugulum* in like manner written *jugulus* and *candelaber*? For if each noun cannot have

---

[1] *i.e.* that the one should be masculine, the other feminine.
[2] *i.e.* does not one of you make the plural of *uter* masc., another neut.?

more than one gender, and if the same word cannot be of this gender and of that (for one gender cannot pass into the other), he commits as great a blunder who utters masculine genders under the laws of feminines, as he who applies masculine articles to feminine genders. And yet we see you using masculines as feminines, and feminines as masculines, and those which you call neuter both in this way and in that, without any distinction. Either, therefore, it is no blunder to employ them indifferently, and [in that case] it is vain for you to say that our works are disfigured with monstrous solecisms; or if the way in which each ought to be employed is unalterably fixed, you also are involved in similar errors, although you have on your side all the Epicadi, Cæsellii, Verrii, Scauri, and Nisi.

60. But, say my opponents, if Christ was God, why did he appear in human shape, and why was he cut off by death after the manner of men? Could that power which is invisible, and which has no bodily substance, have come upon earth and adapted itself to the world and mixed in human society, otherwise than by taking to itself some covering of a more solid substance, which might bear the gaze of the eyes, and on which the look of the least observant might fix itself? For what mortal is there who could have seen him, who could have distinguished him, if he had decreed to come upon the earth such as he is in his own primitive nature, and such as he has chosen to be in his own proper character and divinity? He took upon him, therefore, the form of man; and under the guise of our race he imprisoned his power, so that he could be seen and carefully regarded, might speak and teach, and without encroaching on the sovereignty and government of the King Supreme, might carry out all those objects for the accomplishment of which he had come into the world.

61. What, then, says [my opponent], could not the Supreme Ruler have brought about those things which he had ordained to be done in the world, without feigning himself a man? If it were necessary to do as you say, he perhaps would have done so; because it was not necessary, he acted otherwise.

The reasons why he chose to do it in this way, and did not choose to do it in that, are unknown, being involved in so great obscurity, and comprehensible by scarcely any; but these you might perhaps have understood if you were not already prepared not to understand, and were not shaping your course to brave unbelief, before that was explained to you which you sought to know and to hear.

62. But [you will say] he was cut off by death as men are. Not [Christ] himself; for it is impossible either that death should befall what is divine, or that that should waste away and disappear in death which is one [in its substance], and not compounded, nor formed by bringing together any parts. Who, then [you ask], was seen hanging on the cross? Who dead? The human form,[1] [I reply], which he had put on,[2] and which he bore about with him. It is a tale passing belief, [you say], and wrapt in dark obscurity; if you will, it is not dark, and [is] established by a very close analogy.[3] If the Sibyl, when she was uttering and pouring forth her prophecies and oracular responses, was filled, as you say, with Apollo's power, had been cut down and slain by impious robbers,[4] would Apollo be said to have been slain in her? If Bacis,[5] if Helenus, Marcius,[6] and other soothsayers, had been in like manner robbed of life and light when raving as inspired, would any one say that those who, speaking by

[1] So the MS., followed by Hildebrand and Oehler, reads and punctuates *quis mortuus? homo*, for which all edd. read *mortuus est?* "Who died?"

[2] Here, as in the whole discussion in the second book on the origin and nature of the soul, the opinions expressed are Gnostic, Cerinthus saying more precisely that Christ having descended from heaven in the form of a dove, dwelt in the body of Jesus during his life, but removed from it before the crucifixion.

[3] So the MS. by changing a single letter, with LB. and others, *similitudine proxim-a* (MS. *o*) *constitutum;* while the first ed., Gelenius, Canterus, Ursinus, Orelli, and others, read *·-dini proxime*—" settled very closely to analogy."

[4] In the original *latronibus;* here, as in the next chapter, used loosely to denote lawless men.

[5] So emended by Mercerus for the MS. *vatis*.

[6] So read in the MS.—not *-tius*, as in LB. and Orelli.

their mouths, declared to inquirers what should be done,[1] had perished according to the conditions of human life? The death of which you speak was [that] of the human body which he had assumed,[2] not his own—of that which was borne, not of the bearer; and not even this [death] would he[3] have stooped to suffer, were it not that a matter of such importance was to be dealt with, and the inscrutable plan of fate[4] brought to light in hidden mysteries.

63. What are these hidden and unseen mysteries, you will say, which neither men can know, nor those even who are called gods of the world can in any wise reach by fancy and conjecture; [which] none [can discover],[5] except those whom [Christ] himself has thought fit to bestow the blessing of so great knowledge upon, and to lead into the secret recesses of the inner treasury [of wisdom]? Do you then see that if he had determined that none should do him violence, he should have striven to the utmost to keep off from him his enemies, even by directing his power against them?[6] Could not he [then], who had restored their sight to the blind, make [his enemies] blind if it were necessary? Was it hard or troublesome for him to make them weak, who [had given] strength to the feeble? Did he who bade[7] the lame walk,

---

[1] Lit., "the ways of things"—*vias rerum*.
[2] The MS. reads unintelligibly *assumpti-o hominis fuit*, which was, however, retained in both Roman edd., although Ursinus suggested the dropping of the *o*, which has been done by all later edd.
[3] The MS. reads, *quam nec ipsam perpeti succubuisset vis*—"would his might," *i.e.* "would he with his great power have stooped." Orelli simply omits *vis* as Canterus, and seemingly the other later edd. do.
[4] The MS. and 1st ed. read *sati-s*, which has clearly arisen from *f* being confounded with the old form of *s*.
[5] The construction is a little involved, *quæ nulli nec homines scire nec ipsi qui appellantur dii mundi queunt*—"which none, neither men can know, nor those . . . . of the world can reach, except those whom," etc.
[6] In the Latin, *vel potestate inversa*, which according to Oehler is the MS. reading, while Orelli speaks of it as an emendation of LB. (where it is certainly found, but without any indication of its source), and with most edd. reads *universa*—"by his universal power."
[7] So the MS. according to Hildebrand, reading *præcipi-bat*. Most edd., however, following Gelenius, read *faciebat*—"made them lame."

not know how to take from them all power to move their limbs,[1] by making their sinews stiff?[2] Would it have been difficult for him who drew the dead from their tombs to inflict death on whom he would? But because reason required that those things which had been resolved on should be done here also in the world itself, and in no other fashion than was done, he, with gentleness passing understanding and belief, regarding as but childish trifles the wrongs which men did him, submitted to the violence of savage and most hardened robbers;[3] nor did he think it worth while to take account of what their daring had aimed at, if he only showed to his [disciples] what they were in duty bound to look for from him. For when many things about the perils of souls, many evils about their . . . .; on the other hand, the introducer,[4] the master and teacher directed his laws and ordinances, that they might find their end in fitting duties;[5] did he not destroy the arrogance of the proud? Did he not quench the fires of lust? Did he not check the craving of greed? Did he not wrest the weapons from their hands, and rend from them all the sources[6] of every [form of] corruption? To conclude, was he not himself gentle, peace-

---

[1] Lit., "to bind fast the motions of the members," adopting the reading of most edd., *motus alligare membrorum* (MS. *c-al-igare*).

[2] The MS. reads *nervorum duritia-m*, for which Ursinus, with most edd., reads as above, merely dropping *m*; Hildebrand and Oehler insert *in*, and read, from a conjecture of Ursinus adopted by Elmenhorst, *c-ol-ligare* —" to bind into stiffness."

[3] Ursinus suggested *di-* (" most terrible ") for the MS. *durissimis*.

[4] So the MS. reading, *multa mala de illarum contra insinuator* (*mala* is perhaps in the abl., agreeing with a lost word), which has been regarded by Heraldus and Stewechius, followed by Orelli, as mutilated, and is so read in the first ed., and by Ursinus and LB. The passage is in all cases left obscure and doubtful, and we may therefore be excused discussing its meaning here.

[5] Lit., " to the ends of fitting duties."

[6] In the original, *seminaria abscidit*,—the former word used of nurseries for plants, while the latter may be either as above (from *abscindo*), or may mean "cut off" (from *abscido*); but in both cases the general meaning is the same, and the metaphor is in either slightly confused.

ful, easily approached, friendly when addressed?[1] Did he not, grieving at men's miseries, pitying with his unexampled benevolence all in any wise afflicted with troubles and bodily ills,[2] bring them back and restore them to soundness?

64. What, then, constrains you, what excites you to revile, to rail at, to hate implacably him whom no man[3] can accuse of any crime?[4] Tyrants and your kings, who, putting away [all] fear of the gods, plunder and pillage the treasuries of temples; who by proscription, banishment,[5] and slaughter, strip the state of its nobles; who, with licentious violence, undermine and wrest away the chastity of matrons and maidens,—[these men] you name *indigites* and *divi;* and you worship with couches, altars, temples, and other service, and by celebrating their games and birthdays, those whom it was fitting that you should assail with keenest[6] hatred. And all those, too, who by writing books assail in many forms with biting reproaches public manners; who censure, brand, and tear in pieces your luxurious habits and lives; who carry down to posterity evil reports of their own times[7] in their enduring writings; who [seek to] persuade [men] that the rights of marriage should be held in common;[8] who lie with boys, beautiful, lustful, naked; who declare that

---

[1] Lit., "familiar to be accosted,"—the supine, as in the preceding clause.

[2] So the edd., reading *corporalibus affectos malis*, but the MS. inserts after *malis* the word *morbis* (" with evil bodily diseases "); but according to Hildebrand this word is marked as spurious.

[3] So the edd., reading *nemo h-om-i-n-um*, except Hildebrand and Oehler, who retain the MS. *om-n-i-um*—" no one of all."

[4] John viii. 46: " Which of you convinceth me of sin ? "

[5] So Heraldus and LB., followed by later edd., reading *exiliis* for the MS. *ex-uis*, for which Gelenius, Canterus, and Ursinus read *et suis*— " and by their slaughters."

[6] Here, as frequently in Arnobius, the comparative is used instead of the superlative.

[7] " To posterity evil reports of their own time "—*sui temporis posteris notas*—so emended by Ursinus, followed by Orelli and Hildebrand, for the MS. *in temporis posteri-s*, retained by LB., and with the omission of *s* in the first ed.; but this requires our looking on the passage as defective.

[8] The reference is clearly to the well-known passage in Plato's *Republic*, st. p. 457.

you are beasts, runaways, exiles, and mad and frantic slaves of the most worthless character,—[all these] with wonder and applause you exalt to the stars of heaven, you place in the shrines of your libraries, you present with chariots and statues, and as much as in you lies, gift with a kind of immortality, as it were, by the witness which immortal titles bear to them. Christ alone you would tear in pieces,[1] you would rend asunder, if you could [do so to] a god; nay, [him alone] you would, were it allowed, gnaw with bloody mouths, and break his bones in pieces, and devour him like beasts of the field. For what that he has done, tell, I pray you, for what crime?[2] What has he done to turn aside the course of justice, and rouse you to hatred made fierce by maddening torments? [Is it] because he declared that he was sent by the only [true] King [to be] your soul's guardian, and to bring to you the immortality which you believe that you [already] possess, relying on the assertions of a few men? But [even] if you were assured that he spoke falsely, that he even held out hopes without the slightest foundation, not even in this case do I see [any] reason that you should hate [and] condemn him with bitter reproaches. Nay, if you were kind and gentle in spirit, you ought to esteem him even for this alone, that he promised to you things which you might well wish and hope for; that he was the bearer of good news; that his message was such as to trouble no one's mind, nay, rather to fill [all] with less anxious expectation.[3]

65. Oh ungrateful and impious age, prepared[4] for its own

---

[1] So Gelenius, LB., and Orelli, reading *con-v-ell-e-re* for the MS. *con-p-ell-a-re*, "to accost" or "abuse," which is out of place here. Canterus suggested *com-p-il-are*, "to plunder," which also occurs in the sense "to cudgel."

[2] Supply, "do you pursue him so fiercely?"

[3] These words are followed in the edition of Gelenius by ch. 2-5 of the second book, seemingly without any mark to denote transposition; while Ursinus inserted the same chapters—beginning, however, with the last sentence of the first chapter (read as mentioned in the note on it)—but prefixed an asterisk, to mark a departure from the order of the MS. The later editors have not adopted either change.

[4] So Ursinus suggested in the margin, followed by LB. and Orelli,

destruction by its extraordinary obstinacy! If there had come to you a physician from lands far distant and unknown to you before, offering some medicine to keep off from you altogether every kind of disease and sickness, would you not all eagerly hasten to [him]? Would you not with every kind of flattery and honour receive him into your houses, and treat him kindly? Would you not wish that that kind of medicine should be quite reliable, should be genuine, which promised that even to the utmost limits of life you should be free from such countless bodily distresses? And though it were a doubtful matter, you would yet entrust yourselves [to him]; nor would you hesitate to drink the unknown draught, incited by the hope of health set before you and by the love of safety.[1] Christ shone out and appeared to tell us news of the utmost importance, bringing an omen of prosperity, and a message of safety to those who believe. What, I pray you, means[2] this cruelty, what such barbarity, nay rather, to speak more truly, scornful[3] pride, not only to harass the messenger and bearer of so great a gift with taunting words; but even to assail him with fierce hostility, and with all the weapons which can be showered upon him, and [with all modes of] destruction? Are his words displeasing, and are you offended when you hear them? Count them as [but] a soothsayer's empty tales. Does he speak very stupidly, and promise foolish gifts? Laugh with scorn as wise men, and leave [him in] his folly[4] to be tossed about among his errors. What means this fierceness (to repeat what has been said more than once); what a passion, so murderous? to declare implacable hostility towards one who

reading *in privatam perniciem p-a-r-atum* for the MS. *p-r-iv-atum*, which is clearly derived from the preceding *privatam*, but is, though unintelligible also, retained in the two Roman edd. The conclusion of the sentence is, literally, "obstinacy of spirit."

[1] In the original, *spe salutis proposita atque amore incolumitatis.*
[2] Lit., "is"—*est.*
[3] So all the edd., reading *fastidi-os-um supercilium*, which Crusius says the MS. reads with *os* omitted, i.e. "pride, scorn."
[4] So the edd., reading *fatuita-tem*, for the MS. *fatuita-n-tem*, which may, however, point to a verb not found elsewhere.

has done nothing to deserve it at your hands; to wish, if it were allowed you, to tear him limb from limb, who not only did no man any harm, but with uniform kindness[1] told his enemies what salvation was being brought to them from God Supreme, what must be done that they might escape destruction and obtain an immortality which they knew not of? And when the strange and unheard-of things which were held out staggered the minds of those who heard him, and made them hesitate to believe, [though] master of every power and destroyer of death itself he suffered his human form to be slain, that from the result[2] they might know that the hopes were safe which they had long entertained about the soul's salvation, and that in no other way could they avoid the danger of death.

[1] *i.e.* to friends and foes alike. The MS. reads *æqualiter benignus hostibus dicere*, which is retained by Orelli, supposing an ellipsis of *fuerit, i.e.* "[he was] kind to say," which might be received; but it is more natural to suppose that *-t* has dropped off, and read *diceret* as above, with the two Roman editions and LB. Gelenius, followed by Ursinus, emended *omnibus docuerit*—"with uniform kindness taught to all." It may be well to give here an instance of the very insufficient grounds on which supposed references to Scripture are sometimes based. Orelli considers that Arnobius here refers (*videtur respexisse*, he says) to Col. i. 21, 22, "You, that were sometimes alienated and enemies in mind by wicked works, yet now hath he reconciled in the body of his flesh through death," to which, though the words which follow might indeed be thought to have a very distant resemblance, they can in no way be shown to refer.

[2] *i.e.* from his resurrection, which showed that death's power was broken by him.

BOOK II.

ARGUMENT.

THE question is again asked, Why is Christ so bitterly hated, while it cannot be said that he ever injured any one (1)? Because, an opponent is supposed to reply, he drove religion from the earth by withholding men from worshipping the gods. In this, however, it is shown that he did not assail, but built up religion, as he taught men to worship the creator and source of all things, God supreme, the worship of whom is surely the truest religion (2, 3). It is declared to be mere folly in the heathen to disbelieve Christ's message, for the future alone can prove or disprove the truth of what is foretold; but when there are the two prospects, that if Christ's words are false, his followers lose nothing more than others, but that, on the other hand, if he spoke truly, those who refuse to believe in him suffer an infinite loss, it is more rational to choose the course which tends to no evil and may lead to blessing, rather than that which it is certain leads to no good, and may bring us to terrible woe (4, 5). Is the truth of Christianity not manifested, he goes on to ask, in the readiness with which it has been received by men of every class in all parts of the world, and by the noble constancy with which so many have endured suffering even to death, rather than abandon or dishonour it (5)? And if, as was often the case, any one should say that there were indeed many who received Christ's gospel, but that these were silly and stupid people, Arnobius reminds him that learning and grammatical knowledge alone do not fit a man to decide between truth and falsehood, to say what may and what cannot take place (6); and this is shown by the uncertainty and confusion which surround even those matters which force themselves on our notice every day, such as the nature and origin of man, the end of his being, the mode in which he was quickened into life, and many other similar questions (7). Moreover, the heathen laughed at the faith of the Christians; but in doing so, Arnobius asks, did they not expose themselves to ridicule? For does not the whole conduct of life depend on the belief that the end will correspond to our aims and actions (8)? Again, most men put faith in one or other of the leading philosophers (9); and these, in turn, trust their own fancies, and put faith in their own theories, so that faith is common to all men alike (10). And if the heathen put faith in the philosophers, the Christians have no less reason to put faith in Christ; while, if a comparison be entered into, no other can point to such wonderful powers and such marvellous deeds as are recorded of him (11). Not by such subtle quibbling as men brought against it did the new religion make its way, but by the marvellous and unheard-of miracles which attested its truth, so that it won followers among all tribes on the face of the earth; and if any man was ignorant of these facts, it was because he had not chosen to know them, and had suffered the truth to be obscured by those interested in upholding error (12). Arnobius goes on to show that many Christian doctrines which were ridiculed as such by the heathen, were held by the philosophers also; referring more particularly to the worship of one God, the resurrection of the dead (13), and the quenchless fires of punishment, from which he takes occasion to point out that man's true death comes not at, but after the soul's separation from the body, and to discuss the nature of the soul (14). The soul is not, he maintains, immortal in itself, or of divine origin—if it were born of God, men would be pure and holy, and of one opinion (15)—but has been made vicious and sinful by causes to be found in the world; while, if it had been made by the supreme God, how could his work have been marred by that which was less powerful (16)? Arnobius next endeavours to show that we are in nothing distinguished from the brutes: so far as body, the maintenance of life, and the reproduction of the race are concerned, we are found to be alike, while the heathen are reminded of the doctrine of the transmigration of souls (16); and if stress is laid on man's reason and intelligence as a distinctive characteristic, it is first suggested that all men do not act rationally, and the question is then asked, What is the reason which man possesses, and not the beasts (17)? Man's practical skill is no proof of superior reason, for its exercise is necessitated by his excessive poverty; and it is, moreover, not a faculty native in the soul, but one acquired only after long years under the pressure of necessity (18). The arts, grammar, music, oratory, and geometry are similarly noticed, and the doctrine of reminiscence rejected (19). Arnobius next supposes a boy to be brought up wholly apart from human society, and seeks to establish his position by the supposed results of imaginary questions put to this hypothetical being (20–23); and then goes on to attack the contrary opinions which Plato had sought to establish in a somewhat similar way, by challenging him to question the boy just imagined, who is, of course, found to be exactly what was intended (24); and thus gives his creator a triumph, by showing *conclusively* that man untaught is ignorant as a stock or stone, while on being taught other creatures can learn also—the ox and ass to grind and plough, the horse to run in harness, and the like (25). Pursuing the same subject, it is argued that if the soul loses its former knowledge on uniting with the body, it cannot be incorporeal, and cannot therefore be immortal (26, 27); and further, that if the soul's former knowledge were lost through the influence of the body, the knowledge acquired in this life should in like manner be lost (28). Those who assert the soul's immortality are accused of teaching that which will add to the wickedness of men: for how shall any one be restrained even by the fear of a higher power, who is persuaded that his life cannot be cut short by any power (29)? while if he is threatened with the punishments of the infernal regions, he will laugh them to scorn, knowing that what is incorruptible cannot be affected by mere bodily ills. If the soul is immortal, Arnobius affirms there is no need or ground for philosophy, that is, ethics, whose purpose is to raise man above the brutish pleasures of sense to a virtuous life: for why should not a soul which cannot perish give itself up to any pleasures? while if the soul is mortal, philosophy is in precisely the same position, aiming to do for man what will not profit him if done (30). The soul, he concludes, is neither mortal nor immortal (31); and there is therefore good reason that those who have no confidence in their power to help themselves, should welcome a saviour in one more powerful (32, 33). Christians and heathen alike, then, look for the deliverance of their souls from death; and neither party, therefore, has any reason to mock the other in this (33, 34). Such, too, is the condition of all spirits which are supposed to exist (35); and it is only through God's goodness that any spirit becomes immortal (36). It is next argued at great length, and with some prolixity, that the soul is not sprung from God, on the ground of its vicious and imperfect nature (37–46); and it is then shown that, in denying the soul's divine origin on this ground, we are acting most reasonably, although we cannot say what its real origin is (47, 48); while if any one attempts to show that the soul is not imperfect and polluted by sin by pointing to good and upright men, he is reminded that the whole race cannot take its character from a few individual members, and that these men were not so naturally (49, 50). There is nothing ridiculous, Arnobius goes on to say, in confessing ignorance of such matters; and the preceding statements are to a certain extent supported by Plato's authority, in so far as he separates the formation of man's soul from the divine acts (51, 52). But if this belief be mistaken, what harm does it do to others (53)? From this there naturally follows a discussion of the origin of evil, the existence of which cannot be denied, though its cause is beyond our knowledge; it is enough to know that all God does is good (54, 55). How idle a task it would be to attempt the solution of such problems, is seen when we consider how diverse are the results already arrived at, and that each is supported on plausible grounds (56, 57); which clearly shows that man's curiosity cannot be certainly satisfied, and that one man cannot hope to win general assent to his opinions (57). Arnobius now proposes to his opponents a series of questions as to men and things, after answering which they may with more reason taunt him with his ignorance of the soul's origin (58, 59); and says that, because of the vanity of all these inquiries, Christ had commanded them to be laid aside, and men to strive after the knowledge of God (60), and the deliverance of their souls from the evils which otherwise await them

(61),—a task to be accomplished only through the aid of Him who is all-powerful (62). The condition of those who lived before Christ came to earth is to be learned from his teaching (63); and his bounty extends to all, though all do not accept it (64); for to compel those to turn to him who *will* not come, would be to use violence, not to show mercy (65). No purity therefore, or holiness, can save the man who refuses to accept Christ as his Saviour (66). Arnobius next deals with the objection that Christianity is a thing of yesterday, for which it would be absurd to give up the more ancient religions, by asking if it is thus that we look upon the various improvements which have been suggested from time to time by the increase of knowledge and wisdom (66–68). All things, moreover, have had a beginning—philosophy, medicine, music, and the rest (69), even the gods themselves (70); but all this is wholly beside the mark, for the truth of a religion depends not on its age, but on its divine origin. And if, a few hundred years before, there was no Christianity, the gods were in like manner unknown at a still earlier period (71). But Christianity worships that which was before all, the eternal God, although late in its worship, because there was not the needed revelation sooner (72). Arnobius again asserts that Christianity does not stand alone, for it was at a comparatively late time that the worship of Serapis and Isis, and of others, was introduced; and so Christianity too had sprung up but lately, because it was only then that its teacher had appeared (73): and having considered why Christ was so late in appearing among men (74, 75), and why Christians are allowed to undergo such suffering and trial on earth (76, 77), he earnestly exhorts all to see to the safety of their souls, and flee for salvation to God, seeing that such terrible dangers threaten us, lest the last day come upon us, and we be found in the jaws of death (78).[1]

1. HERE, if any means could be found, I should wish to converse thus with all those who hate the name of Christ, turning aside for a little from the defence primarily set up:—
If you think it no dishonour to answer when asked a ques-

---

[1] There has been much confusion in dealing with the first seven chapters of this book, owing to the leaves of the MS. having been arranged in wrong order, as was pointed out at an early period by some one who noted on the margin that there was some *transposition*. To this circumstance, however, Oehler alone seems to have called attention; but the corruption was so manifest, that the various editors gave themselves full liberty to re-arrange and dispose the text more correctly. The first leaf of the MS. concludes with the words *sine ullius personæ discriminibus inrogavit*, "without any distinction of person," and is followed by one

tion, explain to us and say what is the cause, what the reason, that you pursue Christ with so bitter hostility? or what offences you remember which he did, that at the mention of his name you are roused to bursts of mad and savage fury?[1] Did he ever, in claiming for himself power as king, fill the whole world with bands of the fiercest soldiers; and of nations at peace from the beginning, did he destroy and put an end to some, [and] compel others to submit to his yoke and serve him? Did he ever, excited by grasping[2] avarice, claim as his own by right all that wealth to have abundance of which men strive eagerly? Did he ever, transported with lustful passions, break down by force the barriers of purity, or stealthily lie in wait for other men's wives? Did he ever, puffed up with haughty arrogance, inflict at random injuries and insults, without any distinction of persons? (B) And if he was not worthy that you should listen to and believe [him, yet] he should not have been despised by you even on this account, that he showed to you things concerning your salvation, that he prepared for you a path[3] to

which begins with the words (A, end of c. 5) *et non omnium virtutum,* "and (not) by an eager longing," and ends *tanta experiatur examina,* "undergoes such countless ills" (middle of c. 7). The third and fourth leaves begin with the words (B, end of c. 1) *utrum in cunctos . . . amoverit? qui si dignos,* "Now if he was not worthy" (see notes), and run on to end of c. 5, *quadam dulcedine,* "by some charm;" while the fifth (C, middle of c. 7) begins *atque ne* (or *utrumne*) *illum,* "whether the earth," and there is no further difficulty. This order is retained in the first ed., and also by Hildebrand, who supposes three lacunæ at A, B, and C, to account for the abruptness and want of connection; but it is at once seen that, on changing the order of the leaves, so that they shall run B A C, the argument and sense are perfectly restored. This arrangement seems to have been first adopted in LB., and is followed by the later editors, with the exception of Hildebrand.

[1] Lit., "boil up with the ardours of furious spirits."
[2] Lit., "by the heats of."
[3] So Meursius, reading *a-* for the MS. *o-ptaret,* which is retained by LB., Orelli, and others. The MS. reading is explained, along with the next words *vota immortalitatis,* by Orelli as meaning "sought by his prayers," with reference to John xvii. 24, in which he is clearly mistaken. Heraldus conjectures *p-o-r-ta-s a-p-er-taret,* "opened paths . . . and the gates of immortality."

heaven, and the immortality for which you long; although[1] he neither extended the light of life to all, nor delivered [all] from the danger which threatens them through their ignorance.[2]

2. But indeed, [some one will say], he deserved our hatred because he has driven religion[3] from the world, because he has kept men back from seeking to honour the gods.[4] Is he then denounced as the destroyer of religion and promoter of impiety, who brought true religion into the world, who opened the gates of piety to men blind and verily living in impiety, and pointed out to whom they should bow themselves? Or is there any truer religion—[one] more serviceable,[5] powerful, [and] right—than to have learned to know the supreme God, to know [how] to pray to God supreme, who alone is the source and fountain of all good, the creator,[6] founder, and framer of all that endures, by whom

[1] The words which follow, *ut non in cunctos*, etc., have been thus transposed by Heraldus, followed by later editors; but formerly they preceded the rest of the sentence, and, according to Oehler, the MS. gives *utrum*, thus: "[You ask] whether he has both extended to all . . . ignorance? who, if he was not," etc. Cf. p. 55, note 3.

[2] So the MS., reading *periculum i-g-n-ora-tionis*, for which Meursius suggests *i-n-teri-tionis*—" danger of destruction."

[3] Pl.

[4] This seems the true rationale of the sentence, viewed in relation to the context. Immediately before, Arnobius suggests that the hatred of Christ by the heathen is unjustifiable, because they had suffered nothing at his hands; now an opponent is supposed to rejoin, " But he has deserved our hatred by assailing our religion." The introductory particles *at enim* fully bear this out, from their being regularly used to introduce a rejoinder. Still, by Orelli and other editors the sentence is regarded as interrogative, and in that case would be, " Has he indeed merited our hatred by driving out," etc., which, however, not merely breaks away from what precedes, but also makes the next sentence somewhat lame. The older editors, too, read it without any mark of interrogation.

[5] *i.e.*, according to Orelli, to the wants of men; but possibly it may here have the subjective meaning of "more full of service," *i.e.* to God.

[6] So the MS., reading *perpetuarum pater, fundator, conditor rerum*, but all the editions *pa-ri-ter*, "alike," which has helped to lead Orelli astray. He suggests *et fons est perpetu-us pariter*, etc., "perpetual fountain, . . . of all things alike the founder and framer." It has been also proposed by Oehler (to get rid of the difficulty felt here) to transfer *per metathesin*, the idea of "enduring" to God; but the reference is surely quite clear,

all things on earth and all in heaven are quickened, and filled with the stir of life, and without whom there would assuredly be nothing to bear any name, and [have any] substance? But perhaps you doubt whether there is that ruler of whom we speak, and rather [incline to] believe in the existence of Apollo, Diana, Mercury, Mars. Give a true judgment;[1] and, looking round on all these things which we see, [any one] will rather doubt whether [all] the other gods exist, than hesitate with regard to the God whom we all know by nature, whether when we cry out, O God, or when we make God the witness of wicked [deeds],[2] and raise our face to heaven as though he saw us.

3. But he did not permit men to make supplication to the lesser gods. Do you, then, know who are, or where are the lesser gods? Has mistrust of them, or the way in which they were mentioned, ever touched you, so that you are justly indignant that their worship has been done away with and deprived of all honour?[3] But if haughtiness of mind and arrogance,[4] as it is called by the Greeks, did not stand in your way and hinder you, you might long ago have been able to understand what he forbade to be done, or wherefore; within what limits he would have true religion lie;[5] what danger arose to you from that which you thought obedience; or from what evils you would escape if you broke away from your dangerous delusion.

viewed as a distinction between the results of God's working and that of all other beings.

[1] So the MS. and almost all edd., reading *da verum judicium*, for which Heraldus suggested *da naturæ*, or *verum animæ judicium*, "give the judgment of nature," or "the true judgment of the soul," as if appeal were made to the inner sense; but in his later observations he proposed *da puerum judicem*, "give a boy as judge," which is adopted by Orelli. Meursius, merely transposing *d-a*, reads much more naturally *ad*—"*at* a true judgment."

[2] The MS. reading is *illum testem d-e-um constituimus improb-arum*, retained in the edd. with the change of *-arum* into *-orum*. Perhaps for *deum* should be read *r-e-r-um*, "make him witness of wicked things." With this passage compare iii. 31-33.

[3] It seems necessary for the sake of the argument to read this interrogatively, but in all the edd. the sentence ends without any mark of interrogation.

[4] Typhus—τῦφος.   [5] Lit., "he chose . . . to stand."

4. But all these things will be more clearly and distinctly noticed when we have proceeded further. For we shall show that Christ did not teach the nations impiety, but delivered ignorant and wretched men from those who most wickedly wronged them.[1] We do not believe, you say, that what he says is true. What, then? Have you no doubt as to the things which[2] you say are not true, while, as they are [only] at hand, and not yet disclosed,[3] they can by no means be disproved? But he, too, does not prove what he promises. It is so; for, as I said, there can be no proof of [things still in] the future. Since, then, the nature of the future is such that it cannot be grasped and comprehended by any anticipation,[4] is it not more rational,[5] of two things uncertain and hanging in doubtful suspense, rather to believe that which carries [with it] some hopes, than that which [brings] none at all? For in the one case there is no danger, if that which is said to be at hand should prove vain and groundless; in the other there is the greatest loss, even[6] the loss of salvation, if, when the time has come, it be shown that there was nothing false [in what was declared].[7]

5. What say you, O ignorant ones, for whom we might well weep and be sad?[8] Are you so void of fear that these

[1] Lit., "the ignorance of wretched men from the worst robbers," *i.e.* the false prophets and teachers, who made a prey of the ignorant and credulous. Cf. p. 51, n. 4.

[2] Lit., "Are [the things] clear with you which," etc.

[3] So the MS., followed by both Roman edd., Hildebrand and Oehler, reading *passa*, which Cujacius (referring it to *patior*, as the editors seem to have done generally) would explain as meaning "past," while in all other editions *cassa*, "vain," is read.

[4] Lit., "the touching of no anticipation."

[5] Lit., "purer reasoning."

[6] Lit., "that is." This clause Meursius rejects as a gloss.

[7] *i.e.* If you believe Christ's promises, your belief makes you lose nothing should it prove groundless; but if you disbelieve them, then the consequences to you will be terrible if they are sure. This would seem too clear to need remark, were it not for the confusion of Orelli in particular as to the meaning of the passage.

[8] Lit., "most worthy even of weeping and pity."

things may be true which are despised by you and turned to
ridicule? and do you not consider with yourselves at least,
in your secret thoughts, lest that which to-day with perverse
obstinacy you refuse to believe, time may too late show to
be true,[1] and ceaseless remorse punish [you]? Do not even
these proofs at least give you faith to believe,[2] [viz.] that
already, in so short and brief a time, the oaths of this vast
army have spread abroad over all the earth? that already
there is no nation so rude and fierce that it has not, changed
by his love, subdued its fierceness, and, with tranquillity
hitherto unknown, become mild in disposition?[3] that [men]
endowed with so great abilities, orators, critics, rhetoricians,
lawyers, and physicians, those, too, who pry into the mysteries of philosophy, seek to learn these things, despising those
in which but now they trusted? that slaves choose to be tortured by their masters as they please, wives to be divorced,
children to be disinherited by their parents, rather than be
unfaithful to Christ and cast off the oaths of the warfare of
salvation? that although so terrible punishments have been
denounced by you against those who follow the precepts of
this religion, it[4] increases [even] more, and a great host
strives more boldly against all threats and the terrors which
would keep it back, and is roused to zealous faith by the
very attempt to hinder it? Do you indeed believe that
these things happen idly and at random? that these feelings
are adopted on being met with by chance?[5] Is not this, then,
sacred and divine? Or [do you believe] that, without God['s
grace], their minds are so changed, that although murderous
hooks and other tortures without number threaten, as we said,
those who shall believe, they receive the grounds of faith

[1] *Redarguat.* This sense is not recognised by Riddle and White, and
would therefore seem to be, if not unique, at least extremely rare. The
derivative *redargutio,* however, is in late Latin used for "demonstra-
tion," and this is evidently the meaning here.
[2] *Fidem vobis faciunt argumenta credendi.* Heraldus, joining the two
last words, naturally regards them as a gloss from the margin; but read
as above, joining the first and last, there is nothing out of place.
[3] Lit., "tranquillity being assumed, passed to placid feelings."
[4] *Res,* "the thing." [5] Lit., "on chance encounters."

with which they have become acquainted,[1] as if carried away (A) by some charm, and by an eager longing for all the virtues,[2] and prefer the friendship of Christ to all that is in the world?[3]

6. But perhaps those seem to you weak-minded and silly, who even now are uniting all over the world, and joining together to assent with that readiness of belief [at which you mock].[4] What, then? Do you alone, imbued[5] with the true power of wisdom and understanding, see something wholly different[6] and profound? Do you alone perceive that all these things are trifles? you alone, that those things are mere words and childish absurdities which we declare [are] about to come to us from the supreme Ruler? Whence, pray, has so much wisdom been given to you? whence so

---

[1] *Rationes cognitas.* There is some difficulty as to the meaning of these words, but it seems best to refer them to the *argumenta credendi* (beginning of chapter, " do not even these proofs "), and render as above. Hildebrand, however, reads *tortiones*, " they accept the tortures which they know will befall them."

[2] The MS. reads *et non omnium*, "and by a love *not* of all the virtues," changed in most edd. as above into *atque omnium*, while Oehler proposes *et novo omnium*, " and by fresh love of all," etc. It will be remembered that the transposition of leaves in the MS. (note on ii. 1) occurs here, and this seems to account for the arbitrary reading of Gelenius, which has no MS. authority whatever, but was added by himself when transposing these chapters to the first book (cf. p. 55, n. 4), *atque nectare ebrii cuncta contemnant*—" As if intoxicated with a certain sweetness and nectar, they despise all things." The same circumstance has made the restoration of the passage by Canterus a connecting of fragments of widely separated sentences and arguments.

[3] Lit., " all the things of the world." Here the argument breaks off, and passes into a new phase, but Orelli includes the next sentence also in the fifth chapter.

[4] Lit., " to the assent of that credulity."

[5] So the MS., reading *conditi vi mera*, for which Orelli would read with Oudendorp, *conditae* — " by the pure force of *recondite* wisdom." The MS., however, is supported by the similar phrase in the beginning of c. 8, where *tincti* is used.

[6] So the MS., reading *aliud*, for which Stewechius, adopting a suggestion of Canterus, conjectures, *altius et profundius*—" something deeper and more profound." Others propose readings further removed from the text; while Obbarius, retaining the MS. reading, explains it as " not common."

much subtlety and wit? Or from what scientific training have you been able to gain so much wisdom, to derive so much foresight? Because you are skilled in declining verbs and nouns by cases and tenses, [and][1] in avoiding barbarous words and expressions; because you have learned either to express yourselves in[2] harmonious, and orderly, and fitly-disposed language, or to know when it is rude and unpolished;[3] because you have stamped on your memory the Fornix of Lucilius,[4] and Marsyas of Pomponius; because [you know] what the issues to be proposed in lawsuits are, how many kinds of cases there are, how many ways of pleading, what the genus is, what the species, by what methods an opposite is distinguished from a contrary,—do you therefore think that you know what is false, what true, what can or cannot be done, what is the nature of the lowest and highest? Have the well-known words never rung in[5] your ears, that the wisdom of man is foolishness with God?

7. In the first place, you yourselves, too,[6] see clearly that,

---

[1] Lit., "because [you are]," etc.].

[2] Lit., "either yourselves to utter," etc.

[3] *Incomptus*, for which Heraldus would read *inconditus*, as in opposition to "harmonious." This is, however, unnecessary, as the clause is evidently opposed to the *whole* of the preceding one.

[4] No trace of either of these works has come down to us, and therefore, though there has been abundance of conjecture, we can reach no satisfactory conclusion about them. It seems most natural to suppose the former to be probably part of the lost satires of Lucilius, which had dealt with obscene matters, and the author of the latter to be the Atellane poet of Bononia. As to this there has been some discussion; but, in our utter ignorance of the work itself, it is as well to allow that we must remain ignorant of its author also. The scope of both works is suggested clearly enough by their titles—the statue of Marsyas in the forum overlooking nightly licentious orgies; and their mention seems intended to suggest a covert argument against the heathen, in the implied indecency of the knowledge on which they prided themselves. For *Fornicem Lucilianum* (MS. *Lucialinum*) Meursius reads *Cæcilianum*.

[5] Lit., "Has that [thing] published never struck," etc. There is clearly a reference to 1 Cor. iii. 19, "the wisdom of this world." The argument breaks off here, and is taken up from a different point in the next sentence, which is included, however, in this chapter by Orelli.

[6] So Gelenius, followed by Canterus and Orelli, reading *primum et*

if you ever discuss obscure subjects, and seek to lay bare the mysteries of nature, on the one hand you do not know the very things which you speak of, which you affirm, which you uphold very often with especial zeal, and that each one defends with obstinate resistance his own suppositions as though they were proved and ascertained [truths]. For how can we of ourselves know whether we[1] perceive the truth, even if all ages be employed in seeking out knowledge—[we] whom some envious power[2] brought forth, and formed so ignorant and proud, that, although we know nothing at all, we yet deceive ourselves, and are uplifted by pride and arrogance so as to suppose ourselves possessed of knowledge? For, to pass by divine things, and those plunged in natural obscurity, can any man explain that which in the Phædrus[3] the well-known Socrates cannot comprehend—what man is, or whence he is, uncertain, changeable, deceitful, manifold, of many kinds? for what purposes he was produced? by whose ingenuity he was devised? what he does in the world? (C) why he undergoes such countless ills? whether the earth gave life to him as to worms and mice, being affected with decay through the action of some moisture;[4] or whether he

---

ipsi, by rejecting one word of the MS. (*et quæ*). Canterus plausibly combines both words into *itaque*—" therefore." LB. reads *ecquid*—" do you at all," etc., with which Orelli so far agrees, that he makes the whole sentence interrogative.

[1] So restored by Stewechius; in the first ed. *perspiciam* (instead of *am-us*) " if I perceive the truth," etc.

[2] So the MS. very intelligibly and forcibly, *res . . . invida*, but the common reading is *invid-i-a*—" whom something . . . with envy." The train of thought which is merely started here is pursued at some length a little later.

[3] The MS. gives *fedro*, but all editions, except the first, Hildebrand, and Oehler, read *Phædone*, referring, however, to a passage in the first Alcibiades (st. p. 129), which is manifestly absurd, as in it, while Alcibiades "cannot tell what man is," Socrates at once proceeds to lead him to the required knowledge by the usual dialectic. Nourry thinks that there is a general reference to *Phædr.* st. p. 230,—a passage in which Socrates says that he disregards mythological questions that he may study himself.

[4] Lit., " changed with the rottenness of some moisture." The refer-

received[1] these outlines of body, and [this] cast of face, from the hand of some maker and framer? Can he, I say, know these things, which lie open to all, and are recognisable by[2] the senses common [to all],—by what causes we are plunged into sleep, by what we awake? in what ways dreams are produced, in what they are seen? nay rather—as to which Plato in the *Theætetus*[3] is in doubt—whether we are ever awake, or whether that very state which is called waking is part of an unbroken slumber? and what we seem to do when we say that we see a dream? whether we see by means of rays of light proceeding towards the object,[4] or images of the objects fly to and alight on the pupils of our eyes? whether the flavour is in the things [tasted], or arises from their touching the palate? from what causes hairs lay aside their natural darkness, and do not become gray all at once, but by adding little by little? why it is that all fluids, on mingling, form one whole; [that] oil, [on the contrary], does not suffer the others to be poured into it,[5] but is ever brought together clearly into its own impenetrable[6] substance? finally, why the soul also, which is said by you to be immortal and divine,[7] is sick in [men who are] sick, senseless in children,

ence is probably to the statement by Socrates (*Phædo*, st. p. 96) of the questions with regard to the origin of life, its progress and development, which interested him as a young man.

[1] So the MS., LB., and Oehler, but the other edd. make the verb plural, and thus break the connection.

[2] Lit., "established in the common senses."

[3] Arnobius overstates the fact here. In the passage referred to (*Th.* st. p. 158), Socrates is represented as developing the Protagorean theory from its author's standpoint, not as stating his own opinions.

[4] Lit., "by the stretching out of rays and of light." This, the doctrine of the Stoics, is naturally contrasted in the next clause with that of Epicurus.

[5] Lit., "oil refuses to suffer immersion into itself," *i.e.* of other fluids.

[6] So LB., followed by Orelli, reading *impenetrabil-em* for the MS. *impenetrabil-is*, which is corrected in both Roman edd. by Gelenius, Canterus, and Elmenhorst -*e*, to agree with the subject *oleum*—"being impenetrable is ever," etc.

[7] Lit., "a god."

worn out in doting, silly,[1] and crazy old age? Now the weakness and wretched ignorance of these [theories] is greater on this account, that while it may happen that we at times say something which is true,[2] we cannot be sure even of this very thing, whether we have spoken the truth at all.

8. And since you have been wont to laugh at our faith, and with droll jests to pull to pieces [our] readiness of belief too, say, O wits, soaked and filled with wisdom's pure draught, is there in life any kind of business demanding diligence and activity, which the doers[3] undertake, engage in, and essay, without believing [that it can be done]? Do you travel about, do you sail on the sea without believing that you will return home when your business is done? Do you break up the earth with the plough, and fill it with different kinds of seeds without believing that you will gather in the fruit with the changes of the seasons? Do you unite with partners in marriage,[4] without believing that it will be pure, and a union serviceable to the husband? Do you beget children without believing that they will pass[5] safely through the [different] stages of life to the goal of age? Do you commit your sick bodies to the hands of physicians, without believing that diseases can be relieved by their severity being lessened? Do you wage wars with your enemies, without believing that you will carry off the victory by success in battles?[6] Do you worship and serve the gods without believing that they are, and that they listen graciously to your prayers?

9. What, have you seen with your eyes, and handled[7] with your hands, those things which you write yourselves,

---

[1] So the edd., generally reading *fatua* for the MS. *futura*, which is clearly corrupt. Hildebrand turns the three adjectives into corresponding verbs, and Heinsius emends *deliret* (MS. -*ra*) *et fatue et insane*— "dotes both sillily and crazily." Arnobius here follows Lucr. iii. 445 sqq.

[2] Lit., "something of truth."

[3] The MS. has *a-t-tor-o-s*, corrected by a later writer *a-c-tor-e-s*, which is received in LB. and by Meursius and Orelli.

[4] Lit., "unite marriage partnerships."

[5] Lit., "be safe and come."

[6] Or, "in successive battles"—*præliorum successionibus*.

[7] Lit., "with ocular inspection, and held touched."

which you read from time to time on subjects placed beyond human knowledge? Does not each one trust this author or that? That which any one has persuaded himself is said with truth by another, does he not defend with a kind of assent, as it were, [like that] of faith? Does not he who says that fire[1] or water is the origin of all things, pin his faith to Thales or Heraclitus? he who places the cause [of all] in numbers, to Pythagoras of Samos, [and] to Archytas? he who divides the soul, and sets up bodiless forms, to Plato, the disciple of Socrates? he who adds a fifth element[2] to the primary causes, to Aristotle, the father of the Peripatetics? he who threatens the world with [destruction by] fire, and says that when the time comes it will be [set] on fire, to Panætius, Chrysippus, Zeno? he who is always fashioning worlds from atoms,[3] and destroying [them], to Epicurus, Democritus, Metrodorus? he who [says] that nothing is comprehended by man, and that all things are wrapt in dark obscurity,[4] to Archesilas,[5] to Carneades?—to some teacher, in fine, of the old and later Academy?

10. Finally, do not even the leaders and founders of the schools[6] already mentioned, say those very things[7] which

---

[1] "Fire" is wanting in the MS.

[2] Arnobius here allows himself to be misled by Cicero (*Tusc.* i. 10), who explains ἐντελέχεια as a kind of perpetual motion, evidently confusing it with ἐνδελέχεια (cf. Donaldson, *New Crat.* § 339 sqq.), and represents Aristotle as making it a fifth primary cause. The word has no such meaning, and Aristotle invariably enumerates only four primary causes: the material from which, the form in which, the power by which, and the end for which anything exists (*Physics*, ii. 3; *Metaph.* iv. 2, etc.).

[3] Lit., "with indivisible bodies." [4] Pl.

[5] So the MS., LB., and Hildebrand, reading *Archesilæ*, while the others read *Archesilao*, forgetting that Arcesilas is the regular Latin form, although Archesilaus is found.

[6] *Sententiarum* is read in the first ed. by Gelenius, Canterus, and Ursinus, and seems from Crusius to be the MS. reading. The other edd., however, have received from the margin of Ursinus the reading of the text, *sectarum*.

[7] In the first ed., and that of Ursinus, the reading is, *nonne apud ea*, "in those things which they say, do they not say," etc., which Gelenius emended as in the text, *nonne ipsa ea*.

they do say through belief in their own ideas? For, did Heraclitus see things produced by the changes of fires? Thales, by the condensing of water?[1] [Did] Pythagoras [see them] spring from number?[2] [Did] Plato [see] the bodiless forms? Democritus, the meeting together of the atoms? Or do those who assert that nothing at all can be comprehended by man, know whether what they say is true, so as to[3] understand that the very proposition which they lay down is a declaration of truth?[4] Since, then, you have discovered and learned nothing, and are led by credulity to assert all those things which you write, and comprise in thousands of books; what kind of judgment, pray, is this, so unjust that you mock at faith in us, while you see that you have it in common with our readiness of belief?[5] But [you say] you believe wise men, well versed in all kinds of learning! —those, forsooth, who know nothing, and agree in nothing which they say; who join battle with their opponents on behalf of their own opinions, and are always contending fiercely with obstinate hostility; who, overthrowing, refuting,

---

[1] Cf. Diog. Laert. ix. 9, where Heraclitus is said to have taught that fire—the first principle—condensing becomes water, water earth, and conversely; and on Thales, Arist. *Met.* A, 3, where, however, as in other places, Thales is merely said to have referred the generation and maintenance of all things to moisture, although by others he is represented as teaching the doctrine ascribed to him above. Cf. Cic. *de Nat. Deor.* i. 10, and Heraclides, *Alleg. Hom.* c. 22, where water evaporating is said to become air, and settling, to become mud.

[2] There is some difficulty as to the reading: the MS., first ed., and Ursinus give *numero s-c-ire*, explained by Canterus as meaning "that numbers have understanding," *i.e.* so as to be the cause of all. Gelenius, followed by Canterus, reads *-os scit—*"does Pyth. know numbers," which is absurdly out of place. Heraldus approved of a reading in the margin of Ursinus (merely inserting *o* after *c*), "that numbers unite," which seems very plausible. The text follows an emendation of Gronovius adopted by Orelli, *-o ex-ire.*

[3] So the MS., reading *ut*; but Orelli, and all edd. before him, *aut—*"or do they."

[4] *i.e.* that truth knowable by man exists.

[5] So the MS. reading *nostra in-credulitate*, for which Ursinus, followed by Stewechius, reads *nostra cum.* Heraldus conjectured *vestra*, *i.e.* "in your readiness of belief," you are just as much exposed to such ridicule.

and bringing to nought the one the other's doctrines, have made all things doubtful, and have shown from their very want of agreement that nothing can be known.

11. But, [supposing that] these things do not at all hinder or prevent your being bound to believe and hearken to them in great measure;[1] and what [reason] is there either that you should have more [liberty] in this respect, or that we [should have] less? You believe Plato,[2] Cronius,[3] Numenius, or any one you please; we believe and confide in Christ. How unreasonable it is, that when we both abide[4] by teachers, and have one and the same thing, belief, in common, you should wish it to be granted to you to receive what is so[5] said by them, [but] should be unwilling to hear and see what is brought forward by Christ! And yet, if we chose to compare cause with cause, we are better able to point out what we have followed in Christ, than [you to point out] what you [have followed] in the philosophers. And we, indeed, have followed in him these things—those glorious works and most potent virtues which he manifested and displayed in diverse miracles, by which any one might be led to [feel] the necessity of believing, and [might] decide with confidence that they were not such as might be regarded as man's, but [such as showed] some divine and unknown power. What virtues did you follow in the

---

[1] Heraldus has well suggested that *plurimum* is a gloss arising out of its being met with in the next clause.

[2] So the MS. and edd., reading *Platoni;* but Ursinus suggested *Plotino*, which Heraldus thinks most probably correct. There is, indeed, an evident suitableness in introducing here the later rather than the earlier philosopher, which has great weight in dealing with the next name, and should therefore, perhaps, have some in this case also.

[3] The MS. and both Roman edd. give *Crotonio*, rejected by the others because no Crotonius is known (it has been referred, however, to Pythagoras, on the ground of his having taught in Croton). In the margin of Ursinus *Cronius* was suggested, received by LB. and Orelli, who is mentioned by Eusebius (*Hist. Eccl.* vi. 19, 3) with Numenius and others as an eminent Pythagorean, and by Porphyry (*de Ant. Nymph.* xxi.), as a friend of Numenius, and one of those who treated the Homeric poems as allegories. Gelenius substitutes Plotinus, followed by most edd.

[4] *Stemus*, the admirable correction of Gelenius for the MS. *tem-p-us*.

[5] Orelli, following Stewechius, would omit *ita*.

philosophers, that it was more reasonable for you [to believe] them than for us to believe Christ? Was any one of them ever able by one word, or by a single command, I will not say to restrain, to check[1] the madness of the sea or the fury of the storm; to restore their sight to the blind, or give it to men blind from their birth; to call the dead back to life; to put an end to the sufferings of years; but—and this is much easier[2]—to heal by one rebuke a boil, a scab, or a thorn fixed in the skin? Not that we deny either that they are worthy of praise for the soundness of their morals, or that they are skilled in all kinds of studies and learning: for we know that they both speak in the most elegant language, and [that their words] flow in polished periods; that they reason in syllogisms with the utmost acuteness; that they arrange their inferences in due order;[3] that they express, divide, distinguish principles by definitions; that they say many things about the [different] kinds of numbers, many things about music; that by their maxims and precepts[4] they settle the problems of geometry also. But what [has] that to [do with] the case? Do enthymemes, syllogisms, and other such things, assure us that these [men] know what is true? or are they therefore such that credence should necessarily be given to them with regard to very obscure subjects? A comparison of persons must be decided, not by vigour of eloquence, but by the excellence of the works [which they have] done. He must not[5] be called a good teacher who has expressed himself clearly,[6] but he who accompanies his promises with the guarantee of divine works.

12. You bring forward arguments against us, and specu-

[1] Hildebrand thinks *compescere* here a gloss, but it must be remembered that redundancy is a characteristic of Arnobius.

[2] The superlative is here, as elsewhere, used by Arnobius instead of the comparative.

[3] *i.e.* so as to show the relations existing between them.

[4] Perhaps "axioms and postulates."

[5] According to Crusius, *non* is not found in the MS.

[6] White and Riddle translate *candidule*, "sincerely," but give no other instance of its use, and here the reference is plainly to the previous statement of the literary excellence of the philosophers. Heraldus

lative quibblings,[1] which—may I say this without displeasing him—if Christ himself were to use in the gatherings of the nations, who would assent? who would listen? who would say that he decided[2] anything clearly? or who, though he were rash and utterly[3] credulous, would follow him when pouring forth vain and baseless statements? His virtues [have been] made manifest to you, and that unheard-of power over things, whether that which was openly exercised by him, or that which was used[4] over the whole world by those who proclaimed him: it has subdued the fires of passion, and caused races, and peoples, and nations most diverse in character to hasten with one accord to accept the same faith. For the [deeds] can be reckoned up and numbered which have been done in India,[5] among the Seres, Persians, and Medes; in Arabia, Egypt, in Asia, Syria; among the Galatians, Parthians, Phrygians; in Achaia, Macedonia, Epirus; in all islands and provinces on which the rising and setting sun shines; in Rome herself, finally, the mistress [of the world], in which, although men are[6]

suggests *callidule*, "cunningly," of which Orelli approves; but by referring the adv. to this well-known meaning of its primitive, all necessity for emendation is obviated.

[1] Lit., " subtleties of suspicions." This passage is certainly doubtful. The reading translated, *et suspicionum argutias profer-tis*, is that of LB., Orelli, and the later edd. generally; while the MS. reads *-atis*—" Bring forward arguments to us, and" (for which Heraldus conjectures very plausibly, *nec*, " and not ") " subtleties," etc., which, by changing a single letter, reads in the earlier edd. *profer-etis*—" Will you," or, " You will bring forward," etc.

[2] Meursius conjectures *in-* (for MS. *ju-*) *dicare*—" pointed out," of which Orelli approves.

[3] So the MS. and both Roman edd., supported by Heraldus, reading *solidæ facilitatis*, changed by the edd. into *stolidæ*—" stupid."

[4] So all the edd. except Oehler; but as the first verb is plural in the MS., while the second is singular, it is at least as probable that the second was plural originally also, and that therefore the relative should be made to refer both to " virtues " and " power."

[5] Orelli notes that by India is here meant Ethiopia. If so, it may be well to remember that Lucan (x. 29 sq.) makes the Seres neighbours of the Ethiopians, and dwellers at the sources of the Nile.

[6] Instead of *sint*, Stewechius would read *essent*—" were."

busied with the practices introduced by king[1] Numa, and the superstitious observances of antiquity, they have nevertheless hastened to give up their fathers' mode of life,[2] and attach themselves to Christian truth. For they had seen the chariot[3] of Simon Magus, and his fiery car, blown into pieces by the mouth of Peter, and vanish when Christ was named. They had seen [him], I say, trusting in false gods, and abandoned by them in their terror, borne down headlong by his own weight, lie prostrate with his legs broken; [and] then, when he had been carried to Brunda,[4] worn out with anguish and shame, again cast himself down from the roof of a very lofty house. But all these deeds you neither know nor have wished to know, nor did you ever consider that they were of the utmost importance to you; and while you trust your own judgments, and term [that] wisdom which is overweening conceit, you have given to deceivers—to those guilty [ones], I say, whose interest it is that the Christian name be degraded—an opportunity of raising clouds of darkness, and concealing truths of so much importance; of robbing you of faith, and putting scorn in its place, in order that, as they already feel that an end such as they deserve threatens them, they might excite in you also a feeling through which you should run into danger, and be deprived of the divine mercy.

13. Meantime, however, O you who wonder and are astonished at the doctrines of the learned, and of philosophy,

[1] Instead of the MS. reading, *Numæ regis artibus et antiquis superstitionibus*, Stewechius, followed by Heraldus, would read *ritibus*—" with the rites of Numa," etc.

[2] So the MS., reading *res patrias*, for which Heraldus, *ritus patrios*—" rites."

[3] So the MS., although the first five edd., by changing *r* into *s*, read *cur-s-um*—" course." This story is of frequent occurrence in the later fathers, but is never referred to by the earlier, or by any except Christian writers, and is derived solely from the Apostolic Constitutions. In the Greek version of the Apost. Const. the sixth book opens with a dissertation on schisms and heresies, in which the story of Simon and others is told; but that this was interpolated by some compiler seems clear from the arguments brought forward by Bunsen (*Hippolytus and his Age*, more particularly vol. ii. Pt. 2, § 2, and the second appendix).

[4] Brunda or Brenda, *i.e.* Brundisium.

do you not then think it most unjust to scoff, to jeer at us as though we say foolish and senseless things, when you too are found to say either these or just such things which you laugh at when said and uttered by us? Nor do I address those who, scattered through various bypaths of the schools, have formed this and that [insignificant] party through diversity of opinion. You, you I address, who zealously follow Mercury,[1] Plato, and Pythagoras, and the rest of you who are of one mind, and walk in unity in the same paths of doctrine. Do you dare to laugh at us because we[2] revere and worship the Creator and Lord[3] of the universe, and because we commit and entrust our hopes to Him? What [does] your Plato [say] in the *Theætetus*, to mention him especially? Does he not exhort the soul to flee from the earth, and, as much as in it lies, to be continually engaged in thought and meditation about Him?[4] Do you dare to laugh at us, because we say that there will be a resurrection of the dead? And this indeed we confess that we say, but [maintain] that it is understood by you otherwise than we hold it. What [says] the same Plato in the *Politicus*? Does he not say that, when the world has begun to rise out of the west and tend towards the east,[5] men will again burst forth from the bosom of the earth, aged, grey-haired, bowed down with

---

[1] Hermes Trismegistus. See index.
[2] So the MS., Elmenh., LB., Hildebrand, and Oehler, reading *quod*, for which the other edd. read *qui*—" who."
[3] This seems to be the reading intended by the MS., which according to Hild. gives *dom*, *i.e.* probably *dominum*, which Oehler adopts, but all other edd. read *deum*—" god."
[4] Arnobius rather exaggerates the force of the passage referred to (st. p. 173), which occurs in the beautiful digression on philosophers. Plato there says that only the philosopher's body is here on earth, while his mind, holding politics and the ordinary business and amusements of life unworthy of attention, is occupied with what is above and beneath the earth, just as Thales, when he fell into a ditch, was looking at the stars, and not at his steps.
[5] *In cardinem vergere qui orientis est solis* seems to be the reading of all edd.; but according to Crusius the MS. reads *vertere*—" to turn." Hildebrand, on the contrary, affirms that instead of *t*, the MS. gives *c*.

years; and that when the remoter[1] years begin to draw near, they will gradually sink down[2] to the cradles of their infancy, through the same steps by which they now grow to manhood?[3] Do you dare to laugh at us because we see to the salvation of our souls?—that is, ourselves [care] for ourselves: for what are we men, but souls shut up in bodies? (You, indeed, do not take every pains for their safety,[4] in that you do not refrain from all vice and passion; about this you are anxious, that you may cleave to [your] bodies as though inseparably bound to them.[5]) What mean those mystic rites,[6] in which you beseech some [unknown] powers to be favourable to you, and not put any hindrance in your way to impede you when returning to your native seats?

14. Do you dare to laugh at us when we speak of hell,[7] and fires[8] which cannot be quenched, into which we have

[1] *i.e.* originally earlier.
[2] So most edd., reading *desituros*, for which Stewechius suggests *desulturos*—" leap down; " LB. *exituros*—" go out."
[3] Reference is here made to one of the most extraordinary of the Platonic myths (*Pol.* 269-274), in which the world is represented as not merely material, but as being further possessed of intelligence. It is ever in motion, but not always in the same way. For at one time its motion is directed by a divine governor (τοῦ παντὸς ὁ μὲν κυβερνήτης); but this does not continue, for he withdraws himself from his task, and thereupon the world loses, or rather gives up its previous bias, and begins to revolve in the opposite direction, causing among other results a reverse development of the phenomena which occurred before, such as Arnobius describes. Arnobius, however, gives too much weight to the myth, as in the introduction it is more than hinted that it may be addressed to the young Socrates, as boys like such stories, and he is not much more than a boy. With it should be contrasted the "great year" of the Stoics, in which the universe fulfilled its course, and then began afresh to pass through the same experience as before (Nemesius, *de Nat. Hom.* c. 38).
[4] LB. makes these words interrogative, but the above arrangement is clearly vindicated by the tenor of the argument: You laugh at our care for our souls' salvation; and truly you do not see to their safety by such precautions as a virtuous life, but do you not seek that which you think salvation by mystic rites?
[5] Lit., "fastened with beam" (*i.e.* large and strong) "nails."
[6] Cf. on the intercessory prayers of the Magi, c. 62.
[7] Pl. Cf. Milman's note on Gibbon, vol. 2, c. xi. p. 7.
[8] Lit., "certain fires."

learned that souls are cast by their foes and enemies? What, does not your Plato also, in the book which he wrote on the immortality of the soul, name the rivers Acheron, Styx,[1] Cocytus, and Pyriphlegethon, and assert that in them souls are rolled along, engulfed, and burned up? But [though] a man of no little wisdom,[2] and of accurate judgment and discernment, he essays a problem which cannot be solved; so that, while he says that the soul is immortal, everlasting, and without bodily substance, he yet says that they are punished, and makes them suffer pain.[3] But what man does not see that that which is immortal, which [is] simple,[4] cannot be subject to any pain; that that, on the contrary, cannot be immortal which does suffer pain? And yet his opinion is not very far from the truth. For although the gentle and kindly disposed man thought it inhuman cruelty to condemn souls to death, he yet not unreasonably[5] supposed that they are cast into rivers blazing with masses of flame, and loathsome from their foul abysses. For they are cast in, and being annihilated, pass away vainly in[6] everlasting destruction. For theirs is an intermediate[7] state, as has been learned from Christ's teaching; and [they are] such that they may on the one hand perish if they have not known God, and on the other be delivered from death if they have given heed to his threats[8] and [proffered] favours. And to make

---

[1] Plato, in the passage referred to (*Phædo*, st. p. 113, § 61), speaks of the Styx not as a river, but as the lake into which the Cocytus falls. The fourth river which he mentions in addition to the Acheron, Pyriphlegethon, and Cocytus, which he calls Stygian, is the Ocean stream.

[2] So the MS., according to Hild., reading *parvæ;* but acc. to Rigaltius and Crusius, it gives *pravæ*—" of no mean."

[3] So LB., Hild., and Oehler, reading *doloris afficiat sensu*, by merely dropping *m* from the MS. *sensu-m;* while all the other edd. read *doloribus sensuum*—" affects with the pains of the senses."

[4] *i.e.* not compounded of soul and body.

[5] Or, "not unsuitably," *absone.*

[6] Lit., " in the failure (or ' disappointment') of," etc.

[7] *i.e.* neither immortal nor necessarily mortal.

[8] So Gelenius emended the unintelligible MS. reading *se-mina* by merely adding *s*, followed by all edd., although Ursinus in the margin

manifest[1] what is unknown, this is man's real death, this which leaves nothing behind. For that which is seen by the eyes is [only] a separation of soul from body, not the last end—annihilation:[2] this, I say, is man's real death, when souls which know not God shall[3] be consumed in long-protracted torment with raging fire, into which certain fiercely cruel [beings] shall[3] cast them, *who were* unknown[4] before Christ, and brought to light only by his wisdom.

15. Wherefore there is no reason that that[5] should mislead us, should hold out vain hopes to us, which is said by some men till now unheard of,[6] and carried away by an extravagant opinion of themselves, that souls are immortal, next in point of rank to the God and ruler of the world, descended from that parent and sire, divine, wise, learned, and not within reach of the body by contact.[7] Now, because this is true and certain, and because we have been produced by him who is perfect without flaw, we live unblameably, [I suppose], and therefore without blame; [are] good, just, and upright, in nothing depraved; no passion overpowers, no lust degrades us; we maintain vigorously the unremitting

suggests *se miam, i.e. mi-sericordiam*—" pity ;" and Heraldus conjectures *munia*—" gifts."

[1] So almost all edd., from a conjecture of Gelenius, supplying *ut*, which is wanting in the MS., first ed., and Oehler.

[2] It is worth while to contrast Augustine's words : " The death which men fear is the separation of the soul from the body. The true death, which men do not fear, is the separation of the soul from God " (Aug. in Ps. xlviii., quoted by Elmenhorst).

[3] In the first ed., Gelenius, Canterus, Ursinus, and Orelli, both verbs are made present, but all other edd. follow the MS. as above.

[4] Lit., "and unknown." Here Arnobius shows himself ignorant of Jewish teaching, as in iii. 12.

[5] So the MS. and LB., followed by Oehler ; in the edd. *id* is omitted.

[6] The MS. reading is *a no-b-is quibusdam*, for which LB. reads *nobis a qu.*—" to us," and Hild. *a notis*—" by certain known ;" but all others, as above, from a conjecture of Gelenius, *a no-v-is*, although Orelli shows his critical sagacity by preferring an emendation in the margin of Ursinus, *a bonis*—" by certain good men," in which he sees a happy irony !

[7] Lit., " not touchable by any contact of body," *neque ulla corporis attrectatione contiguas*.

ARNOB. F

practice of all the virtues. And because all our souls have one origin, we therefore think exactly alike; we do not differ in manners, we do not differ in beliefs; we all know God; and there are not as many opinions as there are men in the world, nor [are these] divided in infinite variety.[1]

16. But, [they say], while we are moving swiftly down towards our mortal bodies,[2] causes pursue us from the world's circles,[3] through the working of which we become bad, ay, most wicked; burn with lust and anger, spend our life in shameful deeds, and are given over to the lust of all by the prostitution of our bodies for hire. And how can the material unite with the immaterial? or how can that which God has made, be led by weaker causes to degrade itself through the practice of vice? Will you lay aside your habitual arrogance,[4] O men, who claim God as your Father, and maintain that you are immortal, just as he is? Will you inquire, examine, search what you are yourselves, whose you are, of what parentage you are supposed [to be], what you do in the world, in what way you are born, how you leap to life? Will you, laying aside [all] partiality, consider in the silence of your thoughts that we are creatures either quite like the rest, or separated by no great difference? For what is there to show that we do not resemble them? or what excellence is in us, such that we scorn to be ranked as creatures? Their bodies are built up on bones, and bound closely together by sinews; and our bodies are in like manner built up on

---

[1] Arnobius considers the *reductio ad absurdum* so very plain, that he does not trouble himself to state his argument more directly.

[2] There has been much confusion as to the meaning of Arnobius throughout this discussion, which would have been obviated if it had been remembered that his main purpose in it is to show how unsatisfactory and unstable are the theories of the philosophers, and that he is not therefore to be identified with the views brought forward, but rather with the objections raised to them.

[3] Cf. c. 28, p. 95.

[4] So the MS., followed by Orelli and others, reading *institutum superciliumque*—" habit and arrogance," for the first word of which LB. reads *istum typhum*—" that pride of yours;" Meursius, *isti typhum*—" Lay aside pride, O ye."

bones, and bound closely together by sinews. They inspire the air through nostrils, and in breathing expire it again; and we in like manner draw in the air, and breathe it out with frequent respirations. They have been arranged in classes, female and male; we, too, have been fashioned by our Creator into the same sexes.[1] Their young are born from the womb, and are begotten through union of the sexes; and we are born from sexual embraces, and are brought forth and sent into life from our mothers' wombs. They are supported by eating and drinking, and get rid of the filth which remains by the lower parts; and we are supported by eating and drinking, and that which nature refuses we deal with in the same way. Their care is to ward off death-bringing famine, and of necessity to be on the watch for food. What else is our aim in the business of life, which presses so much upon us,[2] but to seek the means by which the danger of starvation may be avoided, and carking anxiety put away? They are exposed to disease and hunger, and at last lose their strength by reason of age. What, then? are we not exposed to these evils, and are we not in like manner weakened by noxious diseases, destroyed by wasting age? But if that, too, which is said in the more hidden mysteries is true, that the souls of wicked men, on leaving their human bodies, pass into cattle and other creatures,[3] it is [even] more clearly shown that we are allied to them, and not separated by any great interval, since it is on the same ground that both we and they are said to be living creatures, and to act as such.

17. But we have reason, [one will say], and excel the whole race of dumb animals in understanding. I might believe that this was quite true, if all men lived rationally and wisely, never swerved aside from their duty, abstained from what is forbidden, and withheld themselves from baseness, and [if] no one through folly and the blindness of ignorance demanded what is injurious and dangerous to

---

[1] So the edd., reading *in totidem sexus* for the MS. *sexu*—" into so many kinds in sex."

[2] Lit., " in so great occupations of life."

[3] Cf. Plato, *Phædo*, st. p. 81.

himself. I should wish, however, to know what this reason is, through which we are more excellent than all the tribes of animals. [Is it] because we have made for ourselves houses, by which we can avoid the cold of winter and heat of summer? What! do not the other animals show forethought in this respect? Do we not see some build nests as dwellings for themselves in the most convenient situations; others shelter and secure [themselves] in rocks and lofty crags; others burrow in the ground, and prepare for themselves strongholds and lairs in the pits which they have dug out? But if nature, which gave them life, had chosen to give to them also hands to help them, they too would, without doubt, raise lofty buildings and strike out new works of art.[1] Yet, even in those things which they make with beaks and claws, we see that there are many appearances of reason and wisdom which we men are unable to copy, however much we ponder them, although we have hands to serve us dexterously in every kind of work.

18. They have not learned, [I will be told], to make clothing, seats, ships, and ploughs, nor, in fine, the other furniture which family life requires. These are not the gifts of science but the suggestions of most pressing necessity; nor did the arts descend with [men's] souls from the inmost heavens, but here on earth have they all been painfully sought out and brought to light,[2] and gradually acquired in process of time by careful thought. But if the soul[3] had [in itself] the knowledge which it is fitting that a race should have indeed [which is] divine and immortal, all men would from the first know everything; nor would there be an age unacquainted with any art, or not furnished with practical knowledge. But now a life of want and in need of many things

[1] So, by a later writer in the margin of the MS., who gives *artificiosa-novitates*, adopted by Stewechius and Oehler, the *s* being omitted in the text of the MS. itself, as in the edd., which drop the final *s* in the next word also—"would raise and with unknown art strike out lofty buildings."

[2] Lit., "born."

[3] Throughout this discussion, Arnobius generally uses the plural *animæ*—"souls."

noticing some things happen accidentally to its advantage, while it imitates, experiments, and tries, while it fails, remoulds, changes, from continual failure has procured for itself[1] and wrought out some slight acquaintance with the arts, and brought to one issue the advances of many ages.

19. But if men either knew themselves thoroughly, or had the slightest knowledge of God,[2] they would never claim as their own a divine and immortal nature; nor would they think themselves something great because they have made for themselves gridirons, basins, and bowls,[3] because [they have made] under-shirts, outer-shirts, cloaks, plaids, robes of state, knives, cuirasses and swords, mattocks, hatchets, ploughs. Never, I say, carried away by pride and arrogance, would they believe themselves to be deities of the first rank, and fellows of the highest in his exaltation,[4] because they[5] had devised the arts of grammar, music, oratory, and geometry. For we do not see what is [so] wonderful in these arts, that because of their discovery the soul should be believed to be above the sun as well as all the stars, to surpass both in grandeur and essence the whole universe, of which these are parts. For what else do these assert that they can either declare or teach, than that we may learn to know the rules and differences of nouns, the intervals in the sounds of [different] tones, that we may speak persuasively in lawsuits, that we may measure the confines of the earth? Now, if the soul had brought these arts with it from the celestial regions, and it were impossible not to know them, all men

---

[1] So Elmenhorst, Oberthuer, and Orelli, reading *par-a-v-it sibi et* for the MS. *parv-as et*, " from continual failure has wrought out indeed slight smattering of the arts," etc., which is retained in both Roman edd., LB., and Hild.; while Gelenius and Canterus merely substitute *sibi* for *et*, " wrought out for itself slight," etc.

[2] Lit., " or received understanding of God by the breath of any suspicion."

[3] The MS. gives *c-etera-que*, "and the rest," which is retained in both Roman edd., and by Gelenius and Canterus, though rather out of place, as the enumeration goes on.

[4] Lit., " equal to the highness (*summitati*) of the prince."

[5] So LB. and Orelli, reading *qui-a*; the rest, *qui—*." who."

would long before this be busied with them over all the earth, nor would any race of men be found which would not be equally and similarly instructed in them all. But now how few musicians, logicians, and geometricians are there in the world! how few orators, poets, critics! From which it is clear, as has been said pretty frequently, that these things were discovered under the pressure of time and circumstances, and that the soul did not fly hither divinely[1] taught, because neither are all learned, nor can all learn; and[2] there are very many among them somewhat deficient in shrewdness, and stupid, and they are constrained to apply themselves to learning [only] by fear of stripes. But if it were a fact that the things which we learn are but reminiscences[3]—as has been maintained in the systems of the ancients—as we start from the same truth, we should all have learned alike, and remember alike—not have diverse, very numerous, and inconsistent opinions. Now, however, seeing that we each assert different things, it is clear and manifest that we have brought nothing from heaven, but become acquainted with what has arisen here, and maintain what has taken firm root in our thoughts.

20. And, that we may show you more clearly and distinctly what is the worth of man, whom you believe to be very like the higher power, conceive this idea; and because it can be done if we come into direct contact with it, let us conceive it just as if we came into contact. Let us then imagine a place dug out in the earth, fit for dwelling in, formed into a chamber, enclosed by a roof and walls, not cold in winter, not too warm in summer, but so regulated and equable that we suffer neither cold[4] nor the violent heat of summer. To this let there not come any sound or cry whatever,[5] of bird, of beast, of storm, of man—of any noise, in fine, or of the

---

[1] So Gelenius, reading *divinitus* for the MS. *divinas*, *i.e.* " with a divine nature and origin," which is retained in the first ed. and Orelli.

[2] The MS., both Roman edd., Hild., and Oehler, read *ut*, " so that there are."

[3] Cf. on this Platonic doctrine, ch. 24.

[4] Lit., " a feeling of cold."   [5] Lit., " sound of voice at all."

thunder's[1] terrible crash. Let us next devise a way in which it may be lighted not by the introduction of fire, nor by the sight of the sun, but let there be some counterfeit[2] to imitate sunlight, darkness being interposed.[3] Let there not be one door, nor a direct entrance, [but] let it be approached by tortuous windings, and let it never be thrown open unless when it is absolutely necessary.

21. Now, as we have prepared a place for our idea, let us next receive some one born to dwell there, where there is nothing but an empty void,[4]—one of the race of Plato, namely, or Pythagoras, or some one of those who are regarded as of superhuman wit, or have been declared most wise by the oracles of the gods. And when this has been done, he must then be nourished and brought up on suitable food. Let us therefore provide a nurse also, who shall come to him always naked, ever silent, uttering not a word, and shall not open her mouth and lips to speak at all, but after suckling him, and doing what else is necessary, shall leave him fast asleep, and remain day and night before the closed doors; for it is usually necessary that the nurse's care should be near at hand, and that [she] should watch his varying motions. But when the child begins to need to be supported by more substantial food, let it be borne in by the same nurse, still undressed, and maintaining the same unbroken silence. Let the food, too, which is carried in be always precisely the same, with no difference in the material, and without being re-cooked by means of different flavours; but let it be either pottage of millet, or bread of spelt, or, in imitation of the ancients, chestnuts roasted in the hot ashes, or berries plucked

[1] Lit., "of heaven terribly crashing."

[2] So the later edd., adopting the emendation of Scaliger, *nothum*—"spurious," which here seems to approach in meaning to its use by Lucretius (v. 574 sq.), of the moon's light as borrowed from the sun. The MS. and first four edd. read *notum*, "known."

[3] According to Huet (quoted by Oehler), "between that spurious and the true light;" but perhaps the idea is that of darkness interposed at intervals to resemble the recurrence of night.

[4] Lit., "born, and that, too (*et* wanting in almost all edd.), into the hospice of that place which has nothing, and is inane and empty."

from forest trees. Let him, moreover, never learn to drink wine, and let nothing else be used to quench his thirst than pure cold water from the spring, and [that] if possible raised to his lips in the hollow of his hands. For habit, growing into [second] nature, will become familiar from custom; nor will his desire extend[1] further, not knowing that there is [anything] more to be sought after.

22. To what, then, [you ask], do these things tend? [We have brought them forward] in order that—as it has been believed that the souls [of men] are divine, and therefore immortal, and that they come to their human bodies with all knowledge—we may make trial from this [child], whom we have supposed to be brought up in this way, whether this is credible, or has been rashly believed and taken for granted, in consequence of deceitful anticipation. Let us suppose, then, that he grows up, reared in a secluded, lonely spot, spending as many years as you choose, twenty or thirty,—nay, let him be brought into the assemblies of men when he has lived through forty years; and if it is true that he is a part of the divine essence, and[2] lives here sprung from the fountains of life, before he makes acquaintance with anything, or is made familiar with human speech, let him be questioned and answer who he is, or from what father; in what regions he was born, how or in what way brought up; with what work or business he has been engaged during the former part of his life. Will he not, then, stand [speechless], with less wit and sense than any beast, block, stone? Will he not, when brought into contact with[3] strange and previously unknown things, be above all ignorant of himself? If you ask, will he be able to say what the sun is, the earth, seas, stars, clouds, mist, showers, thunder,

---

[1] So most edd., reading *porrigetur* for the MS. *corrigetur*—"be corrected," *i.e.* need to be corrected, which is retained in the first ed.

[2] So Gelenius, followed by Canterus, Elmenh., and Oberthür, reading *portione-m et*, while the words *tam lætam*, "that he is so joyous a part," are inserted before *et* by Stewechius and the rest, except both Roman edd., which retain the MS. *portione jam læta*.

[3] Lit., "sent to."

snow, hail? Will he be able to know what trees are, herbs, or grasses, a bull, a horse, or ram, a camel, elephant, or kite?[1]

23. If you give a grape to him when hungry, a must-cake, an onion, a thistle,[2] a cucumber, a fig, will he know that his hunger can be appeased by all these, or of what kind each should be [to be fit] for eating?[3] If you made a very great fire, or surrounded him with venomous creatures, will he not go through the midst of flames, vipers, tarantulæ,[4] without knowing that they are dangerous, and ignorant even of fear? But again, if you set before him garments and furniture, both for city and country life, will he indeed be able to distinguish[5] for what each is fitted? to discharge what service they are adapted? Will he declare for what purposes of dress the stragula[6] was made, the coif,[7] zone,[8] fillet, cushion, handkerchief, cloak, veil, napkin, furs,[9] shoe, sandal, boot? What, if you go on to ask what a wheel is, or a sledge,[10] a winnowing-fan, jar, tub, an oil-mill, ploughshare, or sieve, a mill-stone, plough-tail, or light hoe; a curved seat, a needle, a strigil, a laver, an open seat, a ladle, a platter, a candlestick, a goblet, a broom, a cup, a bag; a lyre, pipe, silver, brass, gold,[11] a book, a rod, a roll,[12] and the rest of the equipment by which the life of man is sur-

[1] So the MS., reading *milvus*, for which all edd. (except Oberthuer) since Stewechius read *mulus*, "a mule."
[2] *Carduus*, no doubt the esculent thistle, a kind of artichoke.
[3] So, according to an emendation in LB., *esui*, adopted by Orelli and others, instead of the MS. reading *et sui*.
[4] There has been much discussion as to whether the *solifuga* or *solipuga* here spoken of is an ant or spider.
[5] The MS. reads *discriminare, discernere*, with the latter word, however, marked as spurious.
[6] A kind of rug.   [7] *Mitra*.
[8] *Strophium*, passing round the breast, by some regarded as a kind of corset.
[9] *Mastruca*, a garment made of the skins of the *muflone*, a Sardinian wild sheep.
[10] *Tribula*, for rubbing out the corn.
[11] *Aurum* is omitted in all edd., except those of LB., Hild., and Oehler.
[12] *Liber*, a roll of parchment or papyrus, as opposed to the preceding *codex*, a book of pages.

rounded and maintained? Will he not in such circumstances, as we said, like an ox[1] or an ass, a pig, or any beast more senseless, look[2] at these indeed, observing their various shapes, but[3] not knowing what they all are, and ignorant of the purpose for which they are kept? If he were in any way compelled to utter a sound, would he not with gaping mouth shout something indistinctly, as the dumb usually do?

24. Why, O Plato, do you in the *Meno*[4] put to a young slave certain questions relating to the doctrines of number, and strive to prove by his answers that what we learn we do not learn, but that we [merely] call back to memory those things which we knew in former times? Now, if he answers you correctly (for it would not be becoming that we should refuse credit to what you say), he is led [to do so] not by his real knowledge,[5] but by his intelligence; and it results from his having some acquaintance with numbers, through using them every day, that when questioned he follows [your meaning], and that the very process of multiplication always prompts him. But if you are really assured that the souls [of men are] immortal and endowed with knowledge [when they] fly hither, cease to question that youth whom you see to be ignorant[6] and accustomed to the ways of men:[7] call to you that man of forty years, and ask of him, not anything out of the way or obscure about triangles, about squares, [not]

---

[1] The MS. reads *vobis* unintelligibly, corrected by Meursius *bovis*.

[2] So Orelli and modern edd.; but Crusius gives as the MS. reading *conspici-etur* (not -*et*), as given by Ursinus, and commonly received—"Will he not ... be seen?"

[3] The MS. and first five edd. read *et*—"and," changed in LB. to *sed*.

[4] In this dialogue (st. p. 81) Socrates brings forward the doctrine of reminiscence as giving a reasonable ground for the pursuit of knowledge, and then proceeds to give a practical illustration of it by leading an uneducated slave to solve a mathematical problem by means of question and answer.

[5] Lit., "his knowledge of things."

[6] So the MS. and edd., reading *i-gnarum rerum*, except LB., which by merely omitting the *i* gives the more natural meaning, "acquainted with the things," etc.

[7] Lit., "established in the limits of humanity."

what a cube is, or a second power,[1] the ratio of nine to eight, or finally, of four to three; but ask him that with which all are acquainted—what twice two are, or twice three. We wish to see, we wish to know, what answer he gives when questioned—whether he solves the desired problem. In such a case will he perceive, although his ears are open, whether you are saying anything, or asking anything, or requiring some answer from him? and will he not stand like a stock, or the Marpesian rock,[2] as the saying is, dumb and speechless, not understanding or knowing even this—whether you are talking with him or with another, conversing with another or with him;[3] whether that is intelligible speech which you utter, or [merely] a cry having no meaning, but drawn out and protracted to no purpose?

25. What say you, O men, who assign to yourselves too much of an excellence not your own? Is this the learned soul which you describe, immortal, perfect, divine, holding the fourth place under God the Lord of the universe, and under the kindred spirits,[4] and proceeding from the fountains of life?[5] This is that precious [being] man, endowed[6] with the loftiest powers of reason, who is said [to be] a microcosm, and [to be] made and formed after the fashion of the whole [universe], superior, as has been seen, to no brute, more senseless than stock [or] stone; for he is unacquainted with men, and always lives, loiters idly in the still deserts

[1] *i.e.* a square numerically or algebraically. The MS., both Roman edd., and Canterus read *di-bus aut dynam-us*, the former word being defended by Meursius as equivalent to *binio*, "a doubling,"—a sense, however, in which it does not occur. In the other edd., *cubus aut dynamis* has been received from the margin of Ursinus.
[2] *Æneid*, vi. 472.
[3] This clause is with reason rejected by Meursius as a gloss.
[4] Founded on Plato's words (*Phædrus*, st. p. 247), τῷ δ' (*i.e.* Zeus) ἕπεται στρατιὰ θεῶν τε καὶ δαιμόνων, the doctrine became prevalent that under the supreme God were lesser gods made by him, beneath whom again were dæmons, while men stood next. To this Orelli supposes that Arnobius here refers.
[5] The vessels in which, according to Plato (*Timæus*, st. p. 41), the Supreme Being mixed the vital essence of all being. Cf. c. 52.
[6] Lit., "and endowed."

although he were rich,[1] lived years without number, and never escaped from the bonds of the body. But when he goes to school, [you say], and is instructed by the teaching of masters, he is made wise, learned, and lays aside the ignorance which till now clung to him. And an ass, and an ox as well, if compelled by constant practice, learn to plough and grind; a horse, to submit to the yoke, and obey the reins in running;[2] a camel, to kneel down when being either loaded or unloaded; a dove, when set free, to fly back to its master's house; a dog, on finding game, to check and repress its barking; a parrot, too, to articulate words; and a crow to utter names.

26. But when I hear the soul spoken of as something extraordinary, as akin and very nigh to God, [and] as coming hither knowing all about past times, I would have it teach, not learn; and not go back to the rudiments, as the saying is, after being advanced in knowledge, but hold fast the truths it has learned when it enters its earthly body.[3] For unless it were so, how could it be discerned whether [the soul] recalls to memory or learns [for the first time] that which it hears; seeing that it is much easier to believe that it learns what it is unacquainted with, than that it has forgot what it knew [but] a little before, and that its power of recalling former things is lost through the interposition of the body? And what becomes of the doctrine that souls, [being] bodiless, do not have substance? For that which is not connected with[4] any bodily form is not hampered by the opposition of another, nor can anything be led[5] to destroy that which cannot be touched by what is set against it. For

---

[1] The text and meaning are both rather doubtful, and the edd. vary exceedingly. The reading of Orelli, *demoretur iners, valeat in ære quamvis*, has been translated as most akin to the MS., with which, according to Oehler, it agrees, although Orelli himself gives the MS. reading as *aer-io*.

[2] Lit., "acknowledge turnings in the course."

[3] Lit., "but retaining its own things, bind itself in earthly bodies."

[4] Lit., "of."

[5] So the MS. and edd., reading *sua-de-ri*, for which Oehler reads very neatly *sua de vi*—"can anything of its own power destroy," etc.

as a proportion established in bodies remains unaffected and secure, though it be lost to sight in a thousand cases; so must souls, if they are not material, as is asserted, retain their knowledge [1] of the past, however thoroughly they may have been enclosed in bodies.[2] Moreover, the same reasoning not only shows that they are not incorporeal, but deprives them of all [3] immortality even, and refers them to the limits within which life is usually closed. For whatever is led by some inducement to change and alter itself, so that it cannot retain its natural state, must of necessity be considered essentially passive. But that which is liable and exposed to suffering, is declared to be corruptible by that very capacity of suffering.

27. So then, if souls lose all their knowledge on being fettered with the body, they must experience something of such a nature that it makes them become blindly forgetful.[4] For they cannot, without becoming subject to anything whatever, either lay aside their knowledge while they maintain their natural state, or without change in themselves pass into a different state. Nay, we rather think that what is one, immortal, simple, in whatever it may be, must always retain its own nature, and that it neither should nor could be subject to anything, if indeed it purposes to endure and abide within the limits of true immortality. For all suffering is a passage for death and destruction, a way leading to the grave, and bringing an end of life which may not be escaped from; and if souls are liable to it, and yield to its influence and assaults, they indeed have life given to them only for present use, not as a secured possession,[5] although some come to other conclusions, and put faith in their own arguments with regard to so important a matter.

28. And yet, that we may not be as ignorant when we

[1] Lit., "not suffer forgetfulness."

[2] Lit., "however the most solid unions of bodies may have bound them round."

[3] So the edd., reading *privat immortalitate has omni*, for which, according to Hildebrand, the MS. reads *-tatem has omnis*—"all these of immortality."

[4] Lit., "put on the blindness of oblivion."

[5] Cf. Lucretius, iii. 969, where life is thus spoken of.

leave you [as before], let us hear from you[1] how you say that the soul, on being enwrapt in an earthly body, has no recollection of the past; while, after being actually placed in the body itself, and rendered almost senseless by union with it, it holds tenaciously and faithfully the things which many years before, eighty if you choose to say [so], or even more, it either did, or suffered, or said, or heard. For if, through being hampered by the body, it does not remember those things which it knew long ago, and before it came into this world,[2] there is more reason that it should forget those things which it has done from time to time since being shut up in the body, than those which [it did] before entering it,[3] while not yet connected with men. For the same body which[4] deprives of memory the soul which enters it,[5] should cause what is done within itself also to be wholly forgotten; for one cause cannot bring about two results, and [these] opposed to each other, so as to make some things to be forgotten, [and] allow others to be remembered by him who did them. But if souls, as you call them, are prevented and hindered by their [fleshly] members from recalling their former knowledge,[6] how do they remember what has been arranged[7] in [these] very bodies, and know that they are spirits, and have

---

[1] The MS. reads *ne videamu-s*, changed in both Roman edd. into *-amur*—"that we may not be seen by you [as ignorant], how say you," etc. Gelenius proposed the reading of the text, *audiamus*, which has been received by Canterus and Orelli. It is clear from the next words—*quemadmodum dicitis*—that in this case the verb must be treated as a kind of interjection, "How say you, let us hear." LB. reads, to much the same purpose, *scire avemus*, "we desire to know."

[2] Lit., "before man."   [3] Lit., "placed outside."

[4] *Quod enim.*   [5] *Rebus ingressis.*

[6] So read by Orelli, *artes suas antiquas*, omitting *atque*, which, he says, follows in the MS. It is read after *suas*, however, in the first ed., and those of Gelenius, Canterus, Hildebrand; and according to Oehler, it is so given in the MS., "its own and ancient." Oberthür would supply *res*—"its own arts and ancient things."

[7] So the MS., reading *constitut-a*, followed by all edd. except those of Ursinus, Hildebrand, and Oehler, who read *-æ*, "how do they remember when established in the bodies," which is certainly more in accordance with the context.

no bodily substance, being exalted by their condition as immortal beings?[1] [how do they know] what rank they hold in the universe, in what order they have been set apart [from other beings]? how they have come to these, the lowest parts of the universe? what properties they acquired, and from what circles,[2] in gliding along towards these regions? How, I say, do they know that they were very learned, and have lost their knowledge by the hindrance which their bodies afford them? For of this very thing also they should have been ignorant, whether their union with the body had brought any stain upon them; for to know what you were, and what to-day you are not, is no sign that you have lost your memory,[3] but a proof and evidence that it is quite sound.[4]

29. Now, since it is so, cease, I pray you, cease to rate trifling and unimportant things at immense values. Cease to place man in the upper ranks, since he is of the lowest; and in the highest orders, seeing that his person only is taken account of,[5] that he is needy, poverty-stricken in his house and dwelling,[6] and [was] never entitled to be declared of illustrious descent. For while, as just men and upholders of righteousness, you should have subdued pride and arrogance, by the evils[7] of which we are all uplifted and puffed up with empty vanity; you not only hold that these evils arise naturally, but—and this is much worse—you have also added causes by which vice should increase, and wickedness remain incorrigible. For what man is there, although of a disposition which ever shuns what is of bad repute and shameful, who, when he hears it said by very wise men that the soul is immortal, and not subject to the decrees of the fates,[8] would not throw himself headlong into all kinds of

---

[1] Lit., "of immortality." [2] Cf. ch. xvi. p. 82.
[3] Lit., "of a lost memory." [4] Lit., "of [a memory] preserved."
[5] *Capite cum censeatur.*
[6] Lit., "poor in hearth, and of a poor hut."
[7] So the MS., reading *malis*, for which Ursinus suggested *alis*, "on the wings of which."
[8] *i.e.* to death.

vice, [and] fearlessly[1] engage in and set about unlawful things? [who] would not, in short, gratify his desires in all things demanded by his unbridled lust, strengthened even further by its security and freedom from punishment?[2] For what will hinder him from doing so? The fear of a power above and divine judgment? And how shall he be overcome by any fear or dread who has been persuaded that he is immortal, just as the supreme God himself, and that no sentence can be pronounced upon him by God, seeing that there is the same immortality in both, and that the one immortal being cannot be troubled by the other, which is [only] its equal?[3]

30. But [will he not be terrified by][4] the punishments in Hades, of which we have heard, assuming also [as they do] many forms of torture? And who[5] will be so senseless and ignorant of consequences,[6] as to believe that to imperishable spirits either the darkness of Tartarus, or rivers of fire, or marshes with miry abysses, or wheels sent whirling through the air,[7] can in any wise do harm? For that which is beyond reach, and not subject to the laws of destruction, though it be surrounded by all the flames of the raging streams, be rolled in the mire, overwhelmed by the fall of overhanging rocks and by the overthrow of huge mountains,

---

[1] The MS. reads *securus, intrepidus*—"heedless, fearless;" the former word, however, being marked as a gloss. It is rejected in all edd., except LB.

[2] Lit., "by the freedom of impunity."

[3] Lit., "the one [immortality] ... in respect of the equality of condition of the other"—*nec in alterius [immortalitatis] altera [immortalitatas] possit æqualitate conditionis vexari;* the reference being clearly to the immediately preceding clause, with which it is so closely connected logically and grammatically. Orelli, however, would supply *anima*, ἀπὸ τοῦ κοινοῦ, as he puts it, of which nothing need be said. Meursius, with customary boldness, emends *nec vi alterius altera*, "nor by the power of one can the other," etc.

[4] So the ellipse is usually supplied, but it seems simpler and is more natural thus: "But punishments [have been] spoken of" (*memoratæ*), etc.

[5] So MS. and Oehler, for which the edd. read *ec quis*, "will any one."

[6] Lit., "the consequences of things."

[7] Lit., "the moving of wheels whirling."

must remain safe and untouched without suffering any deadly harm.

Moreover, that conviction not only leads on to wickedness, from the very freedom to sin [which it suggests], but even takes away the ground of philosophy itself, and asserts that it is vain to undertake its study, because of the difficulty of the work, which leads to no result. For if it is true that souls know no end, and are ever[1] advancing with all generations, what danger is there in giving themselves up to the pleasures of sense—despising and neglecting the virtues by [regard to] which life is more stinted [in its pleasures], and [becomes] less attractive—and in letting loose their boundless lust to range eagerly and unchecked through[2] all kinds of debauchery? [Is it the danger] of being worn out by such pleasures, and corrupted by vicious effeminacy? And how can that be corrupted which is immortal, which always exists, and [is] subject to no suffering? [Is it the danger] of being polluted by foul and base deeds? And how can that be defiled which has no corporeal substance; or where can corruption seat itself, where there is no place on which the mark of this very corruption should fasten?

But again, if souls draw near to the gates of death,[3] as is laid down in the doctrine of Epicurus, in this case, too, there is no sufficient reason why philosophy should be sought out, even if it is true that by it[4] souls are cleansed and made pure from all uncleanness.[5] For if

[1] Lit., "in the unbroken course of ages"—*perpetuitate ævorum*.
[2] Lit., "and to scatter the unbridled eagerness of boundless lust through," etc.
[3] Lucretius (iii. 417 sqq.) teaches at great length that the soul and mind are mortal, on the ground that they consist of atoms smaller than those of vapour, so that, like it, on the breaking of their case, they will be scattered abroad; next, on the ground of the analogy between them and the body in regard to disease, suffering, etc.; of their ignorance of the past, and want of developed qualities; and finally, on the ground of the adaptation of the soul to the body, as of a fish to the sea, so that life under other conditions would be impossible.
[4] The MS. and first four edd. read *has*, "that these souls," etc.; in the other edd., *hac* is received as above from the margin of Ursinus.
[5] Cf. Plato. *Phædo* (st. p. 64 sq.), where death is spoken of as only a

they all[1] die, and even in the body[2] the feeling characteristic of life perishes, and is lost;[3] it is not only a very great mistake, but [shows] stupid blindness, to curb innate desires, to restrict your mode of life within narrow limits, not yield to your inclinations, and do what our passions have demanded and urged, since no rewards await you for so great toil when the day of death comes, and you shall be freed from the bonds of the body.

31. A certain neutral character, then, and undecided and doubtful nature of the soul, has made room for philosophy, and found out a reason for its being sought after: while, that is, that fellow[4] is full of dread because of evil deeds of which he is guilty; another conceives great hopes if he shall do no evil, and pass his life in obedience to[5] duty and justice. Thence it is that among learned men, and [men] endowed with excellent abilities, there is strife as to the nature of the soul, and some say that it is subject to death, and cannot take upon itself the divine substance; while others [maintain] that it is immortal, and cannot sink under the power of death.[6] But this is brought about by the law of [the soul's] neutral character:[7] because, on the one hand, arguments present themselves to the one party by which it is found that the soul[8] is capable of suffering, and perishable; and, on the other hand, are not wanting to their

carrying further of that separation of the soul from the pleasures and imperfections of the body which the philosopher strives to effect in this life.

[1] Lit., "in common."   [2] Pl.
[3] This refers to the second argument of Lucretius noticed above.
[4] *i.e.* the abandoned and dissolute immortal spoken of in last chapter.
[5] Lit., "with."   [6] Lit., "degenerate into mortal nature."
[7] Arnobius seems in this chapter to refer to the doctrine of the Stoics, that the soul must be material, because, unless body and soul were of one substance, there could be no common feeling or mutual affection (so Cleanthes in *Nemes. de Nat. Hom.* ii. p. 33); and to that held by some of them, that only the souls of the wise remained after death, and these only till the conflagration (Stob. *Ecl. Phys.* p. 372) which awaits the world, and ends the Stoic great year or cycle. Others, however, held that the souls of the wise became dæmons and demigods (Diog. *Laert.* vii. 157 and 151).
[8] Lit., "they"—*eas.*

opponents, by which it is shown that the soul is divine and immortal.

32. Since these things are so, and we have been taught by the greatest teacher that souls are set not far from the gaping[1] jaws of death; that they can, nevertheless, have their lives prolonged by the favour and kindness of the Supreme Ruler, if only they try and study to know him (for the knowledge of him is a kind of vital leaven[2] and cement to bind together that which would otherwise fly apart),—let them,[3] then, laying aside their savage and barbarous nature, return to gentler ways, that they may be able to be ready for that which shall be given.[4] What reason is there that we should be considered by you brutish, as it were, and stupid, if we have yielded and given ourselves up to God our deliverer, because of these fears? We often seek out remedies for wounds and the poisoned bites of serpents, and defend ourselves by means of thin plates[5] sold by Psylli[6] or Marsi, and other hucksters[7] and impostors; and that we may not be inconvenienced by cold or intense heat,[8] we provide with anxious and careful diligence coverings in[9] houses and clothing.

[1] Lit., "from the gapings and," etc.
[2] There may be here some echo of the words (John xvii. 3), "This is eternal life, that they may know thee, the only true God," etc.; but there is certainly not sufficient similarity to found a direct reference on, as has been done by Orelli and others.
[3] *i.e.* souls.
[4] This passage presents no difficulty in itself, its sense being obviously that, as by God's grace life is given to those who serve him, we must strive to fit ourselves to receive his blessing. The last words, however, have seemed to some fraught with mystery, and have been explained by Heraldus at some length as a veiled or confused reference to the Lord's Supper, as following upon baptism and baptismal regeneration, which, he supposes, are referred to in the preceding words, "laying aside," etc.
[5] These "thin plates," *laminæ*, Orelli has suggested, were amulets worn as a charm against serpents.
[6] MS. *Phyllis*.
[7] So the edd., reading *instit-oribus* for the MS. *instit-ut-oribus*, "makers."
[8] Lit., "that colds and violent suns may not," etc.
[9] Lit., "of."

33. Seeing that the fear of death, that is, the ruin of our souls, menaces[1] us, in what are we not acting, as we all are wont, from a sense of what will be to our advantage,[2] in that we hold him fast who assures us that he will be our deliverer from such danger, embrace [him], and entrust our souls to his care,[3] if only that[4] interchange is right? You rest the salvation of your souls on yourselves, and are assured that by your own exertions alone[5] you become gods; but we, on the contrary, hold out no hope to ourselves from our own weakness, for we see that our nature has no strength, and is overcome by its own passions in every strife for anything.[6] You think that, as soon as you pass away, freed from the bonds of your fleshly members, you will find wings[7] with which you may rise to heaven and soar to the stars. We shun such presumption, and do not think[8] that it is in our power to reach the abodes[9] above, since we have no certainty as to this even, whether we deserve to receive life and be freed from the law of death. You suppose that without the aid of others[10] you will return to the master's palace as if to your own home, no one hindering [you]; but we, on the contrary, neither have any expectation that this can be unless by [the will of] the Lord of all, nor think that so much power and licence are given to any man.

34. Since this is the case, what, pray, is so unfair as that we should be looked on by you as silly in that readiness of belief [at which you scoff], while we see that you both

---

[1] Lit., "is set before."

[2] So the MS., first ed., Gelenius, Canterus, Hildebrand, reading *ex commodi sensu*, for which all the other edd., following Ursinus and Meursius, read *ex communi*—"from common sense," *i.e.* wisely.

[3] Perhaps, as Orelli evidently understands it, "prefer him to our own souls"—*animis præponimus*.

[4] So Oehler, reading *ea* for the MS. *ut*, omitted in all edd.

[5] Lit., "by your own and internal exertion."

[6] Lit., "of things."   [7] Lit., "wings will be at hand."

[8] The MS. reads *di*-cimus, "say;" corrected *du*, as above.

[9] The first four edd. read *res*, "things above," for which Stewechius reads, as above, *sedes*.

[10] *Sponte*.

have like beliefs, and entertain the same hopes? If we are thought deserving of ridicule because we hold out to ourselves such a hope, the same ridicule awaits you too, who claim for yourselves the hope of immortality. If you hold and follow a rational course, grant to us also a share in it. If Plato in the *Phædrus*,[1] or another of this band [of philosophers], had promised these joys to us—that is, a way to escape death, or were able to provide it and bring [us] to the end which he had promised,[2] it would have been fitting that we should seek to honour him from whom we look for so great a gift and favour. Now, since Christ has not only promised it, but also shown by his virtues, [which were] so great, that it can be made good, what strange thing do we do, and on what grounds are we charged with folly, if we bow down and worship his name[3] and majesty from whom we expect [to receive] both [these blessings], that we may at once escape a death of suffering, and be enriched with eternal life?[4]

35. But, say [my opponents], if souls are mortal and[5] of neutral character, how can they from their neutral properties become immortal? If we should say that we do not know this, and only believe it because said by[6] [one] mightier [than we], when will our readiness of belief seem mistaken if we believe[7] that to the almighty King nothing is hard,

---

[1] Here, as in c. 7, n. 3, p. 69, the edd. read *Phædone*, with the exception of the first ed. LB., Hildebrand, and Oehler, who follow the MS. as above.

[2] Lit., "to the end of promising."

[3] Meursius suggests *numini*, "deity," on which it may be well to remark once for all, that *nomen* and *numen* are in innumerable places interchanged in one or other of the edd. The change, however, is usually of so little moment, that no further notice will be taken of it.

[4] So the MS., according to Rigaltius and Hildebrand, reading *vitæ æternitate*, while Crusius asserts that the MS. gives *vita et*—"with life and eternity."

[5] The MS. reading is, *mortalis est qualitatis*. The first five edd. merely drop *est*—"of mortal, of neutral," etc.; LB. and the others read, *es et*, as above.

[6] Lit., "heard from."

[7] So the MS., according to Crusius, the edd. reading *cred-id-imus*—"have believed."

nothing difficult, and that[1] what is impossible to us is possible to him and at his command?[2] For is there [anything] which may withstand his will, or does it not follow[3] of necessity that what he has willed [must] be done? Are we to infer from our distinctions what either can or cannot be done; and are we not to consider that our reason is as mortal as we ourselves are, and is of no importance with the Supreme? And yet, O ye who do not believe that the soul is of a neutral character, and that it is held on the line midway between life and death, are not all whatever whom fancy supposes to exist, gods, angels, dæmons, or whatever else is their name, themselves too of a neutral character, and liable to change[4] in the uncertainty of their future?[5] For if we all agree that there is one Father of all, [who] alone [is] immortal and unbegotten, and [if] nothing at all is found before him which could be named,[6] it follows as a consequence that all these whom the imagination of men believes to be gods, have been either begotten by him or produced at his bidding. Are they[7] produced and begotten? they are also later in order and time: if later in order and time, they must have an origin, and beginning of birth and life; but that which has an entrance [into] and beginning of life in its first stages, it of necessity follows, should have an end also.

36. But the gods are said to be immortal. Not by nature, then, but by the goodwill and favour of God their father. In the same way, then, in which the boon[8] of immortality is

---

[1] Lit., " if [we believe] that."

[2] So the MS., reading *ad modum obsecutionis paratum*—" prepared to the mode of compliance;" for which the edd. read *adm. executioni*—" quite prepared for performing," except Hildebrand, who gives *adm. obsecutioni*—" for obedience."

[3] So the MS., according to Crusius, but all edd. read *sequ-a-tur* (for *i*) —" Is there anything which he has willed which it does not follow," etc.

[4] So all edd., reading *mutabiles*, except the two Roman edd. and Oehler, who gives, as the reading of the MS. *nu.*—" tottering."

[5] Lit., " in the doubtful condition of their lot."

[6] Lit., " which may have been of a name."

[7] LB., followed by the later edd., inserted *si*, " if they are," which is certainly more consistent with the rest of the sentence.

[8] The MS. reading is utterly corrupt and meaningless—*immortalitatis*

God's gift to [these who were] assuredly produced,[1] will he deign to confer eternal life upon souls also, although fell death seems able to cut them off and blot them out of existence in utter annihilation.[2] The divine Plato, many of whose thoughts are worthy of God, and not such as the vulgar hold, in that discussion and treatise entitled the *Timæus*, says that the gods and the world are corruptible by nature, and in no wise beyond the reach of death, but that their being is ever maintained[3] by the will of God, [their] king and prince:[4] for that that [even] which has been duly clasped and bound together by the surest bands is preserved [only] by God's goodness; and that by no other than[5] by him who bound [their elements] together can they both be dissolved if necessary, and have the command given which preserves their being.[6] If this is the case, then, and it is not fitting to think or believe otherwise, why do you wonder that we speak of the soul as neutral in its character, when Plato says that it is so even with the deities,[7] but that their life is kept

largiter est donum dei certa prolatis. Gelenius, followed by Canterus, Oberthür, and Orelli, emended *largi-tio . . . certe,* as above. The two Roman edd. read, *-tatem largitus . . . certam*—"bestowed, assured immortality as God's gift on," etc.

[1] *i.e.,* who must therefore have received it if they have it at all.

[2] Lit., "out, reduced to nothing with annihilation, not to be returned from."

[3] Lit., "they are held in a lasting bond," *i.e.* of being.

[4] Plato makes the supreme God, creator of the inferior deities, assure these lesser gods that their created nature being in itself subject to dissolution, his will is a surer ground on which to rely for immortality, than the substance or mode of their own being (*Timæus,* st. p. 41; translated by Cicero, *de Univ.* xi., and criticised *de Nat. Deor.* i. 8 and iii. 12).

[5] The MS. and both Roman edd. read *neque ullo ab-olitio-nis* unintelligibly, for which Gelenius proposed *nexusque abolitione*—"and by the destruction of the bond;" but the much more suitable reading in the margin of Ursinus, translated above, *ullo ab alio nis-i,* has been adopted by later edd.

[6] Lit., "be gifted with a saving order." So the MS., reading *salutari iussione,* followed by both Roman edd.; LB. and Orelli read *vinctione* —"bond;" Gelenius, Canterus, Elmenh., and Oberthuer, *m-issione*— "dismissal."

[7] Lit., "that to the gods themselves the natures are intermediate."

up by God's[1] grace, without break or end? For if by chance you knew it not, and because of its novelty it was unknown to you before, [now, though] late, receive and learn from him who knows and has made it known, Christ, that souls are not the children of the supreme ruler, and did not begin to be self-conscious, and to be spoken of in their own special character after being created by him;[2] but that some other is their parent, far enough removed from the chief in rank and power, of his court, however, and distinguished by his high and exalted birthright.

37. But if souls were, as is said, the Lord's children, and begotten by[3] the supreme power, nothing would have been wanting to make them perfect, [as they would have been] born with the most perfect excellence: they would all have had one mind, and [been of] one accord; they would always dwell in the royal palace; and would not, passing by the seats of bliss in which they had learned and kept in mind the noblest teachings, rashly seek these regions of earth, that[4] they might live enclosed in gloomy bodies amid phlegm and blood, among these bags of filth and most disgusting[5] vessels of urine. But, [an opponent will say], it was necessary that these parts too should be peopled, and therefore Almighty God sent souls hither to [form] some colonies, as it were. And of what use are men to the world, and on account of what are they necessary,[6] so that they may not be believed to

---

[1] Lit., "supreme"—*principali*.

[2] Cf. i. 48. On this passage Orelli quotes Irenæus, i. 21, where are enumerated several gnostic theories of the creation of the world and men by angels, who are themselves created by the "one unknown Father." Arnobius is thought, both by Orelli and others, to share in these opinions, and in this discussion to hint at them, but obscurely, lest his cosmology should be confounded by the Gentiles with their own polytheistic system. It seems much more natural to suppose that we have here the indefinite statement of opinions not thoroughly digested.

[3] Lit., "a generation of."

[4] Canterus, Elmenhorst, Oberthuer, and Orelli omit *ut*, which is retained as above by the rest.

[5] Lit., "obscene."

[6] Elmenhorst endeavours to show that Arnobius coincides in this argument with the Epicureans, by quoting Lucr. v. 165 sqq. and Lact. vii. 5,

have been destined to live here and be the tenants of an earthly body for no purpose? They have a share, [my opponent says,] in perfecting the completeness of this immense mass, and without their addition this whole universe is incomplete and imperfect. What then? If there were not men, would the world cease to discharge its functions? would the stars not go through their changes? would there not be summers and winters? would the blasts of the winds be lulled? and from the clouds gathered and hanging [overhead] would not the showers come down upon the earth to temper droughts? But now[1] all things must go on in their own courses, and not give up following the arrangement established by nature, even if there should be no name of man heard in the world, and this earth should be still with the silence of an unpeopled desert. How then is it alleged that it was necessary that an inhabitant should be given to these regions, since it is clear that by man comes nothing to [aid in] perfecting the world, and that all his exertions regard his private convenience always, and never cease to aim at his own advantage?

38. For, to begin with what is important, what advantage is it to the world that the mightiest kings are here? What, that there are tyrants, lords, [and] other innumerable and very illustrious powers? What, that there are generals of the greatest experience in war, skilled in taking cities; soldiers steady and utterly invincible in battles of cavalry, or in fighting hand to hand on foot? What, that there are orators, grammarians, poets, writers, logicians, musicians, ballet-dancers, mimics, actors, singers, trumpeters, flute and reed players? What, that there are runners, boxers, charioteers, vaulters,[2] walkers on stilts, rope-dancers, jugglers?

---

where the Epicurean argument is brought forward, What profit has God in man, that he should have created him? In doing this, it seems not to have been observed that the question asked by Arnobius is a very different one: What place has man in the *world*, that God should be supposed to have sent him to fill it?

[1] *i.e.* so far from this being the case.

[2] *i.e.* from one horse to another—*desultores*.

What, that there are dealers in salt fish, salters, fishmongers, perfumers, goldsmiths, bird-catchers, weavers of winnowing fans and baskets of rushes? What, that there are fullers, workers in wool, embroiderers, cooks, confectioners, dealers in mules, pimps, butchers, harlots? What, that there are other kinds of dealers? What do [the other kinds] of professors and arts (for the enumeration of which all life would be [too] short) contribute to the plan and constitution[1] of the world, that we should believe[2] that it could not have been founded without men, and would not attain its completeness without the addition of[3] a wretched and useless being's exertion?[4]

39. But perhaps, [some one will urge,] the Ruler of the world sent hither souls sprung from himself for this purpose —a very rash thing for a man to say[5]—that they which had been divine[6] with him, not coming into contact with the body and earthly limits,[7] should be buried in the germs of men, spring from the womb, burst into and keep up the silliest wailings, draw the breasts in sucking, besmear and bedaub themselves with their own filth, then be hushed by the swaying[8] of the frightened nurse and by the sound of rattles.[9] Did he send souls [hither] for this reason, that they which had been but now sincere and of blameless virtue should learn

---

[1] *Rationibus et constitutionibus.*
[2] Lit., "it should be believed."
[3] Lit., "unless there were joined."
[4] So the MS., reading *contentio*, which Orelli would understand as meaning "contents," which may be correct. LB. reads *conditio*—"condition," ineptly; and Ursinus in the margin, *completio*—"the filling up."
[5] So the later edd., from the margin of Ursinus, reading *quod temeritatis est maximæ* for the MS. *quem*—"whom it shows the greatest rashness to speak of."
[6] Lit., "goddesses."
[7] So Gelenius (acc. to Orelli), reading as in the margin of Ursinus, *terrenæ circumscriptionis*, for the unintelligible reading of the MS., *temerariæ*, retained in both Roman edd., Canterus, and (acc. to Ochler) Gelenius. LB. reads *metariæ*—"a limiting by boundaries."
[8] Lit., "motions."
[9] Cf. Lucr. v. 229 sq. The same idea comes up again in iv. 21.

as[1] men to feign, to dissemble, to lie, to cheat,[2] to deceive, to entrap with a flatterer's abjectness; to conceal one thing in the heart,[3] express another in the countenance; to ensnare, to beguile[4] the ignorant with crafty devices, to seek out poisons by means of numberless arts [suggested] by bad feelings, and to be fashioned[5] with deceitful changeableness to suit circumstances? Was it for this he sent souls, that, living [till then] in calm and undisturbed tranquillity, they might find in[6] their bodies causes by which to become fierce and savage, cherish hatred and enmity, make war upon each other, subdue and overthrow states; load themselves with, and give themselves up to the yoke of slavery; and finally, be put the one in the other's power, having changed the condition[7] in which they were born? Was it for this he sent souls, that, being made unmindful of the truth, and forgetful of what God was, they should make supplication to images which cannot move; address as superhuman deities pieces of wood, brass, and stones; ask aid of them[8] with the blood of slain animals; make no mention of Himself: nay more, that some of them should doubt their own existence, or deny altogether that anything exists? Was it for this he sent souls, that they which in their own abodes had been of one mind, equals in intellect and knowledge, after that they put on mortal forms, should be divided by differences of opinion; should have different views as to what is just, useful, and right; should contend about the objects of desire and aver-

[1] Lit., "in."
[2] According to Hildebrand, the MS. reads *dissimular-ent circumscribere*, so that, by merely dropping *nt*, he reads, "to dissemble and cheat;" but according to Crusius, *iri* is found in the MS. between these two words, so that by prefixing *m* Sabæus in the first ed. read *m-ent-iri* as above, followed by all other edd.
[3] Lit., "to roll ... in the mind."
[4] Rigaltius and Hildebrand regard *decipere* as a gloss.
[5] So the MS., reading *formari*, followed by Hildebrand and Oehler; but all the other edd. give the active form, *-are*.
[6] Lit., "from." [7] The condition, *i.e.*, of freedom.
[8] LB., seemingly received by Orelli, though not inserted into his text, reads *poscerent eos* for the MS. *-entur*, which Hildebrand modifies *-ent ea* as above.

sion; should define the highest good and greatest evil differently; that, in seeking to know the truth of things, they should be hindered by their obscurity; and, as if bereft of eyesight, should see nothing clearly,[1] and, wandering from the truth,[2] should be led through uncertain bypaths of fancy?

40. Was it for this he sent souls [hither], that while the other creatures are fed by what springs up spontaneously, and is produced without being sown, and do not seek for themselves the protection or covering of houses or garments, they should be under the sad necessity[3] of building houses for themselves at very great expense and with never-ending toils, preparing coverings for their limbs, making different [kinds of] furniture for the wants[4] of daily life, borrowing help for[5] their weakness from the dumb creatures; using violence to the earth that it might not give forth its own herbs, but might send up the fruits required; and when they had put forth all their strength[6] in subduing the earth, should be compelled to lose the hope with which they had laboured[7] through blight, hail, drought; and at last forced by[8] hunger to throw themselves on human bodies; and when set free, to be parted from their human forms by a wasting sickness? Was it for this that they which, while they abode with him, had never had any longing for property, should have become exceedingly covetous, and with insatiable craving be inflamed to an eager desire of possessing; that they should dig up lofty mountains, and turn the unknown bowels of the earth into materials, and [to] purposes of a different kind; should force their way to remote nations at the risk of life, and, in exchanging goods, always catch at a high price [for what they sell], and a low one[9] [for what they buy], take interest

---

[1] Lit., "certain."   [2] Lit., "by error."
[3] Lit., "the sad necessity should be laid upon them, that," etc.
[4] Lit., "for the want of daily things," *diurnorum egestati*, for which Stewechius would read *diurna egestate*—"from daily necessity."
[5] Lit., "of."   [6] Lit., "poured forth all their blood."
[7] Lit., "of their labour."   [8] Lit., "at last by force of."
[9] So the MS. and edd., reading *vilitatem*, for which Meursius proposed very needlessly *utilitatem*—"and at an advantage."

at greedy and excessive rates, and add to the number of their sleepless nights [spent] in reckoning up thousands[1] wrung from the life-blood of wretched men; should be ever extending the limits of their possessions, and, though they were to make whole provinces one estate, should weary the forum with suits for one tree, for [one] furrow; should hate rancorously their friends and brethren?

41. Was it for this he sent souls, that they which shortly before had been gentle and ignorant [of what it is] to be moved by fierce passions, should build for themselves markets and amphitheatres, places of blood and open wickedness, in the one of which they should see men devoured and torn in pieces by wild beasts, [and] themselves slay others for no demerit but to please and gratify the spectators,[2] and should spend those very days on which such wicked deeds were done in general enjoyment, and keep holiday with festive gaiety; while in the other, again, they should tear asunder the flesh of wretched animals, some snatch one part, others another, as dogs and vultures do, should grind [them] with their teeth, and give to their utterly insatiable[3] maw, and that, surrounded by[4] faces so fierce and savage, those should bewail their lot whom the straits of poverty withheld from such repasts;[5] that their life should be[6] happy and prosperous while such barbarous doings defiled their mouths and face? Was it for this he sent souls, that, forgetting their importance and dignity [as] divine, they should acquire gems,

[1] So, adhering very closely to the MS., which gives *e-t sanguine suppu-tandis augere-t insomnia milibus*, the *t* of *e-t* being omitted and *n* inserted by all. The first five edd. read, *-tandi se angerent insania: millibus*—" harass themselves with the madness of reckoning; by miles should extend," etc.,—the only change in Heraldus and Orelli being a return to *insomnia*—" harass with sleeplessness," etc.

[2] So restored by Cujacius, followed by LB. and Orelli, reading *in grat-i-am* (MS. wants *i*) *voluptatemque*, while the first five edd. merely drop *-que*—" to the grateful pleasure," etc.

[3] Lit., "most cruel."

[4] Lit., "among," *in oris*, the MS. reading, and that of the first four edd., for which the others have received from the margin of Ursinus *moribus*—" [indulging] in so fierce and savage customs."

[5] Lit., "tables." [6] Lit., "they should live."

precious stones, pearls, at the expense of their purity; should entwine their necks with these, pierce the tips of their ears, bind[1] their foreheads with fillets, seek for cosmetics[2] to deck their bodies,[3] darken their eyes with henna; nor, though in the forms of men, blush to curl their hair with crisping-pins, to make the skin of the body smooth, to walk with bare knees, and with every other [kind of] wantonness, both to lay aside the strength of their manhood, and to grow in effeminacy to a woman's habits and luxury?

42. Was it for this he sent souls, that some should infest the highways and roads,[4] others ensnare the unwary, forge[5] false wills, prepare poisoned draughts; that they should break open houses by night, tamper [with slaves], steal and drive away, not act uprightly, and betray [their trust] perfidiously; that they should strike out delicate dainties for the palate; that in cooking fowls they should know how to catch the fat as it drips; that they should make cracknels and sausages,[6] force-meats, tit-bits, Lucanian sausages, with these[7] a sow's udder and iced[8] haggises? Was it for this he sent souls, that beings[9] of a sacred and august race should here practise singing and piping; that they

[1] Lit., "lessen."

[2] In the MS. this clause follows the words "loss of their purity," where it is very much in the way. Orelli has followed Heraldus in disposing of it as above, while LB. inserts it after "tips of their ears." The rest adhere to the arrangement of the MS., Ursinus suggesting instead of *his*—"with these," *catenis*—"with chains;" Heraldus, *linis*—"with strings [of pearls];" Stewechius, *tæniis*—"with fillets."

[3] So LB. and Orelli, reading *con-fic-iendis corporibus* for the MS. *con-sp-iendis*, for which the others read *-spic-*, "to win attention." A conjecture by Oudendorp, brought forward by Orelli, is worthy of notice—*con-spu-endis*, "to cover," *i.e.* so as to hide defects.

[4] Lit., "passages of ways."   [5] Lit., "substitute."

[6] So the later edd., reading *botulos*; the MS. and early edd. give *boletos*—"mushrooms."

[7] For *his*, Heinsius proposes *hiris*—"with the intestines."

[8] Lit., "in a frozen condition." As to the meaning of this there is difference of opinion: some supposing that it means, as above, preserved by means of ice, or at least frozen; while others interpret figuratively, "as hard as ice."

[9] Lit., "things"—*res*.

should swell out their cheeks in blowing the flute; that they should take the lead in singing impure songs, and raising the loud din of the castanets,[1] by which another crowd of souls should be led in their wantonness to abandon themselves to clumsy motions, to dance and sing, form rings of dancers, and finally, raising their haunches and hips, float along with a tremulous motion of the loins?

Was it for this he sent souls, that in men they should become impure, in women harlots, players on the triangle[2] and psaltery; that they should prostitute their bodies for hire, should abandon themselves to the lust of all,[3] ready in the brothels, to be met with in the stews,[4] ready to submit to anything, prepared to do violence to their mouth even?[5]

43. What say you, O offspring and descendants of the Supreme Deity? Did these souls, then, wise, and sprung from the first causes, become acquainted with such forms of baseness, crime, and bad feeling? and were they ordered to dwell here,[6] and be clothed with the garment of the human body, in order that they might engage in, might practise these evil [deeds], and that very frequently? And is there a man with any sense of reason who thinks that the world was

[1] *Scabilla* were a kind of rattles or castanets moved by the feet.

[2] *Sambuca*, not corresponding to the modern triangle, but a stringed instrument of that shape. Its notes were shrill and disagreeable, and those who played on it of indifferent character.

[3] So the MS. and first four edd., reading *virilitatem sui populo publicarent*. Meursius emended *utilitatem*—" made common the use," etc.; and Orelli, from the margin of Ursinus, *vilitatem*—" their vileness."

[4] The MS. reads *in fornicibus obvi-t-æ*, which, dropping *t*, is the reading translated, and was received by Elmenhorst, LB., and Hildebrand, from the margin of Ursinus. The other edd. insert *nc* before *t*—" bound."

[5] The translation does not attempt to bring out the force of the words *ad oris stuprum paratæ*, which are read by Orelli after Ursinus and Gelenius. The text is so corrupt, and the subject so obscene, that a bare reference to the practice may be sufficient.

[6] The MS. reads, *habitare atque habitare juss-e-r-unt*. All edd. omit the first two words, the first ed. without further change; but the active verb is clearly out of place, and therefore all other edd. read *jussæ sunt*, as above. Oehler, however, from *habitare* omitted by the others, would emend *aditare*, " to approach,"—a conjecture with very little to recommend it.

established because of them, and not rather that it was set up as a seat and home, in which every [kind of] wickedness should be committed daily, all evil deeds be done, plots, impostures, frauds, covetousness, robberies, violence, impiety, [all that is] presumptuous, indecent, base, disgraceful,[1] [and] all the other evil deeds which men devise over all the earth with guilty purpose, and contrive for each other's ruin?

44. But, you say, they came of their own accord, not sent[2] by their lord. And[3] where was the Almighty Creator, where the authority of his royal and exalted place,[4] to prevent their departure, and not suffer them to fall into dangerous pleasures? For if he knew that by change of place they would become base—and, as the arranger of all things,[5] he must have known—or that anything would reach them from without which would make them forget their greatness and moral dignity (a thousand times would I beg of him to pardon [my words]), the cause of all is no other than himself, since he allowed them to have freedom to wander[6] who he foresaw would not abide by their state of innocence; and thus it is brought about that it does not matter whether they came of their own accord, or obeyed his command, since in not preventing what should have been prevented, by his inaction he made the guilt his own, and permitted it before [it was done] by neglecting to withhold them [from action].

45. But let this monstrous and impious fancy be put[7] far [from us], that Almighty God, the creator and framer, the author[8] of things great and invisible, should be believed to have begotten souls so fickle, with no seriousness, firmness, and steadiness, prone to vice, inclining to all kinds of sins;

---

[1] These are all substantives in the original.
[2] So the MS., reading *non missione*—"not by the sending;" but, unaccountably enough, all edd. except Hildebrand and Oehler read *jussione*—"not by the command."
[3] So the MS. [4] Lit., "royal sublimity." [5] Lit., "causes."
[6] The MS. and both Roman edd. read *abscondere*—"to hide," for which the other edd. read, as above, *abscedere*, from the margin of Ursinus.
[7] Lit., "go."
[8] By Hildebrand and Oehler, *procreator* is with reason regarded as a gloss.

and while he knew that they were such and of this character, to have bid[1] them enter into bodies, imprisoned in which,[2] they should live exposed to the storms and tempests of fortune every day, and now do mean things, now submit to lewd treatment; that they might perish by shipwreck, accidents, destructive conflagrations; that poverty might oppress some, beggary, others; that some might be torn in pieces by wild beasts, others perish by the venom of flies;[3] that some might limp in walking, others lose their sight, others be stiff with cramped[4] joints; in fine, that they should be exposed to all the diseases which the wretched and pitiable human race endures with agony caused by[5] different sufferings; then that, forgetting that they have one origin, one father and head, they should shake to their foundations and violate the rights of kinship, should overthrow their cities, lay waste their lands as enemies, enslave the free, do violence to maidens and to other men's wives, hate each other, envy the joys and good fortune of others; and further, all malign, carp at, and tear each other to pieces with fiercely biting teeth.

46. But, to say the same things again and again,[6] let this belief, so monstrous and impious, be put far [from us], that God, who preserves[7] all things, the origin of the virtues and chief in[8] benevolence, and, to exalt him with human praise,

---

[1] The MS., both Roman edd., and Hildebrand read *jussisset;* but this would throw the sentence into confusion, and the other edd. therefore drop *t.*

[2] LB., Hildebrand, and Oehler read *quorum indu-c-tæ carceribus*—"led into the prisons of which," all other edd. omitting *c* as above. According to Oehler, the MS. has the former reading.

[3] The MS. and both Roman edd. read *in-f-ernarum paterentut aliæ laniatus muscularum,* which has no meaning, and is little improved by Gelenius changing *ut* into *ur,* as no one knows what "infernal flies" are. LB. and Orelli, adopting a reading in the margin of Ursinus, change *intern.* into *ferarum,* and join *musc.* with the words which follow as above. Another reading, also suggested by Ursinus, seems preferable, however, *internorum . . . musculorum*—" suffer rendings (*i.e.* spasms) of the inner muscles."

[4] Lit., "bound." [5] Lit., " dilaceration of."
[6] Lit., "again and more frequently." [7] Lit., " the salvation of."
[8] Lit., "height of."

most wise, just, making all things perfect, and that permanently,[1] either made anything which was imperfect and not quite correct,[2] or was the cause of misery or danger to any being, or arranged, commanded, and enjoined the very acts in which man's life is passed and employed to flow from his arrangement. These things are unworthy of [3] him, and weaken the force of his greatness; and so far from his being believed to be their author, whoever imagines that man is sprung from Him is guilty of blasphemous impiety, [man,] a being miserable and wretched, who is sorry that he exists, hates and laments his state, and understands that he was produced for no other reason than lest evils should not have something[4] through which to spread themselves, and that there might always be wretched ones by whose agonies some unseen and cruel power,[5] adverse to men, should be gratified.

47. But, you say, if God is not the parent and father of souls, by what sire have they been begotten, and how have they been produced? If you wish to hear unvarnished statements not spun out with vain ostentation of words, we, too,[6] admit that we are ignorant of this, do not know it;[7] and we hold that, to know so great a matter, is not only beyond the reach of our weakness and frailty, but [beyond that] also of all the powers which are in the world, and which have usurped the place of deities in men's belief. But are we bound to show whose they are, because we deny that they are God's? That by no means[8] follows necessarily; for if

---

[1] Lit., "things perfect, and preserving the measure of their completeness," *i.e.* continuing so.

[2] So the MS., LB., Oberthuer, and Oehler, reading *claudum et quod minus esset a recto*. All other edd. read *eminus*—"at a distance from the right."

[3] Lit., "less than." [4] Lit., "material."

[5] Lit., "some power latent and cruelty."

[6] So the MS. and all edd.; but Orelli would change *item* into *iterum*, not seeing that the reference is to the indicated preference of his opponents for the simple truth.

[7] *Nescire* Hildebrand, with good reason, considers a gloss.

[8] *Nihil* for the MS. *mihi*, which makes nonsense of the sentence.

we were to deny that flies, beetles, and bugs, dormice, weevils, and moths,[1] are made by the Almighty King, we should not be required in consequence to say who made and formed them; for without [incurring] any censure, we may not know who, indeed, gave them being, and [yet] assert that not by the Supreme[2] Deity were [creatures] produced so useless, so needless, so purposeless,[3] nay more, at times even hurtful, and causing unavoidable injuries.

48. Here, too, in like manner, when we deny that souls are the offspring of God Supreme, it does not necessarily follow that we are bound to declare from what parent they have sprung, and by what causes they have been produced. For who prevents us from being either ignorant of the source from which they issued and came, or aware that they are not God's descendants? By what method, you say, in what way? Because it is most true and certain[4] that, as has been pretty frequently said, nothing is effected, made, determined by the Supreme, except that which is right and fitting should be done; except that which is complete and entire, and wholly perfect in its[5] integrity. But further, we see that men, that is, these very souls—for what are men but souls bound to bodies?—themselves show by perversely falling into[6] vice, times without number, that they belong to no patrician race, but have sprung from insignificant families. For we see some harsh, vicious, presumptuous, rash, reckless, blinded, false, dissemblers, liars, proud, overbearing, covetous, greedy, lustful, fickle, weak, and unable to observe their own precepts; but they would assuredly not be [so], if their

---

[1] This somewhat wide-spread opinion found an amusing counterpart in the doctrines of Rorarius (mentioned by Bayle, *Dict. Phil.*), who affirmed that the lower animals are gifted with reason and speech, as we are.

[2] Lit., "superior."   [3] Lit., "tending to no reasons."

[4] *Omni vero verissimum est certoque certissimum*—the superlative for the comparative.

[5] Lit., "finished with the perfection of."

[6] Lit., "by perversity"—*s-c-ævitate*, the reading of the MS., LB., Orelli, Hild., and Oehler, all others omitting *c*—"by the rage;" except Stewechius, who reads *servitute*—"slavery."

original goodness defended[1] them, and they traced their honourable descent from the head of the universe.

49. But, you will say, there are good men also in the world,—wise, upright, of faultless and purest morals. We raise no question as to whether there ever were any such, in whom this very integrity which is spoken of was in nothing imperfect. Even if they are very honourable [men], and have been worthy of praise, have reached the utmost height of perfection, and their life has never wavered and sunk into sin, yet we would have you tell us how many there are, or have been, that we may judge from their number whether a comparison[2] has been made [which is] just and evenly balanced.[3] One, two, three, four, ten, twenty, a hundred, yet [are they] at least limited in number, and it may be within the reach of names.[4] But it is fitting that the human race should be rated and weighed, not by a very few good men, but by all the rest [as well]. For the part is in the whole, not the whole in a part; and that which is the whole should draw to it its parts, not the whole be brought to its parts. For what if you were to say that a man, robbed of the use of all his limbs, and shrieking in bitter agony,[5] was quite well, because in[6] one little nail he suffered no pain? or that the earth is made of gold, because in one hillock there are a few small grains from which, when dissolved, gold is produced, and wonder excited at it when formed into a lump?[7] The whole mass shows the nature of an element, not particles fine as air; nor does the sea become forthwith sweet, if you cast or throw into [it] a few drops of less bitter water, for that small quantity is swallowed up in its immense

---

[1] Or, perhaps, "the goodness of the Supreme planted"—*generositas eos adsereret principalis.*

[2] Lit., "opposition," *i.e.* "the setting of one party against the other."

[3] Lit., "weighed with balancing of equality."

[4] Lit., "bounded by the comprehensions of names;" *i.e.* possibly, "the good are certainly few enough to be numbered, perhaps even to be named."

[5] So LB., reading *ex cruciatibus* for the MS. *scruc.*   [6] Lit., "of."

[7] Lit., "admiration is sought for by the putting together"—*congregatione.*

mass; and it must be esteemed, not merely of little importance, but [even] of none, because, being scattered throughout all, it is lost and cut off in the immensity of the vast body [of water].

50. You say that there are good men in the human race; and perhaps, if we compare them with the very wicked, we may be led[1] to believe that there are. Who are they, pray? Tell [us]. The philosophers, I suppose, who[2] assert that they alone are most wise, and who have been uplifted with pride from the meaning attached to this name,[3]—those, forsooth, who are striving with their passions every day, and struggling to drive out, to expel deeply-rooted passions from their minds by the persistent[4] opposition of their better qualities; who, that it may be impossible for them to be led into wickedness at the suggestion of some opportunity, shun riches and inheritances, that they may remove[5] from themselves occasions of stumbling; but in doing this, and being solicitous about it, they show very clearly that [their] souls are, through their weakness, ready and prone to fall into vice. In our opinion, however, that which is good naturally, does not require to be either corrected or reproved;[6] nay more, it should not know what evil is, if the nature of each kind would abide in its own integrity, for neither can two contraries be implanted in each other, nor can equality be contained in inequality, nor sweetness in bitterness. He, then,

[1] Lit., "a comparison of the worst may effect that we," etc.
[2] So all edd. except Hildebrand, who gives as the reading of the MS., *qui-d*—" what! do they assert."
[3] Lit., "by the force of," *vi*,—an emendation of Heraldus for the MS. *in*.
[4] So most edd., reading *pertinaci* for the MS. *-ium*—" by the opposition of persistent virtues," which is retained in both Roman edd., Gelenius, Canterus, Hildebrand, and Oehler.
[5] So Stewechius and later edd., reading *ut . . . auferant*, except Hildebrand, who gives as the MS. reading, *et . . . -unt*—" shun . . . and remove," etc. The first four edd. read *ne . . . afferant*—" that they may not bring upon themselves," etc.
[6] So the MS. and first four edd., Orelli (who, however, seems to have meant to give the other reading), and Oehler, reading *corri-p-i*, for which the others read *-igi*—" corrected," except Hildebrand, who without due reason gives *-rumpi*—" corrupted."

who struggles to amend the inborn depravity of his inclinations, shows most clearly that he is imperfect,[1] blameable, although he may strive with all zeal and stedfastness.

51. But you laugh at our reply, because, while we deny that souls are of royal descent, we do not, on the other hand, say in turn from what causes and beginnings they have sprung. But what kind of crime is it either to be ignorant of anything, or to confess quite openly that you do not know that of which you are ignorant? or whether does he rather seem to you most deserving of ridicule who assumes to himself no knowledge of some dark subject; or he who thinks that he[2] knows most clearly that which transcends human knowledge, and which has been involved in dark obscurity? If the nature of everything were thoroughly considered, you too are in a position like that which you censure in our case. For you do not say anything [which has been] ascertained and set most clearly in the light of truth, because you say that souls descend from the Supreme Ruler himself, and enter into the forms of men. For you conjecture, do not perceive[3] [this]; surmise, do not actually know [it]; for if to know is to retain in the mind that which you have yourself seen or known, not one of those things which you affirm can you say that you have ever seen—that is, that souls descend from the abodes and regions above. You are therefore making use of conjecture, not trusting clear information. But what is conjecture, except a doubtful imagining of things, and directing of the mind upon nothing accessible? He, then, who conjectures, does not comprehend,[4] nor does he walk in the[5] light of knowledge. But if this is true and

---

[1] In the MS. *imperfectum* is marked as a gloss, but is retained in all edd., while *improbabilem* is omitted, except in LB., when *im* is omitted, and *probabilem* joined to the next clause—"however he may strive to be acceptable," in order to provide an object for "strive;" and with a similar purpose Orelli thrusts in *contrarium*, although it is quite clear that the verb refers to the preceding clause, "struggles to amend."

[2] The MS. reads *se esse*, without meaning, from which LB., followed by Hildebrand, and Oehler derived *se ex se*—"himself of himself." The rest simply omit *esse* as above.

[3] Lit., "hold."   [4] Lit., "hold."   [5] Lit., "set in the."

certain in the opinion of proper and very wise judges, your conjectures, too, in which you trust, must be regarded as [showing your] ignorance.

52. And yet, lest you should suppose that none but yourselves can make use of conjectures and surmises, we too are able to bring them forward as well,[1] as your question is appropriate to either side.[2] Whence, you say, are men; and what or whence are the souls of these men? Whence, [we will ask,] are elephants, bulls, stags, mules,[3] asses? Whence lions, horses, dogs, wolves, panthers; and what or whence are the souls of these creatures? For it is not credible that from that Platonic cup,[4] which Timæus prepares and mixes, either their souls came, or [that] the locust,[5] mouse, shrew, cockroach, frog, centipede, should be believed to have been quickened and to live, because[6] they have a cause and origin of birth in[7] the elements themselves, if there are [in these] secret and very little known means[8] for producing the creatures which live in each of them. For we see that some of the wise say that the earth is mother of men, that others join with it water,[9] that others add to these breath of air, but that some [say] that the sun is their framer, and that, having been quickened by his rays, they are filled with the stir of life.[10] What if it is not these, and is something else, another cause, another method, another power, in fine, unheard of

---

[1] Lit., "utter the same [conjectures]," *easdem*, the reading of LB. and Hildebrand, who says that it is so in the MS.; while Crusius asserts that the MS. has *idem*, which, with Orelli's punctuation, gives—"we have the same power; since it is common (*i.e.* a general right) to bring forth what you ask," *i.e.* to put similar questions.

[2] *i.e.* may be retorted upon you.

[3] Here, as elsewhere, instead of *muli*, the MS. reads *milvi*—"kites."

[4] Cf. Plato, *Timæus*, st. p. 41, already referred to.

[5] Or, perhaps, "cray-fish," *locusta*.

[6] The MS. reads *quidem*—"indeed," retained by the first four edd., but changed into *quia*—"because," by Elmenhorst, LB., and Orelli, while Oehler suggests very happily *si quidem*—"if indeed," *i.e.* because.

[7] Lit., "from."   [8] *Rationes*.   [9] Cf. chs. ix. and x.

[10] Orelli, retaining this as a distinct sentence, would yet enclose it in brackets, for what purpose does not appear; more especially as the next sentence follows directly from this in logical sequence.

and unknown to us by name, which may have fashioned the human race, and connected it with things as established;[1] may it not be that men sprang up in this way, and that the cause of their birth does not go back to the Supreme God? For what reason do we suppose that the great Plato had— [a man] reverent and scrupulous in his wisdom—when he withdrew the fashioning of man from the highest God, and transferred it to some lesser [deities], and when he would not have the souls of men formed[2] of that pure mixture of which he had made the soul of the universe, except that he thought the forming of man unworthy of God, and the fashioning of a feeble being not beseeming His greatness and excellence?

53. Since this, then, is the case, we do nothing out of place or foolish in believing that the souls of men are of a neutral character, inasmuch as they have been produced by secondary beings,[3] made subject to the law of death, [and are] of little strength, [and that] perishable; and that they are gifted with immortality, if[4] they rest their hope of so great a gift on God Supreme, who alone has power to grant such [blessings], by putting away corruption. But this, [you say,] we are stupid in believing. What [is that] to you? [In so be-

---

[1] Lit., "the constitutions of things."

[2] Lit., "did not choose the souls of the human race to be mixtures of the same purity," *noluit*, received from the margin of Ursinus by all except the first four edd., which retain the MS. *voluit*—"did choose," which is absurd. Arnobius here refers again to the passage in the *Timæus*, p. 41 sq., but to a different part, with a different purpose. He now refers to the conclusion of the speech of the Supreme God, the first part of which is noticed in ch. xxxvi. (cf. p. 103, n. 4). There the Creator assures the gods he has made of immortality through his grace; now his further invitation that they in turn should form men is alluded to. That they might accomplish this task, the dregs still left in the cup, in which had been mixed the elements of the world's soul, are diluted and given to form the souls of men, to which they attach mortal bodies.

[3] Lit., "things not principal." Orelli here quotes from Tertullian, *de Anim.* xxiii., a brief summary of Gnostic doctrines on these points, which he considers Arnobius to have followed throughout this discussion.

[4] *Si* was first inserted in LB., not being found in the MS., though demanded by the context.

lieving, we act] most absurdly, sillily. In what do we injure you, or what wrong do we do or inflict upon you, if we trust that Almighty God will take care of us when we leave [1] our bodies, and from the jaws of hell, as is said, deliver us?

54. Can, then, anything be made, some one will say, without God's will? We[2] must consider carefully, and examine with no little pains, lest, while we think that we are honouring God[3] by such a question, we fall into the opposite sin, doing despite to his supreme majesty. In what way, [you ask,] on what ground? Because, if all things are brought about by his will, and nothing in the world can either succeed or fail contrary to his pleasure, it follows of necessity that it should be understood that[4] all evils, too, arise by his will. But if, on the contrary, we chose to say that he is privy to and produces no evil, not referring to him the causes of very wicked deeds, the worst things will begin to seem to be done either against his will, or, a monstrous thing to say, while he knows it not, [but] is ignorant and unaware of them. But, again, if we choose to say that there are no evils, as we find some have believed and held, all races will cry out against [us] and all nations together, showing us their sufferings, and the various kinds of dangers with which the human race is every moment[5] distressed and afflicted. Then they will ask of us, Why, if there are no evils, do you refrain from certain deeds and actions? Why do you not do all that eager lust has required or demanded? Why, finally, do you establish punishments by terrible laws for the guilty? For what more monstrous[6] act of folly can be found than to assert that there are no evils, and [at the

---

[1] Lit., "have begun to leave."

[2] The MS. and first three edd. read *vobis*—"you," corrected *nobis*, as above, by Ursinus.

[3] So the MS.; but most edd., following the Brussels transcript, read *dominum*—"Lord."

[4] *Ut* is omitted in the MS., first four edd., and Hild.

[5] So LB., reading *p-uncta* for the MS. *c-uncta*.

[6] So the MS., Hild., and Oehler, reading *imman-ior*; LB., from the margin of Ursinus, *major*—"greater;" the rest, *inanior*—"more foolish."

same time] to kill and condemn the erring as though they were evil?[1]

55. But when, overcome, we agree that there are these things,[2] and expressly allow that all human affairs are full of them, they will next ask, Why, then, the Almighty God does not take away these evils, but suffers them to exist and to go on without ceasing through all the ages?[3] If we have learned of God the Supreme Ruler, and have resolved not to wander in a maze of impious and mad conjectures, we must answer that we do not know these things, and have never sought and striven to know things which could be grasped by no powers [which we have], and that we, even thinking it[4] preferable, rather remain in ignorance and want of knowledge than say that without God nothing is made, so that it should be understood that by his will[5] he is at once both the source of evil[6] and the occasion of countless miseries. Whence then, you will say, are all these evils? From the elements, say the wise, and from their dissimilarity; but how it is possible that things which have not feeling and judgment should be held to be wicked or criminal; or that he should

---

[1] The difficulty felt by Arnobius as to the origin of evil perplexed others also; and, as Elmenhorst has observed, some of the fathers attempted to get rid of it by a distinction between the evil of guilt and of punishment,—God being author of the latter, the devil of the former (Tertullian, *adv. Marcionem*, ii. 14). It would have been simpler and truer to have distinguished deeds, which can be done only if God will, from wickedness, which is in the sinful purpose of man's heart.

[2] *i.e.* ills.

[3] Lit., "with all the ages, in steady continuance."

[4] The MS., followed by Oehler alone, reads *ducetis*—"and you will think;" while all the other edd. read, as above, *ducentes*.

[5] Here, too, there has been much unnecessary labour. These words—*per voluntatem*—as they immediately follow *sine deo dicere nihil fieri*—"to say that without God nothing is made"—were connected with the preceding clause. To get rid of the nonsense thus created, LB. emended *dei . . . voluntate*—"without God's will;" while Heraldus regards them as an explanation of *sine deo*, and therefore interprets the sentence much as LB. Orelli gets rid of the difficulty by calling them a gloss, and bracketing them. They are, however, perfectly in place, as will be seen above.

[6] Pl.

not rather be wicked and criminal, who, to bring about some result, took what was afterwards to become very bad and hurtful,[1]—is for them to consider, who make the assertion. What, then, do we say? whence? There is no necessity that we should answer, for whether we are able to say [whence evil springs], or our power fails us, and we are unable, in either case it is a small matter in our opinion; nor do we hold it of much importance either to know or to be ignorant of it, being content to have laid down but one thing,—that nothing proceeds from God Supreme which is hurtful and pernicious. This we are assured of, this we know, on this one truth of knowledge and science we take our stand,—that nothing is made by him except that which is for the well-being of all, which is agreeable, which is very full of love and joy and gladness, which has unbounded and imperishable pleasures, which every one may ask in all his prayers to befall him, and think that otherwise[2] life is pernicious and fatal.

56. As for all the other things which are usually dwelt upon in inquiries and discussions—from what parents they have sprung, or by whom they are produced—we neither strive to know,[3] nor care to inquire or examine: we leave all things to their own causes, and do not consider that they have been connected and associated with that which we desire should befall us.[4] For what is there which men of ability do

---

[1] It would not be easy to understand why Orelli omitted these words, if we did not know that they had been accidentally omitted by Oberthür also.

[2] Lit., " that apart from these it is pernicious."

[3] It must be observed that this sentence is very closely connected with the last words of the preceding chapter, or the meaning may be obscured. The connection may be shown thus: This one thing—that God is author of no evil—we are assured of; but as for all other questions, we neither know, nor care to know, about them.

[4] This seems the most natural arrangement; but the edd. punctuate thus: " have been connected and associated with us for that which we desire." The last part of the sentence is decidedly obscure; but the meaning may perhaps be, that the circumstances of man's life which absorb so much attention and cause such strife, have no bearing, after all, upon his salvation.

not dare to overthrow, to destroy,[1] from love of contradiction, although that which they attempt to invalidate is unobjectionable[2] and manifest, and evidently bears the stamp of truth? Or what, again, can they not maintain with plausible arguments, although it may be very manifestly untrue, although it may be a plain and evident falsehood? For when a man has persuaded himself that there is or is not something, he likes to affirm what he thinks, and to show greater subtlety than others, especially if the subject discussed is out of the ordinary track, and by nature abstruse and obscure.[3] Some of the wise think that the world was not created, and will never perish;[4] some that it is immortal, although they say that it was created and made;[5] while a third party have chosen to say that it both was created and made, and will perish as other things must.[6] And while of these three opinions one only must be true, they nevertheless all find arguments by which at once to uphold their own doctrines, and undermine and overthrow the dogmas of others. Some teach and declare that this same [world] is composed of four elements, others of two,[7] a third party of one; some say that

[1] So the MS., reading *labefactare dissolvere*; the latter word, however, being marked as spurious.

[2] Lit., "pure."

[3] Lit., "hidden and enwrapt in darkness of nature," *abdita et caligine involuta naturæ*,—the reading of all edd. except Hild. and Oehler, who follow the MS. *abditæ cal.*—'enwrapt in darkness of hidden nature."

[4] This has been supposed to refer to Heraclitus, as quoted by Clem. Alex. *Stromata*, v. p. 599 B., where his words are, "Neither God nor man made the world; but there was always, and is, and will be, an undying flame laying hold of its limits, and destroying them;" on which cf. p. 73, n. 1. Here, of course, fire does not mean that perceived by the senses, but a subtle, all-penetrating energy.

[5] Cf. ch. 52, n. 2, p. 120.

[6] Lit., "by ordinary necessity." The Stoics (Diog. Laert. vii. 134) said that the world was made by God working on uncreated matter, and that it was perishable (§ 141), because made through that of which perception could take cognizance. Cf. ch. 31, n. 7, p. 98.

[7] Orelli thinks that there is here a confusion of the parts of the world with its elements, because he can nowhere find that any philosopher has fixed the number of the elements either above or below four. The Stoics, however (Diog. Laert. vii. 134), said "that the elements ($ἀρχάς$)

[it is composed of] none of these, and that atoms are that from which it is formed,[1] and its primary origin. And since of these opinions only one is true, but[2] not one of them certain, here too, in like manner, arguments present themselves to all with which they may both establish the truth of what they say, and show that there are some things false[3] in the others' opinions. So, too, some utterly deny the existence of the gods; others say that they are lost in doubt as to whether they exist anywhere; others, however, [say] that they do exist, but do not trouble themselves about human things; nay, others maintain that they both take part in the affairs of men, and guide the course of earthly events.[4]

57. While, then, this is the case, and it cannot but be that only one of all these opinions is true, they all nevertheless make use of arguments in striving with each other,—and not one of them is without something plausible to say, whether in affirming his own views, or objecting to the opinions of others. In exactly the same way is the condition of souls discussed. For this one thinks that they both are immortal, and survive the end of our earthly life; that one believes that they do not survive, but perish with the bodies themselves: the opinion of another, however, is that they suffer nothing immediately, but that, after the [form of] man has been laid aside, they are allowed to live a little longer,[5] [and] then come under the power of death. And while all these opinions cannot be alike true, yet all [who hold them] so support their case by strong and very weighty arguments,

---

of the world are two—the active and passive;" while, of course, the cosmic theories of the early philosophers affirm that the world sprang from one, and it seems clear enough that Arnobius here uses the word element in this sense.

[1] Lit., "its material."

[2] A conjecture of Meursius adopted by Oehler, merely dropping *u* from *aut*—" or," which is read in the MS. and edd.

[3] Lit., "refute falsities placed."

[4] Cf. Cicero, *de Nat. Deor.* i. 1, 12, 19, 23, etc.

[5] Lit., "something is given to them to life." So the Stoics taught, although Chrysippus (cf. n. 7, ch. 31, p. 98) held that only the souls of the wise remained at all after death.

that you cannot find out anything which seems false to you, although on every side you see that things are being said altogether at variance with each other, and inconsistent from their opposition to each other;[1] which assuredly would not happen, if man's curiosity could reach any certainty, or if that which seemed [to one] to have been really discovered, was attested by the approval of all the others. It is therefore wholly[2] vain, a useless task, to bring forward something as though you knew it, or to wish to assert that you know that which, although it should be true, you see can be refuted; or to receive that as true which it may be is not, and is brought forward as if by men raving. And it is rightly so, for we do not weigh and guess at[3] divine things by divine, but by human methods; and just as we think that anything should have been made, so we assert that it must be.

58. What, then, are we alone ignorant? do we alone not know who is the creator, who the former of souls, what cause fashioned man, whence ills have broken forth, or why the Supreme Ruler allows them both to exist and be perpetrated, and does not drive them from the world? have you, indeed, ascertained and learned any of these things with certainty? If you chose to lay aside audacious[4] conjectures, can you unfold and disclose whether this world in which we dwell[5] was created or founded at some time? if it was founded and made, by what kind of work, pray, or for what purpose? Can you bring forward and disclose the reason why it does not remain fixed and immoveable, but is ever being carried round in a circular motion? whether it revolves of its own will and choice, or is turned by the influence of some power?

---

[1] The MS., first four edd., and Oehler read *et rerum contrarietatibus dissonare*—" and that they disagree from the oppositions of things." Hild. reads *dissonora*, a word not met with elsewhere, while the other edd. merely drop the last two letters, -*re*, as above; a reading suggested in the margin of Ursinus.

[2] Lit., "a most vain thing," etc.

[3] So the MS., LB., Elmenh., Hild., and Oehler, reading *conjectamus*, the other edd. reading *commetamur* or -*imur*—"measure," except Gelenius and Canterus, who read *commentamur*—"muse upon."

[4] Lit., "audacity of."   [5] Lit., "world which holds us."

what the place, too, and space is in which it is set and revolves, boundless, bounded, hollow, or[1] solid? whether it is supported by an axis resting on sockets at its extremities, or rather itself sustains by its own power, and by the spirit within it upholds itself? Can you, if asked, make it clear, and show most skilfully,[2] what opens out the snow into feathery flakes? what was the reason and cause that day did not, in dawning, arise in the west, and veil its light in the east? how the sun, too, by one and the same influence,[3] produces results so different, nay, even so opposite? what the moon is, what the stars? why, on the one hand, it does not remain of the same shape, or why it was right and necessary that these particles of fire should be set all over the world? why some[4] of them are small, others larger and greater, —these have a dim light, those a more vivid and shining brightness?

59. If that which it has pleased us to know is within reach, and if such knowledge is open to all, declare to us,[5] and say how and by what means showers of rain are produced, so that water is held suspended in the regions above and in mid-air, although by nature it is apt to glide away, and so ready to flow and run downwards. Explain, I say, and tell what it is which sends the hail whirling [through the air], which makes the rain fall drop by drop, which has spread out rain and feathery flakes of snow and sheets of lightning;[6] whence the wind rises, and what it is; why the changes of the seasons were established, when it might have been ordained that there should be only one, and one kind of climate, so that there should be nothing wanting to the world's

[1] The first five edd. insert the mark of interrogation after "hollow:" "Whether does a solid axis," etc.

[2] So the edd. except Hild., who retains the MS. reading *in-scientissime* —"most unskilfully" (the others omitting *in-*), and Oehler, who changes *e* into *i*—"and being most witless show," etc.

[3] Lit., "touch."

[4] So the later edd., reading from the margin of Ursinus *figi? cur alia*, for the MS. *figuralia*, except LB., which reads *figurari*—"be formed."

[5] So the MS.; but all edd. except Hild. and Oehler omit *nobis*.

[6] So the MS., reading *folgora dilatarit*, followed by LB.

completeness. What is the cause, what the reason, that the waters of the sea are salt;[1] or that, of those on land, some are sweet, others bitter or cold? From what kind of material have the inner parts of men's bodies been formed and built up into firmness? From what have their bones been made solid? what made the intestines and veins shaped like pipes, and easily passed through? Why, when it would be better to give us light by several eyes, to [guard against] the risk of blindness, are we restricted to two? For what purpose have so infinite and innumerable kinds of monsters and serpents been either formed or brought forth? what purpose do owls serve in the world,—falcons, hawks? what other birds[2] and winged creatures? what the [different] kinds of ants and worms springing up to be a bane and pest in various ways? what fleas, obtrusive flies, spiders, shrew, and other mice, leeches, water-spinners? what thorns, briers, wild-oats, tares? what the seeds of herbs or shrubs, either sweet to the nostrils, or disagreeable in smell? Nay more, if you think that anything can be known or comprehended, say what wheat is,—spelt, barley, millet, the chick-pea, bean, lentil, melon, cumin, scallion, leek, onion? For [even] if they are useful to you, and are ranked among the different kinds of food, it is not a light or easy thing to know what each is,—why they have been formed with such shapes; [whether] there was any necessity that they should not have had other tastes, smells, and colours than those which each has, or whether they could have taken others also; further, what these very things are,—taste, I mean,[3] and the rest; [and] from what relations they derive their differences of quality. From the elements, you say, and from the first beginnings of things. Are the elements, then, bitter or sweet? have they any odour or[4] stench, that

---

[1] *Salsa*, corrected from the MS. *sola*.

[2] *Alites et volucres;* i.e., according to Orelli, the birds from whose flight auguries were drawn, as opposed to the others.

[3] So Heraldus, whose punctuation also is here followed, omitting *id est sapor*—"that is, taste," which Meursius and LB., followed by Orelli, amend, *ut est*—"as taste is" [in each thing].

[4] *Vel* is here inserted in all edd., most of which read, as above, *oloris*,

we should believe that, from their uniting, qualities were implanted in their products by which sweetness is produced, or something prepared offensive to the senses?

60. Seeing, then, that the origin, the cause, the reason of so many and so important things, escapes you yourselves also, and that you can neither say nor explain what has been made, nor why and wherefore it should not have been [otherwise], do you assail and attack our timidity, who confess that we do not know that which cannot be known, and who do not care to seek out and inquire into those things which it is quite clear cannot be understood, although human conjecture should extend and spread itself through a thousand hearts? And therefore Christ the divine,—although you are unwilling to allow it,—Christ the divine, I repeat (for this must be said often, that the ears of unbelievers may burst and be rent asunder), speaking in the form of man by command of the Supreme God, because he knew that men are naturally[1] blind, and cannot grasp the truth at all, or regard as sure and certain what they might have persuaded themselves as to things set before their eyes, and do not hesitate, for the sake of their[2] conjectures, to raise and bring up questions that cause much strife,—bade us abandon and disregard all these things of which you speak, and not waste our thoughts upon things which have been removed far from our knowledge, but, as much as possible, seek the Lord of the universe with the whole mind and spirit; be raised above these subjects, and give over to him our hearts, as yet hesitating whither to turn;[3] be ever mindful of him; and although no imagination can set him forth as he is,[4] yet form some faint con-

which is found in the MS., in later writing, for the original, *coloris*— "colour," retained by Ursinus, LB., and Oehler.

[1] Lit., " that the nature of man is."

[2] So the MS., according to Crusius, reading *nec pro suis;* while, according to Hild., the reading is *prorsus*—" and are utterly without hesitation," adopted in the edd. with the substitution of *et* for *nec*— " and that they altogether hesitate," which, besides departing from the MS., runs counter to the sense.

[3] Lit., " transfer to him the undecided conversions of the breast."

[4] Lit., " he can be formed by no imagination."

ception of him. For [Christ said] that, of all who are comprehended in the vague notion of what is sacred and divine,[1] he alone is beyond the reach of doubt, alone true, and one about whom only a raving and reckless madman can be in doubt; to know whom is enough, although you have learned nothing besides; and if by knowledge you have indeed been related to[2] God, the head of the world, you have gained the true and most important knowledge.

61. What business of yours is it, he[3] says, to examine, to inquire who made man; what is the origin of souls; who devised the causes of ills; whether the sun is larger than the earth, or measures only a foot in breadth;[4] whether the moon shines with borrowed light, or from her own brightness,— things which there is neither profit in knowing, nor loss in not knowing? Leave these things to God, and allow him to know what is, wherefore, or whence; whether it must have been or not; whether something always existed,[5] or whether it was produced at the first; whether it should be annihilated or preserved, consumed, destroyed, or restored in fresh vigour. Your reason is not permitted to involve you in such questions, and to be busied to no purpose about things so much out of reach. Your interests are in jeopardy, —the salvation, I mean,[6] of your souls; and unless you give yourselves to seek to know the Supreme God, a cruel death awaits you when freed from the bonds of body, not bringing sudden annihilation, but destroying by the bitterness of its grievous and long-protracted punishment.

62. And be not deceived or deluded with vain hopes by that which is said by some ignorant and most presumptuous

[1] Lit., "which the obscurity of sacred divinity contains;" which Orelli interprets, "the most exalted being holds concealed from mortals."

[2] Lit., "and being fixed on."

[3] *i.e.* Christ.

[4] As Heraclitus is reported to have said.

[5] The MS., first five edd., and Oehler read *supernatum*, for which the other edd. read, as above, *semper natum*, from the margin of Ursinus. The soul is referred to.

[6] So the later edd., following Elmenhorst, who emended *dico* for the MS. *dici*, omitted by the first four edd.

pretenders,[1] that they are born of God, and are not subject to the decrees of fate; that his palace lies open to them if they lead a life of temperance, and that after death as men, they are restored without hindrance, as if to their father's abode; nor [by that] which the Magi[2] assert, that they have intercessory prayers, won over by which some powers make the way easy to those who are striving to mount to heaven; nor [by that] which Etruria holds out in the Acherontic books,[3] that souls become divine, and are freed from the law[4] of death, if the blood of certain animals is offered to certain deities. These are empty delusions, and excite vain desires. None but the Almighty God can preserve souls; nor is there any one besides who can give them length of days, and grant to them also a spirit which shall never die,[5] except he who alone is immortal and everlasting, and restricted by no limit of time. For since all the gods, whether those who are real, or those who are merely said to be from hearsay and conjecture, are immortal and everlasting by his good-will and free gift, how can it be that others[6] are able to give that which they themselves have,[7] while they have it as the gift of another, bestowed by a greater power? Let Etruria sacrifice what victims it may, let the wise deny themselves all the pleasures of life,[8] let the Magi soften and soothe all [lesser] powers, [yet,] unless souls have received from the Lord of all things that which reason demands, and [does so] by [his] command, it[9] will hereafter deeply repent having

[1] So most edd., reading *sciolis*, from the emendation of Gelenius; but the MS., first five edd., Hild., and Oehler read *scholis*—" by some schools, and [these] arrogating very much to themselves."

[2] Cf. ch. xiii. p. 79; Plato, *Rep.* ii. st. p. 364, where Glaucon speaks of certain fortune-telling vagrant seers, who persuade the rich that they have power with the gods, by means of charms and sacrifices, to cleanse from guilt; and also Origen, *contra Cels.* i. 69, where the Magi are spoken of as being on familiar terms with evil powers, and thus able to accomplish whatever is within these spirits' power.

[3] Mentioned by Servius (on *Æn.* viii. 399) as composed by Tages (ch. lxix.), and seemingly containing directions as to expiatory sacrifices.

[4] Pl.
[5] Lit., "a spirit of perpetuity."
[6] *i.e.* than the Supreme God.
[7] Lit., "are."
[8] Lit., "all human things."
[9] *i.e.* reason.

made itself a laughing-stock,[1] when it begins to feel the approach[2] of death.

63. But if, my opponents say, Christ was sent by God for this end, that he might deliver unhappy souls from ruin and destruction, of what crime were former ages guilty which were cut off in their mortal state before he came? Can you, then, know what has become of these souls[3] of men who lived long ago?[4] whether they, too, have [not] been aided, provided, and cared for in some way? Can you, I say, know that which could have been learned through Christ's teaching; whether the ages are unlimited in number or not since the human race began to be on the earth; when souls were first bound to bodies; who contrived that binding,[5] nay, rather, who formed man himself; whither the souls of men who lived before us have gone; in what parts or regions of the world they were; whether they were corruptible or not; whether they could have encountered the danger of death, if Christ had not come forward as their preserver at their time of need? Lay aside these cares, and abandon questions to which you can find no answer.[6] The Lord's compassion has been shown to them, too, and the divine kindness[7] has been extended to[8] all alike; they have been preserved, have been delivered, and have laid aside the lot and condition of mortality. Of what kind, [my opponents ask,] what, when? If you were free from presumption, arrogance, and conceit, you might have learned long ago from this teacher.

64. But, [my opponents ask,] if Christ came as the Saviour

---

[1] The MS. reads *fuisse me risui*, which has no meaning; corrected, *fuisse irrisui* in most edd., and *derisui* by Meursius, Hild., and Oehler,—the sense being in either case as above.

[2] Lit., "when it begins to approach to the feeling," *cum ad sensum;* so read by Gelenius for the unintelligible MS. *cum absens cum.*

[3] So the edd., reading *quid sit cum eis animis actum* for the MS. *cum ejus nimis.*

[4] Lit., "of ancient and very old men."

[5] So the MS., LB., Hild., and Ochler, reading *vinctionis;* the other edd. *junctionis*—" union."

[6] Lit., "unknown questions."   [7] Pl.

[8] Lit., "has run over."

of men, as[1] you say, why[2] does he not, with uniform benevolence, free all without exception? [I reply,] does not he free all alike who invites all alike? or does he thrust back or repel any one from the kindness of the Supreme who gives to all alike the power of coming to him,—to men of high rank, to the meanest slaves, to women, to boys? To all, he says, the fountain of life is open,[3] and no one is hindered or kept back from drinking.[4] If you are so fastidious as to spurn the kindly[5] offered gift, nay, more, if your wisdom is so great that you term those things which are offered by Christ ridiculous and absurd, why should he keep on inviting[6] [you], while his only duty is to make the enjoyment of his bounty depend upon your own free choice?[7] God, Plato says, does not cause any one to choose his lot in life;[8] nor can another's choice be rightly attributed to any one, since freedom of choice was put in his power who made it. Must you be even implored to deign to accept the gift of salvation from God; and must God's gracious mercy be poured into your bosom while you reject it with disdain, and

---

[1] So the MS. and Oehler, reading *ut*, which is omitted in all other edd.; in this case, the words in brackets are unnecessary.

[2] So Orelli, reading *cur* (*quur* in most edd.) for the MS. *quos*. Instead of *non*—"not," which follows, the MS., according to Oehler, reads *nos*, and he therefore changes *quos* into *quæso*—"I ask, does he free all of us altogether?"

[3] There is clearly no reference here to a particular passage of Scripture, but to the general tone of Christ's teaching: "Him that cometh unto me, I will in nowise cast out." Orelli, however, with his usual infelicity, wishes to see a direct reference, either to Christ's words to the woman of Samaria (John iv. 13-15), or, which is rather extraordinary, to John vi. 35-37: "I am the bread of life," etc. Cf. n. 6, p. 135.

[4] Lit., "the right of drinking."   [5] Lit., "the kindness of."

[6] Lit., "what waits he for, inviting," *quid invitans expectat;* the reading of the MS., both Roman edd., and Oehler. Gelenius, followed by Canterus and Elmenhorst, changed the last word into *peccat*—"in what does he sin," adopted by the other edd., with the addition of *in te*—"against you."

[7] Lit., "exposes under decision of your own right."

[8] Cf. Plato, *Rep.* ii. st. p. 379: "of a few things God would be the cause, but of many he would not;" and x. st. p. 617 fin.

flee very far from it? Do you choose to take what is offered, and turn it to your own advantage? You will [in that case] have consulted your own interests. Do you reject with disdain, lightly esteem, and despise it? You will [in this case] have robbed yourself of the benefit of the gift.[1] God compels no one, terrifies no one with overpowering fear. For our salvation is not necessary to him, so that he would gain anything or suffer any loss, if he either made us divine,[2] or allowed us to be annihilated and destroyed by corruption.

65. Nay, [my opponent] says, if God is powerful, merciful, willing to save us, let him change our dispositions, and compel us to trust in his promises. This, then, is violence, not kindness nor the bounty of the Supreme God, but a childish and vain[3] strife in seeking to get the mastery. For what is so unjust as to force men who are reluctant and unwilling, to reverse their inclinations; to impress forcibly on their minds what they are unwilling [to receive] and shrink from; to injure before benefiting, and to bring to another way of thinking and feeling, by taking away the former? You who wish yourself to be changed,[4] and to suffer violence, that you may do and may be compelled to take to yourself that which you do not wish, why do you refuse of your own accord to select that which you wish to do, when changed and transformed? I am unwilling, he says, and have no wish. What, then, do you blame God as though he failed you? do you wish [him] to bring you help,[5] whose gifts and bounties you

---

[1] So LB., Orelli, Oehler, adopting the emendation of Ursinus, *tu te muneris commoditate privaveris*, for the unintelligible reading of the MS., *tuti m. c. probaveris*.

[2] *i.e.* immortal, *deos*, so corrected by Gelenius for the MS. *deus*—"if either God made us."

[3] So most edd., reading *inanis* for the MS. *animi*; retained, though not very intelligible, in LB., while Hild. reads *anilis*—"foolish."

[4] So the MS. now reads *verti*; but this word, according to Pithœus, is in a later handwriting, and some letters have been erased.

[5] So the edd., reading *tibi desit? opem desideras tibi*, except Hild. and Oehler, who retain the MS. reading, *t. d. o. desideranti*—"as though he failed you desiring [him] to bring help."

not only reject and shun, but term empty[1] words, and assail with jocose witticisms? Unless, then, [my opponent says,] I shall be a Christian, I cannot hope for salvation. It is just as you yourself say. For, to bring salvation and impart to souls what should be bestowed and must be added, [Christ] alone has had given into his charge and entrusted[2] to him by God the Father, the remote and more secret causes being so disposed. For, as with you, certain gods have fixed offices, privileges, powers, and you do not ask from any of them what is not in his power and permitted to him, so it is the right of[3] Christ alone to give salvation to souls, and assign them everlasting life. For if you believe that father Bacchus can give a good vintage, [but] cannot give relief from sickness; if [you believe] that Ceres [can give] good crops, Æsculapius health, Neptune one thing, Juno[4] another, that Fortune, Mercury, Vulcan, are each the giver of a fixed and particular thing,—this, too, you must needs receive from us,[5] that souls can receive from no one life and salvation, except from him to whom the Supreme Ruler gave this charge and duty. The Almighty Master of the world has determined that this should be the way of salvation,—this the door, so to say, of life; by him[6] alone is there access to the light: nor may men either creep in or enter elsewhere, all other [ways] being shut up and secured by an impenetrable barrier.

66. So, then, even if you are pure, and have been cleansed

---

[1] So Ursinus, reading *in ania cognomines* for the MS. *in alia*, which Orelli would interpret, "call the reverse of the truth."

[2] Lit., "For the parts of bringing ... has enjoined and given over," *partes ... injunctum habet et traditum*, where it will be important to notice that Arnobius, writing rapidly, had carried with him only the general idea, and forgotten the mode in which this was expressed.

[3] *Pontificium.*

[4] Here, too, according to Pithœus, there are signs of erasure.

[5] *i.e.* admit.

[6] This passage at once suggests John x. 9 and xiv. 6, and it is therefore the more necessary to notice the way in which Arnobius speaks ("so to say"), which is certainly not the tone of one quoting a passage with which he is well acquainted.

from every stain of vice, have won over and charmed[1] those powers not to shut the ways against you and bar your passage when returning to heaven, by no efforts will you be able to reach the prize of immortality, unless by Christ's gift you have perceived what constitutes this very immortality, and have been allowed to enter on the true life. For as to that with which you have been in the habit of taunting us, that our religion is new,[2] and arose a few days ago, almost, and that you could not abandon the ancient faith which you had inherited from your fathers, and pass over to barbarous and foreign rites, this is urged wholly without reason. For what if in this way we chose to blame the preceding, even the most ancient ages, because when they discovered how to raise crops,[3] they despised acorns, and rejected with scorn the wild strawberry; because they ceased to be covered with the bark of trees and clad in the hides of wild beasts, after that garments of cloth were devised, more useful and convenient in wearing; or because, when houses were built, and more comfortable dwellings erected, they did not cling to their ancient huts, and did not prefer to remain under rocks and caves like the beasts of the field? It is a disposition possessed by all, and impressed on us almost from our cradles even, to prefer good things to bad, useful to useless things, and to pursue and seek that with more pleasure which has been generally regarded[4] as more [than usually] precious, and to set on that our hopes for prosperity and favourable circumstances.

67. Therefore, when you urge against us that we turn away from the religion[5] of past [ages], it is fitting that you should examine why it is done, not what is done, and not set before you what we have left, but observe especially what we

---

[1] Lit., "bent."   [2] Cf. i. 13 and 58.

[3] Lit., "crops being invented."

[4] So the later edd., reading *constiterit* from the margin of Ursinus; but in the MS. and first four edd. the reading is *constituerit*—"has established," for which there is no subject.

[5] So the later edd., reading *aversionem ex* (LB., and preceding edd. *a*) *religione* for the MS. *et religionem*—"against us the hatred and religion of past ages."

have followed. For if it is a fault or crime to change an opinion, and pass from ancient customs to new conditions and desires, this accusation holds against you too, who have so often changed your habits and mode of life, who have gone over to other customs and ceremonies, so that you are condemned by[1] past ages [as well as we]. Do you indeed have the people distributed into five[2] classes, as your ancestors once had? Do you ever elect magistrates by vote of the people? Do you know what military, urban, and common[3] comitia are? Do you watch the sky, or put an end to public business because evil omens are announced? When you are preparing for war,[4] do you hang out a flag from the citadel, or practise the forms of the Fetiales, solemnly[5] demanding the return of what has been carried off? or, when encountering the dangers of war, do you begin to hope also, because of favourable omens from the points of the spears?[6] In entering on office, do you still observe the laws fixing the proper times? with regard to gifts and presents [to advocates, do you observe] the Cincian and the sumptuary laws in restricting your expenses? Do you maintain fires, ever burning, in gloomy sanctuaries?[7] Do you consecrate tables by putting on them salt-cellars and images of the gods? When you marry, do you spread the couch with a toga, and

---

[1] Lit., " with the condemnation of."

[2] This shows that the division of the people into classes was obsolete in the time of Arnobius.

[3] Turnebus has explained this as merely another way of saying the *comitia centuriata, curiata,* and *tributa.*

[4] So the edd., reading *cum paratis bella* (Oehler reads *reparantes*) for the MS. *reparatis.*

[5] *i.e. per clarigationem,* the solemn declaration of war, if restitution was not made within thirty-three days.

[6] This seems the most natural way to deal with the clause *et ex acuminibus auspicatis,* looking on the last word as an adjective, not a verb, as most edd. seem to hold it. There is great diversity of opinion as to what this omen was.

[7] The MS. reads *in penetralibus et coliginis.* LB., followed by Orelli, merely omits *et,* as above, while the first five edd. read *in pen. Vestæ ignis*—" do you maintain the hearths of Vesta's fire." Many other readings and many explanations of the passage are also proposed.

invoke the genii of husbands? do you arrange the hair of brides with the hasta cœlibaris? do you bear the maidens' garments to the temple of Fortuna Virginalis? Do your matrons work in the halls of your houses, showing their industry openly? do they refrain from drinking wine? are their friends and relations allowed to kiss them, in order that they may show that they are sober and temperate?

68. On the Alban hill, it was not allowed in ancient times to sacrifice any but snow-white bulls: have you not changed that custom and religious observance, and [has it not been] enacted by decree of the senate, that reddish ones may be offered? While during the reigns of Romulus and Pompilius the inner parts, having been quite thoroughly cooked and softened, were burnt up [in sacrificing] to the gods, did you not begin, under king Tullius,[1] to hold them out half-raw and slightly warm, paying no regard to the former usage? While before the arrival of Hercules in Italy supplication was made to father Dis and Saturn with the heads of men by Apollo's advice; have you not, in like manner, changed this custom too, by means of cunning deceit and ambiguous names?[2] Since, then, you yourselves also have followed at one time these customs, at another different laws, and have repudiated and rejected many things on either perceiving your mistakes or seeing something better, what have we done contrary to common sense and the discretion all men have, if we have chosen what is greater and more certain, and have not suffered ourselves to be held back by unreasoning respect for impostures?

69. But our name is new, [we are told,] and the religion which we follow arose but a few days ago. Granting for the present that what you urge against us is not untrue, what is there, [I would ask,] among the affairs of men that is either done by bodily exertion and manual labour, or attained by the mind's learning and knowledge, which did not begin at some time, and pass into general use and practice since

---

[1] *i.e.* Servius Tullius. The first four edd. read *Tullo, i.e.* Tullus Hostilius.
[2] Cf. v. c. 1.

then? Medicine,[1] philosophy, music, and all the other arts by which social life has been built up and refined,—were these born with men, and did they not rather begin to be pursued, understood, and practised lately, nay, rather, but a short time since? Before the Etruscan Tages saw the[2] light, did any one know or trouble himself to know and learn what meaning there was in the fall of thunderbolts, or in the veins of the victims sacrificed?[3] When did the motion of the stars or the art of calculating nativities begin to be known? Was it not after Theutis[4] the Egyptian; or after Atlas, as some say, the bearer, supporter, stay, [and] prop of the skies?

70. But why do I [speak of] these trivial things? The immortal gods themselves, whose temples you now enter [with reverence], whose deity you suppliantly adore, did they not at certain times, as is handed down by your writings and traditions, begin to be, to be known and to be invoked by names and titles which were given to them? For if it is true that Jupiter with his brothers was born of Saturn and his wife, before Ops was married and bore children Jupiter had not existed both the Supreme and the Stygian,[5] no, nor the lord of the sea, nor Juno, nay more, no one inhabited the heavenly seats except the two parents; but from their union [the other gods] were conceived and born, and breathed the breath of life. So, then, at a certain time the god Jupiter began to be, at a certain time to merit worship and sacrifices, at a certain time to be set above his brothers in power.[6] But, again, if Liber, Venus, Diana, Mercury, Apollo, Hercules, the Muses, the Tyndarian brothers,[7] and Vulcan the lord of

---

[1] The MS. reads *edi in filosophia*; the first four edd., *Philos.*; Elmenh. and Orelli, *Etenim phil.*—" For were phil.;" LB., *Ede an phil.*—" say whether phil.," which is, however, faulty in construction, as the indicative follows. Rigaltius, followed by Oehler, emended as above, *Medicina phil.*

[2] Lit., "reached the coasts of."

[3] Lit., "of the intestines"—*extorum*.

[4] In both Roman edd., *Theutatem*, *i.e.* Theutas. Cf. Plato, *Phædrus*, st. p. 274.

[5] *i.e.* Pluto.   [6] Pl.   [7] Lit., "Castors," *i.e.* Castor and Pollux.

fire, were begotten by father Jupiter, and born of a parent sprung from Saturn, before that Memory, Alcmena, Maia, Juno, Latona, Leda, Dione, and Semele also bore children to Diespiter; these [deities], too, were nowhere in the world, nor in any part of the universe, but by Jupiter's embraces they were begotten and born, and began to have some sense of their own existence. So then, these, too, began to be at a certain time, and to be summoned among the gods to the sacred rites. This we say, in like manner, of Minerva. For if, as you assert, she burst forth from Jupiter's head ungenerated,[1] before Jupiter was begotten, and received in his mother's womb the shape and outline of his body,[2] it is quite certain that Minerva did not exist, and was not reckoned among things or as existing at all; but from Jove's head she was born, and began to have a real existence. She therefore has an origin at the first, and began to be called a goddess at a certain time, to be set up in temples, and to be consecrated by the inviolable obligations of religion. Now as this is the case, when you talk of the novelty of our religion, does your own not come into your thoughts, and do you not take care to examine when your gods sprung up,—what origins, what causes they have, or from what stocks they have burst forth and sprung? But how shameful, how shameless it is to censure that in another which you see that you do yourself,—to take occasion to revile and accuse [others] for things which can be retorted upon you in turn!

71. But our rites are[3] new; yours are ancient, and of excessive antiquity, [we are told.] And what help does that give you, or how does it damage our cause and argument? The belief[4] which we hold is new; some day even it, too, will become old: yours is old; but when it arose, it was new and unheard of. The credibility of a religion, however, must not be determined by its age, but by its divinity; and you should consider not when, but what you began to worship. Four hundred years ago, my opponent says, your religion did not exist. And two thousand years ago, [I

---

[1] *i.e. sine ullius seminis jactu.*   [2] Lit., "forms of bodily circumscription."
[3] Lit., "what we do is."   [4] Lit., "thing."

reply,] your gods did not exist. By what reckoning, [you ask,] or by what calculations, can that be inferred? They are not difficult, not intricate, but can be seen by any one who will take them in hand even, as the saying is. Who begot Jupiter and his brothers? Saturn with Ops, as you relate, sprung from Cœlus and Hecate. Who begot Picus, the father of Faunus and grandfather of Latinus? Saturn, as you again hand down by your books and teachers? Therefore, if this is the case, Picus and Jupiter are in consequence united by the bond of kinship, inasmuch as they are sprung from one stock and race. It is clear, then, that what we say is true. How many steps are there in coming down[1] from Jupiter and Picus to Latinus? Three, as the line of succession shows. Will you suppose Faunus, Latinus, and Picus to have each lived a hundred and twenty years, for beyond this it is affirmed that man's life cannot be prolonged? The estimation is well grounded and clear. There are, then, three hundred and sixty years after these?[2] It is just as the calculation shows. Whose father-in-law was Latinus? Æneas'. Whose father [was] he?[3] [He was father] of the founder of the town Alba. How many years did kings reign in Alba? Four hundred and twenty almost. Of what age is the city Rome shown to be in the annals? It reckons fifteen[4] hundred years, or not much less. So, then, from Jupiter, who is the brother of Picus and father of the other and lesser gods, down to the present time, there are nearly, or to add a little to the time, altogether, two thousand years. Now since this cannot be contradicted, not only is the religion to which you adhere shown to have sprung up lately; but [it is also shown] that the gods themselves, to whom you heap up bulls and other vic-

---

[1] Lit., "how many steps are there of race."

[2] *i.e.* Jupiter and Picus.

[3] The MS. reads *genitor . . . Latinus cujus*, some letters having been erased. The reading followed above—*genitor is cujus*—was suggested to Canterus by his friend Gifanius, and is found in the margin of Ursinus and Orelli.

[4] Cf. above, "four hundred years ago," etc., and i. ch. 13. It is of importance to note that Arnobius is inconsistent in these statements.

tims at the risk of bringing on disease, are young and little children, who should still be fed with their mothers' milk.[1]

72. But your religion precedes ours by many years, and is therefore, [you say,] truer, because it has been supported by the authority of antiquity. And of what avail is it that it should precede [ours] as many years as you please, since it began at a certain time? or what[2] are two thousand years, compared with so many thousands of ages? And yet, lest we should seem to betray [our] cause by so long neglect, say, if it does not annoy you, does the Almighty and Supreme God seem to you to be something new; and do those who adore and worship him [seem to you] to support and introduce an unheard-of, unknown, and upstart religion? Is there anything older than him? or can anything be found preceding him in being,[3] time, name? Is not he alone uncreated, immortal, and everlasting? Who is the head[4] and fountain of things? is not he? To whom does eternity owe its name? is it not to him? Is it not because he is everlasting, that the ages go on without end? This is beyond doubt, and true: [the religion] which we follow is not new, then, but we have been late in learning what we should follow and revere, or where we should both fix our hope of salvation, and employ the aid [given] to save us. For he had not yet shone forth who was to point out the way to those wandering [from it], and give the light of knowledge to those who were lying in the deepest darkness, and dispel the blindness of their ignorance.

73. But are we alone in this position?[5] What! have you not introduced into the number of your gods the Egyptian deities named Serapis and Isis, since the consulship of Piso and Gabinius?[6] What! did you not begin both to know

---

[1] Lit., "be nursed with the breasts and dropt milk."
[2] Lit., "of what space."   [3] *i.e.* re.
[4] So the MS., according to Crusius and Livineius, reading *ac;* all edd. except Oehler read *aut*—"head (*i.e.* source) or fountain."
[5] The MS. reads unintelligibly *vertitur solæ;* for which LB., followed by the later edd, reads, as above, *vertimur soli.*
[6] Dr. Schmitz (Smith's *Dict.*, *s. v.* Isis) speaks of these consuls as head-

and be acquainted with, and to worship with remarkable honours, the Phrygian mother—who, it is said, was first set up as a goddess by Midas or Dardanus—when Hannibal, the Carthaginian, was plundering Italy and aiming at the empire of the world?[1] Are not the sacred rites of mother Ceres, which were adopted but a little while ago, called Græca because they were unknown to you, their name bearing witness to their novelty? Is it not said[2] in the writings of the learned, that the rituals of Numa Pompilius do not contain the name of Apollo? Now it is clear and manifest from this, that he, too, was unknown to you, but that at some time afterwards he began to be known also. If any one, therefore, should ask you why you have so lately begun to worship those deities whom we mentioned just now, it is certain that you will reply, either because we were [till] lately not aware that they were gods, or because we have now been warned by the seers, or because, in very trying circumstances, we have been preserved by their favour and help. But if you think that this is well said by you, you must consider that, on our part, a similar reply has been made. Our religion has sprung up just now; for now he has arrived who was sent to declare it to us, to bring [us] to its truth; to show what God is; to summon us from mere conjectures, to his worship.

74. And why, [my opponent] says, did God, the ruler and lord [of the universe], determine that a Saviour, Christ, should be sent to you from the heights of heaven a few hours ago, as it is said? We ask you too, on the other hand, what cause, what reason is there that the seasons sometimes do not recur at their own months, but that winter,

---

ing the popular revolt against the decree of the senate, that the statues of Isis and Serapis should be removed from the Capitol. The words of Tertullian (quoting Varro as his authority) are very distinct: "The consul Gabinius . . . gave more weight to the decision of the senate than to the popular impulse, and forbade their altars (*i.e.* those of Serapis, Isis, Arpocrates, and Anubis) to be set up" (*ad Nationes*, i. 10, cf. *Apol.* 6).

[1] Cf. vii. 49.   [2] Lit., "contained."

summer, and autumn come too late? why, after the crops have been dried up and the corn[1] has perished, showers sometimes fall which should have dropped on them while yet uninjured, and made provision for the wants of the time? Nay, this we rather ask, why, if it were fitting that Hercules should be born, Æsculapius, Mercury, Liber, and some others, that they might be both added to the assemblies of the gods, and might do men some service,—why they were produced so late by Jupiter, that only later ages should know them, while the past ages[2] of those who went before knew them not? You will say that there was some reason. There was then some reason here also that the Saviour of our race came not lately, but to-day. What, then, [you ask,] is the reason? We do not deny that we do not know. For it is not within the power of any one to see the mind of God, or the way in which he has arranged his plans.[3] Man, a blind creature, and not knowing himself even, can[4] in no way learn what should happen, when, or what its nature is: the Father himself, the Governor and Lord of all, alone knows. Nor, if I have been unable to disclose to you the causes why something is done in this way or that, does it straightway follow, that what has been done becomes not done, and that a thing becomes incredible, which has been shown to be beyond doubt by such[5] virtues and[6] powers.

75. You may object and rejoin, Why was the Saviour sent forth so late? In unbounded, eternal ages, [we reply,] nothing whatever should be spoken of as late. For where there is no end and no beginning, nothing is too soon,[7]

---

[1] Pl.   [2] Lit., "antiquity."   [3] Lit., "things."

[4] So Gelenius emended the MS., reading *potens*—"being able," which he changed into *potest*, as above, followed by later edd.

[5] Lit., "by such kinds of."

[6] The MS. and first edd. read *et potestatibus potestatum*—"and by powers of powers;" the other edd. merely omit *potestatibus*, as above, except Oehler, who, retaining it, changes *potestatum* into *protestata*—"being witnessed to by," etc.; but there is no instance adduced in which the participle of this verb is used passively.

[7] These words having been omitted by Oberthür, are omitted by Orelli also, as in previous instances.

nothing too late. For time is perceived from its beginnings and endings, which an unbroken line and endless[1] succession of ages cannot have. For what if the things themselves to which it was necessary to bring help, required that as a fitting time? For what if the condition of antiquity was different from that of later times? What if it was necessary to give help to the men of old in one way, to provide for their descendants in another? Do you not hear your own writings read, telling that there were once men [who were] demi-gods, heroes with immense and huge bodies? Do you not read that infants on their mothers' breasts shrieked like Stentors,[2] whose bones, when dug up in different parts of the earth, have made the discoverers almost doubt that they were the remains of human limbs? So, then, it may be that Almighty God, the only God, sent forth Christ then indeed, after that the human race, [becoming] feebler, weaker, began to be such as we are. If that which has been done now could have been done thousands of years ago, the Supreme Ruler would have done it; or if it had been proper, that what has been done now should be accomplished as many thousands after this, nothing compelled God to anticipate the necessary lapse[3] of time. His plans[4] are executed in fixed ways; and that which has been once decided on, can in no wise be changed again.[5]

76. Inasmuch then, you say, as you serve the Almighty God, and trust that He cares for your safety and salvation, why does He suffer you to be exposed to such storms of persecution, and to undergo all kinds of punishments and tortures? Let us, too, ask in reply, why, seeing that you worship so great and so innumerable gods, and build temples to them, fashion images of gold, sacrifice herds

---

[1] The MS. and first ed. read *etiam moderata continuatio;* corrected, *et immod. con.* by Gelenius.
[2] So the edd., reading *infantes stentoreos,* except Oehler, who retains the MS. reading *centenarios,* which he explains as "having a hundred" heads or hands, as the case might be, *e.g.* Typhon, Briareus, etc.
[3] Lit., "measure." [4] Lit., "things."
[5] Lit., "can be changed with no novelty."

of animals, [and] all heap up¹ boxfuls of incense on the already loaded altars, why you live subject to so many dangers and storms [of calamity], with which many fatal misfortunes vex you every day? Why, I say, do your gods neglect to avert from you so many kinds of disease and sickness, shipwrecks, downfalls, conflagrations, pestilences, barrenness, loss of children, and confiscation of goods, discords, wars, enmities, captures of cities, and the slavery of those who are robbed of their rights of free birth?² But, [my opponent says,] in such mischances we, too, are in no wise helped by God. The cause is plain and manifest. For no hope has been held out to us with respect to this life, nor has any help been promised or³ aid decreed us for what belongs to the husk of this flesh,—nay, more, we have been taught to esteem and value lightly all the threats of fortune, whatever they be; and if ever any very grievous calamity has assailed [us], to count as pleasant in [that] misfortune⁴ the end which must follow, and not to fear or flee from it, that we may be the more easily released from the bonds of the body, and escape from our darkness and⁵ blindness.

77. Therefore that bitterness of persecution of which you speak is our deliverance and not persecution, and our ill-treatment will not bring evil upon us, but will lead us to the light of liberty. As if some senseless and stupid fellow were to think that he never punished a man who had been put into prison⁶ with severity and cruelty, unless he were to rage against the very prison, break its stones in pieces, and

---

¹ Lit., "provide," *conficiatis*, which, however, some would understand "consume."

² Lit., "slaveries, their free births being taken away."

³ Lit., "and."

⁴ So the MS., first five edd., Hild., and Oehler, reading *adscribere infortunio voluptatem*, which is omitted in the other edd. as a gloss which may have crept in from the margin.

⁵ Lit., "our dark."

⁶ The MS. and both Roman edd. read *in carcerem natum inegressum*; LB. and later edd. have received from the margin of Ursinus the reading translated above, *datum*, omitting the last word altogether, which Oehler, however, would retain as equivalent to "not to be passed from."

burn its roof, its wall, its doors; and strip, overthrow, and dash to the ground its other parts, not knowing that thus he was giving light to him whom he seemed to be injuring, and was taking from him the accursed darkness: in like manner, you too, by the flames, banishments, tortures, and monsters with which you tear in pieces and rend asunder our bodies, do not rob us of life, but relieve us of our skins, not knowing that, as far as you assault and seek to rage against these our shadows and forms, so far you free us from pressing and heavy chains, and cutting our bonds, make us fly up to the light.

78. Wherefore, O men, refrain from obstructing what you hope for by vain questions; nor should you, if anything is otherwise than you think, trust your own opinions rather than that which should be reverenced.[1] The times, full of dangers, urge us, and fatal penalties threaten us; let us flee for safety to God our Saviour, without demanding the reason of the offered gift. When that at stake is our souls' salvation and our own interests, something must be done even without reason, as Arrhianus approves of Epictetus having said.[2] We doubt, we hesitate, and suspect the credibility of what is said; let us commit ourselves to God, and let not our incredulity prevail more with us than the greatness of His name and power, lest, while we are seeking out arguments for ourselves, through which that may seem false which we do not wish and deny to be true, the last day steal upon us, and we be found in the jaws of our enemy, death.

[1] Lit., "than an august thing."

[2] Orelli refers to Arrh. i. 12; but the doctrine there insisted on is the necessity of submission to what is unavoidable. Oehler, in addition, refers to Epict. xxxii. 3, where, however, it is merely attempted to show that when anything is withheld from us, it is just as goods are unless paid for, and that we have therefore no reason to complain. Neither passage can be referred to here, and it seems as though Arnobius has made a very loose reference which cannot be specially identified.

BOOK III.

ARGUMENT.

In the two preceding books, Arnobius endeavoured to repel the objections raised against Christianity; but already, he says, it had found able defenders, though strong enough in its own might to need none (1); and therefore, having replied to the charge of neglecting the worship of the gods, by asserting that in worshipping the Supreme God, the Creator of the universe, any other gods, if there are such, receive honour, inasmuch as they are sprung from him (2, 3), he goes on to attack heathenism itself, pointing out that the other gods cannot be proved to exist, their names and number being alike unknown (4, 5). These gods, moreover, are spoken of as male and female, but the divine cannot be liable to such distinctions, as Cicero showed (6); whom it would be well, therefore, for the heathen to refute, instead of merely raising an unreasoning clamour against his writings (7). The use by Christians of a masculine term to denote the Deity, is merely a necessity of speech; but the heathen expressly attributed sex to their deities (8), who would therefore, being immortal, be innumerable; or if the gods did not beget children, why had they sex (9)? Arnobius then inveighs against this opinion as degrading and dishonouring the gods (10), and says that it is far more likely that they would afflict men to punish such insults, than to take vengeance on Christians, who did them no dishonour (11). He then goes on to speak of bodily form, denying that it is attributed to the Deity by Christians (12), while the heathen boldly asserted that their gods had *human* bodies, which, Arnobius shows, makes it necessary to ascribe to some gods the basest offices (13–15). It might, however, be said that the gods were not really supposed to have such bodies, but were so spoken of out of respect. This, Arnobius shows, is not honouring, but insulting, them as much as possible (16). If the Deity has any mortal shape, we do not know it (17); he may hear, see, and speak in his own, but not in our way (18); and it is unbecoming to ascribe even our virtues to God,—we can only say that his nature cannot be declared by man (19).

The offices ascribed to the gods are next derisively commented on (20, 21); and as to the suggestion that the gods impart a knowledge of the arts over which they preside, without being practically acquainted with them, it is asked why the gods should seek this knowledge, when they had no opportunity of turning it to account (22). It might, however, be said that it belonged to the gods to secure a prosperous issue to human undertakings. Why, then, failure, ruin, and destruction (23)? Because, it would be answered, of neglected rites, and sacrifices withheld. Is, then, Arnobius asks, the favour of the gods to be purchased? is it not theirs to give to those utterly destitute (24)? Unxia, Cinxia, Vita, and Potua are held up as foul parodies on Deity (25). Mars and Venus being taken as fair examples (26, 27), the conclusion is reached, that such gods, presiding over lust, discord, and war, cannot be believed in (28). The inconsistent and mutually destructive opinions entertained with regard to Janus, Saturn (29), Jupiter, Juno (30), and other gods, render belief in them impossible (31-34); while if, as some believe, the world is a living being, the deities cannot exist which are said to be parts of it, as the sun, moon, etc., for the whole will have life, not its members (35). Thus the heathen plainly subvert all faith in their religion, however zealous against Christian innovations (36). They do so still further, by the ridiculous inconsistency of their opinions as to the origin and numbers of their gods, in particular of the Muses (37, 38); the Novensiles (38, 39); the Penates (40); and the Lares (41).

Arnobius, having thus shown that the heathen are in doubt and ignorance as to all their gods, a circumstance giving rise to confusion in seeking to celebrate their rites (42, 43), calls upon them to decide on their creed, and abide by it (44).

1. ALL these charges, then, which might truly be better termed abuse, have been long answered with sufficient fulness and accuracy by men of distinction in this respect, and worthy to have learned the truth; and not one point of any inquiry has been passed over, without being determined in a thousand ways, and on the strongest grounds. We need not, therefore, linger further on this part of the case. For neither is the Christian religion unable to stand though it found no advocates, nor will it be therefore proved true if it found many to agree with it, and gained weight through its adherents.[1] Its own strength is sufficient for it, and it rests on the foundations of its own truth, without losing its power, though there were none to defend it, nay, though all voices assailed

---

[1] The MS., followed by Oehler, reads *neque enim res stare . . . non potest, Christiana religio aut*—"for neither can a thing not stand, . . . nor will the Christian religion," etc., while LB. merely changes *aut* into *et*—"for neither can a thing, *i.e.* the Christian religion, . . . nor will it," etc. All other edd. read as above, omitting *et*.

and opposed it, and united with common rancour to destroy all faith[1] in it.

2. Let us now return to the order from which we were a little ago compelled to diverge, that our defence may not, through its being too long broken off, be said to have given our detractors cause to triumph in the establishing of their charge. For they propose these questions: If you are in earnest about religion, why do you not serve and worship the other gods with us, or share your sacred rites with your fellows, and put the ceremonies of the [different] religions on an equality? We may say for the present: In essaying to approach the divine, the Supreme Deity[2] suffices us,—the Deity, I say, who is supreme, the Creator and Lord of the universe, who orders and rules all things: in him we serve all that requires our service; [in him] we worship all that should be adored,—venerate[3] that which demands the homage of our reverence. For as we lay hold of the source of the divine itself, from which the very divinity of all gods whatever is derived,[4] we think it an idle task to approach each personally, since we neither know who they are, nor the names by which they are called; and are further unable to learn, and discover, and establish their number.

3. And as in the kingdoms of earth we are in no wise constrained expressly to do reverence to those who form the royal family as well as to the sovereigns, but whatever honour belongs to them is found to be tacitly[5] implied in the homage

---

[1] According to Crusius and others, the MS. reads *finem;* but, according to Hild., *fidem,* as above.

[2] *Deus primus,* according to Nourry, in relation to Christ; but manifestly from the scope of the chapter, God as the fountain and source of all things.

[3] Lit., "propitiate with venerations."

[4] So the MS., reading *ducitur;* for which Oberthür, followed by Orelli, reads *dicitur*—"is said."

[5] Lit., "whatever belongs to them feels itself to be comprehended with a tacit rendering also of honour in," etc., *tacita et se sentit honorificentia,* read by later edd. for the MS. *ut se sentit*—"but as whatever," retained by Hild. and Oehler; while the first four edd. read *vi*—"feels itself with a silent force comprehended in the honour in," etc.

offered to the kings themselves; in just the same way, these gods, whoever they be, for whose existence you vouch, if they are a royal race, and spring from the Supreme Ruler, even though we do not expressly do them reverence, yet feel that they are honoured in common with their Lord, and share in the reverence shown to him. Now [it must be remembered that] we have made this statement, on the hypothesis only that it is clear and undeniable, that besides the Ruler and Lord himself, there are still other beings,[1] who, when arranged and disposed in order, form, as it were, a kind of plebeian mass. But do not seek to point out to us pictures instead of gods in your temples, and the images [which you set up], for you too know, but are unwilling and refuse to admit, that these are formed of most worthless clay, and are childish figures made by mechanics. And when we converse with you on religion, we ask you to prove this, that there are other gods [than the one Supreme Deity] in nature, power, name, not as we see them manifested in images, but in such a substance as it might fittingly be supposed that perfection of so great dignity should reside.

4. But we do not purpose delaying further on this part of the subject, lest we seem desirous to stir up most violent strife, and engage in agitating contests.

Let there be, as you affirm, that crowd of deities, let there be numberless families of gods; we assent, agree, [and] do not examine [too] closely, nor in any part of the subject do we assail the doubtful and uncertain positions you hold. This, however, we demand, and ask you to tell us, whence you have discovered, or how you have learned, whether there are these gods,[2] whom you believe to be in heaven and serve, or some others unknown by reputation and name? For it may be that beings exist whom you do not believe to do so;

---

[1] So LB. and Orelli, reading *alia etiamnum capita* for the MS. *alienum capita*, read in the first five edd., *alia non capita*—" are others not chiefs;" Hild., followed by Oehler, proposes *alia deûm capita*—" other gods."

[2] According to Orelli's punctuation, " whether there are these gods in heaven whom," etc.

and that those of whose existence you feel assured, are found nowhere in the universe. For you have at no time been borne aloft to the stars of heaven, [at no time] have seen the face and countenance of each; and [then] established here the worship of the same gods, whom you remembered to be there, as having been known and seen [by you]. But this, too, we again would learn from you, whether they have received these names by which you call them, or assumed them themselves on the days of purification.[1] If these are divine and celestial names, who reported them to you? But if, on the other hand, these names have been applied to them by you, how could you give names to those whom you never saw, and whose character or circumstances you in no wise[2] knew?

5. But [let it be assumed] that there are these gods, as you wish and believe, and are persuaded; let them be called also by those names by which the common people suppose that those meaner [gods][3] are known.[4] Whence, however, have you learned who make up the list [of gods] under these names?[5] have any ever become familiar and known [to others] with whose names you were not acquainted?[6] For it cannot be easily known whether their numerous body is settled and fixed [in number]; or whether their multitude cannot be summed up and limited by the numbers of any computation. For let us suppose that you do reverence to a thousand, or rather five thousand gods; but in the uni-

---

[1] So LB. and later edd., from a conj. of Meursius, reading *diebus lustricis* for the MS. *ludibriis;* read by some, and understood by others, as *ludicris, i.e.* festal days.

[2] The MS., followed by Hild. and Oehler, reads *neque . . . in ulla cognatione*—"in no relationship," for which the other edd. give *cognitione,* as above.

[3] So all edd., reading *populares,* except Hild. and Oehler, who receive the conj. of Rigaltius, *populatim*—"among all nations;" the MS. reading *popularem.*

[4] *Censeri, i.e.* "written in the list of gods."

[5] Otherwise, "how many make up the list of this name."

[6] So Orelli, receiving the emendation of Barth, *incogniti nomine,* for the MS. *in cognitione,* -*one* being an abbreviation for *nomine.* Examples of such deities are the Novensiles, Consentes, etc., cc. 38–41.

verse it may perhaps be that there are a hundred thousands; there may be even more than this,—nay, as we said a little before, it may not be possible to compute the number of the gods, or limit them by a definite number. Either, then, you are yourselves impious who serve a few gods, but disregard the duties which you owe to the rest;[1] or if you claim that your ignorance of the rest should be pardoned, you will procure for us also a similar pardon, if in just the same way[2] we refuse to worship those of whose existence we are wholly ignorant.

6. And yet let no one think that we are perversely determined not to submit to[3] the other deities, whoever they are! For we [lift up] pious minds, and stretch forth our hands in prayer,[4] and do not refuse to draw near whithersoever you may have summoned us; if only we learn who those divine beings are whom you press upon us, and with whom it may be right to share the reverence which we show to the king and prince who is over all. It is Saturn, [my opponent] says, and Janus, Minerva, Juno, Apollo, Venus, Triptolemus, Hercules, Æsculapius, and all the others, to whom the reverence of antiquity dedicated magnificent temples in almost every city. You might, perhaps, have been able to attract us to the worship of these deities you mention, had you not been yourselves the first, with foul and unseemly fancies, to devise such tales about them as not merely to stain their honour, but, by the natures assigned to them, to prove that they did not exist at all. For, in the first place, we cannot be led to believe this,—that that immortal and supreme

---

[1] Lit., "who, except a few gods, do not engage in the services of the rest."

[2] Orelli would explain *pro parte consimili* as equivalent to *pro uno vero Deo*—"for the one true God."

[3] Lit., "take the oaths of allegiance," or military oaths, using a very common metaphor applied to Christians in the preceding book, c. 5.

[4] Lit., "suppliant hands." It has been thought that the word *supplices* is a gloss, and that the idea originally was that of a band of soldiers holding out their hands as they swore to be true to their country and leaders; but there is no want of simplicity and congruity in the sentence as it stands, to warrant us in rejecting the word.

nature has been divided by sexes, and that there are some male, others female. But this point, indeed, has been long ago fully treated of by men of ardent genius, both in Latin and Greek; and Tullius, the most eloquent among the Romans, without dreading the vexatiousness of a charge of impiety, has above all, with greater piety,[1] declared—boldly, firmly, and frankly—what he thought of such a fancy; and if you would proceed to receive from him opinions written with true discernment, instead of [merely] brilliant sentences, this case would have been concluded; nor would it require at our weak hands[2] a second pleading,[3] as it is termed.

7. But why should I say that men seek from him subtleties of expression and splendour of diction, when I know that there are many who avoid and flee from his books on this subject, and will not hear his opinions read,[4] overthrowing their prejudices; and when I hear others muttering angrily, and saying that the senate should decree the destruction[5] of these writings by which the Christian religion is maintained, and the weight of antiquity overborne? But, indeed, if you are convinced that anything you say regarding your gods is beyond doubt, point out Cicero's error, refute, rebut his rash and impious words,[6] [and] show [that they are so]. For when you would carry off writings, and suppress a book given forth to the public, you are not defending the gods, but dreading the evidence of the truth.

8. And yet, that no thoughtless person may raise a false

---

[1] *i.e.* than the inventors of such fables had shown.

[2] Lit., "from us infants," *i.e.* as compared with such a man as Cicero.

[3] *Secundas actiones.* The reference is evidently to a second speaker, who makes good his predecessor's defects.

[4] Lit., "are unwilling to admit into their ear the reading of opinions," etc.

[5] Both Christians and heathen, it is probable, were concerned in the mutilation of *de Nat. Deorum*.

[6] So Gelenius, reading *dicta* for the MS. *dictitare*. The last verb is *comprobate*, read *reprobate*—"condemn," by all edd. except Hild. and Oehler.

accusation against us, as though we believe God whom we worship to be male,—for this reason, that is, that when we speak of him we use a masculine word,—let him understand that it is not sex which is expressed, but his name, and its meaning according to custom, and the way in which we are in the habit of using words.[1] For the Deity is not male, but his name is of the masculine gender: but in your ceremonies you cannot say the same; for in your prayers you have been wont to say *whether thou art god or goddess*,[2] and this uncertain description shows, even by their opposition, that you attribute sex to the gods. We cannot, then, be prevailed on to believe that the divine is embodied; for bodies must needs be distinguished by difference of sex, if they are male and female. For who, however mean his capacity,[3] does not know that the sexes of different gender have been ordained and formed by the Creator of the creatures of earth, only that, by intercourse and union of bodies, that which is fleeting and transient may endure being ever renewed and maintained?[4]

9. What, then, shall we say? That gods beget and are begotten?[5] and that therefore they have received organs of generation, that they might be able to raise up offspring, and that, as each new race springs up, a substitution, regularly occurring,[6] should make up for all which had been swept away by the preceding age? If, then, it is so,—that is, if the gods above beget [other gods], and are subject to these conditions of sex,[7] and are immortal, and are not worn out by the chills of age,—it follows, as a consequence, that the world[8] should be full of gods, and that countless heavens could not contain their multitude, inasmuch as they are both them-

---

[1] Lit., "with familiarity of speech."

[2] A formula used when they sought to propitiate the author of some event which could not be traced to a particular deity; referring also to the cases in which there were different opinions as to the sex of a deity.

[3] Lit., "even of mean understanding."

[4] Lit., "by the renewing of perpetual succession."

[5] Lit., "that gods are born."

[6] Lit., "recurring," "arising again."

[7] Lit., "make trial of themselves by these laws of sex."

[8] Lit., "all things," etc.

selves ever begetting, and the countless multitude of their descendants, always being increased, is augmented by means of their offspring; or if, as is fitting, the gods are not degraded by being subjected to sexual impulses,[1] what cause or reason will be pointed out for their being distinguished by those members by which the sexes are wont to recognise each other at the suggestion of their own desires? For it is not likely that they have these [members] without a purpose, or that nature had wished in them to make sport of its own improvidence,[2] in providing them with members for which there would be no use. For as the hands, feet, eyes, and other members which form our body,[3] have been arranged for certain uses, each for its own end, so we may well[4] believe that these members have been provided to discharge their office; or it must be confessed that there is something without a purpose in the bodies of the gods, which has been made uselessly and in vain.

10. What say you, ye holy and pure guardians of religion? Have the gods, then, sexes; and are they disfigured by those parts, the very mention of whose names by modest lips is disgraceful? What, then, now remains, but to believe that they, as unclean beasts, are transported with violent passions, rush with maddened desires into mutual embraces, and at last, with shattered and ruined bodies, are enfeebled by their sensuality? And since some things are peculiar to the female sex, we must believe that the goddesses, too, submit to these conditions at the proper time, conceive and become pregnant with loathing, miscarry, carry the full time, and sometimes are prematurely delivered. O divinity, pure, holy, free from and unstained by any dishonourable blot! The mind longs[5] and burns to see, in the great halls and palaces of heaven,

---

[1] Lit., "if the impurity of sexual union is wanting to the gods."
[2] So the first five edd.
[3] Lit., "the other arrangement of members."
[4] Lit., "it is fitting to believe."
[5] The MS., followed by Hild., reads *habet et animum*—"has it a mind to, and does it," etc.; for which Gelenius, followed by later edd., reads, as above, *avet animus*.

gods and goddesses, with bodies uncovered and bare, the full-breasted Ceres nursing Iaccus,[1] as the muse of Lucretius sings, the Hellespontian Priapus bearing about among the goddesses, virgin and matron, those parts[2] ever prepared for encounter. It longs, I say, to see goddesses pregnant, goddesses with child, and, as they daily increase in size, faltering in their steps, through the irksomeness of the burden they bear about with them; others, after long delay, bringing to birth, and seeking the midwife's aid; others, shrieking as they are attacked by keen pangs and grievous pains, tormented,[3] and, under all these influences, imploring the aid of Juno Lucina. Is it not much better to abuse, revile, and otherwise insult the gods, than, with pious pretence, unworthily to entertain such monstrous beliefs about them?

11. And you dare to charge us with offending the gods, although, on examination, it is found that the ground of offence is most clearly in yourselves, and that it is not occasioned by the insult which you think[4] [we offer them]. For if the gods are, as you say, moved by anger, and burn with rage in their minds, why should we not suppose that they take it amiss, even in the highest degree, that you attribute to them sexes, as dogs and swine have been created, and that, since this is your belief, they are so represented, and openly exposed in a disgraceful manner? This, then, being the case, you are the cause of all troubles— you lead the gods, you rouse them to harass the earth with every ill, and every day to devise all kinds of fresh misfortunes, that so they may avenge themselves, being irritated at suffering so many wrongs and insults from you. By your insults and affronts, I say, partly in the vile stories, partly in the shameful beliefs which your theologians, your

[1] *Cererem ab Iaccho*, either as above, or "loved by Iacchus." Cf. Lucret. iv. 1160: *At tumida et mammosa Ceres est ipsa ab Iaccho*.

[2] *Sensu obscœno*.

[3] The first five edd. read *hortari*—"exhorted," for which LB., followed by later edd., received *tortari*, as above,—a conjecture of Canterus.

[4] So Orelli, reading *nec in contumelia quam opinamini stare* for the MS. *et*, which is retained by all other edd.; Oehler, however, inserts *alia* before *quam*—"and that it is found in an insult other than you think."

poets, you yourselves too, celebrate in disgraceful ceremonies, you will find that the affairs of men have been ruined, and that the gods have thrown away the helm, if indeed it is by their care that the fortunes of men are guided and arranged. For with us, indeed, they have no reason to be angry, whom they see and perceive neither to mock, as it is said, nor worship them, and to think,[1] to believe much more worthily than you with regard to the dignity of their name.

12. Thus far of sex. Now let us come to the appearance and shapes by which you believe that the gods above have been represented, with which, indeed, you fashion, and set them up in their most splendid abodes, your temples. And let no one here bring up against us Jewish fables and those of the sect of the Sadducees,[2] as though we, too, attribute to the Deity forms[3] (for this is supposed to be taught in their writings, and asserted as if with assurance and authority); for these stories either do not concern us, and have nothing at all in common with us, or if they are shared in [by us], as you believe, you must seek out teachers of greater wisdom, through whom you may be able to learn how best to overcome the dark and recondite sayings of those writings. Our opinion on the subject is as follows:—that the whole divine nature, since it neither came into existence at any time, nor will ever come to an end of life, is devoid of bodily features, and does not have anything like the forms with which the termination of the several members usually completes the union of parts.[4] For whatever is of this character, we think mortal and perishable; nor do we believe that that can endure for ever which an inevitable end shuts in, though the boundaries enclosing it be the remotest.

13. But it is not enough that you limit the gods by forms:

[1] So later edd., omitting *quam*, which is read in the MS., both Roman edd., Hild., and Oehler, "to think much more ... than you believe."

[2] It is evident that Arnobius here confuses the sceptical Sadducees with their opponents the Pharisees, and the Talmudists.

[3] The MS. reads *tribuant et nos* unintelligibly, for which LB. and Hild. read *et os*—"as though they attribute form and face;" the other edd., as above, *tribuamus et nos*.

[4] Lit., "the joinings of the members."

—you even confine them to the human figure, and with even less decency enclose them in earthly bodies. What shall we say then? that the gods have a head modelled with perfect symmetry,[1] bound fast by sinews to the back and breast, and that, to allow the necessary bending of the neck, it is supported by combinations of vertebræ, and by an osseous foundation? But if we believe this to be true, it follows that they have ears also, pierced by crooked windings; rolling eyeballs, overshadowed by the edges of the eyebrows; a nose, placed as a channel,[2] through which waste fluids and a current of air might easily pass; teeth to masticate food, of three kinds, and adapted to three services; hands to do their work, moving easily by means of joints, fingers, and flexible elbows; feet to support their bodies, regulate their steps, and prompt the first motions in walking. But if [the gods bear] these things which are seen, it is fitting that they should bear those also which the skin conceals under the framework of the ribs, and the membranes enclosing the viscera; windpipes, stomachs, spleens, lungs, bladders, livers, the long-entwined intestines, and the veins of purple blood, joined with the air-passages,[3] coursing through the whole viscera.

14. Are, then, the divine bodies free from these deformities? and since they do not eat the food of men, are we to believe that, like children, they are toothless, and, having no internal parts, as if they were inflated bladders, are without strength, owing to the hollowness of their swollen bodies? Further, if this is the case, you must see whether the gods are all alike, or are marked by a difference in the contour of their forms. For if each and all have one and the same likeness of shape, there is nothing ridiculous in believing that they err, and are deceived in recognising each other.[4] But

---

[1] Lit., "with smooth roundness."
[2] Lit., "the raised gutter of the nose, easily passed by," etc.
[3] The veins were supposed to be for the most part filled with blood, mixed with a little air; while in the arteries air was supposed to be in excess. Cf. Cicero, de Nat. Deor. ii. 55: "Through the veins blood is poured forth to the whole body, and air through the arteries."
[4] Lit., "in the apprehension of mutual knowledge."

if, on the other hand, they are distinguished by their countenances, we should, consequently, understand that these differences have been implanted for no other reason than that they might individually be able to recognise themselves by the peculiarities of the different marks. We should therefore say that some have big heads, prominent brows, broad brows, thick lips; that others of them have long chins, moles, and high noses; that these have dilated nostrils, those are snub-nosed; some chubby from a swelling of their jaws or growth of their cheeks, dwarfed, tall, of middle size, lean, sleek, fat; some with crisped and curled hair, others shaven, with bald and smooth heads. Now your workshops show and point out that our opinions are not false, inasmuch as, when you form and fashion gods, you represent some with long hair, others smooth and bare, as old, as youths, as boys, swarthy, grey-eyed, yellow, half-naked, bare; or, that cold may not annoy them, covered with flowing garments thrown over them.

15. Does any man at all possessed of judgment, believe that hairs and down grow on the bodies of the gods? that among them age is distinguished? and that they go about clad in dresses and garments of various shapes, and shield themselves from heat and cold? But if any one believes that, he must receive this also as true, that [some] gods are fullers, some barbers; the former to cleanse the sacred garments, the latter to thin their locks when matted with a thick growth of hair. Is not this really degrading, most impious, and insulting, to attribute to the gods the features of a frail and perishing animal? to furnish them with those members which no modest person would dare to recount, and describe, or represent in his own imagination, without shuddering at the excessive indecency? Is this the contempt you entertain, —this the proud wisdom with which you spurn us as ignorant, and think that all knowledge of religion is yours? You mock the mysteries of the Egyptians, because they ingrafted the forms of dumb animals upon their divine causes, and because they worship these very images with much incense, and whatever else is used in such rites: you yourselves adore

images of men, as though they were powerful gods, and are not ashamed to give to these the countenance of an earthly creature, to blame others for their mistaken folly, and to be detected in a similarly vicious error.

16. But you will, perhaps, say that the gods have indeed other forms, and that you have given the appearance of men to them [merely] by way of honour, and for form's sake;[1] which is much more insulting than to have fallen into any error through ignorance. For if you confessed that you had ascribed to the divine forms that which you had supposed and believed, your error, originating in prejudice, would not be so blameable. But now, when you believe one thing and fashion another, you both dishonour those to whom you ascribe that which you confess does not belong to them, and show your impiety in adoring that which you fashion, not that which you think really is, and which is in very truth. If asses, dogs, pigs[2] had any human wisdom and skill in contrivance, and wished to do us honour also by some kind of worship, and to show respect by dedicating statues [to us], with what rage would they inflame us, what a tempest of passion would they excite, if they determined that our images should bear and assume the fashion of their own bodies? How would they, I repeat, fill us with rage, and rouse our passions, if the founder of Rome, Romulus, were to be set up with an ass's face, the revered Pompilius with that of a dog, if under the image of a pig were written Cato's or Marcus Cicero's name? So, then, do you think that your stupidity is not laughed at by your deities, if they laugh [at all]? or, since you believe that they may be enraged, [do you think] that they are not roused, maddened to fury, and that they do not wish to be revenged for so great wrongs and insults, and to hurl on you the punishments usually dictated by chagrin, and devised by bitter hatred? How much better it had been

[1] The MS. and first four edd. read *dotis causa*—"for the sake of a dowry;" corrected as above, *dicis causa* in the later edd.

[2] This argument seems to have been suggested by the saying of Xenophanes, that the ox or lion, if possessed of man's power, would have represented, after the fashion of their own bodies, the gods they would worship.

to give to them the forms of elephants, panthers, or tigers, bulls, and horses! For what is there beautiful in man,—what, I pray you, worthy of admiration, or comely,—unless that which, some poet[1] has maintained, he possesses in common with the ape?

17. But, they say, if you are not satisfied with our opinion, do you point out, tell us yourselves, what is the Deity's form. If you wish to hear the truth, either the Deity has no form; or if he is embodied in one, we indeed know not what it is. Moreover, we think it no disgrace to be ignorant of that which we never saw; nor are we therefore prevented from disproving the opinions of others, because on this we have no opinion of our own to bring forward. For as, if the earth be said to be of glass, silver, iron, or gathered together and made from brittle clay, we cannot hesitate to maintain that this is untrue, although we do not know of what it is made; so, when the form of God is discussed, we show that it is not what you maintain, even if we are [still] less able to explain what it is.

18. What, then, some one will say, does the Deity not hear? does he not speak? does he not see what is put before him? has he not sight? He may in his own, but not in our way. But in so great a matter we cannot know the truth at all, or reach it by speculations; for these are, it is clear, in our case, baseless, deceitful, and like vain dreams. For if we said that he sees in the same way as ourselves, it follows that it should be understood that he has eyelids placed as coverings on the pupils of the eyes, that he closes them, winks, sees by rays or images, or, as is the case in all eyes, can see nothing at all without the presence of other light. So we must in like manner say of hearing, and form of speech, and utterance of words. If he hears by means of ears, these, too, [we must say,] he has, penetrated by winding paths, through which the sound may steal, bearing the meaning of the discourse; or if his words are poured forth from a mouth, that he has lips and teeth, by

---

[1] Ennius (Cic. *de Nat. Deor.* i. 35): *Simia quam similis, turpissima bestia, nobis.*

the contact and various movement of which his tongue utters sounds distinctly, and forms his voice to words.

19. If you are willing to hear our conclusions, [then learn that] we are so far from attributing bodily shape to the Deity, that we fear to ascribe to so great a being even mental graces, and the very excellences by which a few have been allowed with difficulty to distinguish themselves. For who will say that God is brave, firm, good, wise? who [will say] that he has integrity, is temperate, even that he has knowledge, understanding, forethought? that he directs towards fixed moral ends the actions on which he determines? These things are good in man; and being opposed to vices, have deserved the great reputation which they have gained. But who is so foolish, so senseless, as to say that God is great by [merely] human excellences? or that he is above all in the greatness of his name, because he is not disgraced by vice? Whatever you say, whatever in unspoken thought you imagine concerning God, passes and is corrupted into a human sense, and does not carry its own meaning, because it is spoken in the words which we use, and which are suited [only] to human affairs. There is but one thing man can be assured of regarding God's nature, to know and perceive that nothing can be revealed in human language concerning God.

20. This, then, this matter of forms and sexes, is the first affront which you, noble advocates in sooth, and pious writers, offer to your deities. But what is the next, that you represent to us[1] the gods, some as artificers, some physicians, others working in wool, as sailors,[2] players on the harp and flute, hunters, shepherds, and, as there was nothing more, rustics? And that god, he says, is a musician, and this other can divine; for the other gods cannot,[3] and do not know

---

[1] So the MS., followed by Oehler, reading *nobis*, for which all other edd. give *vobis*—"to you."

[2] Meursius would read *naccas*—"fullers," for *nautas;* but the latter term may, properly enough, be applied to the gods who watch over seamen.

[3] Or, "for the others are not gods," *i.e.* cannot be gods, as they do

how to foretell what will come to pass, owing to their want of skill and ignorance of the future. One is instructed in obstetric arts, another trained up in the science of medicine. Is each, then, powerful in his own department; and can they give no assistance, if their aid is asked, in what belongs to another? This one is eloquent in speech, and ready in linking words together; for the others are stupid, and can say nothing skilfully, if they must speak.

21. And, I ask, what reason is there, what unavoidable necessity, what occasion for the gods knowing and being acquainted with these handicrafts as though they were worthless mechanics? For, are songs sung and music played in heaven, that the nine sisters may gracefully combine and harmonize pauses and rhythms of tones? Are there on the mountains[1] of the stars, forests, woods, groves, that[2] Diana may be esteemed very mighty in hunting expeditions? Are the gods ignorant of the immediate future; and do they live and pass the time according to the lots assigned them by fate, that the inspired son of Latona may explain and declare what the morrow or the next hour bears to each? Is he himself inspired by another god, and is he urged and roused by the power of a greater divinity, so that he may be rightly said and esteemed to be divinely inspired? Are the gods liable to be seized by diseases; and is there anything by which they may be wounded and hurt, so that, when there is occasion, he[3] of Epidaurus may come to their assistance? Do they labour, do they bring forth, that Juno may soothe, and Lucina abridge the terrible pangs of childbirth? Do they engage in agriculture, or are they concerned with the duties of war, that Vulcan, the lord of fire, may form for

---

not possess the power of divination. Cf. Lact. i. 11: *Sin autem divinus non sit, ne deus quidem sit.*

[1] The MS., followed by LB. and Hild., reads *sidereis motibus*—"in the motions of the stars;" *i.e.* can these be in the stars, owing to their motion? Oehler conjectures *molibus*—"in the masses of the stars;" the other edd. read *montibus*, as above.

[2] The MS., both Roman edd., and Oehler read *habetur Diana*—"is Diana esteemed;" the other edd., *ut habeatur*, as above.

[3] *i.e.* Æsculapius.

them swords, or forge their rustic implements? Do they need to be covered with garments, that the Tritonian[1] maid may, with nice skill,[2] spin, weave cloth for them, and make[3] them tunics to suit the season, either triple-twilled, or of silken fabric? Do they make accusations and refute them, that the descendant[4] of Atlas may carry off the prize for eloquence, attained by assiduous practice?

22. You err, my opponent says, and are deceived; for the gods are not themselves artificers, but suggest these arts to ingenious men, and teach mortals what they should know, that their mode of life may be more civilised. But he who gives any instruction to the ignorant and unwilling, and strives to make him intelligently expert in some kind of work, must himself first know that which he sets the other to practise. For no one can be capable of teaching a science without knowing the rules of that which he teaches, and having grasped its method most thoroughly. The gods are, then, the first artificers; whether because they inform the minds [of men] with knowledge, as you say yourselves, or because, being immortal and unbegotten, they surpass the whole race of earth by their length of life.[5] This, then, is the question; there being no occasion for these arts among the gods, neither their necessities nor nature requiring in them any ingenuity or mechanical skill, why you should say that they are skilled,[6] one in one craft, another in another, and that individuals are pre-eminently expert[7] in particular departments in which they are distinguished by acquaintance with the several branches of science?

[1] *i.e.* Minerva.
[2] "With nice skill . . . for them," *curiose iis;* for which the MS. and first five edd. read *curiosius*—"rather skilfully."
[3] The MS. reads unintelligibly *et imponere*, for which Meursius emended *componat*, as above.
[4] Mercury, grandson of Atlas by Maia.
[5] Lit., "by the long duration of time."
[6] Lit., "skilled in notions"—*perceptionibus;* for which *præceptionibus, i.e.* "the precepts of the different arts," has been suggested in the margin of Ursinus.
[7] Lit., "and have skill (*sollertias*) in which individuals excel."

23. But you will, perhaps, say that the gods are not artificers, but that they preside over these arts, [and] have their oversight; nay, that under their care all things have been placed, which we manage and conduct, and that their providence sees to the happy and fortunate issue of these. Now this would certainly appear to be said justly, and with some probability, if all we engage in, all we do, or all we attempt in human affairs, sped as we wished and purposed. But since every day the reverse is the case, and the results of actions do not correspond to the purpose of the will, it is trifling to say that we have, set as guardians over us, gods invented by our superstitious fancy, not grasped with assured certainty. Portunus[1] gives to the sailor perfect safety in traversing the seas; but why has the raging sea cast up so many cruelly-shattered wrecks? Consus suggests to our minds courses safe and serviceable; and why does an unexpected change perpetually issue in results other than were looked for? Pales and Inuus[2] are set as guardians over the flocks and herds; why do they, with hurtful laziness,[3] not take care to avert from the herds in their summer pastures, cruel, infectious, and destructive diseases? The harlot Flora,[4] venerated in lewd sports, sees well to it that the fields blossom; and why are buds and tender plants daily nipt and destroyed by most hurtful frost? Juno presides over childbirth, and aids travailing mothers; and why are a thousand mothers every day cut off in murderous throes? Fire is under Vulcan's care, and its source is placed under his control; and why does he, very often, suffer temples and parts of cities to fall into ashes devoured by flames? The soothsayers receive the knowledge of their art from the Pythian god; and why does

---

[1] According to Oehler, Portunus (Portumnus or Palæmon—"the god who protects harbours") does not occur in the MS., which, he says, reads *per maria præstant*—"through the seas they afford;" emended as above by Ursinus, *præstat Portunus*. Oehler himself proposes *permarini*—"the sea gods afford."

[2] Pales, *i.e.* the feeding one; Inuus, otherwise Faunus and Pan.

[3] Otherwise, "from the absence of rain."

[4] So the margin of Ursinus, reading *meretrix*; but in the first four edd., LB., and Oberthür, *genetrix*—"mother," is retained from the MS.

he so often give and afford answers equivocal, doubtful, steeped in darkness and obscurity? Æsculapius presides over the duties and arts of medicine; and why cannot [men in] more kinds of disease and sickness be restored to health and soundness of body? while, on the contrary, they become worse under the hands of the physician. Mercury is occupied with [1] combats, and presides over boxing and wrestling matches; and why does he not make all invincible who are in his charge? why, when appointed to one office, does he enable some to win the victory, while he suffers others to be ridiculed for their disgraceful weakness?

24. No one, says my opponent, makes supplication to the tutelar deities, and they therefore withhold their usual favours and help. Cannot the gods, then, do good, except they receive incense and consecrated offerings?[2] and do they quit and renounce their posts, unless they see their altars anointed with the blood of cattle? And yet I thought but now that the kindness of the gods was of their own free will, and that the unlooked-for gifts of benevolence flowed unsought from them. Is, then, the King of the universe solicited by any libation or sacrifice to grant to the races of men all the comforts of life? Does the Deity not impart the sun's fertilizing warmth, and the season of night, the winds, the rains, the fruits, to all alike,—the good and the bad, the unjust and the just,[3] the free-born and the slave, the poor and the rich? For this belongs to the true and mighty God, to show kindness, unasked, to that which is weary and feeble, and always encompassed by misery of many kinds. For to grant your prayers on the offering of sacrifices, is not to bring help to those who ask it, but to sell the riches of their beneficence. We men trifle, and are foolish in so great a matter; and, forgetting what[4] God is, and the majesty of his name, asso-

---

[1] So LB., reading *cura-t*, the MS. omitting the last letter.

[2] Lit., "salted fruits," the grits mixed with salt, strewed on the victim.

[3] Supplied by Ursinus.

[4] So the edd. reading *quid*, except Hild. and Oehler, who retain the MS. *qui*—" who."

ciate with the tutelar deities whatever meanness or baseness our morbid credulity can invent.

25. Unxia, my opponent says, presides over the anointing [of door-posts]; Cinxia over the loosening of the zone; the most venerable Victa[1] and Potua attend to eating and drinking. O rare and admirable interpretation of the divine powers! would gods not have names if brides did not besmear their husbands' door-posts with greasy ointment; were it not that husbands, when now eagerly drawing near, unbind the maiden-girdle; if men did not eat and drink? Moreover, not satisfied to have subjected and involved the gods in cares so unseemly, you also ascribe to them dispositions fierce, cruel, savage, ever rejoicing in the ills and destruction of mankind.

26. We shall not here mention Laverna, goddess of thieves, the Bellonæ, Discordiæ, Furiæ; and we pass by in utter silence the unpropitious deities whom you have set up. We shall bring forward Mars himself, and the fair mother of the Desires; to one of whom you commit wars, to the other love and passionate desire. My opponent says that Mars has power over wars; whether to quell those which are raging, or to revive them when interrupted, and kindle them in time of peace? For if he calms the madness of war, why do wars rage every day? but if he is their author, we shall then say that the god, to satisfy his own inclination, involves the whole world in strife; sows the seeds of discord and variance between far-distant peoples; gathers so many thousand men from different quarters, and speedily heaps up the field with dead bodies; makes the streams flow with blood, sweeps away the most firmly-founded empires, lays cities in the dust, robs the free of their liberty, and makes them slaves; rejoices in civil strife, in the bloody death of brothers who die in conflict, and, in fine, in the dire, murderous contest of children with their fathers.

27. Now we may apply this very argument to Venus in exactly the same way. For if, as you maintain and believe, she fills men's minds with lustful thoughts, it must be held

---

[1] The MS. reads *Vita*.

in consequence that any disgrace and misdeed arising from such madness should be ascribed to the instigation of Venus. Is it, then, under compulsion of the goddess that even the noble too often betray their own reputation into the hands of worthless harlots; that the firm bonds of marriage are broken; that near relations burn with incestuous lust; that mothers have their passions madly kindled towards their children; that fathers turn to themselves their daughters' desires; that old men, bringing shame upon their grey hairs, sigh with the ardour of youth for the gratification of filthy desires; that wise and brave[1] men, losing in effeminacy the strength of their manhood, disregard the biddings of constancy; that the noose is twisted about their necks; that blazing pyres are ascended;[2] and that in different places men, leaping voluntarily, cast themselves headlong over very high and huge precipices?[3]

28. Can any man, who has accepted the first principles even of reason, be found to mar or dishonour the unchanging nature of Deity with morals so vile? to credit the gods with natures such as human kindness has often charmed away and moderated in the beasts of the field? How,[4] I ask, can it be said that the gods are far removed from any feeling of passion? that they are gentle, lovers of peace, mild? that in the completeness of their excellence they reach[5] the height of perfection, and the highest wisdom also? or, why should we pray them to avert from us misfortunes and calamities, if we find that they are themselves the authors of all the ills by which we are daily harassed? Call us impious as much as you please, contemners of religion, or atheists, you will never make us believe in gods of love and war, that there are gods to sow strife, and to disturb the mind by the stings of

---

[1] *i.e.* those who subdue their own spirits. "Constancy" is the εὐπά-θεια of the Stoics.
[2] Referring to Dido.
[3] As despairing lovers are said to have sought relief in death, by leaping from the Leucadian rock into the sea.
[4] Lit., "where, I ask, is the [assertion] that," etc.
[5] Lit., "hold."

the furies. For either they are gods in very truth, and do not do what you have related; or if[1] they do the things which you say, they are doubtless no gods [at all].

29. We might, however, even yet be able to receive from you these thoughts, most full of wicked falsehoods, if it were not that you yourselves, in bringing forward many things about the gods so inconsistent and mutually destructive, compel us to withhold our minds from assenting. For when you strive individually to excel each other in reputation for more recondite knowledge, you both overthrow the very gods in whom you believe, and replace them by others who have clearly no existence; and different men give different opinions on the same subjects,[2] and you write that those whom general consent has ever received as single persons are infinite in number. Let us, too, begin duly, then, with father Janus, whom certain of you have declared to be the world, others the year, some the sun. But if we are to believe that this is true, it follows as a consequence, that it should be understood that there never was any Janus, who, they say, being sprung from Cœlus and Hecate, reigned first in Italy, founded the town Janiculum, was the father of Fons,[3] the son-in-law of Vulturnus, the husband of Juturna; and thus you erase the name of the god to whom in all prayers you give the first place, and whom you believe to procure for you a hearing from the gods. But, again, if Janus be the year, neither thus can he be a god. For who does not know that the year is a fixed space[4] of time, and that there is nothing divine in that which is formed[5] by the duration of months and lapse of days? Now this very [argument] may, in like manner, be applied to Saturn. For if time is meant under this title, as the expounders of Grecian ideas think, so that that is regarded as Kronos,[6] which is chronos,[7] there is no such deity as Saturn. For who is so

---

[1] In the MS. these words, *aut si*, are wanting.

[2] Stewechius and Orelli would omit *rebus*, and interpret "about the same gods." Instead of *de*—"about," the MS. has *deos*.

[3] The MS. reads *fonti*, corrected by Meursius *Fontis*, as above.

[4] Lit., "circuit." [5] Lit., "finished." [6] *i.e.* the god. [7] *i.e.* time.

senseless as to say that time is a god, when it is but a certain space measured off[1] in the unending succession of eternity? And thus will be removed from the rank of the immortals that deity too, whom the men of old declared, and handed down to their posterity, to be born of father Cœlus, the progenitor of the *dii magni*, the planter of the vine, the bearer of the pruning-knife.[2]

30. But what shall we say of Jove himself, whom the wise have repeatedly asserted to be the sun, driving a winged chariot, followed by a crowd of deities;[3] some, the ether, blazing with mighty flames, and wasting fire which cannot be extinguished? Now if this is clear and certain, there is, then, according to you, no Jupiter at all; who, born of Saturn his father and Ops his mother, is reported to have been concealed in the Cretan territory, that he might escape his father's rage. But now, does not a similar mode of thought remove Juno from the list of gods? For if she is the air, as you have been wont to jest and say, repeating in reversed order the [syllables] of the Greek name,[4] there will be found no sister and spouse of almighty Jupiter, no Fluonia,[5] no Pomona, no Ossipagina, no Februtis, Populonia, Cinxia, Caprotina; and thus the invention of that name, spread abroad with a frequent but vain[6] belief, will be found to be wholly[7] useless.

31. Aristotle, a man of most powerful intellect, and distinguished for learning, as Granius tells, shows by plausible arguments that Minerva is the moon, and proves it by the authority of learned men. Others have said that this very goddess is the depth of ether, and utmost height; some [have maintained] that she is memory, whence her name even, Minerva, has arisen, as if she were some goddess of

---

[1] Lit., "the measuring of a certain space included in," etc.
[2] Cf. vi. 12.   [3] Cf. Plato, *Phædr.* st. p. 246.
[4] Lit., "the reversed order of the Greek name being repeated," *i.e.* instead of ἤ-ρα, ἀ-ήρ.
[5] The MS. gives Fluvionia.
[6] Lit., "with the frequency (or fame) of vain," etc.
[7] Lit., "very."

memory. But if this is credited, it follows that there is no daughter of Mens, no daughter of Victory, no discoverer of the Olive, born from the head of Jupiter, no [goddess] skilled in the knowledge of the arts, and in different branches of learning. Neptune, they say, has received his name and title because he covers the earth with water. If, then, by the use of this name is meant the outspread water, there is no god Neptune at all; and thus is put away, and removed [from us], the full brother of Pluto and Jupiter, armed with the iron trident, lord of the fish, great and small, king of the depths of the sea, and shaker of the trembling earth.[1]

32. Mercury, also, has been named as though he were a kind of go-between; and because conversation passes between two speakers, and is exchanged by them, that which is expressed by this name has been produced.[2] If this, then, is the case, Mercury is not the name of a god, but of speech and words exchanged [by two persons]; and in this way is blotted out and annihilated the noted Cyllenian bearer of the caduceus, born on the cold mountain top,[3] contriver of words and names, [the god] who presides over markets, and over the exchange of goods and commercial intercourse. Some of you have said that the earth is the Great Mother,[4] because it provides all things living with food; others declare that the same [earth] is Ceres, because it brings forth crops of useful fruits;[5] while some maintain that it is Vesta, because it alone in the universe is at rest, its other members being, by their constitution, ever in motion. Now if this is propounded and maintained on sure grounds, in like manner, on your interpretation, three deities have no existence: neither Ceres nor Vesta are to be reckoned in the number[6] of the gods; nor, in fine, can the mother of the gods herself, whom Nigidius thinks to have been married to Saturn, be rightly

---

[1] So Meursius emended the MS. *sali*—"sea."

[2] Lit., "the quality of this name has been adjusted."

[3] So Orelli, reading *monte vertice;* the last word, according to Oehler, not being found in the MS.

[4] *i.e.* Cybele. Cf. Lucr. ii. 991 sqq.   [5] Lit., "seeds."

[6] *Fasti*—"list," "register."

declared a goddess, if indeed these are all names of the one earth, and it alone is signified by these titles.

33. We here leave Vulcan unnoticed, to avoid prolixity; whom you all declare to be fire, with one consenting voice. [We pass by] Venus, named because [love] assails all, and Proserpina, named because plants steal gradually forth into the light,—where, again, you do away with three deities; if indeed the first is the name of an element, and does not signify a living power; the second, of a desire common to all living creatures; while the third refers to seeds rising above ground, and the upward movements[1] of growing crops. What! when you maintain that Bacchus, Apollo, the Sun, are one deity, [seemingly] increased in number by the use of three names, is not the number of the gods lessened, and their vaunted reputation overthrown, by your opinions? For if it is true that the sun is also Bacchus and Apollo, there can consequently be in the universe no Apollo or Bacchus; and thus, by yourselves, the son of Semele [and] the Pythian god are blotted out [and] set aside,—one the giver of drunken merriment, the other the destroyer of Sminthian mice.

34. Some of your learned men[2]—men, too, who do not chatter [merely] because their humour leads them—maintain that Diana, Ceres, Luna, are but one deity in triple union;[3] and that there are not three distinct persons, as there are three different names; that in all these Luna is invoked, and that the others are a series of surnames added to her name. But if this is sure, if this is certain, and the facts of the case show it to be so, again is Ceres but an empty name, and Diana: and thus the discussion is brought to this issue, that you lead and advise us to believe that she whom you maintain to be the discoverer of the earth's fruits has no existence, and Apollo is robbed of his sister, whom

---

[1] Lit., "motions."
[2] Cf. Servius ad Virg. *Georg.* i. 7: "The Stoics say that Luna, Diana, Ceres, Juno, and Proserpina are one; following whom, Virgil invoked Liber and Ceres for Sol and Luna."
[3] *Triviali*—"common," "vulgar," seems to be here used for *triplici*.

once the horned hunter[1] gazed upon as she washed her limbs from [sweat and] impurity in a pool, and paid the penalty of his curiosity.

35. Men worthy to be remembered in the study of philosophy, who have been raised by your praises to its highest place, declare, with commendable earnestness, as their conclusion, that the whole mass of the world, by whose folds we all are encompassed, covered, and upheld, is one animal[2] possessed of wisdom and reason; yet if this is a true, sure, and certain opinion,[3] they also will forthwith cease to be gods whom you set up a little ago in its parts without change of name.[4] For as one man cannot, while his body remains entire, be divided into many men; nor can many men, while they continue to be distinct and separate from each other,[5] be fused into one sentient individual: so, if the world is a single animal, and moves from the impulse of one mind, neither can it be dispersed in several deities; nor, if the gods are parts of it, can they be brought together and changed into one living creature, with unity of feeling throughout all its parts. The moon, the sun, the earth, the ether, the stars, are members and parts of the world; but if they are parts and members, they are certainly not themselves[6] living creatures; for in no thing can parts be the very thing which the whole is, or think and feel for themselves, for this cannot be effected by their own actions, without the whole creature's joining in; and this being established and settled, the whole matter comes back to this, that neither Sol, nor Luna, nor Æther, Tellus, and the rest, are gods. For they are parts of the world, not the proper names of deities; and thus it is brought about that,

---

[1] Actæon.   [2] Plato, *Timæus*, st. p. 30.

[3] Lit., "of which things, however, if the opinion," etc.

[4] *i.e.* deifying parts of the universe, and giving them, as deities, the same names as before.

[5] Lit., "the difference of their disjunction being preserved"—*multi disjunctionis differentia conservata*, suggested in the margin of Ursinus for the MS. *multitudinis junctionis d. c.*, retained in the first five edd.

[6] Lit., "of their own name."

by your disturbing and confusing all divine things, the world is set up as the sole god in the universe, while all the rest are cast aside, and that [as] having been set up vainly, uselessly, and without any reality.

36. If we sought to subvert the belief in your gods in so many ways, by so many arguments, no one would doubt that, mad with rage and fury, you would demand for us the stake, the beasts, and swords, with the other kinds of torture by which you usually appease your thirst in its intense craving for our blood. But while you yourselves put away almost the whole race of deities with a pretence of cleverness and wisdom, you do not hesitate to assert that, because of us, men suffer ill at the hands of the gods;[1] although, indeed, if it is true that they anywhere exist, and burn with anger and[2] rage, there can be no better reason for their showing anger against you,[3] than that you deny their existence, and [say] that they are not [found] in any part of the universe.

37. We are told by Mnaseas that the Muses are the daughters of Tellus and Cœlus; others declare [that they are] Jove's by his wife Memory, or Mens; some relate that they were virgins, others that they were matrons. For now we wish to touch briefly on the points where you are shown, from the difference of your opinions, to make different statements about the same thing. Ephorus, then, says that they are three[4] in number; Mnaseas, whom we mentioned, [that they are] four;[5] Myrtilus[6] brings forward seven; Crates

---

[1] Lit., "for the sake of our name, men's affairs are made harassing."

[2] Lit., "with flames of," etc.

[3] The MS., according to Crusius, reads nos—"us."

[4] Three was the most ancient number; and the names preserved by Pausanias, are Μελέτη, Ἀοιδή, Μνήμη.

[5] Cicero (de Nat. Deor. iii. 21, a passage where there is some doubt as to the reading) enumerates as the four muses, Thelxiope, Aœde, Arche, Melete.

[6] The MS. reads Murtylus. Seven are said to have been mentioned by Epicharmus,—Neilous, Tritone, Asopous, Heptapolis, Acheloïs, Tipoplous, and Rhodia.

asserts that there are eight; finally Hesiod, enriching heaven and the stars with gods, comes forward with nine names.[1]

If we are not mistaken, such want of agreement marks those who are wholly ignorant of the truth, and does not spring from the real state of the case. For if their number were clearly known, the voice of all would be the same, and the agreement of all would tend to and find issue in the same conclusion.[2]

38. How, then, can you give to religion its whole power, when you fall into error about the gods themselves? or summon us to their solemn worship, while you give us no definite information how to conceive of the deities themselves? For, to take no notice of the other[3] authors, either the first[4] makes away with and destroys six divine Muses, if they are certainly nine; or the last[5] adds six who have no existence to the three who alone really are; so that it cannot be known or understood what should be added, what taken away; and in the performance of religious rites we are in danger[6] of either worshipping that which does not exist, or passing that by which, it may be, does exist. Piso believes that the Novensiles are nine gods, set up among the Sabines at Trebia.[7] Granius thinks that they are the Muses, agreeing with Ælius; Varro teaches that they are nine,[8] because, in doing anything, [that number] is always reputed most powerful and greatest; Cornificius,[9] that they watch over the renewing of things,[10] because, by their care, all things are afresh renewed in strength, and endure; Manilius, that they

---

[1] The nine are Clio, Euterpe, Thalia, Melpomene, Terpsichore, Erato, Polymnia, Ourania, and Calliope (*Theog.* 77-79).

[2] Lit., "into the end of the same opinion."

[3] Lit., "in the middle," "intermediate."

[4] *i.e.* Ephorus.   [5] *i.e.* Hesiod.

[6] Lit., "the undertaking of religion itself is brought into the danger," etc.

[7] An Umbrian village.

[8] Lit., "that the number is nine."

[9] A grammarian who lived in the time of Augustus, not to be confounded with Cicero's correspondent.

[10] *Novitatum*.

are the nine gods to whom alone Jupiter gave power to wield his thunder.[1] Cincius declares them to be deities brought from abroad, named from their very newness, because the Romans were in the habit of sometimes individually introducing into their families the rites[2] of conquered cities, while some they publicly consecrated; and lest, from their great number, or in ignorance, any god should be passed by, all alike were briefly and compendiously invoked under one name—Novensiles.

39. There are some, besides, who assert that those who from being men became gods, are denoted by this name,—as Hercules, Romulus, Æsculapius, Liber, Æneas. These are all, as is clear, different opinions; and it cannot be, in the nature of things, that those who differ in opinion can be regarded as teachers of one truth. For if Piso's opinion is true, Ælius and Granius say what is false; if what they say is certain, Varro, with all his skill,[3] is mistaken, who substitutes things most frivolous and vain for those which really exist. If they are named Novensiles because their number is nine,[4] Cornificius is shown to stumble, who, giving them might and power not their own, makes them the divine overseers of renovation.[5] But if Cornificius is right in his belief, Cincius is found [to be] not wise, who connects with the power of the dii Novensiles the gods of conquered cities. But if they are those whom Cincius asserts [them to be], Manilius will be found to speak falsely, who comprehends those who wield another's thunder under this name.[6] But if that which Manilius holds is true and certain, they are utterly mistaken who suppose that those raised to divine honours, and deified mortals, are [thus] named because of

[1] The Etruscans held (Pliny, *H. N.* ii. 52) that nine gods could thunder, the bolts being of different kinds: the Romans so far maintained this distinction as to regard thunder during the day as sent by Jupiter, at night by Summanus.
[2] So LB., reading *relig-* for the MS. *reg-iones.*
[3] Lit., "the very skilful."
[4] Lit., "if the number nine bring on the name of," etc.
[5] Lit., "gives another's might and power to gods presiding."
[6] Lit., "the title of this name."

the novelty of their rank. But if the Novensiles are those who have deserved to be raised to the stars after passing through the life of men,[1] there are no dii Novensiles at all. For as slaves, soldiers, masters, are not names of persons comprehended under them,[2] but of offices, ranks, and duties, so, when we say that Novensiles is the name[3] of gods who by their virtues have become[4] gods from being men, it is clear and evident that no individual persons are marked out particularly, but that newness itself is named by the title Novensiles.

40. Nigidius taught that the dii Penates were Neptune and Apollo, who once, on fixed terms, girt Ilium[5] with walls. He himself again, in his sixteenth book, following Etruscan teaching, shows that there are four kinds of Penates; and that one of these pertains to Jupiter, another to Neptune, the third to the shades below, the fourth to mortal men, making some unintelligible assertion. Cæsius himself, also, following this [teaching], thinks that they are Fortune, and Ceres, the genius Jovialis,[6] and Pales, but not the female [deity] commonly received,[7] but some male attendant and steward of Jupiter. Varro thinks that they are the gods of whom we speak who are within, and in the inmost recesses of heaven, and that neither their number nor names are known. The Etruscans say that these are the *Consentes* and *Complices*,[8] and name them because they rise and fall together,

---

[1] Lit., "after they have finished the mortality of life," *i.e.* either as above, or "having endured its perishableness."

[2] Lit., "lying under."

[3] So most edd., following Gelenius, who reads *esse nomen* for the MS. *si omnes istud*.

[4] Lit., "who have deserved to," etc.

[5] The MS. reads *immortalium*, corrected in the edd. *urbem Ilium*.

[6] Supposed to be either the genius attending Jupiter; the family god as sent by him; or the chief among the genii, sometimes mentioned simply as *Genius*.

[7] Lit., "whom the commonalty receives."

[8] *Consentes* (those who are together, or agree together, *i.e.* councillors) and *Complices* (confederate, or agreeing) are said by some to be the twelve gods who composed the great council of heaven; and, in

six of them being male, and as many female, with unknown names and pitiless dispositions,[1] but they are considered the counsellors and princes of Jove supreme. There were some, too, who said that Jupiter, Juno, and Minerva were the dii Penates, without whom we cannot live and be wise, and by whom we are ruled within in reason, passion, and thought. As you see, even here, too, nothing is said harmoniously, nothing is settled with the consent of all, nor is there anything reliable on which the mind can take its stand, drawing by conjecture very near to the truth. For their opinions are so doubtful, and one supposition so discredited[2] by another, that there is either no truth in them all, or if it is uttered by any, it is not recognised amid so many different statements.

41. We can, if it is thought proper, speak briefly of the Lares also, whom the mass think to be the gods of streets and ways, because the Greeks name streets *lauræ*. In different parts of his writings, Nigidius [speaks of them] now as the guardians of houses and dwellings; now as the Curetes, who are said to have once concealed, by the clashing of cymbals,[3] the infantile cries of Jupiter; now the five Digiti Samothracii, who, the Greeks tell [us], were named Idæi Dactyli. Varro, with like hesitation, says at one time that

accordance with this, the words *una oriantur et occidant una* might be translated "rise and sit down together," *i.e.* at the council table. But then, the names and number of these are known; while Arnobius says, immediately after, that the names of the dii Consentes are not known, and has already quoted Varro, to the effect that neither names nor number are known. Schelling (*über die Gotth. v. Samothr.*, quoted by Orelli) adopts the reading (see following note), "of whom very little mention is made," *i.e.* in prayers or rites, because they are merely Jove's councillors, and exercise no power over men, and identifies them with the Samothracian Cabiri—Κάβειροι and Consentes being merely Greek and Latin renderings of the name.

[1] So the MS. and all edd. reading *miserationis parcissimæ*, except Gelenius, who reads *nationis barbarissimæ*—"of a most barbarous nation;" while Ursinus suggested *memorationis parc.*—"of whom very little mention is made,"—the reading approved by Schelling.

[2] Lit., "shaken to its foundations."

[3] *Æribus.* Cf. Lucretius, ii. 633-6.

they are the Manes,[1] and therefore the mother of the Lares was named Mania; at another time, again, he maintains that they are gods of the air, and are termed heroes; at another, following the opinion of the ancients, he says that the Lares are ghosts, as it were a kind of tutelary demon, spirits of dead [2] men.

42. It is a vast and endless task to examine each kind separately, and make it evident even from your religious books that you neither hold nor believe that there is any god concerning whom you have not [3] brought forward doubtful and inconsistent statements, expressing a thousand different beliefs. But, to be brief, and avoid prolixity,[4] it is enough to have said what has been said; it is, further, too troublesome to gather together many things into one mass, since it is made manifest and evident in different ways that you waver, and say nothing with certainty of these things which you assert. But you will perhaps say, Even if we have no personal knowledge of the Lares, Novensiles, Penates, still the very agreement of our authors proves their existence, and that such a race [5] takes rank among the celestial gods. And how can it be known whether there *is* any god, if what he is shall be wholly unknown?[6] or how can it avail even to ask for benefits, if it is not settled and determined who should be invoked at each inquiry?[7] For every one who seeks to obtain an answer from any deity, should of necessity know to whom he makes supplication, on whom he calls, from whom he asks help for the affairs and occasions of human life; especially as you yourselves declare that all the gods do not have all power, and [8] that the wrath and anger of each are appeased by different rites.

---

[1] The MS. reads *manas*, corrected as above by all edd. except Hild., who reads *Manias*.

[2] The MS. reads *effunctorum;* LB. *et funct.*, from the correction of Stewechius; Gelenius, with most of the other edd., *def.*

[3] The MS. and first ed. omit *non*. [4] Lit., "because of aversion."

[5] Lit., "the form of their race." [6] *i.e. ignorabitur et nescietur.*

[7] The MS. reads *consolationem*—"for each consolation," *i.e.* to comfort in every distress.

[8] The MS. omits *et*.

43. For if this [deity]¹ requires a black, that² a white skin; [if] sacrifice must be made to this one with veiled, to that with uncovered head;³ this one is consulted about marriages,⁴ the other relieves distresses,—may it not be of some importance whether the one or the other is Novensilis, since ignorance of the facts and confusion of persons displeases the gods, and leads necessarily to the contraction of guilt? For suppose that I myself, to avoid some inconvenience and peril, make supplication to any one of these deities, saying, Be present, be near, divine Penates, thou Apollo, and thou, O Neptune, and in your divine clemency turn away all these evils, by which I am annoyed,⁵ troubled, and tormented: will there be any hope that I shall receive help from them, if Ceres, Pales, Fortune, or the genius Jovialis,⁶ not Neptune and Apollo, shall be the dii Penates? Or if I invoked the Curetes instead of the Lares, whom some of your writers maintain to be the Digiti Samothracii, how shall I enjoy their help and favour, when I have not given them their own names, and *have* given to the others names not their own? Thus does our interest demand that we should rightly know the gods, and not hesitate or doubt about the power, the name of each; lest,⁷ if they be invoked with rites and titles not their own, they have at once their ears stopped [against our prayers], and hold us involved in guilt which may not be forgiven.

44. Wherefore, if you are assured that in the lofty palaces of heaven there dwells, there is, that multitude of deities

---

¹ The *dii inferi*.   ² The *dii superi*.
³ Saturn and Hercules were so worshipped.   ⁴ Apollo.

⁵ The MS., first five edd., and Oehler read *terreor*—" terrified;" the others *tor.*, as above, from the conjecture of Gifanius.

⁶ Cf. ch. 40, note 6. It may further be observed that the Etruscans held that the superior and inferior gods and men were linked together by a kind of intermediate beings, through whom the gods took cognizance of human affairs, without themselves descending to earth. These were divided into four classes, assigned to Tina (Jupiter), Neptune, the gods of the nether world, and men respectively.

⁷ So LB., Hild., and Oehler, reading *nomine ne*; all others *ut*, the MS. having no conjunction.

whom you specify, you should make your stand on one proposition,[1] and not, divided by different and inconsistent opinions, destroy belief in the very things which you seek to establish. If there is a Janus, let Janus be; if a Bacchus, let Bacchus be; if a Summanus,[2] let Summanus be: for this is to confide, this to hold, to be settled in the knowledge of something ascertained, not to say after the manner of the blind and erring, The Novensiles are the Muses, in truth they are the Trebian gods, nay, their number is nine, or rather, they are the protectors of cities which have been overthrown; and bring so important matters into this danger, that while you remove some, and put others in their place, it may well be doubted of them all if they anywhere exist.

[1] Lit., "it is fitting that you stand in the limits of," etc.
[2] *i.e.* Summus Manium, Pluto.

BOOK IV.

ARGUMENT.

ARNOBIUS now attacks the heathen mythology, pointing out that such deities as Piety, Concord, Safety, and the like, could only be mere abstractions (1, 2); while, as to many others, it would be difficult to suppose—especially when facts are compared with theories—that they were seriously spoken of as deities, *e.g.* Luperca, Præstana, Pantica (3), and Pellonia (4); the sinister deities (5); Lateranus, a god degraded to the kitchen (6); and others to whom were assigned obscene and trifling offices (7); and asking whether the existence of these deities depended on the things for which they cared, or the performance of the offices over which they were set, and how, if they were first in the order of existence, they could be named from things which did not then exist, and how their names were known (8). Common-sense will not allow us to believe in gods of Gain, Lust, Money, and the rest (9); and besides, we could not stop here, for if there were gods to preside over bones, honey, thresholds, we should find it impossible to deny that everywhere and for everything there are special gods (10). What proof, it is asked, do the gods give of their existence? do they appear when invoked? do they give true oracles (11)? how were they made known to men, and how could it be certain that some one did not take the place of all those supposed to be present at different rites (12)? Arnobius next goes on to point out that several deities were spoken of under one name, while, on the contrary, several names were sometimes applied to one deity (13); *e.g.* there were three Jupiters, five Suns and Mercuries, five Minervas (14), four Vulcans, three Dianas and Æsculapii, six called Hercules, and four called Venus, and others, in like manner, from which would arise much confusion (15); for if Minerva were invoked, the five might be supposed to appear, each claiming the honour of deity as her own, in which case the position of the worshipper would be one of danger and perplexity (16). The others might be similarly referred to, and this alone would make it impossible to believe in these deities (17). And if it should be said that these writings are false, it might be answered that it is only of such published statements that notice could be taken; and that, if they were discredited, this fact should be made evident; and, finally, that from them all the religious ideas of the heathen were drawn (18). In saying that a god was sprung from such a father and mother, the thought might have suggested itself, that in this there was something human, something not befitting deity (19); but, so far from this, they had added everything degrading and horrible (20). Jupiter had such an origin, they said, and the Thunderer was once a helpless infant tended by his nurse (21); and—which was even more degrading and unseemly—in turn he, too, was subject to lust and passion, even descending to intercourse with mortals (22, 23). Here, Arnobius says, would be found the cause of all the miseries of which they complained, and these, therefore, were to be laid to the account, not of the Christians, but of the heathen, for it was they who devised such hideous, absurd, and blasphemous tales about the deities, which are either utterly false, or conclusively disprove the existence of such gods (24–28). Here it might have been shown that all the gods were originally men, by referring to various historians (29); but this is not done, because the purpose of Arnobius was merely to show that it was the heathen, not the Christians, who did the gods dishonour. True worship is not ritual observance, but right thoughts; and therefore the resentment of the gods would be excited rather by the infamous tales of the heathen, than by the neglect of the Christians (30, 31); and whoever might have invented them, the great body of the people were to blame, in that they allowed it to be done, and even took pleasure in reading or hearing such stories, although they had secured not merely the great, but even private persons from libels and calumnies by the strictest laws (32–34). But not merely did they suffer things to be written with impunity which dishonoured the gods, similar plays were also acted on the stage (35); and in these the gods were even made a laughing-stock, to the great delight of crowded audiences (35, 36). And yet, though they were so open and unblushing in the insults which they offered the gods, they did not hesitate to accuse the Christians of impiety, who were not guilty in this respect at all (37). If, therefore, the gods are angry, it is not because of the Christians, but because of their own worshippers (38).

1. WE would ask you, and you above all, O Romans, lords and princes of the world, whether you think that Piety, Concord, Safety, Honour, Virtue, Happiness, and other such names, to which we see you rear[1] altars and splendid temples, have divine power, and live in heaven?[2] or, as is usual, have you classed them with the deities merely for form's sake, because we desire and wish these blessings to fall to our lot? For

---

[1] Lit., "see altars built."
[2] Lit., "in the regions of heaven."

if, while you think them empty names without any substance, you yet deify them with divine honours,[1] you will have to consider whether that is a childish frolic, or tends to bring your deities into contempt,[2] when you make equal, and add to their number vain and feigned names. But if you have loaded them with temples and couches, holding with more assurance that these, too, are deities, we pray you to teach [us in] our ignorance, by what course, in what way, Victory, Peace, Equity, and the others mentioned among the gods, can be understood to be gods, to belong to the assembly of the immortals?

2. For we (but, perhaps, you [would] rob and deprive us of common-sense) feel and perceive that none of these has divine power, or possesses a form of its own;[3] but that, [on the contrary,] they are the excellence of manhood,[4] the safety of the safe, the honour of the respected, the victory of the conqueror, the harmony of the allied, the piety of the pious, the recollection of the observant, the good fortune, indeed, of him who lives happily and without exciting any ill-feeling. Now it is easy to perceive that, in speaking thus, we speak most reasonably when we observe[5] the contrary qualities opposed [to them], misfortune, discord, forgetfulness, injustice, impiety, baseness of spirit, and unfortunate[6] weakness of body. For as these things happen accidentally, and[7] depend on human acts [and] chance moods, so their contraries, named[8] after more agreeable qualities, must be

[1] The MS. reads *tam* (corrected by the first four edd. *tamen*) *in regionibus*—"in the divine seats;" corrected, *religionibus*, as above, by Ursinus.

[2] Lit., "to the deluding of your deities."

[3] Lit., "is contained in a form of its own kind."

[4] *i.e.* manliness.

[5] Lit., "which it is easy to perceive to be said by us with the greatest truth from," etc.,—so most edd. reading *nobis;* but the MS., according to Crusius, gives *vobis*—"you," as in Orelli and Oberthür.

[6] Lit., "less auspicious."

[7] The MS., first four edd., and Elmenhorst, read *quæ*—"which;" the rest, as above, *que*.

[8] Lit., "what is opposed to them named," *nominatum;* a correction by Oehler for the MS. *nominatur*—"is named."

found in others; and from these, originating in this wise, have arisen those invented names.

3. With regard, indeed, to your bringing forward to us other bands of unknown[1] gods, we cannot determine whether you do that seriously, and from a belief in its certainty; or, [merely] playing with empty fictions, abandon yourselves to an unbridled imagination. The goddess Luperca, you tell us on the authority of Varro, was named because the fierce wolf spared the exposed children. Was that goddess, then, disclosed, not by her own power, [but] by the course of events? and was it [only] after the wild beast restrained its cruel teeth, that she both began to be herself and was marked by[2] her name? or if she was already a goddess long before the birth of Romulus and his brother, show us what was her name and title. Præstana was named, according to you, because, in throwing the javelin, Quirinus excelled all in strength;[3] and the goddess Panda, or Pantica, was named because Titus Tatius was allowed to open up and make passable a road, that he might take the Capitoline. Before these events, then, had the deities never existed? and if Romulus had not held the first place in casting the javelin, and if the Sabine king had been unable to take the Tarpeian rock, would there be no Pantica, no Præstana? And if you say that they[4] existed before that which gave rise to their name, a question which has been discussed in a preceding section,[5] tell us also what they were called.

4. Pellonia is a goddess mighty to drive back enemies. Whose enemies, say, if it is convenient? Opposing armies meet, and fighting together, hand to hand, decide the battle; and to one this side, to another that, is hostile. Whom, then, will Pellonia turn to flight, since on both sides there will be

---

[1] The MS. and both Roman edd. read *signatorum*—"sealed;" the others, except Hild., *ignotorum*, as above.

[2] Lit., "drew the meaning of her name."

[3] Lit., "excelled the might of all."

[4] MS., "that these, too," *i.e.* as well as Luperca.

[5] No such discussion occurs in the preceding part of the work, but the subject is brought forward in the end of ch. viii.

fighting? or in favour of whom will she incline, seeing that she should afford to both sides the might and services of her name? But if she indeed[1] did so, that is, if she gave her good-will and favour to both sides, she would destroy the meaning of her name, which was formed with regard to the beating back of one side. But you will perhaps say, She is goddess of the Romans only, and, being on the side of the Quirites alone, is ever ready graciously to help them.[2] We wish, indeed, that it were so, for we like the name; but it is a very doubtful matter. What! do the Romans have gods to themselves, who do not help[3] other nations? and how can they be gods, if they do not exercise their divine power impartially towards all nations everywhere? and where, I pray you, was this goddess Pellonia long ago, when the national honour was brought under the yoke at the Caudine Forks? when at the Trasimene lake the streams ran with blood? when the plains of Diomede[4] were heaped up with dead Romans? when a thousand other blows were sustained in countless disastrous battles? Was she snoring and sleeping; or, as the base often do, had she deserted to the enemies' camp?

5. The sinister deities preside over the regions on the left hand only, and are opposed to those[5] on the right. But with what reason this is said, or with what meaning, we do not understand ourselves; and we are sure that you cannot in any degree cause it to be clearly and generally understood.[6] For in the first place, indeed, the world itself has in itself neither right nor left, neither upper nor under regions, neither fore nor after [parts]. For whatever is round, and bounded on every side by the circumference[7] of a solid sphere, has no beginning, no end; where there is no end and begin-

---

[1] In the first sentence the MS. reads *utrique*, and in the second *utique*, which is reversed in most edd., as above.

[2] Lit., "ever at hand with gracious assistances."

[3] Lit., "are not of."   [4] *i.e.* the field of Cannæ.

[5] Lit., "the parts."

[6] Lit., "it cannot be brought into any light of general understanding by you."

[7] Lit., "convexity."

ning, no part can have[1] its own name and form the beginning. Therefore, when we say, This is the right, and that the left side, we do not refer to anything[2] in the world, which is everywhere very much the same, but to our own place and position, we being[3] so formed that we speak of some things as on our right hand, of others as on our left; and yet these very things which we name left, and the others [which we name] right, have in us no continuance, no fixedness, but take their forms from our sides, just as chance, and the accident of the moment, may have placed us. If I look towards the rising sun, the north pole and the north are on my left hand; and if I turn my face thither, the west will be on my left, for it will be regarded as behind the sun's back. But, again, if I turn my eyes to the region of the west, the wind and country of the south are now said to be on[4] my left; and if I am turned to this side by the necessary business of the moment, the result is, that the east is said [to be] on the left, owing to a further change of position,[5]—from which it can be very easily seen that nothing is either on our right or on our left by nature, but from position, time,[6] and according as our bodily position with regard to surrounding objects has been taken up. But in this case, by what means, in what way, will there be gods of the regions of the left, when it is clear that the same regions are at one time on the right, at another on the left? or what have the regions of the right done to the immortal gods, to deserve that they should be without any to care for them, while they have ordained that these should be fortunate, and ever [accompanied] by lucky omens?

[1] Lit., "be of."   [2] Lit., "to the state of the world."
[3] Lit., "who have been so formed, that some things are said by us," *nobis*, the reading of Oberthür and Orelli for the MS. *in nos*—"with regard to us," which is retained by the first four edd., Elm., Hild., and Oehler.
[4] *i.e. transit in vocabulum sinistri; in* being omitted in the MS. and both Roman edd.
[5] Lit., "the turning round of the body being changed."
[6] So Oehler, reading *positione, sed tempore sed*, for the MS. *positionis et temporis et*.

6. Lateranus,[1] as you say, is the god and genius of hearths, and received this name because men build that kind of fireplace of unbaked bricks. What then? if hearths were made of baked clay, or any other material whatever, will they have no genii? and will Lateranus, whoever he is, abandon his duty as guardian, because the kingdom which he possesses has not been formed of bricks of clay? And for what purpose,[2] I ask, has that god received the charge of hearths? He runs about the kitchens of men, examining and discovering with what kinds of wood the heat in their fires is produced; he gives strength[3] to earthen vessels, that they may not fly in pieces, overcome by the violence of the flames; he sees that the flavour of unspoilt dainties reaches the taste of the palate with their own pleasantness, and acts the part of a taster, and tries whether the sauces have been rightly prepared. Is not this unseemly, nay—to speak with more truth—disgraceful, impious, to introduce some pretended deities for this only, not to do them reverence with fitting honours, but to appoint them over base things, and disreputable actions?[4]

7. Does Venus Militaris, also, preside over the evil-doing[5] of camps, and the debaucheries of young men? Is there one Perfica,[6] also, of the crowd of deities, who causes those base and filthy delights to reach their end with uninterrupted pleasure? Is there also Pertunda, who presides over the marriage[7] couch? Is there also Tutunus, on whose huge members[8] and horrent *fascinus* you think it auspicious, and desire, that your matrons should be borne? But if facts

---

[1] No mention is made of this deity by any other author.
[2] Lit., "that he may do what."
[3] Lit., "[good] condition," *habitudinem*.
[4] Lit., "a disreputable act."
[5] So the MS. reading *flagitiis*, followed by all edd. except LB. and Orelli, who read *plagiis*—"kidnapping."
[6] Of this goddess, also, no other author makes mention, but the germ may be perhaps found in Lucretius (ii. 1116-7), where nature is termed *perfica*, *i.e.* "perfecting," or making all things complete.
[7] *i.e. in cubiculis præsto est virginalem scrobem effodientibus maritis.*
[8] The first five edd. read *Mutunus*. Cf. ch. 11.

themselves have very little effect in suggesting to you a right understanding of the truth, are you not able, even from the very names, to understand that these are the inventions of a most meaningless superstition, and the false gods of fancy?[1] Puta, you say, presides over the pruning of trees, Peta over prayers; Nemestrinus[2] is the god of groves; Patellana is a deity, and Patella, of whom the one has been set over things brought to light, the other over those yet to be disclosed. Nodutis is spoken of as a god, because he[3] brings that which has been sown to the knots; and she who presides over the treading out of grain, Noduterensis;[4] the goddess Upibilia[5] delivers from straying from the [right] paths; parents bereaved of their children are under the care of Orbona,—those very near to death, under that of Nœnia. Again,[6] Ossilago herself is mentioned [as she] who gives firmness and solidity to the bones of young children. Mellonia is a goddess, strong and powerful in regard to bees, caring for and guarding the sweetness of their honey.

8. Say, I pray you (that Peta, Puta, Patella may graciously favour you), if there were no[7] bees at all on the earth then, or if we men were born without bones, like some worms, would there be no goddess Mellonia;[8] or would Ossilago, who gives bones their solidity, be without a name of her own? I ask truly, and eagerly inquire whether you think that gods, or men, or bees, fruits, twigs, and the rest, are the more

---

[1] Lit., the "fancies" or "imaginations of false gods." Meursius proposed to transpose the whole of this sentence to the end of the chapter, which would give a more strictly logical arrangement; but it must be remembered that Arnobius allows himself much liberty in this respect.

[2] Of these three deities no other mention is made.

[3] The MS., LB., Hild., and Oehler read *qui*—"who brings;" the other edd., as above, *quia*.

[4] So the MS. (cf. ch. 11), first five edd., Oberth., Hild., and Oehler; the other edd. read *Nodutim Ter*.

[5] So the MS., both Roman edd., and Oehler; the other edd. reading *Vibilia*, except Hild., *Viabilia*.

[6] The MS. reads *nam*—"for," followed by all edd. except Orelli, who reads *jam* as above, and Oehler, who reads *etiam*—"also."

[7] Orelli omits *non*, following Oberthür.

[8] Both in this and the preceding chapter the MS. reads *Melonia*.

ancient in nature, time, long duration? No man will doubt that you say that the gods precede all things whatever by countless ages and generations. But if it is so, how, in the nature of things, can it be that, from things produced afterwards, they received those names which are earlier in point of time? or that the gods were charged with the care[1] of those things which were not yet produced, and assigned to be of use to men? Or were the gods long without names; and was it only after things began to spring up, and be on the earth, that you thought it right that they should be called by these names[2] and titles? And whence could you have known what name to give to each, since you were wholly ignorant of their existence; or that they possessed [any] fixed powers, seeing that you were equally unaware which of them had any power, and over what he should be placed to suit his divine might?

9. What then? you say; do you declare that these gods exist nowhere in the world, and have been created by unreal fancies? Not we alone, but truth itself, and reason, say so, and that common-sense in which all men share. For who is there who believes that there are gods of gain, and that they preside over the getting of it, seeing that it springs very often from the basest employments, and is always at the expense of others? Who believes that Libentina, who that Burnus,[3] is set over [those] lusts which wisdom bids us avoid, and which, in a thousand ways, vile and filthy wretches[4] attempt and practise? Who that Limentinus and Lima have the care of thresholds, and do the duties of their keepers, when every day we see [the thresholds] of temples and private houses destroyed and overthrown, and that the in-

---

[1] Lit., "obtained by lot the wardships."
[2] Lit., "signs."
[3] So the MS., both Roman edd., Hild., and Oehler; the others reading *Liburnum*, except Elm., who reads *-am*, while Meursius conjectured *Liberum*—"Bacchus."
[4] Lit., "shameful impurity seeks after;" *expetit* read by Gelenius, Canterus, and Oberthür, for the unintelligible MS. reading *expeditur*, retained in both Roman edd.; the others reading *experitur*—"tries."

famous approaches to stews are not without them? Who believes that the Limi[1] watch over obliquities? who that Saturnus presides over the sown crops? who that Montinus is the guardian of mountains; Murcia,[2] of the slothful? Who, finally, would believe that Money is a goddess, whom your writings declare (as though [she were] the greatest deity) to give golden rings,[3] the front seats at games and shows, honours in the greatest number, the dignity of the magistracy, and that which the indolent love most of all,— an undisturbed ease, by means of riches.

10. But if you urge that the bones, [different kinds of] honey, thresholds, and all the other things which we have either run over rapidly, or, to avoid prolixity, passed by altogether, have[4] their own peculiar guardians, we may in like manner introduce a thousand other gods, who should care for and guard innumerable things. For why should a god have charge of honey only, and not of gourds, rape, cunila, cress, figs, beets, cabbages? Why should the bones alone have found protection, and not the nails, hair, and all the other things which are placed in the hidden parts and members of which we feel ashamed, and are exposed to very many accidents, and stand more in need of the care and attention of the gods? Or if you say that these parts, too, act under the care of their own tutelar deities, there will begin to be as many gods as there are things; nor will the cause be stated why the divine care does not protect all things, if you say that there are certain things over which the deities preside, and for which they care.

[1] The MS. reads *Lemons;* Hild. and Oehler, *Limones;* the others, *Limos,* as above.

[2] The MS., LB., Hild., and Oehler read *Murcidam;* the others, *Murciam,* as above.

[3] *i.e.* equestrian rank.

[4] The MS. reading is *quid si haberet in sedibus suos,* retained by the first five edd., with the change of *-ret* into *-rent*—" what if in their seats the bones had their own peculiar guardians;" Ursinus in the margin, followed by Hild. and Oehler, reads *in se divos suos*—" if for themselves the bones had gods as their own peculiar," etc.; the other edd. reading, as above, *si habere insistitis suos.*

11. What say you, O fathers of new religions, and powers?[1] Do you cry out, and complain that these gods are dishonoured by us, and neglected with profane contempt, viz., Lateranus, the genius of hearths; Limentinus, who presides over thresholds; Pertunda,[2] Perfica, Noduterensis?[3] and do you say that things have sunk into ruin, and that the world itself has changed its laws and constitution, because we do not bow humbly in supplication to Mutunus[4] and Tutunus? But now look and see, lest while you imagine such monstrous things, and form such conceptions, you may have offended the gods who most assuredly exist, if only there are any who are worthy to bear and hold that most exalted title; and it be for no other reason that those evils, of which you speak, rage, and increase by accessions every day.[5] Why, then, some one of you will perhaps say, do you maintain[6] that it is not true that these gods exist? And, when invoked by the diviners, do they obey the call, and come when summoned by their own names, and give answers which may be relied on, to those who consult them? We can show that what is said is false, either because in the whole matter there is the greatest room for distrust, or because we, every day, see many of their pre-

---

[1] *i.e.* deities. So LB. and Orelli, reading *quid potestatum?*—" what, [O fathers] of powers." The MS. gives *qui*—" what say you, O fathers of new religions, who cry out, and complain that gods of powers are indecently dishonoured by us, and neglected with impious contempt," etc. Heraldus emends thus: " . . . fathers of great religions and powers? Do you, then, cry out," etc. "Fathers," *i.e.* those who discovered, and introduced, unknown deities and forms of worship.

[2] The MS. reads *pertus quæ-* (marked as spurious) *dam;* and, according to Hild., *naeniam* is written over the latter word.

[3] So the MS. Cf. ch. 7.

[4] The MS. is here very corrupt and imperfect,—*supplices hoc est uno procumbimus atque est utuno* (Orelli omits *ut-*), emended by Gelenius, with most edd., *supp. Mut-uno proc. atque Tutuno*, as above; Elm. and LB. merely insert *humi*—" on the ground," after *supp.*

[5] Meursius is of opinion that some words have slipped out of the text here, and that some arguments had been introduced about augury and divination.

[6] *Contendis,* not found in the MS.

dictions either prove untrue, or wrested with baffled expectation [to suit] the opposite issues.

12. But let them[1] be true, as you maintain, yet will you have us also believe[2] that Mellonia, for example, introduces herself into the entrails, or Limentinus, and that they set themselves to make known[3] what you seek to learn? Did you ever see their face, their deportment, their countenance? or can even these be seen in lungs or livers? May it not happen, may it not come to pass, although you craftily conceal it, that the one should take the other's place, deluding, mocking, deceiving, and presenting the appearance of the [deity] invoked? If the magi, [who are] so much akin to[4] soothsayers, relate that, in their incantations, pretended gods[5] steal in frequently instead of those invoked; that some of these, moreover, are spirits of grosser substance,[6] who pretend that they are gods, and delude the ignorant by their lies and deceit,—why[7] should we not similarly believe that here, too, others substitute themselves for those who are not, that they may both strengthen your superstitious beliefs, and rejoice that victims are slain in sacrifice to them under names not their own?

13. Or if you refuse to believe this on account of its novelty,[8] how can you know whether there is not some one, who comes in place of all whom you invoke, and substituting himself in all parts of the world,[9] shows to you what appear to be[10] many gods and powers? Who is that one? some one will ask. We may perhaps, being instructed by truthful authors, be able to say; but, lest you should be unwilling to

---

[1] *i.e.* the predictions.
[2] Lit., "will you make the same belief."
[3] Lit., "adapt themselves to the significations of the things which."
[4] Lit., "brothers of."   [5] *i.e.* demons.
[6] Perhaps "abilities"—*materiis*.
[7] The MS. reads *cum*—"with similar reason we may believe," instead of *cur*, as above.
[8] Lit., "novelty of the thing."
[9] Lit., "of places and divisions," *i.e.* places separated from each other.
[10] Lit., "affords to you the appearance of."

believe us, let my opponent ask the Egyptians, Persians, Indians, Chaldæans, Armenians, and all the others who have seen and become acquainted with these things in the more recondite arts. Then, indeed, you will learn who is the one god, or who the very many under him are, who pretend to be gods, and make sport of men's ignorance.

Even now we are ashamed to come to the point at which not only boys, young and pert, but grave men also, cannot restrain their laughter, and [men who have been] hardened into a strict and stern humour.[1] For while we have all heard it inculcated and taught by our teachers, that in declining [the names] of the gods there was no plural number, because the gods were individuals, and the ownership of each name could not be common to a great many;[2] you in forgetfulness, and putting away the memory of your early lessons, both give to several gods the same names, and, although you are elsewhere more moderate as to their number, have multiplied them, again, by community of names; which subject, indeed, men of keen discernment and acute intellect have before now treated both in Latin and Greek.[3] And that might have lessened [our labour,[4]] if it were not that at the same time we see that some know nothing of these books; and, also, that the discussion which we have begun, compels us to bring forward something on these subjects, although [it has been already] laid hold of, and related by those [writers].

14. Your theologians, then, and authors on unknown antiquity, say that in the universe there are three Joves, one of whom has Æther for his father; another, Cœlus;

[1] Lit., "a severity of stern manner"—*moris* for the MS. *mares*.
[2] Orelli here introduces the sentence, "For it cannot be," etc., with which this book is concluded in the MS. Cf. ch. 37, n.
[3] There can be no doubt that Arnobius here refers to Clemens Alexandrinus (Λόγος Προτρεπτικὸς πρὸς Ἕλληνας), and Cicero (*de Nat. Deor.*), from whom he borrows most freely in the following chapters, quoting them at times very closely. We shall not indicate particular references without some special reason, as it must be understood these references would be required with every statement.
[4] Lit., "given to us an abridging," *i.e.* an opportunity of abridging.

the third, Saturn, born and buried[1] in the island of Crete. [They speak of] five Suns and five Mercuries,—of whom, as they relate, the first Sun is called the son of Jupiter, and is regarded as grandson of Æther; the second [is] also Jupiter's son, and the mother who bore him Hyperiona;[2] the third the son of Vulcan, not [Vulcan] of Lemnos, but the son of the Nile; the fourth, whom Acantho bore at Rhodes in the heroic age, [was] the father of Ialysus; [while] the fifth is regarded as the son of a Scythian king and subtle Circe. Again, the first Mercury, who is said to have lusted after Proserpina,[3] is son of Cœlus, [who is] above all. Under the earth is the second, who boasts that he is Trophonius. The third [was] born of Maia, his mother, and the third Jove;[4] the fourth is the offspring of the Nile, whose name the people of Egypt dread and fear to utter. The fifth is the slayer of Argus, a fugitive and exile, and the inventor of letters in Egypt. But there are five Minervas also, they say, just as [there are five] Suns and Mercuries; the first of whom is no virgin, but the mother of Apollo by Vulcan; the second, the offspring of the Nile, who is asserted to be the Egyptian Sais; the third is descended from Saturn, and is the one who devised the use of arms; the fourth is sprung from Jove, and the Messenians name her Cory-

---

[1] Lit., "committed to sepulture and born in," etc.

[2] Arnobius repeats this statement in ch. xxii., or the name would have been regarded as corrupt, no other author making mention of such a goddess; while Cicero speaks of one Sun as born of Hyperion. It would appear, therefore, to be very probable that Arnobius, in writing from memory or otherwise, has been here in some confusion as to what Cicero did say, and thus wrote the name as we have it. It has also been proposed to read "born of Regina" (or, with Gelenius, Rhea), "and his father Hyperion," because Cybele is termed βασίλεια; for which reading there seems no good reason.—Immediately below, Ialysus is made the son, instead of, as in Cicero, the grandson of the fourth; and again, Circe is said to be mother, while Cicero speaks of her as the daughter of the fifth Sun. These variations, viewed along with the general adherence to Cicero's statements (de N. D. iii. 21 sqq.), seem to give good grounds for adopting the explanation given above

[3] i.e. in Proserpinam genitalibus adhinnivisse subrectis.

[4] Lit., "of Jupiter, but the third."

phasia; and the fifth is she who slew her lustful[1] father, Pallas.

15. And lest it should seem tedious and prolix to wish to consider each person singly, the same theologians say that there are four Vulcans and three Dianas, as many Æsculapii and five Dionysi, six Hercules and four Venuses, three sets of Castors and the same number of Muses, three winged Cupids, and four named Apollo;[2] whose fathers they mention in like manner, in like manner their mothers, [and] the places where they were born, and point out the origin and family of each. But if it is true and certain, and is told in earnest as a [well] known matter, either they are not all gods, inasmuch as there cannot be several under the same name, as we have been taught; or if there is one of them, he will not be known and recognised, because he is obscured by the confusion of very similar names. And thus it results from your own action, however unwilling you may be that it should be so, that religion is brought into difficulty and confusion, and has no fixed end to which it can turn itself, without being made the sport of equivocal illusions.

16. For suppose that it had occurred to us, moved either by suitable influence or violent fear of you,[3] to worship Minerva, for example, with the rites you deem sacred, and the usual ceremony: if, when we prepare sacrifices, and approach to make [the offerings] appointed for her on the flaming altars, all the Minervas shall fly thither, and striving for the right to that name, each demand that the offerings prepared be given to herself; what drawn-out animal shall we place among them, or to whom shall we direct the sacred offices which are our duty?[4] For the first one of whom we spoke will perhaps say, *The name Minerva is mine,*

---

[1] *i.e. incestorum appetitorem.*

[2] So Cicero (iii. 23); but Clemens (p. 24) speaks of five, and notes that a sixth had been mentioned.

[3] Lit., "by the violence of your terror." The preceding words are read in the MS. *ideo motos*—" so moved by authority," and were emended *idonea*, as in the text, by Gelenius.

[4] Lit., "to what parts shall we transfer the duties of pious service."

mine[1] *the divine majesty, who bore Apollo and Diana, and by the fruit of my womb enriched heaven with deities, and multiplied the number of the gods. Nay, Minerva, the fifth will say, are you speaking,[2] who, being a wife, and so often a mother, have lost the sanctity of spotless purity? Do you not see that in all temples*[3] *the images of Minervas are those of virgins, and that all artists refrain from giving to them the figures of matrons?*[4] *Cease, therefore, to appropriate to yourself a name not rightfully*[5] *yours. For that I am Minerva, begotten of father Pallas, the whole band of poets bear witness, who call me Pallas, the surname being derived from my father. What say you,* the second will cry on hearing this; *do you, then, bear the name of Minerva, an impudent parricide, and one defiled by the pollution of lewd lust, who, decking yourself with rouge and a harlot's arts, roused upon yourself even your father's passions, full of maddening desires? Go further, then, seek for yourself another name; for this belongs to me, whom the Nile, greatest of rivers, begot from among his flowing waters, and brought to a maiden's state from the condensing of moisture.*[6] *But if you inquire into the credibility of the matter, I too will bring as witnesses the Egyptians, in whose language I am called Neith, as Plato's* Timæus[7]

---

[1] The MS. reads *cum numen*; Rigaltius, followed by Oehler, emending, as above, *meum*; the first four edd., with Oberthür, *tum*—"then the deity [is mine];" while the rest read *cum numine*—"with the deity."

[2] So LB., Orelli, and Oehler, reading *tu tinnis* for the MS. *tutunis*.

[3] *Capitoliis*. In the Capitol were three shrines,—to Jove, Juno, and Minerva; and Roman colonies followed the mother-state's example. Hence the present general application of the term, which is found elsewhere in ecclesiastical Latin.

[4] Lit., "Nor are the forms of married persons given to these by all artists;" *nec* read in all edd. for the MS. *et*—"and of married," etc. which is opposed to the context.

[5] Lit., "not of your own right."

[6] *Concretione roris*—a strange phrase. Cf. Her. iv. 180: "They say that Minerva is the daughter of Poseidon and the Tritonian lake."

[7] St. p. 21. The MS. reads *quorum Nili lingua latonis*; the two Roman edd. merely insert *p.*, *Plat.*; Gelenius and Canterus adding *dicor*—"in whose language I am called the Nile's," *Nili* being changed into *Neith* by Elmenhorst and later edd.

attests. What, then, do we suppose will be the result? Will she indeed cease to say that she is Minerva, who is named Coryphasia, either to mark her mother, or because she sprung forth from the top of Jove's head, bearing a shield, and girt with the terrors of arms? Or [are we to suppose] that she who is third will quietly surrender the name? and not argue[1] and resist the assumption of the first [two] with such words as these, *Do you thus dare to assume the honour of my name, O Sais,[2] sprung from the mud and eddies of a stream, and formed in miry places? Or do you usurp[3] another's rank, who falsely say that you were born a goddess from the head of Jupiter, and persuade very silly men that you are reason? Does he conceive and bring forth children from his head? That the arms you bear might be forged and formed, was there even in the hollow of his head a smith's workshop? [were there] anvils, hammers, furnaces, bellows, coals, and pincers? Or if, as you maintain, it is true that you are reason, cease to claim for yourself the name which is mine; for reason, of which you speak, is not a certain form of deity, but the understanding of difficult questions.* If, then, as we have said, five Minervas should meet us when we essay to sacrifice,[4] and contending as to whose this name is, each demand that either fumigations of incense be offered to her, or sacrificial wines poured out from golden cups; by what arbiter, by what judge, shall we dispose of so great a dispute? or what examiner will there be, what umpire of so great boldness as to attempt, with such personages, either to give a just decision, or to declare their causes not founded on right? Will he not rather go home, and, keeping himself apart from such matters, think it safer to have nothing to do with them, lest he should either make enemies of the rest, by giving to one what belongs to all, or be charged with folly for yielding[5] to all what should be the property of one?

---

[1] Lit., "take account of herself."
[2] So Ursinus suggested in the margin for the MS. *si verum*.
[3] The third Minerva now addresses the fourth.
[4] Lit., "approaching the duties of religion."
[5] According to the MS. *sic*—"for so (*i.e.* as you do) yielding," etc.

17. We may say the very same things of the Mercuries, the Suns,—indeed of all the others whose numbers you increase and multiply. But it is sufficient to know from one case that the same principle applies to the rest; and, lest our prolixity should chance to weary our audience, we shall cease to deal with individuals, lest, while we accuse you of excess, we also should ourselves be exposed to the charge of excessive loquacity. What do you say, you who, by [the fear of] bodily tortures, urge us to worship the gods, and constrain us to undertake the service of your deities? We can be easily won, if only something befitting the conception of so great a race be shown to us. Show us Mercury, but [only] one; give us Bacchus, but [only] one; one Venus, and in like manner one Diana. For you will never make us believe that there are four Apollos, or three Jupiters, not even if you were to call Jove himself as witness, or make the Pythian [god] your authority.

18. But some one on the opposite side says, How do we know whether the theologians have written what is certain and well known, or set forth a wanton fiction,[1] as they thought and judged? That has nothing to do with the matter; nor does the reasonableness of your argument depend upon this,—whether the facts are as the writings of the theologians state, or are otherwise and markedly different. For to us it is enough to speak of things which come before the public; and [we need] not inquire what is true, but [only] confute and disprove that which lies open to all, and [which] men's thoughts have generally received. But if they are liars, declare yourselves what is the truth, and disclose the unassailable mystery. And how can it be done when the services of men of letters are set aside? For what is there which can be said about the immortal gods that has not reached men's thoughts from what has been written by men on these subjects?[2] Or can you relate anything yourselves

---

[1] So all the edd., though Orelli approves of *fictione* (edd. *-em*), which is, he says, the MS. reading, "set forth with wanton fiction."

[2] The MS. and earlier edd., with Hild. and Oehler, read *ex hominum de scriptis;* LB. and Orelli inserting *his* after *de*, as above.

about their rites and ceremonies, which has not been recorded in books, and made known by what authors have written? Or if you think these of no importance, let all the books be destroyed which have been composed about the gods for you by theologians, pontiffs, [and] even some devoted to the study of philosophy; nay, let us rather suppose that from the foundation of the world no man ever wrote[1] anything about the gods: we wish to find out, and desire to know, whether you can mutter or murmur in mentioning the gods,[2] or conceive those in thought to whom no idea[3] from any book gave shape in your minds. But when it is clear that you have been informed of their names and powers by the suggestions of books,[4] it is unjust to deny the reliableness of these books by whose testimony and authority you establish what you say.

19. But perhaps these things will turn out to be false, and what you say to be true. By what proof, by what evidence [will it be shown]? For since both parties are men, both those who have said the one thing and those who have said the other, and on both sides the discussion was of doubtful matters, it is arrogant to say that that is true which seems so to you, but that that which offends your feelings manifests wantonness and falsehood. By the laws of the human race, and the associations of mortality itself, when you read and hear, That god was born of this [father] and of that mother, do you not feel in your mind[5] that something is said which belongs to man, and relates to the meanness of our earthly race? Or, while you think that it is so,[6] do you conceive no anxiety lest you should in something offend the gods themselves, whoever they are, because you believe that it is owing to filthy intercourse . . . [7] that they have

---

[1] The MS. and both Roman edd. read *esse*, which is clearly corrupt; for which LB. gives *scripsisse* (misprinted *scripse*), as above.
[2] *i.e.* "speak of them at all."   [3] Lit., "an idea of no writing."
[4] Lit., "been informed by books suggesting to you," etc.
[5] Lit., "does it not touch the feeling of your mind."
[6] Ursinus would supply *eos*—"that they are so."
[7] *Atque ex seminis actu*, or *jactu*, as the edd. except Hild. read it.

reached the light they knew not of, thanks to lewdness?
For we, lest any one should chance to think that we are
ignorant of, do not know, what befits the majesty of that
name, assuredly[1] think that the gods should not know birth;
or if they are born at all, we hold and esteem that the Lord
and Prince of the universe, by ways which he knew himself,
sent them forth spotless, most pure, undefiled, ignorant of
sexual pollution,[2] and brought to the full perfection of their
natures as soon as they were begotten.[3]

20. But you, on the contrary, forgetting how great[4] their
dignity and grandeur are, associate with them a birth,[5] and
impute [to them] a descent,[5] which men of at all refined
feelings regard as at once execrable and terrible. From
Ops, you say, his mother, and from his father Saturn,
Diespiter was born with his brothers. Do the gods, then,
have wives; and, the matches having been previously planned,
do they become subject to the bonds of marriage? Do they
take upon themselves[6] the engagements of the bridal couch
by prescription, by the cake of spelt, and by a pretended
sale?[7] Have they their mistresses,[8] their promised wives,
their betrothed brides, on settled conditions? And what
do we say about their marriages, too, when indeed you say
that some celebrated their nuptials, and entertained joyous
throngs, and that the goddesses sported at these; and that
[some] threw all things into utter confusion with dissensions
because they had no share in [singing] the Fescennine

---

[1] The MS. reads *dignitati-s aut;* corrected, as above, *d. sane*, in the first five edd., Oberthür, and Orelli.

[2] *Quæ sit fœditas ista cocundi.*

[3] Lit., "as far as to themselves, their first generation being completed."

[4] Lit., "forgetting the so great majesty and sublimity."

[5] Both plural.

[6] The MS., first four edd., and Oberthür read *conducunt*—"unite;" for which the rest read *condic-unt*, as above.

[7] *i.e. usu, farre, coemptione.*

[8] The word here translated mistresses, *speratas*, is used of maidens loved, but not yet asked in marriage.

verses, and occasioned danger and destruction[1] to the next generation of men?[2]

21. But perhaps this foul pollution may be less apparent in the rest. Did, then, the ruler of the heavens, the father of gods and men, who, by the motion of his eyebrow, and by his nod, shakes the whole heavens and makes them tremble, —did he find his origin in man and woman? And unless both sexes abandoned [themselves] to degrading pleasures in sensual embraces,[3] would there be no Jupiter, greatest of all; and even to this time would the divinities have no king, and heaven stand without its lord? And why do we marvel that you say Jove sprang from a woman's womb, seeing that your authors relate that he both had a nurse, and in the next place maintained the life given to him by nourishment [drawn from] a foreign[4] breast? What say you, O men? Did, then, shall I repeat, [the god] who makes the thunder crash, lightens and hurls the thunderbolt, and draws together terrible clouds, drink in the streams of the breast, wail as an infant, creep about, and, that he might [be persuaded to] cease his crying most foolishly protracted, was he made silent by the noise of rattles,[5] and put to sleep lying in a very soft cradle, and lulled with broken words? O devout assertion [of the existence] of gods, pointing out and declaring the venerable majesty of their awful grandeur! Is it thus in your opinion, I ask, that the exalted powers[6] of heaven are produced? do your gods come forth to the light by modes of birth such as these, by which asses, pigs, dogs, by which the whole of this unclean herd[7] of earthly beasts is conceived and begotten?

22. And, not content to have ascribed these carnal unions to the venerable Saturn,[8] you affirm that the king of the

[1] Lit., "dangers of destructions."
[2] Instead of "occasioned," *sevisse*, which the later editions give, the MS. and first four edd. read *sævisse*—"that danger and destruction raged against," etc.
[3] *Copulatis corporibus.*
[4] *i.e.* not his mother's, but the dug of the goat Amalthea.
[5] Lit., "rattles heard."   [6] Lit., "the eminence of the powers."
[7] Lit., "inundation."   [8] Lit., "Saturnian gravity."

world himself begot children even more shamefully than he was himself born and begotten. Of Hyperiona,[1] as his mother, you say, and Jupiter, who wields the thunderbolt, was born the golden and blazing Sun; of Latona and the same, the Delian archer, and Diana,[2] who rouses the woods; of Leda and the same,[3] those named in Greek Dioscori; of Alcmena and the same, the Theban Hercules, whom his club and hide defended; of him and Semele, Liber, who is named Bromius, and was born a second time from his father's thigh; of him, again, and Maia, Mercury, eloquent in speech, and bearer of the harmless snakes. Can any greater insult be put upon your Jupiter, or is there anything else which will destroy and ruin the reputation of the chief of the gods, further than that you believe him to have been at times overcome by vicious pleasures, and to have glowed with the passion of a heart roused to lust after women? And what had the Saturnian king to do with strange nuptials? Did Juno not suffice him; and could he not stay the force of his desires on the queen of the deities, although so great excellence graced her, [such] beauty, majesty of countenance, and snowy and marble whiteness of arms? Or did he, not content with one wife, taking pleasure in concubines, mistresses, and courtezans, a lustful god, show[4] his incontinence in all directions, as is the custom with dissolute[5] youths; and in old age, after intercourse with numberless persons, did

---

[1] Cf. ch. 14, note 2.

[2] It is worth while to compare this passage with ch. 16. Here Arnobius makes Latona the mother of Apollo and Diana, in accordance with the common legend; but there he represents the first Minerva as claiming them as her children.

[3] In the MS. there is here an evident blunder on the part of the copyist, who has inserted the preceding line ("the archer Apollo, and of the woods") after "the same." Omitting these words, the MS. reading is literally, " the name in Greek is to the Dioscori." Before "the name" some word is pretty generally supposed to have been lost, some conjecturing "to whom;" others (among them Orelli, following Salmasius) "Castores." But it is evidently not really necessary to supplement the text.

[4] Lit., "scatter."

[5] Orelli reads, with the MS., LB., and Hild., *babecali*, which he interprets *belli*, *i.e.* "handsome."

he renew his eagerness for pleasures [now] losing their zest? What say you, profane ones; or what vile thoughts do you fashion about your Jove? Do you not, then, observe, do you not see with what disgrace you brand him? of what wrong-doing you make him the author? or what stains of vice, how great infamy you heap upon him?

23. Men, though prone to lust, and inclined, through weakness of character, to [yield to] the allurements of sensual pleasures, still punish adultery by the laws, and visit with the penalty of death those whom they find to have possessed themselves of others' rights by forcing the marriage-bed. The greatest of kings, [however, you tell us,] did not know how vile, how infamous the person of the seducer and adulterer was; and he who, as is said, examines our merits and demerits, did not, owing to the reasonings of his abandoned heart, see what was the fitting course [for him] to resolve on. But this misconduct might perhaps be endured, if you were to conjoin him with persons at least his equals, and [if] he were made by you the paramour of the immortal goddesses. But what beauty, what grace was there, I ask you, in human bodies, which could move, which could turn to it[1] the eyes of Jupiter? Skin, entrails, phlegm, and all that filthy mass placed under the coverings of the intestines, which not Lynceus only with his searching gaze can shudder at, but any other also can [be made to] turn from even by merely thinking. O wonderful reward of guilt, O fitting and precious joy, for which Jupiter, the greatest, should become a swan, and a bull, and beget white eggs!

24. If you will open your minds' eyes, and see the real[2] truth without gratifying any private end, you will find that the causes of all the miseries by which, as you say, the human race has long been afflicted, flow from such beliefs which you held in former times about your gods; and which you have refused to amend, although the truth was placed before your eyes. For what about them, pray, have we indeed

---

[1] MS. and first five edd. read *inde*—"thence;" the others *in se*, as above.

[2] Orelli, without receiving into the text, approves of the reading of Stewechius, *promptam*, "evident," for the MS. *propriam*.

ever either imagined which was unbecoming, or put forth in shameful writings that the troubles which assail men and the loss of the blessings of life[1] should be used to excite a prejudice against us? Do we say that certain gods were produced from eggs,[2] like storks and pigeons? [Do we say] that the radiant Cytherean Venus grew up, having taken form from the sea's foam and the severed genitals of Cœlus? that Saturn was thrown into chains for parricide, and relieved from their weight only on his own days?[3] that Jupiter was saved from death[4] by the services of the Curetes? that he drove his father from the seat of power, and by force and fraud possessed a sovereignty not his own? Do we say that his aged sire, when driven out, concealed himself in the territories of the Itali, and gave his name as a gift to Latium,[5] because he had been [there] protected from his son? Do we say that Jupiter himself incestuously married his sister? or, instead of pork, breakfasted in ignorance upon the son of Lycaon, when invited to his table? that Vulcan, limping on one foot, wrought as a smith in the island of Lemnos? that Æsculapius was transfixed by a thunderbolt because of his greed and avarice, as the Bœotian Pindar[6] sings? that Apollo, having become rich, by his ambiguous responses, deceived the very kings by whose treasures and gifts he had been enriched? Did we declare that Mercury was a thief? that Laverna is [so] also, and along with him presides over secret frauds? Is the writer Myrtilus one of us, who declares that the Muses were the handmaids of Megalcon,[7] daughter of Macarus?[8]

---

[1] Lit., "the benefits diminished by which it is lived."

[2] The MS. reads *ex Jovis;* the first five edd. *Jove*—"from Jove," which is altogether out of place; the others, as above, *ex ovis.* Cf. i. 36.

[3] The MS. reads *et ablui diebus tantis . . . elevari;* LB., Hild., and Oehler, *statis* or *statutis . . . et levari*—"and was loosed and released on fixed days;" Elm., Oberthür, and Orelli receive the conjecture of Ursinus, *et suis diebus tantum . . . rel.,* as above.

[4] Cf. iii. 41.

[5] *i.e.* hiding-place. Virg. *Æn.* viii. 322: *Quoniam latuisset tutus in oris.*

[6] *Pyth.* iii. 102 sq.   [7] MS. *Meglac.*

[8] The MS. and most edd. give *filias,* making the Muses daughters of

25. Did we say[1] that Venus was a courtezan, deified by a Cyprian king named Cinyras? Who reported that the palladium was formed from the remains of Pelops? Was it not you? Who that Mars was Spartanus? was it not your writer Epicharmus? Who that he was born within the confines of Thrace? was it not Sophocles the Athenian, with the assent of all his spectators? Who [that he was born] in Arcadia? was it not you? Who that he was kept a prisoner for thirteen months?[2] was it not the son of the river Meles? Who [said] that dogs were sacrificed to him by the Carians, asses by the Scythians? was it not Apollodorus especially, along with the rest? Who that in wronging another's marriage couch, he was caught entangled in snares? was it not your writings, your tragedies? Did we ever write that the gods for hire endured slavery, as Hercules at Sardis[3] for lust and wantonness; as the Delian Apollo, [who served] Admetus, as Jove's brother, [who served] the Trojan Laomedon, whom the Pythian also [served], but with his uncle; as Minerva, who gives light, and trims the lamps to secret lovers? Is not he one of your poets, who represented Mars and Venus as wounded by men's hands? Is not Panyassis

Macarus; but Orelli, Hild., and Oehler adopt, as above, the reading of Canterus, *filiæ*, in accordance with Clem. Alex.

[1] So the MS. reading *numquid dictatum*, which would refer this sentence to the end of the last chapter. Gelenius, with Canth., Oberth., and Orelli, reads *quis ditatam*, and joins with the following sentence thus: "Who related that Venus, a courtezan enriched by C., was deified...? who that the palladium," etc. Cf. v. 19.

[2] The MS. reads *quis mensibus in Arcadia tribus et decem vinctum*—"Who that he was bound thirteen months in Arcadia? was it not the son," etc. To which there are these two objections,—that Homer never says so; and that Clemens Alexandrinus (*Protrept.* p. 25), from whom Arnobius here seems to draw, speaks of Homer as saying only that Mars was so bound, without referring to Arcadia. The MS. reading may have arisen from carelessness on the part of Arnobius in quoting (cf. ch. 14, n. 2), or may be a corruption of the copyists. The reading translated is an emendation by Jortin, adopted by Orelli.

[3] *Sardibus*,—a conjecture of Ursinus, adopted by LB., Hild., and Oehler for the MS. *sordibus;* for which the others read *sordidi*—" for the sake of base lust."

one of you, who relates that father Dis and queenly Juno were wounded by Hercules? Do not the writings of your Polemo say that Pallas[1] was slain,[2] covered with her own blood, overwhelmed by Ornytus? Does not Sosibius declare that Hercules himself was afflicted by the wound and pain he suffered at the hands of Hipocoon's children? Is it related at our instance that Jupiter was committed to the grave in the island of Crete? Do we say that the brothers,[3] who were united in their cradle, were buried in the territories of Sparta and Lacedæmon? Is the author of our number, who is termed Patrocles the Thurian in the titles of his writings, who relates that the tomb and remains of Saturn are found[4] in Sicily? Is Plutarch of Chæronea[5] esteemed one of us, who said that Hercules was reduced to ashes on the top of Mount Œta, after his loss of strength through epilepsy?

26. But what shall I say of the desires with which it is written in your books, and contained in your writers, that the holy immortals lusted after women? For is it by us that the king of the sea is asserted in the heat of maddened passion to have robbed of their virgin purity Amphitrite,[6] Hippothoe, Amymone, Menalippe, Alope?[7] that the spotless Apollo, Latona's son, most chaste and pure, with the passions of a breast not governed by reason, desired Arsinoe, Æthusa, Hypsipyle, Marpessa, Zeuxippe, and Prothoe, Daphne, and Sterope?[6] Is it shown in our poems that the aged Saturn, already long covered with grey hair, and now cooled by weight of years, being taken by his wife in adultery, put on the form of one of the lower animals, and neighing [loudly], escaped in the shape of a beast? Do you not accuse Jupiter

---

[1] Lit., "the masculine one."
[2] As this seems rather extravagant when said of one of the immortals, *læsam*, "hurt," has been proposed by Meursius.
[3] Castor and Pollux. [4] Lit., "contained."
[5] The MS. reads *Hieronymus Pl.*—"is Hier., is Pl.," while Clem. Alex. mentions only "Hieronymus the philosopher."
[6] These names are all in the plural in the original.
[7] So LB. and Orelli, reading *Alopas*, from Clem. Alex., for the MS. *Alcyonas*.

himself of having assumed countless forms, and concealed by mean deceptions the ardour of his wanton lust? Have we ever written that he obtained his desires by deceit, at one time changing into gold, at another into a sportive satyr; into a serpent, a bird, a bull; and, to pass beyond all limits of disgrace, into a little ant, that he might, forsooth, make Clitor's daughter the mother of Myrmidon, in Thessaly? Who represented him as having watched over Alcmena for nine nights without ceasing? was it not you?—that he indolently abandoned himself to his lusts, forsaking his post in heaven? was it not you? And, indeed, you ascribe[1] [to him] no mean favours; since, in your opinion, the god Hercules was born to exceed and surpass in such matters his father's powers. He in nine nights begot[2] with difficulty one son; but Hercules, a holy god, in one night taught the fifty daughters of Thestius at once to lay aside their virginal title, and to bear a mother's burden. Moreover, not content to have ascribed to the gods love of women, do you also say that they lusted after men? Some one loves Hylas; another is engaged with Hyacinthus; that one burns with desire for Pelops; this one sighs more ardently for Chrysippus; Catamitus is carried off to be a favourite and cup-bearer; and Fabius, that he may be called Jove's darling, is branded on the soft parts, and marked in the hinder.

27. But among you, is it only the males who love; and has the female sex preserved its purity?[3] Is it not proved in your books that Tithonus was loved by Aurora; that Luna lusted after Endymion; the Nereid after Æacus; Thetis after Achilles' father; Proserpina after Adonis; her mother, Ceres, after some rustic Jasion, and afterwards Vulcan, Phaeton,[4] Mars; Venus herself, the mother of Æneas, and founder of the Roman power, to marry Anchises?

---

[1] Lit., "you add."

[2] In the original, somewhat at large—*unam potuit prolem extundere, concinnare, compingere.*

[3] All edd. read this without mark of interrogation.

[4] The MS. reads *Phætontem*: for which, both here and in Clem., Potter proposed *Phaonem*, because no such amour is mentioned elsewhere.

While, therefore, you accuse, without making [any] exception, not one only by name, but the whole of the gods alike, in whose existence you believe, of such acts of extraordinary shamefulness and baseness, do you dare, without violation of modesty, to say either that we are impious, or that you are pious, although they receive from you much greater occasion for offence on account of all the shameful acts which you heap up to their reproach, than in connection with the service and duties required by their majesty, honour, and worship? For either all these things are false which you bring forward about them individually, lessening their credit and reputation; and it is [in that case] a matter quite deserving, that the gods should utterly destroy the race of men; or if they are true and certain, and perceived without any reasons for doubt, it comes to this issue, that, however unwilling you may be, we believe them to be not of heavenly, but of earthly birth.

28. For where there are weddings, marriages, births, nurses, arts,[1] and weaknesses; where there is liberty and slavery; where there are wounds, slaughter, and [shedding of] blood; where there are lusts, desires, sensual pleasures; where there is every mental passion arising from disgusting emotions,—there must of necessity be nothing godlike there; nor can that cleave to a superior nature which belongs to a fleeting race, and to the frailty of earth. For who, if only he recognises and perceives what the nature of that power is, can believe either that a deity had the generative members, and was deprived of them by a very base operation; or that he at one time cut off the children sprung from himself, and was punished by suffering imprisonment; or that he, in a way, made civil war upon his father, and deprived him of the right of governing; or that he, filled with fear of one younger when overcome, turned to flight, and hid in remote solitudes, like a fugitive and exile? Who, I say, can believe

---

[1] *i.e.* either the arts which belong to each god (cf. the words in ii. 18: "these [arts] are not the gifts of science, but the discoveries of necessity"), or, referring to the words immediately preceding, obstetric arts.

that the deity reclined at men's tables, was troubled on account of his avarice, deceived his suppliants by an ambiguous reply, excelled in the tricks of thieves, committed adultery, acted as a slave, was wounded, and in love, and submitted to the seduction of impure desires in all the forms of lust? But yet you declare all these things both were, and are, in your gods; and you pass by no form of vice, wickedness, error, without bringing it forward, in the wantonness of your fancies, to the reproach of the gods. You must, therefore, either seek out other gods, to whom all these [reproaches] shall not apply, for they are a human and earthly race to whom they apply; or if there are only these whose names and character you have declared, by your beliefs you do away with them: for all the things of which you speak relate to men.

29. And here, indeed, we can show that all those whom you represent to us as and call gods, were [but] men, by quoting either Euhemerus of Acragas,[1] whose books were translated by Ennius into Latin that all might be thoroughly acquainted [with them]; or Nicanor[2] the Cyprian; or the Pellaean Leon; or Theodorus of Cyrene; or Hippo and Diagoras of Melos; or a thousand other writers, who have minutely, industriously, and carefully[3] brought secret things to light with noble candour. We may, I repeat, at pleasure, declare both the acts of Jupiter, and the wars of Minerva and the virgin[4] Diana; by what stratagems Liber strove to make himself master of the Indian empire; what was the condition, the duty, the gain[5] of Venus; to whom the great mother was bound in marriage; what hope, what joy was aroused in her by the comely Attis; whence [came] the Egyptian Serapis and Isis, or for what reasons their very names[6] were formed.

[1] Lit., "Euhemerus being opened."

[2] So Elm. and Orelli, reading *Nicanore* for the MS. *Nicagora*, retained by all other edd.

[3] Lit., "with the care of scrupulous diligence."

[4] Meursius would join *virginis* to Minerva, thinking it an allusion to her title Παρθένος.

[5] These terms are employed of hetærœ.

[6] Lit., "the title itself of their names was."

30. But in the discussion which we at present maintain, we do not undertake this trouble or service, to show and declare who all these were. [But] this is what we proposed to ourselves, that as you call us impious and irreligious, [and,] on the other hand, maintain that you are pious and serve the gods, we should prove and make manifest that by no men are they treated with less respect than by you. But if it is proved by the very insults that it is so, it must, as a consequence, be understood that it is you who rouse the gods to fierce and terrible rage, because you either listen to or believe, or yourselves invent about them, stories so degrading. For it is not he who is anxiously thinking of religious rites,[1] and slays spotless victims, who gives piles of incense to be burned with fire, not he must be thought to worship the deities, or alone discharge the duties of religion. True worship is in the heart, and a belief worthy of the gods; nor does it at all avail to bring blood and gore, if you believe about them things which are not only far remote from and unlike their nature, but even to some extent stain and disgrace both their dignity and virtue.

31. We wish, then, to question you, and invite you to answer a short question, Whether you think it a greater offence to sacrifice to them no victims, because you think that so great a being neither wishes nor desires these; or, with foul beliefs, to hold opinions about them so degrading, that they might rouse any one's spirit to a mad desire for revenge? If the relative importance of the matters be weighed, you will find no judge so prejudiced as not to believe it a greater crime to defame by manifest insults any one's reputation, than to treat it with silent neglect. For this, perhaps, may be held and believed from deference to reason; [but] the other course manifests an impious spirit, and a blindness despaired of in fiction. If in your ceremonies and rites neglected sacrifices and expiatory offerings may be demanded, guilt is said to have been contracted; if by a momentary

---

[1] *Qui sollicite relegit.* *Relegit* is here used by Arnobius to denote the root of *religio*, and has therefore some such meaning as that given above. Cf. Cicero, *de Nat. Deorum*, ii. 28.

forgetfulness[1] any one has erred either in speaking or in pouring wine;[2] or again,[3] if at the solemn games and sacred races the dancer has halted, or the musician suddenly become silent,—you all cry out immediately that something has been done contrary to the sacredness of the ceremonies; or if the boy termed patrimus let go the thong in ignorance,[4] or could not hold [to] the earth:[5] and [yet] do you dare to deny that the gods are ever being wronged by you in sins so grievous, while you confess yourselves that, in less matters, they are often angry, to the national ruin?

32. But all these things, they say, are the fictions of poets, and games arranged for pleasure. It is not credible, indeed, that men by no means thoughtless, who sought to trace out the character of the remotest antiquity, either did not[6] insert in their poems the fables which survived in men's minds[7] and common conversation;[8] or that they would have assumed to themselves so great licence as to foolishly feign what was almost sheer madness, and might give them reason to be afraid of the gods, and bring them into danger with men. But let us grant that the poets are, as you say, the inventors and authors of tales so disgraceful; you are not, however, even thus free from the guilt of dishonouring the gods, who either are remiss in punishing such offences, or have not, by passing laws, and by severity of punishments, opposed such

[1] Lit., "an error of inadvertence."
[2] Lit., "with the sacrificial bowl."
[3] So the MS., both Roman edd., Elm., Hild., and Oehler, reading *rursus;* the others *in cursu*—"in the course."
[4] *Patrimus, i.e.* one whose father is alive, is probably used loosely for *patrimus et matrimus,* to denote one both of whose parents were alive, who was therefore eligible for certain religious services.
[5] So the MS. reading *terram tenere,* for which Hild. would read *tensam,* denoting the car on which were borne the images of the gods, the thongs or reins of which were held by the *patrimus et matrimus;* Lipsius, *siserram,* the sacrificial victim. The reading of the text has been explained as meaning to touch the ground with one's hands; but the general meaning is clear enough,—that it was unlucky if the boy made a slip, either with hands or feet.
[6] Oberthür and Orelli omit *non.* [7] Lit., "notions."
[8] Lit., "placed in their ears."

indiscretion, and determined[1] that no man should henceforth say that which tended to the dishonour,[2] or was unworthy of the glory of the gods.[3] For whoever allows the wrongdoer to sin, strengthens his audacity; and it is more insulting to brand and mark any one with false accusations, than to bring forward and upbraid their real offences. For to be called what you are, and what you feel yourself to be, is less offensive, because [your resentment] is checked by the evidence supplied against you on privately reviewing your life;[4] but that wounds very keenly which brands the innocent, and defames a man's honourable name and reputation.

33. Your gods, it is recorded, dine on celestial couches, and in golden chambers, drink, and are at last soothed by the music of the lyre, and singing. You fit them with ears not easily wearied;[5] and do not think it unseemly to assign to the gods the pleasures by which earthly bodies are supported, and which are sought after by ears enervated by the frivolity of an unmanly spirit. Some of them are brought forward in the character of lovers, destroyers of purity, to commit shameful and degrading deeds not only with women, but with men also. You take no care as to what is said about matters of so much importance, nor do you check, by any fear of chastisement at least, the recklessness of your wanton literature; others, through madness and frenzy, bereave themselves, and by the slaughter of their own relatives cover themselves with blood, just as though it were that of an enemy. You wonder at these loftily expressed impieties; and that which it was fitting should be subjected to all punishments, you extol with praise that spurs them on, so as to rouse their recklessness to greater vehemence. They mourn over the wounds of their bereavement, and with unseemly

---

[1] Lit., "and it has [not] been established by you,"—a very abrupt transition in the structure of the sentence.

[2] Lit., "which was very near to disgrace."

[3] So the margin of Ursinus, followed by later edd., prefixing *d* before the MS. *-corum*.

[4] Lit., "has less bite, being weakened by the testimony of silent reviewing," *recognitionis*.

[5] Lit., "most enduring."

wailings accuse the cruel fates; you are astonished at the force of their eloquence, carefully study [and] commit to memory that which should have been wholly put away from human society,[1] and are solicitous that it should not perish through any forgetfulness. They are spoken of as being wounded, maltreated, making war upon each other with hot and furious contests; you enjoy the description; and, to enable you to defend so great daring in the writers, pretend that these things are allegories, and contain the principles of natural science.

34. But why do I complain that you have disregarded the insults[2] offered to the other deities? That very Jupiter, whose name you should not have spoken without fear and trembling over your whole body, is described as confessing his faults when overcome by love[3] of his wife, and, hardened in shamelessness, making known, as if he were mad and ignorant,[4] the mistresses he preferred to his spouse, the concubines he preferred to his wife; you say that those who have uttered so marvellous things, are chiefs and kings among poets endowed with godlike genius, that they are persons most holy; and so utterly have you lost sight of your duty in the matters of religion which you bring forward, that words are of more importance, in your opinion, than the profaned majesty of the immortals. So then, if only you felt any fear of the gods, or believed with confident and unhesitating assurance that they existed at all, should you not, by bills, by popular votes, by fear of the senate's decrees, have hindered, prevented, [and] forbidden any one to speak at random of the gods otherwise than in a pious manner?[5] Nor have they obtained this honour even at your hands, that you should repel insults offered to them by the same laws by

---

[1] *Coetu.* The MS. and most edd. read *coalitu,*—a word not occurring elsewhere; which Gesner would explain, "put away that it may not be established among men," the sense being the same in either case.

[2] Lit., "complain of the neglected insults of the other gods."

[3] Lit., "as a lover by." Cf. Homer, *Il.* 14, 312.

[4] *i.e.* of himself.

[5] Lit., "except that which was full of religion."

which you ward them off from yourselves. They are accused of treason among you who have whispered any evil about your kings. To degrade a magistrate, or use insulting language to a senator, you have made by decree [a crime], followed by the severest punishment. To write a satirical poem, by which a slur is cast upon the reputation and character of another, you determined, by the decrees of the decemvirs, should not go unpunished; and that no one might assail your ears with too wanton abuse, you established formulæ[1] for severe affronts. With you only the gods are unhonoured, contemptible, vile; against whom you allow any one liberty to say what he will, to accuse them of the deeds of baseness which his lust has invented and devised. And [yet] you do not blush to raise against us the charge of want of regard for deities so infamous, although it is much better to disbelieve the existence of the gods than to think that they are such, and of such repute.

35. But is it only poets whom you have thought proper[2] to allow to invent unseemly tales about the gods, and to turn them shamefully into sport? What do your pantomimists, the actors, that crowd of mimics and adulterers?[3] Do they[4] not abuse your gods to make to themselves gain, and [do not the others][5] find enticing pleasures in[6] the wrongs and insults offered to the gods? At the public games, too, the colleges of all the priests and magistrates take their places, the chief Pontiffs, and the chief priests of the curiæ; the Quindecemviri take their places, [crowned] with wreaths of laurel, and the flamines diales with their mitres; the augurs take their places, who disclose the divine mind and will; and the chaste maidens also, who cherish and guard the ever burning fire; the whole people and the senate take their places; the

---

[1] *i.e.* according to which such offences should be punished.
[2] Lit., "have willed."
[3] Lit., "full-grown race," *exoleti*, a word frequently used, as here, *sensu obscœno*.
[4] *i.e.* the actors, etc.
[5] *i.e.* the crowd of adulterers, as Orelli suggests.
[6] Lit., "draw enticements of pleasures from."

fathers who have done service as consuls, princes next to the gods, and most worthy of reverence; and, shameful to say, Venus, the mother of the race of Mars, and parent of the imperial people, is represented by gestures as in love,[1] and is delineated with shameless mimicry as raving like a Bacchanal, with all the passions of a vile harlot.[2] The Great Mother, too, adorned with her sacred fillets, is represented by dancing; and that Pessinuntic Dindymene[3] is, to the dishonour of her age, represented as with shameful desire using passionate gestures in the embrace of a herdsman; and also in the Trachiniæ of Sophocles,[4] that son of Jupiter, Hercules, entangled in the toils of a death-fraught garment, is exhibited uttering piteous cries, overcome by his violent suffering, and at last wasting away and being consumed, as his intestines soften and are dissolved.[5] But in [these] tales even the Supreme Ruler of the heavens himself is brought forward, without any reverence for his name and majesty, as acting the part of an adulterer, and changing his countenance for purposes of seduction, in order that he might by guile rob of their chastity matrons, who were the wives of others, and putting on the appearance of their husbands, by assuming the form of another.

36. But this crime is not enough: the persons of the most sacred gods are mixed up with farces also, and scurrilous plays. And that the idle onlookers may be excited to laughter and jollity, the deities are hit at in jocular quips, the spectators shout and rise up, the whole pit resounds with the clapping of hands and applause. And to the debauched scoffers[6] at the gods gifts and presents are ordained, ease, freedom from public burdens, exemption and relief, together with triumphal

[1] Or, "Venus, the mother ... and loving parent," etc.
[2] Lit., "of meretricious vileness."
[3] *i.e.* Cybele, to whom Mount Dindymus in Mysia was sacred, whose rites, however, were celebrated at Pessinus also, a very ancient city of Galatia.
[4] MS. *Sofocles*, corrected in LB. *Sophocles.* Cf. Trach. 1022 sqq.
[5] Lit., "towards (*in*) the last [of the] wasting consumed by the softening of his bowels flowing apart."
[6] Lit., "debauched and scoffers."

garlands,—a crime for which no amends can be made by any apologies. And after this do you dare to wonder whence these ills come with which the human race is deluged and overwhelmed without any interval, while you daily both repeat and learn by heart all these things, with which are mixed up libels upon the gods and slanderous sayings; and when[1] you wish your inactive minds to be occupied with useless dreamings, demand that days be given to you, and exhibition made without any interval? But if you felt any real indignation on behalf of your religious beliefs, you should rather long ago have burned these writings, destroyed those books of yours, and overthrown these theatres, in which evil reports of your deities are daily made public in shameful tales. For why, indeed, have our writings deserved to be given to the flames? our meetings to be cruelly broken up,[2] in which prayer is made to the Supreme God, peace and pardon are asked for all in authority, for soldiers, kings, friends, enemies, for those still in life, and those freed from the bondage of the flesh;[3] in which all that is said is such as to make [men] humane,[4] gentle, modest, virtuous, chaste, generous in dealing

[1] So Orelli, reading *et quando;* MS. and other edd. *et si*—" and if ever."

[2] Arnobius is generally thought to refer here to the persecution under Diocletian mentioned by Eusebius, *Hist. Eccl.* viii. 2.

[3] The service in which these prayers were offered was presided over by the bishop, to whom the dead body was brought: hymns were then sung of thanksgiving to God, the giver of victory, by whose help and grace the departed brother had been victorious. The priest next gave thanks to God, and some chapters of the Scriptures were read; afterwards the catechumens were dismissed; the names of those at rest were then read in a clear voice, to remind the survivors of the success with which others had combated the temptations of the world. The priest again prayed for the departed, at the close beseeching God to grant him pardon, and admission among the undying. Thereafter the body was kissed, anointed, and buried.—(Dionysius, *Eccl. Hier.*, last chapter quoted by Heraldus. Cf. *Const. Apost.* viii. 41.) With the church's advance in power there was an accession of pomp to these rites.

[4] Cf. the younger Pliny, Epist. x. 97: "They affirmed that they bound themselves by oath not for any wicked purpose, but to pledge themselves not to commit theft, robbery, or adultery, nor break faith, or prove false to a trust."

with their substance, and inseparably united to all embraced in our brotherhood?[1]

37. But this is the state of the case, that as you are exceedingly strong in war and in military power, you think you excel in knowledge of the truth also, and are pious before the gods,[2] whose might you have been the first to besmirch with foul imaginings. Here, if your fierceness allows, and madness suffers, we ask you to answer us this: Whether you think that anger finds a place in the divine nature, or that the divine blessedness is far removed from such passions? For if they are subject to passions so furious,[3] and are excited by feelings of rage as your imaginings suggest (for you say that they have often shaken the earth with their roaring,[4] and bringing woful misery on men, corrupted with pestilential contagion the character of the times,[5] both because their games had been celebrated with too little care, and because their priests were not received with favour, and because some small spaces were desecrated, and because their rites were not duly performed), it must consequently be understood that they feel no little wrath on account of the opinions which have been mentioned. But if, as follows of necessity, it is admitted that all these miseries with which men have long been overwhelmed flow from such fictions, if the anger of the deities is excited by these causes, you are the occasion of so terrible misfortunes, because you never cease to jar upon the feelings of the gods, and excite them to a fierce desire for vengeance. But if, on the other hand, the gods are not subject to such passions, and do not know at all what it is to be enraged, then indeed there is no ground for saying that they who know not what anger is are angry with us, *and they are free from its presence,*[6] *and the dis-*

---

[1] Lit., "whom [our] society joins together," *quos solidet germanitas.*
[2] *i.e.* in their sight or estimation.   [3] Lit., "conceive these torches."
[4] Lit., "have roared with tremblings of the earth."
[5] The MS. reads *conru-isse auras temporum*, all except the first four edd. inserting *p* as above. Meursius would also change *temp.* into *ventorum*—"the breezes of the winds."
[6] So the MS., reading *comptu*—tie, according to Hild., followed by LB. and Orelli.

order[1] [*it causes*]. *For it cannot be, in the nature of things, that what is one should become two; and that unity, which is naturally uncompounded, should divide and go apart into separate things.*[2]

---

[1] Lit., "mixture."

[2] The words in italics are bracketed in LB. as spurious or corrupt, or at least as here out of place. Orelli transposes them to ch. 13, as was noticed there, although he regards them as an interpolation. The clause is certainly a very strange one, and has a kind of affected abstractness, which makes it seem out of place; but it must be remembered that similarly confused and perplexing sentences are by no means rare in Arnobius. If the clause is to be retained, as good sense can be made from it here as anywhere else. The general meaning would be: The gods, if angry, are angry with the pagans; but if they are not subject to passion, it would be idle to speak of them as angry with the Christians, seeing that they cannot possibly at once be incapable of feeling anger, and yet at the same time be angry with them.

BOOK V.

ARGUMENT.

It might be said that these charges were founded by Arnobius on the writings of poets and actions of stage-players, and that the heathen generally could not therefore be held guilty. Such a defence, however, would not avail those who in their histories and religious rites were not less impious and insulting to the deities. Arnobius proceeds, therefore, to narrate the story, told by Antias, of Jupiter's being tricked by Numa (1), and criticises it minutely, showing the manifest absurdity and impiety of representing man as overcoming and deluding the gods (2–4). He next relates from Timotheus the origin of Acdestis (5); the base and degrading expedients which the gods were compelled to adopt in order that they might rid themselves of his audacity; and the extraordinary birth (6) and death of Attis, and institution of the rites of the Great Mother in memory of him (7). This story also is criticised at great length, its absurdity, indecency, and silliness being brought prominently forward (8–14); while it is pointed out that the truth or falsehood of the story is of no consequence to the argument, as all that Arnobius wishes to prove is, that any deities which exist are more grossly insulted by their own worshippers than by Christians (15). But, he says, how can you maintain that this story is false, when the ceremonies you are ever observing always refer to the events of which it speaks (16, 17)?

Neglecting many similar stories as too numerous to be related, he merely mentions Fenta Fauna, the birth of Servius Tullius (18), the Omophagia, rites of Venus, Corybantia, and the Bacchanalia which relate the dismembering of Bacchus (19). The story is next related of Jupiter's amours with Ceres as a bull, and with Proserpine as a serpent (20, 21), in which, Arnobius says, it might be thought that it was wished to make Jupiter an embodiment of all the vices (22); and then notes, with bitter irony, how the Supreme Ruler is belittled by their trivial and degrading tales (23). Passing now to the other deities, Arnobius narrates the wanderings of Ceres, and the origin, in consequence, of the Thesmophoria and Eleusinia (24–27). So, too, the obscene Alimontia are shown to have an origin as shameful (28); and Arnobius indignantly asks, whether such a tale does not strike at the foundation of all morality? and whether Christians are to be forced, by fear of torment and death, to worship such deities (29), for disbelief in whom he cannot but wonder that men are called atheists? (30). Since, then, it is the heathen who so insult their own deities, the wrath of the gods must be against their worshippers, not against Christians (31).

The suggestion that these stories are allegories (32) he scouts as utterly absurd, pointing out the impossibility of finding any meaning in some parts of the fables, insisting that as every detail is not allegorical, no part can be, and supposing that he thus shows that these must be accounts of actual events (33-39). If, however, these tales are allegories, do they not, Arnobius asks, do the gods wrong by imputing to them as crimes what are merely natural phenomena (40)? that is, do they not turn into obscenity that which is pure and honourable in itself, while allegory is rather used to hide under a cloak of decency what is indecent (41)? There is but one other pretext, that the gods themselves would have their mysteries made allegories, not choosing that they should be generally understood. But how was this ascertained? and why would they not allow the truth to be told, against which no objection could be taken, preferring indecent and shameful allegory (42)? These explanations, then, are merely attempts to get rid of difficulties (43); attempts, too, which could not be very successful, for many shameful tales do not admit of explanation as allegories (44). What remarkable modesty is this, to blush at the mention of bread and wine, and to say fearlessly Venus for a shameful act! (45.)

1. ADMITTING that all these things which do the immortal gods dishonour, have been put forth by poets merely in sport, what [are we to say of] those found in grave, serious, and careful histories, and handed down by you in hidden mysteries? have they been invented by the licentious fancy of the poets? Now if they seemed[1] to you stories of such absurdity, some of them you would neither retain in their constant use, nor celebrate as solemn festivals from year to year, nor would you maintain them among your sacred rites as shadows of real events. With strict moderation, I shall adduce only one of these stories which are so numerous; that in which Jupiter himself is brought on the stage as stupid and inconsiderate, being tricked by the ambiguity of words. In the second book of Antias—lest any one should think, perchance, that we are fabricating charges calumniously—the following story is written: The famous king Numa, not knowing how to avert evil portended by thunder, and being eager to learn, by advice of Egeria con-

---

[1] So most edd., inserting *er;* in MS. and Oehler, *vid-entur.*

cealed beside a fountain twelve chaste youths provided with chains; so that when Faunus and Martius[1] Picus came to this place[2] to drink (for hither they were wont to come[3] to draw water), they might rush on them, seize and bind them. But, that this might be done more speedily, the king filled many[4] cups with wine and with mead,[5] and placed them about the approaches to the fountain, where they would be seen—a crafty snare for those who should come. They, as was their usual custom, when overcome by thirst, came to their well-known haunts. But when they had perceived cups with sweetly smelling liquors, they preferred the new to the old; rushed eagerly upon them; charmed with the sweetness of the draught, drank too much; and becoming drunk, fell fast asleep. Then the twelve [youths] threw themselves upon the sleepers, [and] cast chains round them, lying soaked with wine; and they,[6] when roused, immediately taught the king by what methods and sacrifices Jupiter could be called down to earth. With this knowledge the king performed the sacred ceremony on the Aventine, drew down Jupiter to the earth, and asked from him the due form of expiation. Jupiter having long hesitated, said, *Thou shalt avert what is portended by thunder with a head.*[7] The king answered, *With an onion.*[8] Jupiter again, *With a man's.* The king returned, *But with hair.*[9] The deity in turn, *With the life.*[10] With a

[1] So named either because he was said to have made use of the bird of Mars, *i.e.* a woodpecker (*picus*), in augury, or because according to the legend he was changed into one by Circe.

[2] *i.e.* the Aventine. The story is told by Plutarch in his Life of Numa, c. 15, and by Ovid, *Fasti*, iii. 291 sqq.

[3] The MS. reads, *sollemniter hæc,* corrected, as above, *solenne iter huc* by all edd. except Hild.

[4] So the MS. and most edd., reading *pocula non parvi numeri*, for which Elm. and Orelli have received from the margin of Ursinus, *poc. non parva mero*—" cups of great size, with pure wine."

[5] *i.e. mulsum.*   [6] *i.e.* Faunus and Picus.
[7] *Capite.*   [8] *Cæpitio.*

[9] Jupiter is supposed to say *humano*, meaning *capite*, to be understood, *i.e.* "with a man's head," while the king supplies *capillo*—"with a man's hair."

[10] *Anima* (MS. *l'a*).

fish,[1] rejoined Pompilius. Then Jupiter, being ensnared by the ambiguous terms used, uttered these words: *Thou hast overreached me, Numa; for I had determined that evils portended by thunder should be averted with [sacrifices of] human heads, not*[2] *with hair [and] an onion. Since, however, your craft has outwitted me, have the mode which you wished; and always undertake the expiation of thunder-portents with those things which you have bargained for.*

2. What the mind should take up first, what last, or what it should pass by silently, it is not easy to say, nor is it made clear by any amount of reflection; for all have been so devised and fitted to be laughed at, that you should strive that they may be believed to be false—even if they are true—rather than pass current as true, and suggest as it were something extraordinary, and bring contempt upon deity itself. What, then, do you say, O you—? Are we to believe[3] that that Faunus and Martius Picus (if they are of the number of the gods, and of that everlasting and immortal substance) were once parched with thirst, and sought the gushing fountains, that they might be able to cool with water their heated veins? Are we to believe that, ensnared by wine, and beguiled by the sweetness of mead, they dipped so long into the treacherous cups, that they even got into danger of becoming drunk? Are we to believe that, being fast asleep, and plunged in the forgetfulness of most profound slumbers, they gave to creatures of earth an opportunity to bind them? On what parts, then, were those bonds and chains flung? Did they have any solid substance, or had their hands been formed of hard bones, so that it might be possible to bind them with halters and hold them fast by tightly drawn knots? For I do not ask, I do not inquire

---

[1] *Mæna.* There is here a lacuna in the text; but there can be no difficulty in filling it up as above, with Heraldus from Plutarch, or with Gelenius from Ovid, *piscis*—" [with the life] of a fish."

[2] The MS. and both Roman edd. read *Numa*, corrected by Gelenius, as above, *non.*

[3] The MS. and edd. read *cred-i-musne*—" do we believe," for which Meursius suggests *-e-* as above.

whether they could have said anything when swaying to and fro in their drunken maunderings; or whether, while Jupiter was unwilling, or rather unwitting, any one could have made known the way to bring him down to earth. This only do I wish to hear, why, if Faunus and Picus are of divine origin and power, they did not rather themselves declare to Numa, as he questioned them, that which he desired to learn from Jove himself at a greater risk? Or[1] did Jupiter alone have knowledge of this—for from him the thunderbolts fall—how training in some kind of knowledge should avert impending dangers? Or, while he himself hurls these fiery bolts, is it the business of others to know in what way it is fitting to allay his wrath and indignation? For truly it would be most absurd to suppose that he himself appoints[2] the means by which may be averted that which he has determined should befall men through the hurling of his thunderbolts. For this is to say, By such ceremonies you will turn aside my wrath; and if I shall at any time have foreshown by flashes of lightning that some evil is close at hand, do this and that, so that[3] what I have determined should be done may be done altogether in vain, and may pass away idly through the force[4] of these rites.

3. But let us admit that, as is said, Jupiter has himself appointed against himself ways and means by which his own declared purposes might fittingly be opposed: are we also to believe that a deity of so great majesty was dragged down to earth, and, standing on a petty hillock with a mannikin, entered into a wrangling dispute? And what, I ask, was the charm which forced Jupiter to leave the all-important[5] direction of the universe, and appear at the bidding of mortals? the sacrificial meal, incense, blood, the scent of burning laurel-

[1] Lit., "or whether." Below the MS. reads corruptly *ad ipsum*—"to him."
[2] The MS. reads *scire*, but "knows" would hardly suit the context. Instead of adopting any conjecture, however, it is sufficient to observe, with Oehler, that *scire* is elsewhere used as a contraction for *sciscere*.
[3] The MS. omits *ut*.
[4] So Cujacius, inserting *vi*, omitted by the MS.
[5] Lit., "so great."

boughs,[1] and muttering of spells? And were all these more powerful than Jupiter, so that they compelled him to do unwillingly what was enjoined, or to give himself up of his own accord to their crafty tricks? What! will what follows be believed, that the son of Saturn had so little foresight, that he either proposed terms by the ambiguity of which he was himself ensnared, or did not know what was going to happen, how the craft and cunning of a mortal would overreach him? You shall make expiation, he says, with a head when thunderbolts have fallen. The phrase is still incomplete, and the meaning is not fully expressed and defined; for it was necessarily right to know whether Diespiter ordains that this expiation be effected with the head of a wether, a sow, an ox, or any other animal. Now, as he had not yet fixed this specifically, and his decision was still uncertain and not yet determined, how could Numa know that Jupiter would say the head of a man, so as to[2] anticipate [and] prevent [him], and turn his uncertain and ambiguous words[3] into " an onion's head?"

4. But you will perhaps say that the king was a diviner. Could he be more so than Jupiter himself? But for a mortal's anticipating[4] what Jupiter (whom[5] he overreached) was going to say, could the god not know in what ways a man was preparing to overreach him? Is it not, then, clear and manifest that these are puerile and fanciful inventions, by which, while a lively wit is assigned[6] to Numa, the greatest want of foresight is imputed to Jupiter? For what shows so little foresight as to confess that you have been ensnared by the subtlety of a man's intellect, and while you are vexed at being deceived, to give way to the wishes of him who has overcome you, and to lay aside the means which you had

---

[1] Lit., "the fumigation of *verbenæ*," i.e. of boughs of the laurel, olive, or myrtle.
[2] The MS. omits *ut*.
[3] Lit., "the uncertain [things] of that ambiguity."
[4] Lit., "unless a mortal anticipated"—*præsumeret*, the MS. reading.
[5] So Oehler, supplying *quem*.
[6] Lit., "liveliness of heart is procured."

proposed? For if there was reason and some natural fitness that[1] expiatory sacrifice for that which was struck with lightning should have been made with a man's head, I do not see why the proposal of an onion's was made by the king; but if it could be performed with an onion also, there was a greedy lust for human blood. And both parts are made to contradict themselves: so that, on the one hand, Numa is shown not to have wished to know what he did wish; and, on the other, Jupiter is shown to have been merciless, because he said that he wished expiation to be made with the heads of men, which could have been done by Numa with an onion's head.

5. In Timotheus, who was no mean mythologist, and also in others equally well informed, the birth of the Great Mother of the gods, and the origin of her rites, are thus detailed, being derived (as he himself writes and suggests) from learned books of antiquities, and from [his acquaintance with] the most secret mysteries:—Within the confines of Phrygia, he says, there is a rock of unheard-of wildness in every respect, the name of which is Agdus, so named by the natives of that district. Stones taken from it, as Themis by her oracle[2] had enjoined, Deucalion and Pyrrha threw upon the earth, at that time emptied of men; from which this Great Mother, too, as she is called, was fashioned along with the others, and animated by the Deity. Her, given over to rest and sleep on the very summit of the rock, Jupiter assailed with lewdest[3] desires. But when, after long strife, he could not accomplish what he had proposed to himself, he, baffled, spent his lust on the stone. This the rock received, and with many groanings Acdestis[4] is born in the tenth month, being named from his mother rock. In him there had been resistless might, and a fierceness of disposition beyond control, a lust

[1] Lit., "why."
[2] So Ovid also (*Metam.* i. 321), and others, speak of Themis as the first to give oracular responses.
[3] So the MS. and edd., reading *quam incestis*, except Orelli, who adopts the conjecture of Barthius, *nequam*—"lustful Jupiter with lewd desires."
[4] So the MS. and edd., except Hildebrand and Oehler, who throughout spell *Agdestis*, following the Greek writers, and the derivation of the word from *Agdus*.

made furious, and [derived] from both sexes.¹ He violently plundered and laid waste; he scattered destruction wherever the ferocity of his disposition had led him; he regarded not gods or men, nor did he think anything more powerful than himself; he contemned earth, heaven, and the stars.

6. Now, when it had been often considered in the councils of the gods, by what means it might be possible either to weaken or to curb his audacity, Liber, the rest hanging back, takes upon himself this task. With the strongest wine he drugs a spring much resorted to by Acdestis,² where he had been wont to assuage the heat and burning thirst³ roused [in him] by sport and hunting. Hither runs Acdestis to drink when he felt the need;⁴ he gulps down the draught too greedily into his gaping veins. Overcome by what he is quite unaccustomed to, he is in consequence sent fast asleep. Liber is near the snare [which he had set]; over his foot he throws one end of a halter⁵ formed of hairs, woven together very skilfully; with the other end he lays hold of his privy members. When the fumes of the wine passed off, Acdestis starts up furiously, and his foot dragging the noose, by his own strength he robs himself of his⁶ sex; with the tearing asunder of [these] parts there is an immense flow of blood; both⁷ are carried off and swallowed up by the earth; from them there suddenly springs up, covered with fruit, a pomegranate tree, seeing the beauty of which, with admiration, Nana,⁸ daughter of the king or river Sangarius, gathers and places in her bosom [some of the fruit]. By this she becomes

---

¹ So Ursinus suggested, followed by later edd., *ex utroque* (MS. *utra.*) *sexu*; for which Meursius would read *ex utroque sexus*—"and a sex of both," *i.e.* that he was a hermaphrodite, which is related by other writers.

² Lit., "him."   ³ Lit., "of thirsting."   ⁴ Lit., "in time of need."

⁵ So the reading of the MS. and edd., *unum laqueum*, may be rendered; for which Canterus conjectured *imum*—"the lowest part of the noose."

⁶ So the edd., reading *eo quo* (MS. *quod*) *fuerat privat sexu*; for which Hild. and Oehler read *fu-tu-erat*—"of the sex with which he had been a fornicator."

⁷ Lit., "these (*i.e.* the parts and the blood) are," etc.

⁸ The MS. here reads *Nata*, but in c. 13 the spelling is Nana, as in other writers.

pregnant; her father shuts her up, supposing that she had been[1] debauched, and seeks to have her starved to death; she is kept alive by the mother of the gods with apples, and other food,[2] [and] brings forth a child, but Sangarius[3] orders it to be exposed. One Phorbas having found the child, takes it home,[4] brings it up on goats' milk; and as handsome fellows are so named in Lydia, or because the Phrygians in their own way of speaking call their goats *attagi*, it happened in consequence that [the boy] obtained the name Attis. Him the mother of the gods loved exceedingly, because he was of most surpassing beauty; and Acdestis, [who was] his companion, as he grew up fondling him, and bound [to him] by wicked compliance with his lust in the only way now possible, leading him through the wooded glades, and presenting him with the spoils of many wild beasts, which the boy Attis at first said boastfully were won by his own toil and labour. Afterwards, under the influence of wine, he admits that he is both loved by Acdestis, and honoured by him with the gifts brought from the forest; whence it is unlawful for those polluted by [drinking] wine to enter into his sanctuary, because it discovered his secret.[5]

7. Then Midas, king of Pessinus, wishing to withdraw the youth from so disgraceful an intimacy, resolves to give him his own daughter in marriage, and caused the [gates of the] town to be closed, that no one of evil omen might disturb their marriage joys. But the mother of the gods, knowing the fate of the youth, and that he would live among men in safety [only] so long as he was free from the ties of marriage, that no disaster might occur, enters the closed city, raising its

[1] Lit., "as if."
[2] The MS. reads *t-abulis*, corrected as above *p-* by Jos. Scaliger, followed by Hild. and Oehler. The other edd. read *bacculis*—"berries."
[3] So all the edd., except Hild. and Oehler, who retain the MS. reading *sanguinarius*—"bloodthirsty."
[4] So Salmasius, Orelli, and Hild., reading *repertum nescio quis sumit Phorbas, lacte;* but no mention of any Phorbas is made elsewhere in connection with this story, and Oehler has therefore proposed *forma ac lacte*—"some one takes [the child] found, nourishes it with sweet pottage of millet (*forma*) and milk," etc. [5] Lit., "his silence."

walls with her head, which began to be crowned with towers in consequence. Acdestis, bursting with rage because of the boy's being torn from himself, and brought to seek a wife, fills all the guests with frenzied madness:[1] the Phrygians shriek aloud, panic-stricken at the appearance of the gods;[2] a daughter of adulterous[3] Gallus cuts off her breasts; Attis snatches the pipe borne by him who was goading them to frenzy; and he, too, now filled with furious passion, raving franticly [and] tossed about, throws himself down at last, and under a pine tree mutilates himself, saying, *Take these,*[4] *Acdestis, for which you have stirred up so great and terribly perilous commotions.*[5] With the streaming blood his life flies; but the Great Mother of the gods gathers the parts which had been cut off, and throws earth on them, having first covered them, and wrapped[6] them in the garment of the dead. From the blood which had flowed springs a flower, the violet, and with[7] this the tree[8] is girt. Thence the custom began and arose, whereby you even now veil and wreath with flowers the sacred pine. The virgin who had been the bride (whose name, as Valerius[9] the pontifex relates, was Ia) veils the breast of the lifeless [youth] with soft wool, sheds tears with Acdestis, and slays herself. After her death her blood is changed

[1] Lit., "fury and madness."

[2] The MS., first five edd., and Oberthür, read *exterriti adorandorum Phryges;* for which Ursinus suggested *ad ora deorum*—"at the faces of gods," adopted by Oehler; the other edd. reading *ad horam*—"at the hour, *i.e.* thereupon."

[3] It seems probable that part of this chapter has been lost, as we have no explanation of this epithet; and, moreover (as Oehler has well remarked), in c. 13 this Gallus is spoken of as though it had been previously mentioned that he too had mutilated himself, of which we have not the slightest hint.

[4] *i.e. genitalia.*   [5] Lit., "so great motions of furious hazards."

[6] So most edd., reading *veste prius tectis atque involutis* for the MS. reading, retained by Hild. and Oehler, *tecta atque involuta*—"his vest being first drawn over and wrapt about them;" the former verb being found with this meaning in no other passage, and the second very rarely.

[7] Lit., "from."   [8] *i.e.* the pine.

[9] Nourry supposes that this may refer to M. Valerius Messala, a fragment from whom on auspices has been preserved by Gellius (xiii. 15); while Hild. thinks that Antias is meant, who is mentioned in c. 1.

into purple violets. The mother of the gods shed tears also,[1] from which springs an almond tree, signifying the bitterness of death.[2] Then she bears away to her cave the pine tree, beneath which Attis had unmanned himself; and Acdestis joining in her wailings, she beats and wounds her breast, [pacing] round the trunk of the tree now at rest.[3] Jupiter is begged by Acdestis that Attis may be restored to life: he does not permit it. What, however, fate allowed,[4] he readily grants, that his body should not decay, that his hairs should always grow, that the least of his fingers should live, and should be kept ever in motion; content with which favours, [it is said] that Acdestis consecrated the body in Pessinus, [and] honoured it with yearly rites and priestly services.[5]

8. If some one, despising the deities, and furious with a savagely sacrilegious spirit, had set himself to blaspheme your gods, would he dare to say against them anything more severe than this tale relates, which you have reduced to form, as though [it were] some wonderful narrative, and have honoured without ceasing,[6] lest the power of time and the remoteness[7] of antiquity should cause it to be forgotten? For what is there asserted in it, or what written about the gods, which, if said with regard to a man brought up with bad habits and a pretty rough training, would not make you liable to be accused of wronging and insulting him, and expose you to hatred and

---

[1] So Orelli punctuates and explains; but it is doubtful whether, even if this reading be retained, it should not be translated, "bedewed these [violets]." The MS. reads, *suffodit et as* (probably *has*)—"digs under these," emended as above in LB., *suffudit et has*.

[2] Lit., "burial."

[3] So it has been attempted to render the MS., reading *pausatæ circum arboris robur*, which has perplexed the different edd. Heraldus proposed *pausate*—"at intervals round the trunk of the tree;" LB. reads *-ata* —"round . . . tree having rested." Reading as above, the reference might be either to the rest from motion after being set up in the cave, or to the absence of wind there.

[4] Lit., "could be done through (*i.e.* as far as concerns) fate."

[5] So Oehler, reading *sacerdotum antistitiis* for the MS. *anti-stibus*, changed in both Roman edd. and Hild. to *-stitibus*—"with priests (or overseers) of priests." Salmasius proposed *intestibus*—"with castrated priests."

[6] *i.e.* in the ever recurring festival of Cybele.   [7] Lit., "length."

dislike, accompanied by implacable resentment? From the stones, you say, which Deucalion and Pyrrha threw, was produced the mother of the gods. What do you say, O theologians? what, ye priests of the heavenly powers? Did the mother of the gods, then, not exist at all for the sake of the deluge? and would there be no cause or beginning of her birth, had not violent storms of rain swept away the whole race of men? It is through man, then, that she feels herself to exist, and she owes it to Pyrrha's kindness that she sees herself addressed as a real being;[1] but if that is indeed true, this too will of necessity not be false, that she was human, not divine. For if it is certain that men are sprung originally from the casting of stones, it must be believed that she too was one of us, since she was produced by means of the same causes. For it cannot be, for nature would not suffer it,[2] that from one kind of stones, and from the same mode of throwing [them], some should be formed to rank among the immortals, others with the condition of men. Varro, that famous Roman, distinguished by the diversity of his learning, and unwearied in his researches into ancient times, in the first of four books which he has left in writing on the race of the Roman people, shows by careful calculations, that from the time of the deluge, which we mentioned before, down to the consulship of Hirtius and Pansa,[3] there are not quite two thousand years; and if he is to be believed, the Great Mother, too, must be said to have her whole life bounded by the limits of this number. And thus the matter is brought to this issue, that she who is said to be parent of all the deities is not their mother, but their daughter; nay, rather a [mere] child, a little girl, since we admit that in the never-ending series of ages neither beginning nor end has been ascribed to the gods.

9. But why do we speak of your having bemired the great mother of the gods with the filth of earth, when you have not

---

[1] So the edd., reading *orari in alicujus substantiæ qualitate* for the MS. *erari* restored by Oehler, *num-erari*—"numbered in the quality of some substance," from the reading of an old copy adopted by Livineius.

[2] Lit., "through the resistance of nature." [3] B.C. 43.

been able for but a little time even to keep from speaking evil of Jupiter himself? While the mother of the gods was then sleeping on the highest peak of Agdus, her son, you say, tried stealthily to surprise her chastity while she slept. After robbing of their chastity virgins and matrons without number, did Jupiter hope to gratify his detestable passion upon his mother? and could he not be turned from his fierce desire by the horror which nature itself has excited not only in men, but in some [other] animals also, and by common[1] feeling? Was he then regardless of piety[2] and honour, who is chief in the temples? and could he neither reconsider nor perceive how wicked was his desire, his mind being madly agitated? But, as it is, forgetting his majesty and dignity, he crept forward to steal those vile pleasures, trembling and quaking with fear, holding his breath, walking in terror on tiptoe, and, between hope and fear, touched her secret parts, trying how soundly his mother slept, and what she would suffer.[3] Oh, shameful representation! oh, disgraceful plight of Jupiter, prepared to attempt a filthy contest! Did the ruler of the world, then, turn to force, when, in his heedlessness and haste, he was prevented from stealing on by surprise;[4] and when he was unable to snatch his pleasure by cunning craft, did he assail his mother with violence, and begin without any concealment to destroy the chastity which he should have revered? Then, having striven for a very long time when she is unwilling, did he go off conquered, vanquished, and overcome? and did his spent lust part him whom piety was unable to hold back from execrable lust after his mother?

10. But you will perhaps say the human race shuns and execrates such unions;[5] among the gods there is no incest.

[1] Lit., "the feeling commonly implanted."

[2] Lit., "was regard of piety wanting"—*defuit*, an emendation of Salmasius (according to Orelli) for the MS. *depuit*.

[3] Lit., "the depth and patience of his sleeping mother."

[4] Lit., "from the theft of taking by surprise"—*obreptionis*, for which the MS., first four edd., Oberth., Hild., and Oehler read *object.*—"of what he proposed."

[5] So Heraldus, reading *conventionis hujusmodi cœtum* for the MS. *cœptum*.

And why, [then,] did his mother resist with the greatest vehemence her son when he offered her violence? Why did she flee from his embraces, as if she were avoiding unlawful approaches? For if there was nothing wrong in so doing, she should have gratified him without any reluctance, just as he eagerly wished to satisfy the cravings of his lust. And here, indeed, very thrifty men, and frugal even about shameful works, that that sacred seed may not seem to have been poured forth in vain—the rock, one says, drank up Jupiter's foul incontinence. What followed next, I ask? Tell. In the very heart of the rock, and in that flinty hardness, a child was formed and quickened to be the offspring of great Jupiter. It is not easy to object to conceptions so unnatural and so wonderful. For as the human race is said by you to have sprung and proceeded from stones, it must be believed that the stones both had genital parts, and drank in the seed cast on them, and when their time was full were pregnant,[1] and at last brought forth, travailing in distress as women do. That impels our curiosity to inquire, since you say that the birth occurred after ten months, in what womb of the rock was he enclosed at that time? with what food, with what juices, was he supplied? or what could he have drawn to support him from the hard stone, as unborn infants usually [receive] from their mothers? He had not yet reached the light, [my informant] says; and already bellowing and imitating his father's thunderings, he reproduced [their sound].[2] And after it was given him to see the sky and the light of day, attacking all things which lay in his way, he made havoc of them, and assured himself that he was able to thrust down from heaven the gods themselves. O cautious and foreseeing mother of the gods, who, that she might not undergo the ill-will of so[3] arrogant a son, or that his bellowing while still unborn might not disturb her slumbers or break her repose, withdrew herself, and sent far from her that most hurtful seed, and gave it to the rough rock.

[1] *Sustulisse alvos graves.*   [2] Most edd. read as an interrogation.

[3] Perhaps, "that she might not be subject to ill-will for having borne so."

11. There was doubt in the councils of the gods how that unyielding and fierce violence was to be subdued; and when there was no other way, they had recourse to one means, that he should be soaked with much wine, and bereft of his members, by their being cut off. As if, indeed, those who have suffered the loss of these parts become less arrogant, and [as if] we do not daily see those who have cut them away from themselves become more wanton, and, neglecting all the restraints of chastity and modesty, throw themselves headlong into filthy vileness, making known abroad their shameful deeds. I should like, however, to see—were it granted me to be born at those times—father Liber, who overcame the fierceness of Acdestis, having glided down from the peaks of heaven after the very venerable meetings of the gods, cropping the tails of horses,[1] plaiting pliant halters, drugging the waters harmless while pure with much strong wine, and after that drunkenness sprung from drinking, to have carefully introduced his hands, handled the members of the sleeper, and directed his care skilfully[2] to the parts which were to perish, so that the hold of the nooses placed round [them] might surround them all.

12. Would any one say this about the gods who had even a very low opinion of them? or, if they were taken up with such affairs, considerations, cares, would any man of wisdom either believe that they are gods, or reckon them among men even? Was that Acdestis, pray, the lopping off of whose lewd members was to give a sense of security to the immortals, [was he] one of the creatures of earth, or one of the gods, and possessed of[3] immortality? For if he was thought [to be] of our lot and in the condition of men, why did he cause the deities so much terror? But if he was a god, how could he be deceived, or [how] could anything be cut off from a

---

[1] *i.e.* to form nooses with. The reading translated is an emendation of Jos. Scaliger, adopted by Orelli, *peniculamenta decurtantem cantheriorum*, for the MS. *peniculantem decurtam tam cantherios*, emended by each ed. as he has thought fit.

[2] Lit., "the cares of art."

[3] Lit., "endowed with the honour of."

divine body?¹ But we raise no issue on this point: he may have been of divine birth, or one of us, if you think it more correct to say so. Did a pomegranate tree, also, spring from the blood which flowed and from the parts which were cut off? or at the time when² that member was concealed in the bosom of the earth, did it lay hold of the ground with a root, and spring up into a mighty tree, put forth branches loaded with blossoms,³ and in a moment bare mellow fruit perfectly and completely ripe? And because these sprang from red blood, is their colour therefore bright purple, with a dash of yellow? Say further that they are juicy also, that they have the taste of wine, because they spring from the blood of one filled with it, and you have finished your story consistently. O Abdera, Abdera, what occasions for mocking [you would give⁴] to men, if such a tale had been devised by you! All fathers relate it, and haughty states peruse it; and you are considered foolish, and utterly dull and stupid.

13. Through her bosom, we are told,⁵ Nana conceived a son by an apple. The opinion is self-consistent; for where rocks and hard stones bring forth, there apples must have their time of generating.⁶ The Berecyntian goddess fed the imprisoned maiden with nuts⁷ and figs, fitly and rightly; for it was right that she should live on apples who had been made a mother by an apple. After her offspring was born, it was ordered by Sangarius to be cast far away: that which he believed to be divinely conceived long before, he would not have⁸ called the offspring of his child. The infant was brought up on he-goats' milk. O story ever opposed and most inimical to the male sex, in which not only do men lay aside their virile powers, but beasts even which were males

---

¹ The MS. here inserts *de*—" from the body from a divine [being]."

² So the edd. (except Oehler), reading *tum cum* for the MS. *tum quæ quod.*

³ *Balaustiis*, the flowers of the wild pomegranate.

⁴ *Dares* supplied by Salmasius.   ⁵ Lit., " he says."

⁶ Lit., "must rut"—*suriant*, as deer. The MS., first four edd., and Elm. read *surgant*—" rise," corrected as above in the margin of Ursinus.

⁷ Lit., " acorns"—*glandibus*.

⁸ The MS. reads *des-*, emended as above *ded-ignatus* by Stewechius, followed by Heraldus and Orelli.

become mothers!¹ He was famous for his beauty, and distinguished by his remarkable² comeliness. It is wonderful enough that the noisome stench of goats did not cause him to be avoided and fled from. The Great Mother loved him—if as a grandmother her grandson, there is nothing wrong; but if as the theatres tell, her love is infamous and disgraceful. Acdestis, too, loved him above all, enriching him with a hunter's gifts. There could be no danger to his purity from one emasculated, [you say]; but is it not easy to guess what Midas dreaded? The Mother entered bearing³ the very walls. Here we wondered, indeed, at the might and strength of the deity; but again⁴ we blame her carelessness, because when she remembered the decree of fate,⁵ she heedlessly laid open the city to its enemies. Acdestis excites to fury and madness those celebrating the nuptial vows. If King Midas had displeased [him] who was binding the youth to a wife, of what had Gallus been guilty, and his concubine's daughter, that he should rob himself of his manhood, she herself of her breasts? *Take and keep these*, says he,⁶ *because of which you have excited such commotions to the overwhelming of* [*our*] *minds with fear*. We should none of us yet know what the frenzied Acdestis had desired in his paramour's body, had not the boy thrown to him, to appease his wrath,⁷ the parts cut off.

14. What say you, O races and nations, given up to such beliefs? When these things are brought forward, are you not ashamed and confounded to say things so indecent? We wish to hear or learn from you something befitting the gods; but you, on the contrary, bring forward to us the cutting off of breasts, the lopping off of men's members,

---

¹ *i.e.* he-goats are made to yield milk.
² Lit., "praiseworthy." ³ Lit., "with."
⁴ So the MS., both Roman edd., LB., Hild., and Oehler, reading *rursus*, for which the others receive the emendation of Gelenius, *regis*—"the king's carelessness."
⁵ Lit., "the law and fate." ⁶ *i.e.* Attis.
⁷ The MS. reads *satietati-s objecisset offensi*, corrected as above by Hild. (omitting *s*), followed by Oehler. The conjectures of previous edd. are very harsh and forced.

ragings, blood, frenzies, the self-destruction of maidens, and flowers and trees begotten from the blood of the dead. Say, again, did the mother of the gods, then, with careful diligence herself gather in her grief the scattered genitals with the shed blood?[1] With her own sacred, her own divine[2] hands, did she touch and lift up the instruments of a disgraceful and indecent office? Did she also commit them to the earth to be hid from sight; and lest in this case they should, being uncovered, be dispersed in the bosom of the earth, did she indeed wash and anoint them with fragrant gums before wrapping and covering them with his dress? For whence could the violet's sweet scent have come had not the addition of those ointments modified the putrefying smell of the member? Pray, when you read such tales, do you not seem to yourselves to hear either girls at the loom wiling away their tedious working hours, or old women seeking diversions for credulous children, and to be declaring manifold fictions under the guise of truth? Acdestis appealed to[3] Jupiter to restore life to his paramour: Jupiter would not consent, because he was hindered by the fates more powerful [than himself]; and that he might not be in every respect very hard-hearted, he granted one favour—that the body should not decay through any corruption; that the hair should always grow; that the least of his fingers alone in his body should live, alone keep always in motion. Would any one grant this, or support it with an unhesitating assent, that hair grows on a dead body,—that part[4] perished, and that the [rest of his] mortal body, free from the law of corruption, remains even still?

15. We might long ago have urged you to ponder this, were it not foolish to ask proofs of such things, as well as to say[5] them. But this story is false, and is wholly untrue. It is

[1] Lit., "flows."
[2] Lit., "herself with sacred, herself with divine."
[3] Lit., "spoke with."
[4] *i.e.* the part cut off and buried separately.
[5] So the MS., according to Crusius, the edd. inserting *s*, *di-s-cere*—"to learn."

no matter to us, indeed, because of whom you maintain that the gods have been driven from the earth, whether it is consistent and rests on a sure foundation,[1] or is, on the contrary, framed and devised in utter falsehood. For to us it is enough—who have proposed this day to make it plain—that those deities whom you bring forward, if they are anywhere on earth, and glow with the fires of anger, are not more excited to furious hatred by us than by you; and that that [story] has been classed as an event and committed to writing by you, and is willingly read over by you every day, and handed down in order for the edifying of later times. Now, if this [story] is indeed true, we see that there is no reason in it why the celestial gods should be asserted to be angry with us, since we have neither declared things so much to their disgrace, nor committed them to writing at all, nor brought them publicly to light[2] by the celebration of sacred rites; but if, as you think, it is untrue, and made up of delusive falsehoods, no man can doubt that you are the cause of offence, who have either allowed certain persons to write such stories, or have suffered [them], when written, to abide in the memory of ages.

16. And yet how can you assert the falsehood of this story, when the very rites which you celebrate throughout the year testify that you believe [these things] to be true, and consider them perfectly trustworthy? For what is the meaning of that pine[3] which on fixed days you always bring into the sanctuary of the mother of the gods? Is it not in imitation of that tree, beneath which the raging and ill-fated youth laid hands upon himself, and [which] the parent of the gods consecrated to relieve her sorrow?[4] What mean the fleeces of wool with which you bind and surround the trunk of the

---

[1] Lit., "on firmness of faith."
[2] Lit., "sent to public testifying."
[3] The festival of Cybele began on the 22d of March, when a pine tree was introduced into the mysteries, and continued until the 27th, which was marked by a general purification (*lavatio*), as Salmasius observed from a calendar of Constantine the Great.
[4] Lit., "for solace of so great a wound."

tree? Is it not to recall the wools with which Ia[1] covered the dying [youth], and thought that she could procure some warmth for his limbs [fast] stiffening with cold? What [mean] the branches of the tree girt round and decked with wreaths of violets? Do they not mark this, how the Mother adorned with early flowers the pine which indicates and bears witness to the sad mishap? What [mean] the *Galli*[2] with dishevelled hair beating their breasts with their palms? Do they not recall to memory those lamentations with which the tower-bearing Mother, along with the weeping Acdestis, wailing aloud,[3] followed the boy? What [means] the abstinence from eating bread which you have named *castus*? Is it not in imitation of the time when the goddess abstained from Ceres' fruit in her vehement sorrow?

17. Or if the things which we say are not so, declare, say yourselves—those effeminate and delicate [men] whom we see among you in the sacred rites of this deity—what business, [what] care, [what] concern have they there; and why do they like mourners wound their arms and[4] breasts, and act as those dolefully circumstanced? What [mean] the wreaths, what the violets, what the swathings, the coverings of soft wools? Why, finally, is the very pine, but a little before swaying to and fro among the shrubs, an utterly inert log, set up in the temple of the mother of the gods next, like some propitious and very venerable deity? For either this is the cause which we have found in your writings and treatises, and [in that case] it is clear that you do not celebrate divine rites, but give a representation of sad events; or if there is any other reason which the darkness of the mystery has with-

---

[1] So Stewechius, followed by Orelli and Oehler, reading *quibus Ia* for the MS. *jam*, which would refer the action to Cybele, whereas Arnobius expressly says (c. 7) that it was the newly wedded wife who covered the breast of Attis with wools. *Jam* is, however, received from the MS. by the other edd., except Hild., who asserts that the MS. reads *Iam*, and Elmenh., who reads *Ion*.

[2] *i.e.* priests of Cybele, their name being derived from the Phrygian river Gallus, whose waters were supposed to bring on frenzy ending in self-mutilation.

[3] Lit., "with wailing." [4] Lit., "with."

held from us, even it also must be involved in the infamy of some shameful deed. For who would believe that there is any honour in that which the worthless *Galli* begin, effeminate debauchees complete?

18. The greatness of the subject, and our duty to those on their defence also,[1] demand that we should in like manner hunt up the other forms of baseness, whether those which the histories of antiquity record, or those contained in the sacred mysteries named *initia*,[2] and not divulged[3] openly to all, but to the silence of a few; but your innumerable sacred rites, and the loathsomeness of them all,[4] will not allow us to go through them all bodily: nay, more, to tell the truth, we turn aside ourselves from some purposely and intentionally, lest, in striving to unfold all things, we should be defiled by contamination in the very exposition. Let us pass by Fauna[5] Fatua, therefore, who is called Bona Dea, whom Sextus Clodius, in his sixth book in Greek on the gods, declares to have been scourged to death with rods of myrtle, because she drank a whole jar of wine without her husband's knowledge; and this is a proof, that when women show her divine honour a jar of wine is placed [there, but] covered from sight, and that it is not lawful to bring in twigs of myrtle, as Butas[6] mentions in his Causalia. But let us pass by with similar neglect[7] the *dii conserentes*, whom Flaccus and others relate to have buried themselves, changed *in humani penis similitudinem* in the cinders under a pot of *exta*.[8] And when Tanaquil, skilled in the arts of Etruria,[9] disturbed these, the gods erected themselves, and became rigid. She then commanded a captive woman from Corni-

---

[1] Lit., "and the duty of defence itself."
[2] *i.e.* secret rites, to which only the initiated were admitted.
[3] Lit., "which you deliver"—*traditis*; so Elmenh., LB., and latter edd., for the unintelligible MS. *tradidisse*, retained in both Roman edd.
[4] Lit., "deformity affixed to all." [5] MS. *fetam f.* Cf. i. 36, n. 1.
[6] So Heraldus, from Plutarch, *Rom.* 21, where Butas is said to have written on this subject (αἰτίαι) in elegiacs, for the MS. Putas.
[7] Lit., "in like manner and with dissimulation."
[8] *i.e.* heart, lungs, and liver, probably of a sacrifice.
[9] *i.e.* "divination, augury," etc.

culum to learn and understand what was the meaning of
this: Ocrisia, a woman of the greatest wisdom *divos inseruisse
genitali, explicuisse motus certos.* Then the holy and burning
deities poured forth the power of Lucilius,[1] and [thus] Servius
king of Rome was born.

19. We shall pass by the wild Bacchanalia also, which are
named in Greek Omophagia, in which with seeming frenzy
and the loss of your senses you twine snakes about you;
and, to show yourselves full of the divinity and majesty of
the god, tear in pieces with gory mouths the flesh of loudly-
bleating goats. Those hidden mysteries of Cyprian Venus
we pass by also, whose founder is said to have been King
Cinyras,[2] in which being initiated, they bring stated fees as to
a harlot, and carry away *phalli,* given as signs of the propitious deity. Let the rites of the Corybantes also be con-
signed to oblivion, in which is revealed that sacred mystery,
a brother slain by his brothers, parsley sprung from the blood
of the murdered one, that vegetable forbidden to be placed
on tables, lest the *manes* of the dead should be unappeasably
offended. But those other Bacchanalia also we refuse to proclaim, in which there is revealed and taught to the initiated
a secret not to be spoken; how Liber, when taken up with
boyish sports, was torn asunder by the Titans; how he was
cut up limb by limb by them also, and thrown into pots
that he might be cooked; how Jupiter, allured by the sweet
savour, rushed unbidden to the meal, and discovering what
had been done, overwhelmed the revellers with his terrible
thunder, and hurled them to the lowest part of Tartarus.
As evidence and proof of which, the Thracian [bard] handed
down in his poems the dice, mirror, tops, hoops, and smooth
balls, and golden apples taken from the virgin Hesperides.

20. It was our purpose to leave unnoticed those mysteries
also into which Phrygia is initiated, and all that[3] race, were
it not that the name of Jupiter, [which has been] introduced
by them, would not suffer us to pass cursorily by the wrongs

---

[1] *Vis Lucilii, i.e. semen.*   [2] Cf. iv. 24.

[3] So the MS. and edd., reading *gens illa,* for which Memmius proposed
Ilia—"and all the Trojan race."

and insults offered to him; not that we feel any pleasure in discussing[1] mysteries so filthy, but that it may be made clear to you again and again what wrong you heap upon those whose guardians, champions, worshippers, you profess to be. Once upon a time, they say, Diespiter, burning after his mother Ceres with evil passions and forbidden desires (for she is said by the natives of that district [to be] Jupiter's mother), and yet not daring to seek by open[2] force that for which he had conceived a shameless longing, hits upon a clever trick by which to rob of her chastity his mother, who feared nothing of the sort. Instead of a god, he becomes a bull; and concealing his purpose and daring under the appearance of a beast lying in wait,[3] he rushes madly with sudden violence upon her, thoughtless and unwitting, obtains his incestuous desires; and the fraud being disclosed by his lust, flies off known and discovered. His mother burns, foams, gasps, boils with fury and indignation; and being unable to repress the storm[4] and tempest of her wrath, received the name Brimo[5] thereafter from her ever-raging passion: nor has she any other wish than to punish as she may her son's audacity.

21. Jupiter is troubled enough, being overwhelmed with fear, and cannot find means to soothe the rage of his violated [mother]. He pours forth prayers, and makes supplication; her ears are closed by grief. The whole order of the gods is sent [to seek his pardon]; no one has weight enough to win a hearing. At last, the son seeking how to make satisfaction, devises this means: *Arietem nobilem bene grandibus cum testiculis deligit, exsecat hos ipse et lanato exuit ex folliculi tegmine.* Approaching his mother sadly and with downcast looks, and as if by his own decision he had condemned himself, he casts and throws these[6] into her bosom. When she saw what his pledge was,[7] she is somewhat softened, and allows

---

[1] Lit., "riding upon"—*inequitare*.   [2] Lit., "most open."
[3] *Subsessoris.*   [4] Lit., "growling"—*fremitum*.
[5] The MS. reads *primo*, emended as above by the brother of Canterus, followed by later edd.
[6] *i.e. testiculi*.   [7] *Virilitate pignoris visa.*

herself to be recalled to the care of the offspring which she had conceived.[1] After the tenth month she bears a daughter, of beautiful form, whom later ages have called now Libera, now Proserpine; whom when Jupiter Verveceus[2] saw to be strong, plump, and blooming, forgetting what evils and what wickedness, and how great recklessness, he had a little before fallen into,[3] he returns to his former practices; and because it seemed too[4] wicked that a father openly be joined as in marriage with his daughter, he passes into the terrible form of a dragon: he winds his huge coils round the terrified maiden, and under a fierce appearance sports and caresses [her] in softest embraces. She, too, is in consequence filled with the seed of the most powerful Jupiter, but not as her mother [was], for she[5] bore a daughter like herself; but from the maiden was born something like a bull, to testify to her seduction by Jupiter. If any one asks[6] who narrates this, then we shall quote the well-known senarian verse of a Tarentine poet which antiquity sings,[7] saying: *The bull begot a dragon, and the dragon a bull.* Lastly, the sacred rites themselves, and the ceremony of initiation even, named Sebadia,[8] might attest the truth; for in them a golden snake is let down into the bosom of the initiated, and taken away again from the lower parts.

---

[1] So Ursinus suggested, followed by Stewechius and later edd., *concepti foetus revocatur ad curam*; the MS. reads *concepit*—"is softened and conceived," etc.

[2] Jupiter may be here called *Verveceus*, either as an epithet of Jupiter Ammon—"like a wether," or (and this seems most probable from the context), "dealing with wethers," referring to the mode in which he had extricated himself from his former difficulty, or "stupid." The MS. reads *virviriceus*.

[3] Lit., "encountered"—*aggressus*.   [4] Lit., "sufficiently."

[5] *i.e.* Ceres.   [6] Lit., "will any one want."

[7] *i.e.* handed down by antiquity.

[8] These seem to have been celebrated in honour of Dionysius as well as Zeus, though, in so far as they are described by Arnobius, they refer to the intrigue of the latter only. Macrobius, however (*Saturn.* i. 18), mentions that in Thrace, Liber and Sol were identified and worshipped as Sebadius; and this suggests that we have to take but one more step to explain the use of the title to Jupiter also.

22. I do not think it necessary here also with many words to go through each part, and show how many base and unseemly things there are in each particular. For what mortal is there, with but little sense even of what becomes a man, who does not himself see clearly the character of all these things, how wicked [they are], how vile, and what disgrace is brought upon the gods by the very ceremonies of their mysteries, and by the unseemly origin of their rites? Jupiter, it is said, lusted after Ceres. Why, I ask, has Jupiter deserved so ill of you, that there is no kind of disgrace, no infamous adultery, which you do not heap upon his head, as if on some vile and worthless person? Leda was unfaithful to her nuptial vow; Jupiter is said to be the cause of the fault. Danae could not keep her virginity; the theft is said [to have been] Jupiter's. Europa hastened to the name of woman; he is again declared [to have been] the assailant of her chastity. Alcmena, Electra, Latona, Laodamia, a thousand other virgins, and a thousand matrons, and with them the boy Catamitus, were robbed of their honour and[1] chastity. It is the same story everywhere—Jupiter. Nor is there any kind of baseness in which you do not join and associate his name with passionate lusts; so that the wretched being seems to have been born for no other reason at all except that he might be a field fertile in[2] crimes, an occasion of evil-speaking, a kind of open place into which should gather all filthiness from the impurities of the stage.[3] And yet if you were to say that he had intercourse with strange women, it would indeed be impious, but the wrong done in slandering him might be bearable. [But] did he lust[4] after his mother also, after his daughter too, with furious desires; and could no sacredness in his parent, no

---

[1] Lit., "of."

[2] Lit., "that he might be a crop of"—*seges*, a correction in the margin of Ursinus for the MS. *sedes*—"a seat."

[3] So all edd., reading *scenarum* (MS. *scr-*, but *r* marked as spurious), except LB., followed by Orelli, who gives *sentinarum*—"of the dregs." Oehler supplies *e*, which the sense seems to require.

[4] Lit., "neigh with appetites of an enraged breast."

reverence for her, [no] shrinking even from the child which had sprung from himself, withhold him from conceiving so detestable a plan?

23. I should wish, therefore, to see Jupiter, the father of the gods, who ever controls the world and men,[1] adorned with the horns of an ox, shaking his hairy ears, with his feet contracted into hoofs, chewing green grass, and [having] behind him[2] a tail, hams,[3] and ankles smeared over with soft excrement,[4] and bedaubed with the filth cast forth. I should wish, I say (for it must be said over and over again), to see him who turns the stars [in their courses], and who terrifies and overthrows nations pale with fear, pursuing the flocks of wethers, *inspicientem testiculos aretinos*, snatching these away with that severe[5] and divine hand with which he was wont to launch the gleaming lightnings and to hurl in his rage the thunderbolt.[6] Then, indeed, [I should like to see him] ransacking their inmost parts with glowing knife;[7] and all witnesses being removed, tearing away the membranes *circumjectas prolibus*, and bringing them to his mother, still hot with rage, as a kind of fillet[8] to draw forth her pity, with downcast countenance, pale, wounded,[9] pretending to be in agony; and to make this believed, defiled with the blood of the ram, and covering his pretended wound with bands of wool and linen. [Is it possible] that this can be heard and read in this world,[10] and that those who discuss these things wish themselves to be thought pious, holy, and defenders of religion? Is there any greater sacrilege than this, or can

---

[1] This clearly refers to the *Æneid*, x. 18.
[2] Lit., "on the rear part."   [3] *Suffragines*.
[4] So the margin of Ursinus, Elmenh., LB., Oberth., Orelli, and Oehler, reading *molli fimo* for the MS. *molissimo*.
[5] Lit., "censorial."   [6] Lit., "rage with thunders."
[7] So Gelenius, followed by Stewechius and Orelli, reading *smila* for the corrupt and unintelligible MS. *nullas*.
[8] *Infulæ*, besides being worn by the priest, adorned the victim, and were borne by the suppliant. Perhaps a combination of the two last ideas is meant to be suggested here.
[9] *i.e.* seemingly so.
[10] Lit., "under this axis of the world."

any mind[1] be found so imbued with impious ideas as to believe such stories, or receive them, or hand them down in the most secret mysteries of the sacred rites? If that Jupiter [of whom you speak], whoever he is, really[2] existed, or was affected by any sense of wrong, would it not be fitting that,[3] roused to anger, he should remove the earth from under our feet, extinguish the light of the sun and moon; nay more, that he should throw all things into one mass, as of old?[4]

24. But, [my opponent] says, these are not the rites of our state. Who, pray, says this, or who repeats it? [Is he] Roman, Gaul, Spaniard, African, German, or Sicilian? And what does it avail your cause if these stories are not yours, while those who compose them are on your side? Or of what importance is it whether you approve of them or not, since what you yourselves say[5] are found to be either just as foul, or of even greater baseness? For do you wish that we should consider the mysteries and those ceremonies which are named by the Greeks Thesmophoria,[6] in which those holy vigils and solemn watchings were consecrated [to the goddess] by the Athenians? Do you wish us, I say, to see what beginnings they have, what causes, that we may prove that Athens

[1] So the MS., followed by Hild. and Oehler; the other edd. reading *gens* for *mens*.

[2] Lit., "felt himself to be."

[3] Lit., "would the thing not be worthy that angry and roused."

[4] *i.e.* reduce to chaos, in which one thing would not be distinguished from another, but all be mixed up confusedly.

[5] Lit., "what are your proper things."

[6] Every one since Salmasius (*ad Solinum*, p. 750) has supposed Arnobius to have here fallen into a gross error, by confounding the Eleusinian mysteries with the Thesmophoria; an error the less accountable, because they are carefully distinguished by Clemens Alexandrinus, whom Arnobius evidently had before him, as usual. There seems to be no sufficient reason, however, for charging Arnobius with such a blunder, although in the end of ch. 26 he refers to the story just related, as showing the base character of the Eleusinia (*Eleusiniorum vestrorum notas*); as he here speaks of *mysteria* (*i.e.* Eleusinia, cf. Nepos, *Alc.* 3, 16) *et illa divina quæ Thesmophoria nominantur a Græcis*. It should be remembered also that there was much in common between these mys-

itself also, distinguished in the arts and pursuits of civilisation, says things as insulting to the gods as others, and that stories are there publicly related under the mask of religion just as disgraceful as are thrown in [our] way by the rest of you? Once, they say, when Proserpine, not yet a woman and still a maiden, was gathering purple flowers in the meadows of Sicily, and when her eagerness to gather them was leading her hither and thither in all directions, the king of the shades, springing forth through an opening of unknown depth, seizes and bears away with him the maiden, and conceals himself again in the bowels[1] of the earth. Now when Ceres did not know what had happened, and had no idea where in the world her daughter was, she set herself to seek the lost one all over the[2] world. She snatches up two torches lit at the fires of Ætna;[3] and giving herself light by means of these, goes on her quest in all parts of the earth.

25. In her wanderings on that quest, she reaches the confines of Eleusis as well as other countries[4]—that is the name of a canton in Attica. At that time these parts were inhabited by aborigines[5] named Baubo, Triptolemus, Eubuleus, Eumolpus,[6] Dysaules: Triptolemus, who yoked oxen;

teries: the story of Ceres' wanderings was the subject of both; in both there was a season of fasting to recall her sadness; both had indecent allusions to the way in which that sadness was dispelled; and both celebrated with some freedom the recovery of cheerfulness by the goddess, the great distinguishing feature of the Thesmophoria being that only women could take part in its rites. Now, as it is to the points in which the two sets of mysteries were at one that allusion is made in the passage which follows, it was only natural that Arnobius should not be very careful to distinguish the one from the other, seeing that he was concerned not with their differences, but with their coincidence. It seems difficult, therefore, to maintain that Arnobius has here convicted himself of so utter ignorance and so gross carelessness as his critics have imagined.

[1] Lit., "caverns."   [2] Lit., "in the whole."
[3] The MS. is utterly corrupt—*flammis onere pressas etneis*, corrected as above by Gelenius from c. 35, f. *comprehensas.*—ÆL.
[4] Lit., "also."   [5] Lit., "[they were] earth-born who inhabited."
[6] The MS. wants this name; but it has evidently been omitted by accident, as it occurs in the next line.

Dysaules, a keeper of goats; Eubuleus, of swine; Eumolpus, of sheep,[1] from whom also flows the race of Eumolpidæ, and [from whom] is derived that name famous among the Athenians,[2] and those who afterwards flourished as *caduceatores*,[3] hierophants, and criers. So, then, that Baubo who, we have said, dwelt in the canton of Eleusis, receives hospitably Ceres, worn out with ills of many kinds, hangs about her with pleasing attentions, beseeches her not to neglect to refresh her body, brings to quench her thirst wine thickened with spelt,[4] which the Greeks term *cyceon*. The goddess in her sorrow turns away from the kindly offered services,[5] and rejects [them]; nor does her misfortune suffer her to remember what the body always requires.[6] Baubo, on the other hand, begs and exhorts her—as is usual in such calamities— not to despise her humanity; Ceres remains utterly immoveable, and tenaciously maintains an invincible austerity. But when this was done several times, and her fixed purpose could not be worn out by any attentions, Baubo changes her plans, and determines to make merry by strange jests her whom she could not win by earnestness. That part of the body by which women both bear children and obtain the name of mothers,[7] this she frees from longer neglect: she makes it assume a purer appearance, and become smooth like a child, not yet hard and rough with hair. In this wise she returns[8] to the sorrowing goddess; and while trying the common expedients by which it is usual to break the force of grief, and moderate it, she uncovers herself, and baring her

[1] Lit., "of woolly flock."   [2] *Cecropios et qui*.
[3] *i.e.* staff-bearers.
[4] *Cinnus*, the chief ingredients, according to Hesychius (quoted by Oehler), being wine, honey, water, and spelt or barley.
[5] Lit., "offices of humanity."
[6] Lit., "common health." Arnobius is here utterly forgetful of Ceres' divinity, and subjects her to the invariable requirements of nature, from which the divine might be supposed to be exempt.
[7] So the conjecture of Livineius, adopted by Oehler, *gene-t-ricum* for the MS. *genericum*.
[8] So Stewechius, followed by Oehler, reading *redit ita* for the MS. *red-ita*; the other edd. merely drop *a*.

groins, displays all the parts which decency hides;[1] and then the goddess fixes her eyes upon these,[2] and is pleased with the strange form of consolation. Then becoming more cheerful after laughing, she takes and drinks off the draught spurned [before], and the indecency of a shameless action forced that which Baubo's modest conduct was long unable to win.

26. If any one perchance thinks that we are speaking wicked calumnies, let him take the books of the Thracian soothsayer,[3] which you speak of as of divine antiquity; and he will find that we are neither cunningly inventing anything, nor seeking means to bring the holiness of the gods into ridicule, and doing so: for we shall bring forward the very verses which the son of Calliope uttered in Greek,[4] and published abroad in his songs to the human race throughout all ages:

"With these words she at the same time drew up her garments from
   the lowest [hem],
And exposed to view *formatas inguinibus res*,
Which Baubo grasping [5] with hollow hand, for
Their appearance was infantile, strikes, touches gently.
Then the goddess, fixing her orbs of august light,
Being softened, lays aside for a little the sadness of her mind;
Thereafter she takes the cup in her hand, and laughing,
Drinks off the whole draught of cyceon with gladness."[6]

---

[1] *Omnia illa pudoris loca.*   [2] *Pubi.*

[3] Orpheus, under whose name there was current in the time of Arnobius an immense mass of literature freely used, and it is probable sometimes supplemented, by Christian writers. Cf. c. 19.

[4] Lit., "put forth with Greek mouth."   [5] Lit., "tossing."

[6] It may be well to observe that Arnobius differs from the Greek versions of these lines found in Clem. Alex. (*Protrept.* p. 17) and Eusebius (*Præpar. Evang.* ii. 3), omitting all mention of Iacchus, who is made very prominent by them; and that he does not adhere strictly to metrical rules, probably, as Heraldus pointed out, because, like the poets of that age, he paid little heed to questions of quantity. Whether Arnobius has merely paraphrased the original as found in Clement and Eusebius, or had a different version of them before him, is a question which can only be discussed by means of a careful comparison between the Greek and Latin forms of the verses with the context in both cases.

What say you, O wise sons of Erectheus?[1] what, you citizens of Minerva?[2] The mind is eager to know with what words you will defend what it is so dangerous to maintain, or what arts you have by which to give safety to personages and causes wounded so mortally. This[3] is no false mistrust, nor are you assailed with lying accusations:[4] the infamy of your Eleusinia is declared both by their base beginnings and by the records of ancient literature, by the very signs, in fine, which you use when questioned in receiving the sacred things,—*I have fasted, and drunk the draught;*[5] *I have taken out of the [mystic] cist,*[6] *and put into the wicker-basket; I have received again, and transferred to the little chest.*

27. Are then your deities carried off by force, and do they seize by violence, as their holy and hidden mysteries relate? do they enter into marriages sought stealthily and by fraud?[7] is their honour snatched from virgins[8] resisting and unwilling? have they no knowledge of impending injury, no acquaintance with what has happened to those carried off by force? Are they, when lost, sought for as men are? and do they traverse the earth's vast extent with lamps and torches when the sun is shining most brightly? Are they afflicted? are they troubled? do they assume the squalid garments of mourners, and the signs of misery? and that they may be able to turn their mind to victuals and the taking of food, is use made not of reason, not of the right time, not of some weighty words or pressing courtesy, but is a display made of the shameful and indecent parts of the body? and are those members exposed which the shame felt by all, and the natural law of modesty, bid us conceal, which it is not permissible to

---

[1] So LB., Hild., and Oehler, reading *Erechthidæ O* (inserted by Hild.) for the MS. *erithideo*.

[2] *i.e.* Athenians.

[3] The MS., 1st ed., Hild., and Oehler read *ita*—"It is thus not," etc.; the others as above, *ista*.

[4] *Delatione calumniosa.*   [5] *Cyceon.*

[6] The MS. reads *exci-ta*, corrected as above, *ex cista*, in the margin of Ursinus.

[7] Lit., "by stealthy frauds."

[8] Lit., "is the honour of virginity snatched from them?"

name among pure ears without permission, and saying, "*by your leave?*"[1] What, I ask you, was there in such a sight,[2] what in the privy parts of Baubo, to move to wonder and laughter a goddess of the same sex, and formed with similar parts? what was there such that, when presented to the divine eyes[3] and sight, it should at the same time enable her to forget her miseries, and bring her with sudden cheerfulness to a happier state of mind? Oh, what have we had it in our power to bring forward with scoffing and jeering, were it not for respect for the reader,[4] and the dignity of literature!

28. I confess that I have long been hesitating, looking on every side, shuffling, doubling Tellene perplexities;[5] while I am ashamed to mention those Alimontian[6] mysteries in which Greece erects *phalli* in honour of father Bacchus, and the whole district is covered with images of men's *fascina*. The meaning of this is obscure perhaps, and it is asked why it is done. Whoever is ignorant of this, let him learn, and, wondering at what is so important, ever keep it with reverent care in a pure heart.[7] While Liber, born at Nysa,[8] and son of Semele, was still among men, the story goes, he wished to become acquainted with the shades below, and to inquire into what went on in Tartarus; but this wish was hindered by some difficulties, because, from ignorance of the route, he did not

---

[1] *Sine veniâ ac sine honoribus præfatis.*

[2] So Stewechius, LB., and Orelli, reading *spec-t-u in t-ali* for the MS. *in specu ali.*

[3] Lit., "light."   [4] So the MS., Hild., and Oehler, reading *noscentis.*

[5] This allusion is somewhat obscure. Heraldus regards *tricas Tellenas* as akin in sense to *t. Atellanas, i.e.* "comic trifles;" in which case the sense would be, that Arnobius had been heaping up any trifles which would keep him back from the disagreeable subject. Ausonius Popma (quoted by Orelli) explains the phrase with reference to the capture of Tellenæ by Ancus Martius as meaning "something hard to get through."

[6] The MS. reads *alimoniæ,* corrected from Clem. Alex. by Salmasius, *Alimontia, i.e.* celebrated at Halimus in Attica.

[7] Lit., "in pure senses."

[8] Cicero (*de Nat. Deor.* iii. 23) speaks of five Dionysi, the father of the fifth being Nisus. Arnobius had this passage before him in writing the fourth book (cf. c. 15, and n. 2), so that he may here mean to speak of Liber similarly.

know by what way to go and proceed. One Prosumnus starts up, a base lover of the god, and [a fellow] too prone to wicked lusts, who promises to point out the gate of Dis, and the approaches to Acheron, if the god will gratify him, and suffer *uxorias voluptates ex se carpi*. The god, without reluctance, swears to put himself[1] in his power and at his disposal, but [only] immediately on his return from the lower regions, having obtained his wish and desire.[2] Prosumnus politely tells him the way, and sets him on the very threshold of the lower regions. In the meantime, while Liber is inspecting[3] and examining carefully Styx, Cerberus, the Furies, and all other things, the informer passed from the number of the living, and was buried according to the manner of men. Evius[4] comes up from the lower regions, and learns that his guide is dead. But that he might fulfil his promise, and free himself from the obligation of his oath, he goes to the place of the funeral, and *ficorum ex arbore ramum validissimum præsecans dolat, runcinat, levigat et humani speciem fabricatur in penis, figit super aggerem tumuli, et posticâ ex parte nudatus accedit, subsidit, insidit. Lascivia deinde surientis assumptâ, huc atque illuc clunes torquet et meditatur ab ligno pati quod jamdudum in veritate promiserat.*

29. Now, to prevent any one from thinking that we have devised what is so impious, we do not call upon him to believe Heraclitus as a witness, nor to receive from his account what he felt about such mysteries. Let him[5] ask the whole of Greece what is the meaning of these *phalli* which ancient custom erects and worships throughout the country, throughout the towns: he will find that the causes are those which we say; or if they are ashamed to declare the truth honestly, of what avail will it be to obscure, to conceal the cause and origin of the rite, while[6] the accusation holds good against the very act of worship? What say

---

[1] Lit., "that he will be."
[2] So the MS., acc. to Hild., reading *expe-titionis;* acc. to Crusius, the MS. gives *-ditionis*—"[having accomplished] his expedition."
[3] Lit., "is surveying with all careful examination."
[4] MS. *cuius*.   [5] i.e. the sceptic.   [6] *Cum* wanting in the MS.

you, O peoples? what, ye nations busied with the services of the temples, and given up [to them]? Is it to these rites you drive us by flames, banishment, slaughter, and any other kind of punishments, and by fear of cruel torture? Are these the gods whom you bring to us, whom you thrust and impose upon us, like whom you would neither wish yourselves to be, nor any one related to you by blood and friendship?[1] Can you declare to your beardless sons, still wearing the dress of boys, the agreements which Liber formed with his lovers? Can you urge your daughters-in-law, nay, even your own wives, to [show] the modesty of Baubo, and [enjoy] the chaste pleasures of Ceres? Do you wish your young men to know, hear, [and] learn what even Jupiter showed himself to more matrons than one? Would you wish your grown-up maidens and still lusty fathers to learn how the same deity sported with his daughter? Do you wish full brothers, already hot with passion, and sisters sprung from the same parents, to hear that he again did not spurn the embraces, the couch of his sister? Should we not then flee far from such gods; and should not our ears be stopped altogether, that the filthiness of so impure a religion may not creep into the mind? For what man is there who has been reared with morals so pure, that the example of the gods does not excite him to similar madness? or who can keep back his desires from his kinsfolk, and those of whom he should stand in awe, when he sees that among the gods above nothing is held sacred in the confusion caused by[2] their lusts? For when it is certain that the first and perfect nature has not been able to restrain its passion within right limits, why should not man give himself up to his desires without distinction, being both borne on headlong by his innate frailty, and aided by the teaching of the holy deities?[3]

---

[1] Lit., "by right of friendship." [2] Lit., "of."

[3] Lit., "of holy divinity." Orelli thinks, and with reason, that Arnobius refers to the words which Terence puts into the mouth of Chaerea (*Eun.* iii. v. vv. 36–43), who encourages himself to give way to lust by asking, "Shall I, a man, not do this?" when Jove had done as much.

30. I confess that, in reflecting on such monstrous stories in my own mind, I have long been accustomed to wonder that you dare to speak of those as atheists,[1] impious, sacrilegious, who either deny that there are [any] gods at all, or doubt [their existence], or assert that they were men, and have been numbered among the gods for the sake of some power and good desert; since, if a true examination be made, it is fitting that none should be called by such names, more than yourselves, who, under the pretence of showing them reverence, heap up in so doing[2] more abuse and accusation, than if you had conceived the idea of doing this openly with avowed abuse. He who doubts the existence of the gods, or denies it altogether, although he may seem to adopt monstrous opinions from the audacity of his conjectures, yet refuses to credit what is obscure without insulting any one; and he who asserts that they were mortals, although he brings them down from the exalted place of inhabitants of heaven, yet heaps upon them other[3] honours, since he supposes that they have been raised to the rank of the gods[4] for their services, and from admiration of their virtues.

31. But you who assert that you are the defenders and propagators of their immortality, have you passed by, have you left untouched, any one of them, without assailing him[5] with your abuse? or is there any kind of insult so damnable in the eyes of all, that you have been afraid to use it upon them, even though hindered[6] by the dignity of their name? Who declared that the gods loved frail and mortal bodies? [was it] not you? Who that they perpetrated those most charming thefts on the couches of others? [was it] not you? Who that children had intercourse with their mothers; [and] on the other hand, fathers with their virgin daughters? [was it]

---

[1] Lit., "to speak of any one as atheist . . . of those who," etc.

[2] So the MS. and edd., reading *in eo*, for which we should perhaps read *in eos*—"heap upon them."

[3] *Subsicivis laudibus.*

[4] Lit., "to the reward (*meritum*) of divinity."

[5] Lit., "unwounded."

[6] So the edd., reading *tardati* for the MS. *tradatis*, except Hild., who reads *tardatis*.

not you? Who that pretty boys, and even grown-up [men] of very fine appearance, were wrongfully lusted after? [was it] not you? Who [declared that they[1] were] mutilated, debauched,[2] skilled in dissimulation, thieves, held in bonds and chains, finally assailed with thunderbolts, [and] wounded, that they died, [and] even found graves on earth? [was it] not you? While, then, so many and grievous charges have been raised by you to the injury of the gods, do you dare to assert that the gods have been displeased because of us, while it has long been clear that you are the guilty causes of such anger, and the occasion of the divine wrath?

32. But you err, says [my opponent], and are mistaken, and show, even in criticising [these] things, that you are rather ignorant, unlearned, and boorish. For all those stories which seem to you disgraceful, and tending to the discredit of the gods, contain in them holy mysteries, theories wonderful and profound, and not such as any one can easily become acquainted with by force of understanding. For that is not meant and said which has been written and placed on the surface of the story; but all these things are understood in allegorical senses, and by means of secret explanations privately supplied.[3] Therefore he who says[4] Jupiter lay with his mother, does not mean the incestuous or shameful embraces of Venus, but names Jupiter instead of rain, and Ceres instead of the earth. And he, again, who says that he[5] dealt lasciviously with his daughter, speaks of no filthy pleasures, but puts Jupiter for the name of a shower, and by his daughter means[6] the crop sown. So, too, he who says that Proserpina was carried off by father Dis, does not say (as you suppose[7]) that the maiden was carried off to [gratify] the basest desires; but because we cover the seed with clods, he signifies that the goddess has sunk under the

---

[1] *i.e.* the gods.   [2] *Exoletos.* Cf. iv. c. 35, n. 3.

[3] *Subditivis secretis.*

[4] Both Roman edd. and MS. read *dicet*—"shall say;" all others as above—*dicit.*

[5] *i.e.* Jupiter.   [6] Lit., "in the signification of his daughter."

[7] So the margin of Ursinus—*ut reris* for the MS. *ut ce-reris.*

earth, and unites with Orcus to bring forth fruit. In like manner in the other stories also one thing indeed is said, but something else is understood; and under a commonplace openness of expression there lurks a secret doctrine, and a dark profundity of mystery.

33. These are all quirks, as is evident, and quibbles with which they are wont to bolster up weak cases before a jury; nay, rather, to speak more truly, they are pretences, such as are used in[1] sophistical reasonings, by which not the truth is sought after, but always the image, and appearance, and shadow of the truth. For because it is shameful and unbecoming to receive as true the correct accounts, you have had recourse[2] to this expedient, that one thing should be substituted for another, and that what was in itself shameful should, in being explained, be forced into the semblance of decency. But what is it to us whether other senses and other meanings underlie [these] vain stories? For we who assert that the gods are treated by you wickedly and impiously, need only[3] receive what is written, what is said,[4] and need not care as to what is kept secret, since the insult to the deities consists not in the idea hidden in its meanings,[5] but in what is signified by the words as they stand out. And yet, that we may not seem unwilling to examine what you say, we ask this first of you, if only you will bear with us, from whom have you learned, or by whom has it been made known, either that these things were written allegorically, or that they should be understood in the same way? Did the writers summon you to [take] counsel [with them]? or did you lie hid in their bosoms at the time[6] when they put one thing for another, without regard to truth? Then, if they chose, from

---

[1] Lit., "colours of."

[2] The MS. and both Roman edd. read *indecorum est*, which leaves the sentence incomplete. LB., followed by later edd., proposed *decursum est*, as above (Oehler, *inde d.*—"from these recourse has been had"), the other conjectures tending to the same meaning.

[3] "We need only;" lit., "it is enough for us to."

[4] Lit., "heard."

[5] Lit., "in the obscure mind of senses."

[6] "Or at the time," *aut tum*, the correction of LB. for the MS. *sutum*.

religious awe[1] and fear on any account, to wrap those mysteries in dark obscurity, what audacity it shows in you to wish to understand what they did not wish, to know yourselves and make all acquainted with that which they vainly attempted to conceal by words which did not suggest the truth!

34. But, agreeing with you that in all these stories stags are spoken of instead of Iphigenias, yet, how are you sure, when you either explain or unfold these allegories, that you give the same explanations or have the same ideas which were entertained by the writers themselves in the silence of their thoughts, but expressed by words not adapted[2] to what was meant, but to something else? You say that the falling of rain into the bosom of the earth was spoken of as the union of Jupiter and Ceres; another may both devise with greater subtlety, and conjecture with some probability, something else; a third, a fourth may [do the same]; and as the characteristics of the minds of the thinkers show themselves, so each thing may be explained in an infinite number of ways. For since all that allegory, as it is called, is taken from narratives expressly made obscure,[3] and has no certain limit within which the meaning of the story,[4] as it is called, should be firmly fixed and unchangeable, it is open to every one to put the meaning into it which he pleases, and to assert that that has been adopted[5] to which his thoughts and surmises[6] led him. But this being the case, how can you obtain certainty from what is doubtful, and attach one sense only to an expression which you see to be explained in innumerable different ways?[7]

35. Finally, if you think it right, returning to our inquiry, we ask this of you, whether you think that all stories about the gods,[8] that is, without any exception,[9] have been written

---

[1] Lit., "fear of any reason and of religion."   [2] Lit., "proper."
[3] Lit., "from shut up things."   [4] *Rei.*   [5] Lit., "placed."
[6] Lit., "his suspicion and conjectural (perhaps "probable") inference."
[7] Lit., "to be deduced with variety of expositions through numberless ways."
[8] The MS., first four edd., and Hild. read *de his*—"about these," corrected in the others *dis* or *diis*, as above.
[9] Lit., "each."

throughout with a double meaning and sense, and in a way[1] admitting of several interpretations; or that some parts of them are not ambiguous at all, [while], on the contrary, others have many meanings, and are enveloped in the veil of allegory which has been thrown round them? For if the whole structure and arrangement of the narrative have been surrounded with a veil of allegory from beginning to end, explain [to us], tell [us] what we should put and substitute for each thing which every story says, and to what other things and meanings we should refer[2] each. For as, to take an example, you wish Jupiter to be said instead of the rain, Ceres for the earth, and for Libera[3] and father Dis the sinking and casting of seed [into the earth], so you ought to say what we should understand for the bull, what for the wrath and anger of Ceres; what the word Brimo[4] means; what the anxious prayer of Jupiter; what the gods sent to make intercession for him, but not listened to; what the castrated ram; what the parts[5] of the castrated ram; what the satisfaction made with these; what the further dealings with his daughter, still more unseemly in their lustfulness; so, in the other story also, what the grove and flowers of Henna are; what the fire taken from Ætna, and the torches lit with it; what the travelling through the world with these; what the Attic country, the canton of Eleusin, the hut of Baubo, and her rustic hospitality; what the draught of *cyceon* means, the refusal of it, the shaving and disclosure of the privy parts, the shameful charm of the sight, and the forgetfulness of her bereavement produced by such means. Now, if you point out what should be put in the place of all these, changing the one for the other,[6] we shall admit your assertion;

[1] Pl.   [2] Lit., "call."
[3] *i.e.* Proserpine. The readiness with which Arnobius breaks the form of the sentence should be noted. At first the gods represent physical phenomena, but immediately after natural events are put for the gods. In the MS. two copyists have been at work, the earlier giving *Libero*, which is rather out of place, and is accordingly corrected by the later, *Libera*, followed by LB., Oberthür, Orelli, Hild., and Oehler.
[4] The MS. reads *primo*. Cf. c. 20.   [5] *Proles*.
[6] Lit., "by change of things."

but if you can neither present another supposition in each case, nor appeal to[1] the context as a whole, why do you make that obscure,[2] by means of fair-seeming allegories, which has been spoken plainly, and disclosed to the understanding of all?

36. But you will perhaps say that these allegories are not [found] in the whole body of the story, but that some parts are written so as to be understood by all, while others have a double meaning, and are veiled in ambiguity. That is refined subtlety, and can be seen through by the dullest. For because it is very difficult for you to transpose, reverse, and divert [to other meanings] all that has been said, you choose out some things which suit your purpose, and by means of these you strive to maintain that false and spurious versions were thrown about the truth which is under them.[3] But yet, supposing that we should grant to you that it is just as you say, how do you know, or whence do you learn, which part of the story is written without any double meaning,[4] which, on the other hand, has been covered with jarring and alien senses? For it may be that what you believe to be so[5] is otherwise, that what you believe to be otherwise[6] has been produced with different, and [even] opposite modes of expression. For where, in a consistent whole, one part is said to be written allegorically, the other in plain and trustworthy language, while there is no sign in the thing itself to point out the difference between what is said ambiguously and what is said simply, that which is simple may as well be thought to have a double meaning, as what has been written ambiguously be believed to be wrapt in obscurity.[7] But, indeed, we confess that we do not understand at all by whom this[8] is either done, or can be believed to be possible.

---

[1] The MS. omits *ad*, supplied by Ursinus.

[2] So all edd., except Hild. and Oehler, reading *obscur-atis* for the MS. *-itatibus*.

[3] Lit., "were placed above the interior truth."

[4] Lit., "with simple senses."   [5] *i.e.* involved in obscurity.

[6] *i.e.* free from ambiguity.   [7] Lit., "of shut off obscurities."

[8] The reference is to the words in the middle of the chapter, "how do

37. Let us examine, then, what is said in this way. In the grove of Henna, my opponent says, the maiden Proserpine was once gathering flowers: this is as yet uncorrupted, and has been told in a straightforward manner, for all know without any doubt what a grove and flowers are, what Proserpine is, and a maiden. Summanus sprung forth from the earth, borne along in a four-horse chariot: this, too, is just as simple, for a team of four horses, a chariot, and Summanus need no interpreter. Suddenly he carried off Proserpine, and bore her with himself under the earth: the burying of the seed, my opponent says, is meant by the rape of Proserpine. What has happened, pray, that the story should be suddenly turned to something else? that Proserpine should be called the seed? that she who was for a long time held to be a maiden gathering flowers, after that she was taken away and carried off by violence, should begin to signify the seed sown? Jupiter, my opponent says, having turned himself into a bull, longed to have intercourse with his mother Ceres: as was explained before, under these names the earth and falling rain are spoken of. I see the law of allegory expressed in the dark and ambiguous terms. Ceres was enraged and angry, and received the parts[1] of a ram as the penalty demanded by[2] vengeance: this again I see to be expressed in common language, for both anger and *testes* [and] satisfaction are spoken of in their usual circumstances.[3] What, then, happened here,—that from Jupiter, who was named [for] the rain, and Ceres, who was named [for] the earth, the story passed to the true Jove, and to a most straightforward account of events?

38. Either, then, they must all have been written and put forward allegorically, and the whole should be pointed out to us; or nothing has been so written, since what is supposed to be [allegorical] does not seem as if it were part of the nar-

you know which part is simple?" etc.; Arnobius now saying that he does not see how this can be known.

[1] *Proles.*
[2] Lit., "for penalty and."
[3] Lit., "in their customs and conditions."

rative.[1] These are all written allegorically, [you say]. This seems by no means certain. Do you ask for what reason, for what cause? Because [I answer] all that has taken place and has been set down distinctly in any book cannot be turned into an allegory, for neither can that be undone which has been done, nor can the character of an event change into one which is utterly different. Can the Trojan war be turned into the condemnation of Socrates? or the battle of Cannæ become the cruel proscription of Sulla? A proscription may indeed, as Tullius says[2] in jest, be spoken of as a battle, and be called that of Cannæ; but what has already taken place, cannot be at the same time a battle and a proscription; for neither, as I have said, can that which has taken place be anything else than what has taken place; nor can that pass over into a substance foreign to it which has been fixed down firmly in its own nature and peculiar condition.

39. Whence, then, do we prove that all these narratives are records of events? From the solemn rites and mysteries of initiation, it is clear, whether those which are celebrated at fixed times and on set days, or those which are taught secretly by the heathen without allowing the observance of their usages to be interrupted. For it is not to be believed that these have no origin, are practised without reason or meaning, and have no causes connected with their first beginnings. That pine which is regularly borne into the sanctuary of the Great Mother,[3] is it not in imitation of that tree beneath which Attis mutilated and unmanned himself, which also, they relate, the goddess consecrated to relieve her grief? That erecting of *phalli* and *fascina*, which Greece worships and celebrates in rites every year, does it not recall the deed by which Liber[4] paid his debt? Of what do those

---

[1] *i.e.* if historical, the whole must be so, as bits of allegory would not fit in.
[2] Cicero, *pro Rosc. Am.* c. 32.
[3] The MS. and edd. read *matris deæ*—" of the mother goddess;" for which Meursius proposed *deûm*—" mother of the gods," the usual form of the title. Cf. cc. 7 and 16.
[4] The name is wanting in the MS. Cf. c. 28.

Eleusinian mysteries and secret rites contain a narrative? Is it not of that wandering in which Ceres, worn out in seeking for her daughter, when she came to the confines of Attica, brought wheat [with her], graced with a hind's skin the family of the Nebridæ,[1] and laughed at that most wonderful sight in Baubo's groins? Or if there is another cause, that is nothing to us, so long as they are all produced by [some] cause. For it is not credible that these things were set on foot without being preceded by any causes, or the inhabitants of Attica must be considered mad to have received[2] a religious ceremony got up without any reason. But if this is clear and certain, that is, if the causes and origins of the mysteries are traceable to past events, by no change can they be turned into the figures of allegory; for that which has been done, [which] has taken place, cannot, in the nature of things, be undone.[3]

40. And yet, even if we grant you that this is the case, that is, even if the narratives give utterance to one thing in words, [but] mean[4] something else, after the manner of raving seers, do you not observe in this case, do you not see how dishonouring, how insulting to the gods, this is which is said to be done?[5] or can any greater wrong be devised than to term and call the earth and rain, or anything else (for it does not matter what change is made in the interpretation), the intercourse of Jupiter and Ceres? and to signify the descent of rain from the sky, and the moistening of the earth, by charges against the gods? Can anything be either

---

[1] No Attic family of this name is mentioned anywhere; but in Cos the Nebridæ were famous as descendants of Æsculapius through Nebros. In Attica, on the other hand, the initiated were robed in fawn-skins (νεβρίδες), and were on this account spoken of as νεβρίζοντες. Salmasius has therefore suggested (*ad Solinum*, p. 864, E) that Arnobius, or the author on whom he relied, transferred the family to Attica on account of the similarity of sound.

[2] Lit., "who have attached to themselves."

[3] Arnobius would seem to have been partial to this phrase, which occurs in the middle of c. 38.

[4] Lit., "say."

[5] Lit., "with what shame and insult of the gods this is said to be done."

thought or believed more impious than that the rape of Proserpine speaks of seeds buried in the earth, or anything else (for in like manner it is of no importance), and that it speaks of the pursuit of agriculture to[1] the dishonour of father Dis? Is it not a thousand times more desirable to become mute and speechless, and to lose that flow of words and noisy and[2] unseemly loquacity, than to call the basest things by the names of the gods; nay, more, to signify commonplace things by the base actions of the gods?

41. It was once usual, in speaking allegorically, to conceal under perfectly decent ideas, and clothe[3] with the respectability of decency, what was base and horrible to speak of openly; but now venerable things are at your instance vilely spoken of, and what is quite pure[4] is related[5] in filthy language, so that that which vice[6] formerly concealed from shame, is now meanly and basely spoken of, the mode of speech which was fitting[7] being changed. In speaking of Mars and Venus as having been taken in adultery by Vulcan's art, we speak of lust, says [my opponent], and anger, as restrained by the force and purpose of reason. What, then, hindered, what prevented you from expressing each thing by the words and terms proper to it? nay, more, what necessity was there, when you had resolved[8] to declare something or other, by means of treatises and writings, to resolve that that should not be the meaning to which you point, and in one narrative to take up at the same time opposite positions—the eagerness of one wishing to teach, the niggardliness of one reluctant to make public?[9] Was there no risk in speaking of the gods

---

[1] Lit., "with."
[2] Lit., "din of."
[3] *Passive.*
[4] Lit., "strong in chastity."
[5] The MS., first three edd., Elm., and Oehler read *commorantur*—"lingers," *i.e.* "continues to be spoken of;" the other edd. receive *commemorantur*, as above, from the *errata* in the 1st ed.
[6] The MS., first four edd., and Oehler read *gravitas*—seriousness; corrected *pr.* as above, in all edd. after Stewechius.
[7] So, perhaps, the unintelligible MS. *dignorum* should be emended *digna rerum.*
[8] So all edd. since Stewechius, adding *s* to the MS. *voluisse.*
[9] *i.e.* the mere fact that the stories were published, showed a wish to

as unchaste? The mention of lust and anger, [my opponent says], was likely to defile the tongue and mouth with foul contagion.[1] But, assuredly, if this were done,[2] and the veil of allegorical obscurity were removed, the matter would be easily understood, and at the same the dignity of the gods would be maintained unimpaired. But now, indeed, when the restraining of vices is said to be signified by the binding of Mars and Venus, two most inconsistent[3] things are done at the very same time; so that, on the one hand, a description of something vile suggests an honourable meaning, and on the other, the baseness occupies the mind before any regard for religion can do so.

42. But you will perhaps say (for this only is left which you may think[4] can be brought forward by you) that the gods do not wish their mysteries to be known by men, and that the narratives were therefore written with allegorical ambiguity. And whence have you learned[5] that the gods above do not wish their mysteries to be made public? whence have you become acquainted with these? or why are you anxious to unravel them by explaining them as allegories? Lastly, and finally, what do the gods mean, that while they do not wish honourable, they allow unseemly, even the basest things, to be said about them? When we name Attis, says [my opponent], we mean and speak of the sun; but if Attis is the sun, as you reckon [him] and say, who will that Attis be whom your books record and declare to have been born in Phrygia, to have suffered certain things, to have done certain things also, whom all the theatres know in the scenic shows, to whom every year we see divine honours paid expressly by name amongst the [other] religious ceremonies? Whether was this name made to pass from the sun to a man,

teach; but their being allegories, showed a reluctance to allow them to be understood.

[1] The edd. read this sentence interrogatively.

[2] *i.e.* "if you said exactly what you mean." The reference is not to the immediately preceding words, but to the question on which the chapter is based—"what prevented you from expressing," etc.

[3] Lit., "perverse."   [4] *Passive*.   [5] Lit., "is it clear to you."

or from a man to the sun? For if that name is derived in the first instance from the sun, what, pray, has the golden sun done to you, that you should make that name to belong to him in common with an emasculated person? But if it is [derived] from a goat, and is Phrygian, of what has the sire of Phaethon, the father of this light and brightness, been guilty, that he should seem worthy to be named from a mutilated man, and should become more venerable when designated by the name of an emasculated body?

43. But what the meaning of this is, is already clear to all. For because you are ashamed of such writers and histories, and do not see that these things can be got rid of which have once been committed to writing in filthy language, you strive to make base things honourable, and by every kind of subtlety you pervert and corrupt the real senses[1] of words for the sake of spurious interpretations;[2] and, as ofttimes happens to the sick, whose senses and understanding have been put to flight by the distempered force of disease, you toss about confused and uncertain [conjectures], and rave in empty fictions.

Let it be [granted] that the irrigation of the earth was meant by the union of Jupiter and Ceres, the burying of the seed[3] by the ravishing [of Proserpine] by father Dis, wines scattered over the earth by the limbs of Liber torn asunder [by the Titans], that the restraining[4] of lust and rashness has been spoken of as the binding of the adulterous Venus and Mars.

44. But if you come to the conclusion that these fables have been written allegorically, what is to be done with the rest, which we see cannot be forced into such changes [of sense]? For what are we to substitute for the wrigglings[5]

---

[1] Lit., "natures."   [2] Lit., "things."

[3] So most edd., reading *occultatio* for the MS. *occupatio*.

[4] So all edd., reading *com-*, except Hild. and Oehler, who retain the MS. reading, *im-pressio*—"the assault of," *i.e.* "on."

[5] Lit., "waves"—*fluctibus*, the reading of the MS., LB., Hild., and Oehler; the other edd. reading *fustibus*—"stakes."

into which the lustful heat[1] of Semele's offspring forced him upon the sepulchral mound? and what for those Ganymedes who were carried off[2] and set to preside over lustful practices? what for that conversion of an ant into which Jupiter, the greatest [of the gods], contracted the outlines of his huge body?[3] what for swans and satyrs? what for golden showers, which the same seductive [god] put on with perfidious guile, amusing himself by changes of form? And, that we may not seem to speak of Jupiter only, what allegories can there be in the loves of the other deities? what in their circumstances as hired servants and slaves? what in their bonds, bereavements, lamentations? what in their agonies, wounds, sepulchres? Now, while in this you might be held guilty in one respect for writing in such wise about the gods, you have added to your guilt beyond measure[4] in calling base things by the names of deities, and again in defaming the gods by [giving to them] the names of infamous things. But if you believed without any doubt[5] that they were here close at hand, or anywhere at all, fear would check you in making mention of them, and your beliefs and unchanged thoughts should have been exactly[6] as if they were listening to you and heard your words. For among men devoted to the services of religion, not only the gods themselves, but even the names of the gods, should be reverenced, and there should be quite as much grandeur in their names as there is in those even who are thought of under these names.

---

[1] So Meursius, changing the MS. *o*- into *u-rigo*.

[2] The first four edd. retain the MS., reading *partis*—" brought forth ;" the others adopt a suggestion of Canterus, *raptis*, as above.

[3] Lit., " vastness."

[4] *Addere garo gerrem*, a proverb ridiculing a worthless addition, which nullifies something in itself precious, *garum* being a highly esteemed sauce (or perhaps soup), which would be thrown away upon *gerres*, a worthless kind of salt fish. Arnobius merely means, however, that while such stories are wrong, what follows is unspeakably worse.

[5] Lit., " with indubitable knowledge."

[6] Lit., " it ought to have been so believed, and to be held fixed in thought just," etc.

45. Judge fairly, and you are deserving of censure in this,[1] that in your common conversation you name Mars when you mean[2] fighting, Neptune when you mean the seas, Ceres when you mean bread, Minerva when you mean weaving,[3] Venus when you mean filthy lusts. For what reason is there, that, when things can be classed under their own names, they should be called by the names of the gods, and that such an insult should be offered to the deities as not even we men endure, if any one applies and turns our names to trifling objects? But language, [you say], is contemptible, if defiled with such words.[4] O modesty,[5] worthy of praise! you blush to name bread and wine, and are not afraid to speak of Venus instead of carnal intercourse!

[1] Lit., "are in this part of censure."
[2] Lit., "for."
[3] Lit., "the warp," *stamine*.
[4] *i.e.* if things are spoken of under their proper names.
[5] The MS. reads *ac* unintelligibly.

BOOK VI.

ARGUMENT.

HAVING shown how impious were the opinions entertained by the heathen about their own gods, Arnobius next meets the charge of impiety made against Christians because they neither built temples, nor set up statues, nor offered sacrifices. This, however, he asserts was not the fruit of impiety, but of nobler beliefs (1). For, admitting that they are gods, they must be free from all imperfection, and therefore self-sufficient, not dependent on aid from without, nor afflicted with the desires and passions of mortals. To think thus, he adds, is not to hold the gods in contempt (2). But if they are such, of what use would temples be to them? Is it not sheer madness to think that you honour your superiors when you judge of them by your own necessities? Do the gods need shelter from cold and heat, from rain or storm? And although to men temples may seem magnificent, to the gods of heaven they can be only mean cells (3). But, it might be said, temples are built not to shelter the gods, but that we may address them face to face, as it were. Then, if prayers were offered to the gods under the open heaven, they would not be heard. But the true God must hear prayers wherever offered, nay, must be present even in the silent recesses of the heart, to know what is thought, what is desired, even though it be not expressed, for it is his to fill all things with his power, and not to be present in one place only (4). Otherwise there could be no hope of help; for if prayers were made to one deity from different parts of the earth, while he could be present only in one, then either all would be alike neglected, or one only would be heard and answered (5).

These temples, however, which were said to have been built in honour of the gods, were in reality places of sepulture. Thus Cecrops was buried in the temple of Minerva at Athens, and others, both men and women, in various well-known shrines (6), even the Capitol being only the sepulchre of Olus; and thus the heathens are shown to have been guilty either of worshipping the dead as gods, or of dishonouring the gods by making tombs their temples (7).

As to images, if there are really gods in heaven to whom supplication can be made, why, Arnobius asks, should figures of them be made on earth? and if they are not believed to be in heaven, it is still more difficult to say of what use these images are (8). We worship the gods, the heathen said, by means of their images. Can the gods, therefore, Arnobius asks, receive homage only when offered to statues? What can be more insulting than to believe in a god, and pray to a statue, to hope for aid from a deity, but to ask it from his image (9)? Moreover, how could it be known that those figures were indeed images of the gods? The moon is ever in motion; how could the figure of a woman which never stirred be her likeness? But if the gods were not such as their statues—which no one supposed—what audacity was shown in giving to them whatever figures men pleased (10)! Little occasion had they to laugh at the superstitious worship of rivers, stones, sabres, and pieces of wood by ancient and barbarous peoples, while they themselves prayed to little figures of men. Did they, then, believe that the gods were like men? No, Arnobius says; only they found themselves committed to a false position, and would rather maintain it with violence and cruelty than admit that they were in error (11). Hence it was that such extraordinary forms and equipments were given to the gods. But if the images were secretly removed from their proper places, and the insignia of one given to another, it would be impossible to say which was Jupiter, which Mars. How absurd to form images of the gods, which depend for their individuality on the dresses put upon them (12)! It was a small thing, however, to distinguish the gods by means of reaping-hooks, tridents, horns, or hammers; but it was no light matter that the gods should be fashioned like lewd men and women, and that thus divine honours should be paid to harlots (13). Arnobius next insists that images are but dead matter, moulded, cut, filed, and hewn into form by men; and that it is therefore absurd for a man to worship what he has himself made (14). No one would worship, he says, a mass of metal or a heap of stones, or even fragments of images; but why, while the parts are thus regarded as merely dead matter, should they, when formed into an image, become divine (15)? Still men asked blessings from earthenware, copper, and ivory, and supposed that their prayers were heard by senseless figures, forgetting how and from what they were formed; that it was man's skill which gave them all their grandeur, for within them there was only hideous emptiness; and that they were destroyed by time, used as coverts by mean and loathsome creatures, and bemired by birds, the dumb animals thus teaching their master, man, that the images which he worshipped were beneath his notice (16). But, was the reply of the heathen, we worship not the images, but the deities, which are brought into them by their consecration. Do the gods, then, quit heaven to give dignity to what is base? And if so, do they enter these images willingly or unwillingly? If unwillingly, is their majesty not lessened? If willingly, what can they find there to entice them from their starry seats (17)? It is further asked, Do the gods always remain in these images, or come and go at will? If the former, how wretched is their case! If the latter, how is it to be known when the god is in the image so that he should be worshipped, and when he has quitted it so that it may be safely neglected? Moreover, in small figures, do the gods become small? in those represented as sitting, do they sit? and do they thus conform in all respects to their images (18)? But there are either as many gods as statues, or no statue can be tenanted by a god, because one god cannot occupy different images (19). But if the gods dwell in their own images, why do they not themselves defend these, instead of leaving it to dogs and geese and watchers to protect their effigies from fire or thieves (20)? Nay, more, why do they allow themselves to be robbed and insulted by the stripping from their images of what is valuable (21)? It might be said that the gods despised such trifles; but if so, that showed that they despised the images as well. Arnobius then relates the stories of men falling in love with statues of Venus, and asks, where was the goddess, that she did not repel and punish such insulting wantonness, or at least recall the frenzied youths to their senses (22)? If any explanation could be found for this, there was none, however, for the fact that so many temples had been destroyed by fire and spoiled by robbers, without the interference of their presiding deities (23). Finally, if it were said that images had been devised in ancient times to terrify men from their wickedness by the belief that gods were at hand to see and punish their crimes, Arnobius admits that there would be some reason in this, if temples and images caused peace, justice, and purity to prevail on the earth; but points out that this had not been the result, for crime and wickedness abound everywhere; and temples, and even the images which were to force men to be just, are plundered without fear (24). He then asks what power Saturn's sickle, the winged shoes of Mercury, or any of the other insignia of the gods possess, to move men's minds to fear (25); and whether it had ever been thought that men could be frightened by a hideous face, as children by some bugbear. The enactment of laws, however, shows clearly that images or temples have no such power (26). He next proceeds to meet the charge, that Christians are atheists because they offer none of the usual divine honours to God. The fact he admits, but asserts that in so doing Christians really comply with God's will (27).

1. HAVING shown briefly how impious and infamous [are the] opinions [which] you have formed about your gods, we have now to[1] speak of their temples, their images also, and sacrifices, and of the other things which are[2] united and closely related to them. For you are here in the habit of fastening upon us a very serious charge of impiety because we do not rear temples for the ceremonies of worship, do not set

[1] Lit., "it remains that we."   [2] Lit., "series which is," etc.

up statues and images[1] of any god, do not build altars,[2] do not offer the blood of creatures slain [in sacrifices], incense, nor sacrificial meal, and finally, do not bring wine flowing in libations from sacred bowls; which, indeed, we neglect to build and do, not as though we cherish impious and wicked dispositions, or have conceived any madly desperate feeling of contempt for the gods, but because we think and believe that they[3] (if only they are true gods, and are called by this exalted name[4]) either scorn such honours, if they give way to scorn, or endure [them] with anger, if they are roused by feelings of rage.

2. For—that you may learn what are our sentiments and opinions about that race—we think that they (if only they are true gods, that the same things may be said again till you are wearied hearing them[5]) should have all the virtues in perfection, should be wise, upright, venerable (if only our heaping upon them human honours is not a crime), strong in excellences within themselves, and should not give themselves[6] up to external props, because the completeness of their unbroken bliss is made perfect; [should be] free from all agitating and disturbing passions; should not burn with anger, should not be excited by any desires; should send misfortune to none, should not find a cruel pleasure in the ills of men; should not terrify by portents, should not show prodigies to cause fear; should not hold [men] responsible and liable to be punished for the vows which they owe, nor demand expiatory sacrifices by threatening omens; should not bring on pestilences [and] diseases by corrupting the air, should not burn up the fruits with droughts; should take no part in the slaughter of war and devastation of cities; should not wish ill to one party, and be favourable to the success of another; but, as becomes great minds, should weigh all in a just

[1] Singular.

[2] *Non altaria, non aras*, i.e. neither to the superior nor inferior deities. Cf. Virgil, *Ecl.* v. 66.

[3] The earlier edd. prefix *d* to the MS. *cos*—"that the gods," etc.

[4] Lit., "endowed with the eminence of this name."

[5] Lit., "and to satiety."

[6] The MS. wants *se*, which was supplied by Stewechius.

balance, and show kindness impartially to all. For it belongs to a mortal race and human weakness to act otherwise ;[1] and the maxims and declarations of wise men state distinctly, that those who are touched by passion live a life of suffering,[2] [and] are weakened by grief,[3] and that it cannot be but that those who have been given over to disquieting feelings, have been bound by the laws of mortality. Now, since this is the case, how can we be supposed to hold the gods in contempt, who we say are not gods, and cannot be connected with the powers of heaven, unless they are just and worthy of the admiration which great minds excite?

3. But, [we are told], we rear no temples to them, and do not worship their images; we do not slay victims in sacrifice, we do not offer incense and libations of wine. And what greater honour or dignity can we ascribe to them, than that we put them in the same position as the Head and Lord of the universe, to whom the gods owe it in common with us,[4] that they are conscious that they exist, and have a living being?[5] For do we honour Him with shrines, and by building temples?[6] Do we even slay victims [to Him]? Do we give [to Him] the other things, to take which and pour them

---

[1] *i.e.* not act impartially and benevolently, which may possibly be the meaning of *contrariis agere*, or, as Oehler suggests, "to assail [men] with contrary, *i.e.* injurious things." All edd. read *egere*, except Oehler, who can see no meaning in it; but if translated, "to wish for contrary things," it suits the next clause very well.

[2] Lit., "whom passion touches, suffer."

[3] So the MS., Stewechius, Hild., and Oehler, while the first four edd. and Oberthür merely add *m* to *dolore*, and join with the preceding *pati* —" suffer pain, are weakened."

[4] The MS. and most edd. read *di-vina nobiscum*—"the divine things along with us;" Heraldus rejects *div.* as a gloss, while Meursius, followed by Orelli, corrects *dii una*, and Oehler *divi una*, as above.

[5] Lit., "are contained in vital substance."

[6] Arnobius here expressly denies that the Christians had any temples. There has been some controversy on the subject (Mosheim, B. i. cent. 1, ch. 4, sec. 5, Soames' ed.), surely as needless as controversy could be; for as the Christians must at all times have had stated places of meeting (although in time of persecution these might be changed frequently), it is clear that, in speaking thus, the meaning must be only, that their buildings had no architectural pretensions, and their service no splendour of ritual.

forth in libation shows not a careful regard to reason, but heed to a practice maintained[1] [merely] by usage? For it is perfect folly to measure greater powers by your necessities, and to give the things useful to yourself to the gods who give [all things], and to think this an honour, not an insult. We ask, therefore, to do what service to the gods, or to meet what want, do you say that temples have been reared,[2] and think that they should be again built? Do they feel the cold of[3] winter, or are they scorched by summer suns? Do storms of rain flow over them, or whirlwinds shake them? Are they in danger of being exposed to the onset of enemies, or the furious attacks of wild beasts, so that it is right and becoming to shut them up in places of security,[4] or guard them by throwing up a rampart of stones? For what are these temples? If you ask human weakness[5]—something vast and spacious; if you consider the power of the gods— small caves, as it were,[6] and even, to speak more truly, the narrowest kind of caverns formed and contrived with sorry judgment.[7] Now, if you ask to be told who was their first founder[8] and builder, either Phoroneus or the Egyptian Merops[9] will be mentioned to you, or, as Varro relates in his [treatise, *de*] *Admirandis*, Æacus the offspring of Jupiter. Though these, then, should be built of heaps of marble, or shine resplendent with ceilings fretted with gold, [though] precious stones sparkle here, and gleam like stars set at varying intervals, all these things are made up of earth, and of the

[1] Lit., "drawn out."

[2] So the edd., reading *constructa* for the corrupt MS. *conscripta*— "written."

[3] *i.e.* to suppose that temples are necessary to the gods, is to make them subject to human weakness.

[4] Lit., "with fortifications of roofs."

[5] *i.e.* if you have regard merely to the weakness of men, a temple may be something wonderful.

[6] Lit., "some." [7] Lit., "formed by contrivance of a poor heart."

[8] *Institutor*, wanting in all edd., except Hild. and Oehler.

[9] Arnobius here agrees with Clemens Alexandrinus, but Jos. Scaliger has pointed out that the name should be Cecrops. It is possible that Arnobius may have been misled by what was merely a slip of Clement's pen.

lowest dregs of [even] baser matter. For not even, if you value these more highly, is it to be believed that the gods take pleasure in them, or that they do not refuse and scorn to shut themselves up, and be confined within these barriers. This, [my opponent] says, is the temple of Mars, this [that] of Juno and of Venus, this [that] of Hercules, of Apollo, of Dis. What is this but to say this is the house of Mars, this of Juno and Venus,[1] Apollo dwells here, in this [house] abides Hercules, in that Summanus? Is it not, then, the very[2] greatest affront to hold the gods kept fast[3] in habitations, to give to them little huts, to build lockfast places and cells, and to think that the things are[4] necessary to them which are needed by men, cats, emmets, and lizards, by quaking, timorous, and little mice?

4. But, says [my opponent], it is not for this reason that we assign temples to the gods as though we [wished to] ward off from them drenching storms of rain, winds, showers, or the rays of the sun; but in order that we may be able to see them in person and close at hand, to come near and address them, and impart to them, when in a measure present, the expressions of our reverent feelings. For if they are invoked under the open heaven, and the canopy of ether, they hear nothing [I suppose]; and unless prayers are addressed to them [by those] near at hand, they will stand deaf and immoveable as if nothing were said. And yet we think that every god whatever—if only he has the power of this name—should hear what every one said from every part of the world, just as if he were present; nay, more, should foresee, without waiting to be told,[5] what every one conceived in his secret and silent[6] thoughts. And as the stars, the sun, the moon, while

[1] The preceding words, from "this of Hercules," are omitted by the first four edd. and Elmenh., and were first restored from the MS. by Stewechius.

[2] Lit., "first and."

[3] So the edd., reading *habere districtos* for the MS. *destructos*.

[4] Lit., "that the things be thought to be."

[5] Lit., "knowledge being anticipated."

[6] These words, *et tacitis*, omitted by Oberthür, are similarly omitted by Orelli without remark.

they wander above the earth, are steadily and everywhere in sight of all those who gaze at them without any exception; so, too,[1] it is fitting that the ears of the gods should be closed against no tongue, and should be ever within reach, although voices should flow together to them from widely separated regions. For this [it is that] belongs specially to the gods,— to fill all things with their power, to be not partly at any place, but all everywhere, not to go to dine with the Æthiopians, and return after twelve days to their own dwellings.[2]

5. Now, if this be not the case, all hope of help is taken away, and it will be doubtful whether you are heard[3] by the gods or not, if ever you perform the sacred rites with due ceremonies. For, to make it clear,[4] let us suppose that there is a temple of some deity in the Canary Islands, [another] of the same [deity] in remotest Thyle, also among the Seres, among the tawny Garamantes, and any others[5] who are debarred from knowing each other by seas, mountains, forests, and the four quarters of the world. If they all at one time beg of the deity with sacrifices what their wants compel each one to think about,[6] what hope, pray, will there be to all of obtaining the benefit, if the god does not hear the cry sent up to him everywhere, and [if] there shall be any distance to which the words of the suppliant for help cannot penetrate? For either he will be nowhere present, if he may at times not be anywhere,[7] or he will be at one place

---

[1] So the edd., inserting *quo-* into the MS. reading *ita-que*—"it is therefore fitting," which is absurd, as making the connection between the members of the sentence one not of analogy, but of logical sequence.

[2] Cf. the speech of Thetis, *Iliad*, i. 423-5.

[3] So the margin of Ursinus, Elm., LB., and Orelli, with Meursius, reading *audiamini* for the MS. *audiamur*—"we are heard," which does not harmonize with the next clause.

[4] Lit., "for the purpose of coming to know the thing."

[5] Lit., "if there are any others."

[6] So the MS., reading *c-ogitare*, corrected *r-*—"to beg," in the margin of Ursinus and Elm. For the preceding words the MS. reads, *poscantque de numine*. The edd. omit *que* as above, except Oehler, who reads *quæ*— "what hope will there be, what, pray, to all," etc.

[7] So the MS., reading *si uspiam poterit aliquando non esse*, which may be understood in two senses, either not limited by space, or not in space, *i.e.*

only, since he cannot give his attention generally, and without making any distinction. And thus it is brought about, that either the god helps none at all, if being busy with something he has been unable to hasten to give ear to their cries, or one only goes away with his prayers heard, [while] the rest have effected nothing.

6. What [can you say] as to this, that it is attested by the writings of authors, that many of these temples which have been raised with golden domes and lofty roofs cover bones and ashes, and are sepulchres of the dead? Is it not plain and manifest, either that you worship dead men for immortal gods, or that an inexpiable affront is cast upon the deities, whose shrines and temples have been built over the tombs of the dead? Antiochus,[1] in the ninth [book] of his *Histories*, relates that Cecrops was buried in the temple of Minerva,[2] at Athens; again, in the temple of the same goddess, which is in the citadel of Larissa,[3] it is related and declared that Acrisius was laid, [and] in the sanctuary of Polias,[4] Erichthonius; [while] the brothers Dairas and Immarnachus [were buried] in the enclosure of Eleusin, which lies near the city. What say you as to the virgin daughters of Celeus? are they not said to be buried[5] in the temple of Ceres at Eleusin? [and] in the shrine of Diana, which was set up in the temple of the Delian Apollo, are not Hyperoche and Laodice buried, who are said to have been brought thither from the country of

---

not existing; but the reading and meaning must be regarded as alike doubtful.

[1] A Syracusan historian. The rest of the chapter is almost literally translated from Clement (p. 39), who is followed by Eusebius also (*Præp. Evang.* ii. 6).

[2] *i.e.* the Acropolis.

[3] In Thessaly, whither (acc. to Pausanias) he had fled in vain, to avoid the fulfilment of the oracle that he should be killed by his daughter's son.

[4] *i.e.* Athena Polias, or guardian of cities. Immediately below, the MS. reads *Immarnachus*, corrected in LB. and Orelli *Immarus* from Clem., who speaks of "Immarus, son of Eumolpus and Daeira."

[5] So the unintelligible reading of the MS., *humation-ibus officia*, was emended by Heraldus, followed by LB. and Orelli, *-is habuisse*.

the Hyperboreans? In the Milesian Didymæon,[1] Leandrius says that Cleochus had the last honours of burial paid to him. Zeno of Myndus openly relates that the monument of Leucophryne is in the sanctuary of Diana at Magnesia. Under the altar of Apollo, which is seen in the city of Telmessus, is it not invariably declared by writings that the prophet Telmessus lies buried? Ptolemæus, the son of Agesarchus, in the first book of the *History of Philopator*[2] which he published, affirms, on the authority of literature, that Cinyras, king of Paphos, was interred in the temple of Venus with all his family, nay, more, with all his stock. It would be[3] an endless and boundless task to describe in what sanctuaries they all are throughout the world; nor is anxious care required, although[4] the Egyptians fixed a penalty for any one who should have revealed the places in which Apis lay hid, as to those *Polyandria*[5] of Varro,[6] by what temples they are covered, and what heavy masses they have laid upon them.

7. But why [do] I [speak] of these trifles? What man is there who is ignorant that in the Capitol of the imperial people is the sepulchre of Tolus[7] Vulcentanus? Who is there, I say, who does not know that from beneath[8] its

---

[1] *i.e.* the temple near Didyma, sacred to Apollo, who was worshipped then under the name Didymus.

[2] *i.e.* "lover of his father," the name given ironically to the fourth Ptolemy, because he murdered his father.

[3] Lit., "is."

[4] So the MS., both Rom. edd., Hild., and Oehler, reading *quamvis pænam;* Gelenius, Canterus, Elm., and Oberthür omit *vis*, and the other edd. *v*, *i.e.* "as to what punishment the Egyptian," etc. This must refer to the cases in which the sacred bull, having outlived the term of twenty-five years, was secretly killed by the priests, while the people were taught that it had thrown itself into the water.

[5] *i.e.* "burial-places." By this Oehler has attempted to show is meant the *Hebdomades vel de Imaginibus* of Varro, a series of biographical sketches illustrated with portraits, executed in some way which cannot be clearly ascertained.

[6] MS. *Barronis.*

[7] So the MS., first four edd., and Oberthür, reading *Toli*, corrected *Oli* in the others, from Servius (*ad. Æn.* viii. 345). Arnobius himself gives the form *Aulus*, *i.e. Olus*, immediately below, so that it is probably correct.

[8] Lit., "the seats of."

foundations there was rolled a man's head, buried for no very long time before, either by itself without the other parts [of the body] (for some relate this), or with all its members? Now, if you require this to be made clear by the testimonies of authors, Sammonicus, Granius, Valerianus,[1] and Fabius will declare to you whose son Aulus[2] was, of what race and nation, how[3] he was bereft of life and light by the slave of his brother, of what crime he was guilty against his fellow-citizens, that he was denied burial in his father[4] land. You will learn also—although they pretend to be unwilling to make this public—what was done with his head when cut off, or in what place it was shut up, and the whole affair carefully concealed, in order that the omen which the gods had attested might stand without interruption,[5] unalterable, and sure. Now, while it was proper that this [story] should be suppressed, and concealed, and forgotten in the lapse of time, the composition of the name published it, and, by a testimony which could not be got rid of, caused it to remain [in men's minds], together with its causes, so long as it endured itself ;[6] and the state [which is] greatest [of all], and worships all deities, did not blush in giving a name to the temple, to name it from the head of Olus[7] Capitolium rather than from the name of Jupiter.

8. We have therefore—as I suppose—shown sufficiently, that to the immortal gods temples have been either reared in vain, or built in consequence of insulting opinions [held]

[1] Ursinus suggested *Valerius Antias*, mentioned in the first chapter of the fifth book ; a conjecture adopted by Hild.

[2] The MS., LB., Hild., and Oehler read Aulus, and, acc. to Oehler, all other edd. *Tolus*. Orelli, however, reads *Olus*, as above.

[3] The MS. and both Roman edd. read *germani servuli vita* without meaning, corrected as above by Gelenius, Canterus, Elm., and Oberthür, *ut a g. servulo*, and *ut a g. servulis*—"by the slaves," in the others, except Oehler who reads as above, *g. servulo ut*.

[4] The MS. and both Roman edd. read unintelligibly *patientiæ*, corrected *paternæ* in Hild. and Oehler, *patriæ* in the rest.

[5] Lit., "the perpetuity of the omen sealed might stand."

[6] Lit., "through the times given to itself."

[7] The MS. reads *s-oli*,—changed into *Toli* by the first four edd., Elm., and Oberthür. The others omit *s*.

to their dishonour and to the belittling of the power believed [to be in their hands]. We have next to say something about statues and images, which you form with much skill, and tend with religious care,—wherein if there is any credibility, we can by no amount of consideration settle in our own minds whether you do this in earnest and with a serious purpose, or amuse yourselves in childish dreams by mocking at these very things.[1] For if you are assured that the gods exist whom you suppose, and that they live in the highest regions of heaven, what cause, what reason, is there that those images should be fashioned by you, when you have true beings to whom you may pour forth prayers, and [from whom you may] ask help in trying circumstances? But if, on the contrary, you do not believe, or, to speak with moderation, are in doubt, in this case, also, what reason is there, pray, to fashion and set up images of doubtful [beings], and to form[2] with vain imitation what you do not believe to exist? Do you perchance say, that under these images of deities there is displayed to you their presence, as it were, and that, because it has not been given you to see the gods, they are worshipped in this fashion,[3] and the duties owed [to them] paid? He who says and asserts this, does not believe that the gods exist; and he is proved not to put faith in his own religion, to whom it is necessary to see what he may hold, lest that which [being] obscure is not seen, may happen to be vain.

9. We worship the gods, you say, by means of images. What then? Without these, do the gods not know that they are worshipped, and will they not think that any honour is shown to them by you? Through by-paths, as it were, then, and by assignments to a third party,[4] as they are called, they receive and accept your services; and before those to whom

---

[1] *i.e.* " which you pretend to worship."

[2] So the edd., reading *formar-e*, except Hild. and Oehler, who retain the MS. reading *i*—" that images be formed."

[3] The MS. and both Roman edd. read corruptly *insolidi*, corrected *ita* or *sic coli*, as above, in all except the last two edd.

[4] *i.e.* you do not seek access to the gods directly, and seek to do them honour by giving that honour to the idols instead.

that service is owed experience it, you first sacrifice to images, and transmit, as it were, some remnants to them at the pleasure of others.[1] And what greater wrong, disgrace, hardship, can be inflicted than to acknowledge one god, and [yet] make supplication to something else—to hope for help from a deity, and pray to an image without feeling? Is not this, I pray you, that which is said in the common proverbs: *to cut down the smith when you strike at the fuller;*[2] *and when you seek a man's advice, to require of asses and pigs their opinions as to what should be done?*

10. And whence, finally, do you know whether all these images which you form and put in the place of[3] the immortal gods reproduce and bear a resemblance to the gods? For it may happen that in heaven one has a beard who by you is represented[4] with smooth cheeks; that [another] is rather advanced in years to whom you give the appearance of a youth;[5] that here he is fair, [with blue eyes],[6] who really has grey ones; that he has distended nostrils whom you make and form with a high nose. For it is not right to call or name that an image which does not derive from the face of the original features like [it]; which[7] can be recognised to be clear and certain from things which are manifest. For while all we men see that the sun is perfectly round by our eyesight, which cannot be doubted, you have given[8] to him the features of a man, and

---

[1] *i.e.* the transmission of the sacrifice to the gods is made dependent on idols.

[2] This corresponds exactly to the English, "to shoot at the pigeon and hit the crow."

[3] Lit., "with vicarious substitution for."

[4] The MS. reads *effi-gitur*, corrected as above, *effin.*, in all edd. except Hild., who reads *efficitur*—"is made," and Stewechius, *effigiatur*—"is formed."

[5] Lit., "boy's age."

[6] *Flavus*, so invariably associated with blue eyes, that though these are the feature brought into contrast, they are only suggested in this way, and not directly mentioned—a mode of speech very characteristic of Arnobius.

[7] *i.e.* a fact which can be seen to be true by appealing to analogy.

[8] So the MS., LB., Hild., and Oehler, reading *donastis*, the others *donatis*—"you give."

of mortal bodies. The moon is always in motion, and in its restoration every month puts on thirty faces:[1] with you, as leaders and designers, that is [represented as] a woman, and has one countenance, which passes through a thousand different states, changing each day.[2] We understand that all the winds are [only] a flow of air driven and impelled in mundane ways: in your hands they take[3] the forms of men filling with breath twisted trumpets by blasts from out their breasts.[4] Among [the representations of] your gods we see [that there is] the very stern face of a lion[5] smeared with pure vermilion, and that it is named *Frugifer*. If all these images are likenesses of the gods above, there must then be said to dwell in heaven also a god such as the image which has been made to represent his form and appearance;[6] and, of course, as here that [figure] of yours, so there the deity himself[7] is a mere mask and face, without the rest of the body, growling with fiercely gaping jaws, terrible, red as blood,[8]

---

[1] As the appearance of the moon is the same in some of its phases as in others, it is clear that Arnobius cannot mean that it has thirty distinct forms. We must therefore suppose that he is either speaking very loosely of change upon change day after day, or that he is referring to some of the lunar theories of the ancients, such as that a new moon is created each day, and that its form is thus ever new (*Lucr.* v. 729-748).

[2] Lit., "is changed through a thousand states with daily instability."

[3] Lit., "are."   [4] Lit., "intestine and domestic."

[5] The MS. reads *leon-e-s torvissimam faciem*, emended, as above, *leonis t. f.*, in LB., Orelli, Hild., and Oehler, and *l. torvissima facie*—"lions of very stern face," in the others. Nourry supposes that the reference is to the use of lions, or lion-headed figures, as architectural ornaments on temples (cf. the two lions rampant surmounting the gate of Mycenæ), but partially coincides in the view of Elm., that mixed figures are meant, such as are described by Tertullian and Minucius Felix (ch. 28: "You deify gods made up of a goat and a lion, and with the faces of lions and of dogs"). The epithet *frugifer*, however, which was applied to the Egyptian Osiris, the Persian Mithras, and Bacchus, who were also represented as lions, makes it probable that the reference is to symbolic statues of the sun.

[6] Lit., "such a god to whose form and appearance the likeness of this image has been directed."

[7] Lit., "that."

[8] The MS. and both Roman edd. read unintelligibly *sanguineo decotoro*,

holding an apple fast with his teeth, and at times, as dogs [do] when wearied, putting his tongue out of his gaping mouth.[1] But if,[2] indeed, this is not the case, as we all think that it is not, what, pray, is the meaning of so great audacity to fashion to yourself whatever form you please, and to say [3] that it is an image of a god whom you cannot prove to exist at all?

11. You laugh because in ancient times the Persians worshipped rivers, as is told in the writings which hand down [these things] to memory; the Arabians an unshapen stone;[4] the Scythian nations a sabre; the Thespians a branch instead of Cinxia;[5] the Icarians[6] an unhewn log instead of Diana; the people of Pessinus a flint instead of the mother of the gods; the Romans a spear instead of Mars, as the muses of Varro point out; and, before they were acquainted with the statuary's art, the Samians a plank[7] instead of Juno, as Aëthlius[8] relates: and you do not laugh when, instead of the

for which *s. de colore*, as above, has been suggested by Canterus, with the approval of Heraldus.

[1] The MS. here inserts *puetuitate*, for which no satisfactory emendation has been proposed. The early edd. read *pituitate*, a word for which there is no authority, while LB. gives *potus aviditate*—" drunk with avidity "—both being equally hopeless.

[2] MS. *sic*, corrected by Gelenius *si*.

[3] So Meursius, *ac dicere*, for MS. *-cidere*.

[4] It is worthy of notice that although in this passage, as often elsewhere, Arnobius adheres pretty closely to the argument proposed by Clemens Alexandrinus, he even in such passages sometimes differs from it, and not at random. Thus Clement speaks merely of a "stone," and Arnobius of an "unshaped stone." The former expression harmonizes with the words of Maximus Tyrius (*Serm.* xxxviii. p. 225, Steph.), "The Arabians worship I know not whom, but the image which I saw was a square stone;" while Suidas (Küster's ed., s. v. θεὺς "Ἀρης) agrees with Arnobius in calling it a "stone, black, square, unfashioned" (ἀτύπωτος). This is the more noteworthy, as at times Arnobius would almost seem to be following Clement blindly.

[5] So Arnobius renders Clement's *Cithæronian Hera*.

[6] So corrected in the notes of Canterus from Clem. for the MS. reading *Carios*, retained by the first four edd. and Elmenh. In Icaria there was a temple of Diana called Ταυροπόλιον.

[7] The MS. and first four edd. read *p-uteum*—"a well," corrected *plut.*, as above, by Gifanius, and in the notes of Canterus.

[8] The MS. reads *ethedius*, corrected in the notes of Canterus.

immortal gods, you make supplication to little images of men and human forms—nay, you even suppose that these very little images are gods, and besides these you do not believe that anything has divine power. What say you, O ye ——! Do the gods of heaven have ears, then, and temples, an occiput, spine, loins, sides, hams, buttocks, houghs,[1] ankles, and the rest of the other members with which we have been formed, which were also mentioned in the first part [of this book][2] a little more fully, and cited with greater copiousness of language? Would that it were possible[3] to look into the sentiments and very recesses of your mind, in which you revolve various and enter into the most obscure considerations: we should find that you yourselves even feel as we do, and have no other opinions as to the form of the deities. But what can we do with obstinate prejudices? what with those who are menacing [us] with swords, and devising new punishments [against us]? In your rage[4] you maintain a bad cause, [and that although you are] perfectly aware [of it]; and that which you have once done without reason, you defend lest you should seem to have ever been in ignorance; and you think it better not to be conquered, than to yield and bow to acknowledged truth.

12. From such causes as these this also has followed, with your connivance, that the wanton fancy of artists has found full scope in [representing] the bodies of the gods, and giving forms to them, at which even the sternest might laugh. And so Hammon is even now formed and represented with a ram's horns; Saturn with his crooked sickle, like some guardian of the fields, [and] pruner of too luxuriant branches; the son of Maia with a broad-brimmed travelling cap, as if he were preparing to take the road, and avoiding the sun's rays and the dust; Liber with tender limbs, and with a woman's perfectly free and easily flowing

---

[1] So all edd., except both Roman edd., which retain the MS. reading in the singular, *suffraginem*.

[2] *i.e.* iii. 6.   [3] Lit., "it was allowed."

[4] So Meursius suggested *amentes* for the MS. reading *animantis*, for which Heraldus proposed *argumentis*—" by arguments."

lines of body;[1] Venus, naked and unclothed, just as if you said that she exposed publicly, and sold to all comers,[2] the beauty of her prostituted body; Vulcan with his cap and hammer, but with his right hand free, and with his dress girt up as a workman prepares[3] for his work; the Delian god with a plectrum and lyre, gesticulating like a player on the cithern and an actor about to sing; the king of the sea with his trident, just as if he had to fight in the gladiatorial contest: nor can any figure of any deity be found[4] which does not have certain characteristics[5] bestowed [on it] by the generosity of its makers. Lo, if some witty and cunning king were to remove the Sun from [his place before] the gate[6] and transfer him to that of Mercury, [and] again were to carry off Mercury and make him migrate to the shrine of the Sun (for both are made beardless by you, and with smooth faces), and to give to this one rays [of light], to place a little cap[7] on the Sun's head, how will you be able to distinguish between them, whether this is the Sun, or that Mercury, since dress, not the peculiar appearance of the face, usually points out the gods to you? Again, if, having transported them in like manner, he were to take away his horns from the unclad Jupiter, and fix them upon the temples of Mars, and to strip Mars of his arms, and, on the other hand, invest Hammon with them, what distinction can there be between them, since he who had been Jupiter can be also supposed to be Mars, and he who had been Mavors can assume the appearance of Jupiter Hammon? To such an extent is there wantonness in fashioning those images and consecrating names, as if [they were] peculiar to them; since, if you take away their dress, the [means of] recognising each is put an end to, god may be believed to be god, one may seem to be the other, nay, more, both may be considered both!

---

[1] Lit., "and most dissolved with the laxity of feminine liquidity."
[2] *Divendere.*   [3] Lit., "with a workman's preparing."
[4] Lit., "is there any figure to find."   [5] *Habitus.*
[6] *Ex foribus.* Cf. Tertull. *de Idol.* ch. 15: "In Greek writers we also read that Apollo Θυραῖος and the *dæmones Antelii* watch over doors."
[7] So the edd., reading *petas-un-culum* for the MS. *-io-*.

13. But why do I laugh at the sickles and tridents which have been given to the gods? why at the horns, hammers, and caps, when I know that certain images have[1] the forms of certain men, and the features of notorious courtezans? For who is there that does not know that the Athenians formed the *Hermæ* in the likeness of Alcibiades? Who does not know—if he read Posidippus over again—that Praxiteles, putting forth his utmost skill,[2] fashioned the face of the Cnidian Venus on the model of the courtezan Gratina, whom the unhappy man loved desperately? But is this the only Venus to whom there has been given beauty taken from a harlot's face? Phryne,[3] the well-known native of Thespia— as those who have written [on] Thespian affairs relate—when she was at the height of her beauty, comeliness, and youthful vigour, is said to have been the model of all the Venuses which are [held] in esteem, whether throughout the cities of Greece or here,[4] whither has flowed the longing and eager desire for such figures. All the artists, therefore, who lived at that time, and to whom truth gave the greatest ability to portray likenesses, vied in transferring with all painstaking and zeal the outline of a prostitute to the images of the Cytherean. The beautiful [thoughts][5] of the artists were full of fire; and they strove each to excel the other with emulous rivalry, not that Venus might become more august, but that Phryne[3] might stand for Venus. And so it was brought to this, that sacred honours were offered to courtezans instead of the immortal gods, and an unhappy system of worship was led astray by the making of statues. That well-known and[6] most distinguished statuary, Phidias, when he had raised the form of Olympian Jupiter with immense

---

[1] Lit., "are." [2] Lit., "with strife of skills."

[3] MS. *Phyrna*, but below *Phryna*, which is read in both instances by Hild. and Oehler.

[4] So Meursius, followed by Orelli, reading *istic* for the MS. *iste*.

[5] *i.e.* either the conceptions in their minds, or realized in their works. Orelli, followed by the German translator Besnard, adopting the former view, translates "the ideas of the artists (die Ideale der Künstler) were full of fire and life."

[6] So Gelenius and Canterus, reading *et* for MS. *est*.

labour and exertion,[1] inscribed on the finger of the god PAN-TARCES[2] [is] BEAUTIFUL ([this], moreover, was the name of a boy loved by him, and that with lewd desire), and was not moved by any fear or religious dread to call the god by the name of a prostitute; nay, rather, to consecrate the divinity and image of Jupiter to a debauchee. To such an extent is there wantonness and childish feeling in forming those little images, adoring them as gods, heaping upon them the divine virtues, when we see that the artists themselves find amusement in fashioning them, and set them up as monuments of their own lusts! For what [reason] is there, if you should inquire, why Phidias should hesitate to amuse himself, and be wanton when he knew that, but a little before, the very Jupiter which he had made was gold, stones, and ivory,[3] formless, separated, confused, and that it was he himself who brought all these together and bound them fast, that their appearance[4] had been given to them by himself in the imitation[5] of limbs [which he had] carved; and, which is more than[6] all, that it was his own free gift, that [Jupiter] had been produced and was adored among men?[7]

14. We would here, as if all nations on the earth were present, make one speech, and pour into the ears of them all, words which should be heard in common: Why, pray, is this, O men! that of your own accord you cheat and deceive yourselves by voluntary blindness? Dispel the darkness now, and, returning to the light of the mind, look more closely and see what that is which is going on, if only you retain your right,[8] and are not beyond the reach[9] of the reason and prudence

---

[1] Lit., "with exertion of immense strength."
[2] MS. Pantarches. This was a very common mode of expressing love among the ancients, the name of the loved one being carved on the bark of trees (as if the Loves or the mountain nymphs had done it), on walls, doors, or, as in this case, on statues, with the addition "beautiful" (Suidas, s. v. Καλοί and 'Ραμνουσία Νέμεσις, with Küster's notes).
[3] Lit., "bones." [4] Lit., "conditions," habitus.
[5] Lit., "similitude." [6] Lit., "first among."
[7] Lit., "human things."
[8] i.e. the faculty of discernment, which is properly man's.
[9] Lit., "are in the limits of."

given to you.[1] Those images which fill you with terror, and which you adore prostrate upon the ground[2] in all the temples, are bones, stones, brass, silver, gold, clay, wood taken from a tree, or glue mixed with gypsum. Having been heaped together, it may be, from a harlot's gauds or from a woman's[3] ornaments, from camels' bones or from the tooth of the Indian beast,[4] from cooking-pots [and] little jars, from candlesticks and lamps, or from other less cleanly vessels, [and] having been melted down, they were cast into these shapes and came out into the forms which you see, baked in potters' furnaces, produced by anvils and hammers, scraped with the silversmith's, and filed down with [ordinary] files, cleft [and] hewn with saws, with augers,[5] with axes, dug [and] hollowed out by the turning of borers, [and] smoothed with planes. Is not this, then, an error? Is it not, to speak accurately, folly to believe [that] a god which you yourself made with care, to kneel down trembling in supplication to that which has been formed by you, and while you know, and are assured that it is the product[6] of the labour of your hands,[7]—to cast [yourself] down upon your face, beg aid suppliantly, and, in adversity and time of distress, [ask it] to succour[8] [you] with gracious and divine favour?

15. Lo, if some one were to place before you copper in the lump, and not formed[9] into any works [of art], masses of unwrought silver, and gold not fashioned into shape, wood, stones, and bones, with all the other materials of which statues

---

[1] The MS. reads *his*—"these," emended, as above, *vobis* in the margin of Ursinus, Elm., and LB.

[2] Lit., "and humble."   [3] *i.e.* a respectable woman.

[4] *i.e.* the elephant's tusk.

[5] So Salmasius, followed by Orelli, Hild., and Oehler, reading *furfuraculis*, and LB., reading *perforaculis* for the MS. *furfure aculeis*.

[6] So the margin of Ursinus, Meursius (according to Orelli), Hild., and Oehler, reading *part-u-m* for the MS. *-e-*—"is a part of your labour," etc.

[7] Lit., "of thy work and fingers."

[8] So the MS., both Roman edd., Elm., and Orelli, reading *numinis favore*, for which LB. reads *favorem*—"the favour of the propitious deity to succour [you]."

[9] Lit., "thrown together."

and images of deities usually consist,—nay, more, if some one were to place before you the faces of battered gods, images melted down[1] and broken, and were also to bid you slay victims to the bits and fragments, and give sacred and divine honours to masses without form,—we ask you to say to us, whether you would do this, or refuse to obey. Perhaps you will say, why? Because there is no man so stupidly blind that he will class among the gods silver, copper, gold, gypsum, ivory, potter's clay, and say that these very things have, and possess in themselves, divine power. What reason is there, then, that all these bodies should want the power of deity and the rank of celestials if they remain untouched and unwrought, [but] should forthwith become gods, and be classed and numbered among the inhabitants of heaven if they receive the forms of men, ears, noses, cheeks, lips, eyes, and eyebrows? Does the fashioning add any newness to these bodies, so that from this addition you are compelled[2] to believe that something divine and majestic has been united to them? Does it change copper into gold, or compel worthless earthenware to become silver? Does it cause things which but a little before were without feeling, to live and breathe?[3] If they had any natural properties previously,[4] all these they retain[5] when built up in the bodily forms of statues. What stupidity it is —for I refuse to call it blindness—to suppose that the natures of things are changed by the kind of form [into which they are forced], and that that receives divinity from the appearance given to it, which in its original body has been inert, and unreasoning, and unmoved by feeling![6]

16. And so unmindful and forgetful of what the substance and origin of the images are, you, men, rational

[1] Rigaltius suggested *confracta*—" shattered," for MS. *-flata*.
[2] So the edd., reading *cog-* for the MS. *cogit-amini*.
[3] Lit., "be moved with agitation of breathing."
[4] Lit., "outside," *i.e.* before being in bodily forms.
[5] So Ursinus and LB., reading *retin-e-nt* for the MS. *-ea-*, which can hardly be correct. There may possibly be an ellipsis of *si* before this clause, so that the sentence would run: "If they had any natural properties, [if] they retain all these, what stupidity," etc.
[6] Lit., "deprived of moveableness of feeling."

ARNOB.   T

beings[1] and endowed with the gift of wisdom and discretion, sink down before pieces of baked earthenware, adore plates of copper, beg from the teeth of elephants good health, magistracies, sovereignties, power, victories, acquisitions, gains, very good harvests, and very rich vintages; and while it is plain [and] clear that you are speaking to senseless things, you think that you are heard, and bring yourselves into disgrace of your own accord, by vainly and credulously deceiving yourselves.[2] Oh, would that you might enter into some statue! rather, would that you might separate[3] and break up into parts[4] those Olympian and Capitoline Jupiters, and behold all those parts alone and by themselves which make up the whole of their bodies! You would at once see that these gods of yours, to whom the smoothness [of their] exterior gives a majestic appearance by its alluring[5] brightness, are [only] a framework of flexible[6] plates, particles without shape joined together; that they are kept from falling into ruin and fear of destruction, by dove-tails and clamps and brace-irons; and that lead is run into the midst of all the hollows and where the joints meet, and causes delay[7] useful in preserving them. You would see, I say, at once [that they have] faces only without the rest of the head,[8] imperfect hands without arms, bellies and sides in halves, incomplete feet,[9] and, which is most ridiculous, [that they] have been put together without

---

[1] Lit., "a rational animal."

[2] Lit., "with deceit of vain credulity." The edd. read this as an interrogation: "Do you, therefore, sink down, adore, and bring yourselves into disgrace?"

[3] So Orelli, Hild., and Oehler, adopting a conjecture of Grævius, *di-*, for the MS. *de-ducere*—" to lead down."

[4] Lit., "resolved into members."

[5] Lit., "by the charm of."

[6] The MS. reads *flev-ilium*, for which Hild. suggests *flex-*, as above, previous edd. reading *flat-* —" of cast plates;" which cannot, however, be correct, as Arnobius has just said that the images were in part made of ivory.

[7] Lit., "delays salutary for lastingnesses." The sense is, that the lead prevents the joints from giving way, and so gives permanence to the statue.

[8] *Occipitiis.*   [9] *Plantarum vestigia.*

uniformity in the construction of their bodies, being in one part made of wood, but in the other of stone. Now, indeed, if these things could not be seen through the skill with which they were kept out of sight,[1] even those at least which lie open to all should have taught and instructed you that you are effecting nothing, and giving your services in vain to dead things. For, in this case,[2] do you not see that these images, which seem to breathe,[3] whose feet and knees you touch and handle when praying, at times fall into ruins from the constant dropping of rain, at other times lose the firm union of their parts from their decaying and becoming rotten,[4]—how they grow black, being fumigated and discoloured by the steam [of sacrifices], and by smoke,—how with continued neglect they lose their position[5] [and] appearance, and are eaten away with rust? In this case, I say, do you not see that newts, shrews, mice, and cockroaches, which shun the light, build their nests and live under the hollow parts of these statues? that they gather carefully into these all kinds of filth, and other things suited to their wants, hard and half-gnawed bread, bones dragged [thither] in view of [probable] scarcity,[6] rags, down, [and] pieces of paper to make their nests soft, and keep their young warm? Do you not see sometimes over the face of an image cobwebs and treacherous nets spun by spiders, that they may be able to entangle in them buzzing and imprudent flies while on the wing? Do you not see, finally, that swallows full of filth, flying within the very domes of the temples, toss [themselves] about, and bedaub now the very

---

[1] Lit., "from the art of obscurity."

[2] *i.e.* if the nature of the images is really concealed by the skill displayed in their construction.

[3] Lit., "breathing."

[4] Lit., "are relaxed from decay of rottenness."

[5] *i.e.* fall from their pedestals. For the MS. reading *situs* (retained in LB., as above), the margin of Ursinus, followed by the other edd. except the first four, and Oberthür, read *situ*—"lose their appearance from mould."

[6] So LB. and Oehler, reading *famis in spem* for the MS. *pannis*, omitted in other edd. All prefix *p*, as above, to the next word, *annos*.

faces, now the mouths of the deities, the beard, eyes, noses, and all the other parts on which their excrements[1] fall? Blush, then, even [though it is] late, and accept true methods and views from dumb creatures, and let these teach you that there is nothing divine in images, into which they do not fear or scruple to cast unclean things in obedience to the laws of their being, and led by their unerring instincts.[2]

17. But you err, [says my opponent], and are mistaken, for we do not consider either copper, or gold and silver, or those other materials of which statues are made, to be in themselves gods and sacred deities; but in them we worship and venerate those whom their[3] dedication as sacred introduces and causes to dwell in statues made by workmen. The reasoning [is] not vicious nor despicable by which any one — the dull, and also the most intelligent—can believe that the gods, forsaking their proper seats—that is, heaven—do not shrink back and avoid entering earthly habitations; nay, more, that impelled by the rite of dedication, they are joined to images! Do your gods, then, dwell in gypsum and in figures of earthenware? Nay, rather, are the gods the minds, spirits, and souls of figures of earthenware and of gypsum? and, that the meanest things may be able to become of greater importance, do they suffer themselves to be shut up and concealed and confined in[4] an obscure abode? Here, then, in the first place, we wish and ask to be told this by you: do they do this against their will—that is, do they enter the images as dwellings, dragged to [them] by the rite of dedication—or are they ready and willing? and do you not summon them by any considerations of necessity? Do they do this unwillingly?[5] and how can it be possible that they should be compelled [to submit] to any necessity without their dignity

---

[1] *Deonerati proluvies podicis.*

[2] Lit., "incited by the truth of nature." The MS. and both Roman edd. read *d-*, all others *instincta*, as above.

[3] Lit., "the sacred dedication."

[4] Lit., "concealed in the restraint of."

[5] The MS. reads *inrogati* (the next letter being erased, having probably been *s* redundant) *si inviti*, corrected in the margin of Ursinus and Oehler, as above, *-tis in*.

being impaired? With ready assent?[1] And what do the gods seek for in figures of earthenware that they should prefer these prisons[2] to their starry seats,—that, having been all but fastened to them, they should ennoble[3] earthenware and the other substances of which images are made?

18. What then? Do the gods remain always in such substances, and do they not go away to any place, even though summoned by the most momentous affairs? or do they have free passage, when they please to go any whither, and to leave their own seats and images? If they are under the necessity of remaining, what can be more wretched than they, what more unfortunate than if hooks and leaden bonds hold them fast in this wise on their pedestals? but [if] we allow that they prefer [these images] to heaven and the starry seats, they have lost their divine power.[4] But if, on the contrary, when they choose, they fly forth, and are perfectly free to leave the statues empty, the images will then at some time cease to be gods, and it will be doubtful when sacrifices should be offered,—when it is right and fitting to withhold them. Oftentimes we see that by artists these images are at one time made small, and reduced to the size of the hand, at another raised to an immense height, and

---

[1] Lit., "with the assent of voluntary compliance." "Do you say," or some such expression, must be understood, as Arnobius is asking his opponent to choose on which horn of the dilemma he wishes to be impaled.

[2] Lit., "bindings."

[3] So Gelenius, Canterus, Elm., Oberth., and Orelli, reading *nobilitent*. No satisfactory emendation has been proposed, and contradictory accounts are given as to the reading of the MS. Immediately after this sentence, LB., followed by Orelli, inserts a clause from the next chapter. Cf. the following note.

[4] It will be seen that these words fit into the indirect argument of Arnobius very well, although transposed in LB. to the end of last chapter, and considered a gloss by Orelli and Hildebrand. "See the consequences," Arnobius says, "of supposing that the gods do not quit these images: not merely are they in a wretched case, but they must further lose their power as divinities." Meursius, with more reason, transposes the clause to the end of the next sentence, which would be justifiable if necessary.

built up to a wonderful size. In this way, then, it follows that we should understand that the gods contract themselves in[1] little statuettes, and are compressed till they become like[2] a strange body; or, again, [that they] stretch themselves out to a great length, and extend to immensity in images of vast bulk. So, then, if this is the case, in sitting statues also the gods should be said to be seated, and in standing ones to stand, to be running in those stretching forward to run, to be hurling javelins in those [represented as] casting [them], to fit and fashion themselves to their countenances, and to make themselves like[3] the other characteristics of the body formed by the [artist].

19. The gods dwell in images—each wholly in one, or divided into parts, and into members? For neither is it possible that there can be at one time one god in several images, nor, again, divided into parts by his being cut up.[4] For let us suppose that there are ten thousand images of Vulcan in the whole world: is it possible at all, as I said, that at one time one [deity] can be in all the ten thousand? I do not think [so]. [Do you ask] wherefore? Because things which are naturally single and unique, cannot become many while the integrity of their simplicity[5] is maintained. And this they are further unable [to become] if the gods have the forms of men, as your belief declares; for either a hand separated from the head, or a foot divided from the body, cannot manifest the perfection of the whole, or it must be said that parts can be the same as the whole, while the whole cannot exist unless it has been made by gathering together its parts. Moreover, if the same [deity] shall be said to be in all [the statues], all reasonableness and sound-

---

[1] Perhaps "into," as Arnobius sometimes uses the abl. after *in* instead of the acc.

[2] Lit., "compressed to the similitude of."

[3] Lit., "to adapt their similitude to."

[4] Lit., "a cutting taking place."

[5] *i.e.* of their character as independent and not compounded. This is precisely such an expression as that which closes the fourth book, and its occurrence is therefore an additional ground for regarding the earlier passage as genuine.

ness is lost to the truth, if this is assumed that at one time one can remain in [them] all; or each of the gods must be said to divide himself from himself, so that he is both himself and another, not separated by any distinction, but himself the same as another. But as nature rejects and spurns and scorns this, it must either be said and confessed that there are Vulcans without number, if we decide that he exists and is in all the images; or he will be in none, because he is prevented by nature from being divided among several.

20. And yet, O you—if it is plain and clear to you that the gods live, and that the inhabitants of heaven dwell in the inner parts of the images, why do you guard, protect, and keep them shut up under the strongest keys, and under fastenings of immense size, under iron bars, bolts,[1] and other such things, and defend them with a thousand men and a thousand women to keep guard, lest by chance some thief or nocturnal robber should creep in? Why do you feed dogs in the capitols?[2] Why do you give food and nourishment to geese? Rather, if you are assured that the gods are there, and that they do not depart to any place from their figures and images, leave to them the care of themselves, let their shrines be always unlocked and open; and if anything is secretly carried off by any one with reckless fraud, let them show the might of divinity, and subject the sacrilegious robbers to fitting punishments at the moment[3] of their theft and [wicked] deed. For it is unseemly, and subversive of their power and majesty, to entrust the guardianship of the highest deities to the care of dogs, and when you are seeking for some means of frightening thieves so as to keep them away, not to beg it from [the gods] themselves, but to set and place it in the cackling of geese.

21. They say that Antiochus of Cyzicum took from its

---

[1] *Claustris repagulis pessulis.*

[2] Cf. p. 198, n. 3. Geese as wells as dogs guarded the Capitol, having been once, as the well-known legend tells, its only guards against the Gauls.

[3] The MS., first four edd., and Elm. read *nomine*—"under the name of," corrected *momine* by Meursius and the rest.

shrine a statue of Jupiter made of gold ten[1] cubits [high], and set up in its place one made of copper covered with thin plates of gold. If the gods are present, and dwell in their own images, with what business, with what cares, had Jupiter been entangled that he could not punish the wrong done to himself, and avenge his being substituted in baser metal? When the famous Dionysius (but [it was] the younger)[2] despoiled Jupiter of his golden vestment, and put instead of it one of wool, [and], when mocking [him] with pleasantries also, he said that that [which he was taking away] was cold in the frosts of winter, this warm, that that one was cumbrous in summer, that this, again, was airy in hot weather,—where was the king of the world that he did not show his presence by some terrible deed, and recall the jocose buffoon to soberness by bitter torments? For why should I mention that the dignity of Æsculapius was mocked by him? For when Dionysius was spoiling him of his very ample beard, [which was] of great weight and philosophic thickness,[3] he said that it was not right that a son sprung from Apollo, a father smooth and beardless, and very like a mere boy,[4] should be formed with such a beard that it was left uncertain which of them was father, which son, or rather whether they were of the same[5] race and family. Now, when all these things were being done, and the robber was speaking with impious

---

[1] So the MS., reading *decem;* but as Clement says πεντεκαίδεκα πηχῶν, we must either suppose that Arnobius mistook the Greek, or transcribed it carelessly, or, with the margin of Ursinus, read *quindecim*—" fifteen."

[2] Stewechius and Heraldus regard these words as spurious, and as having originated in a gloss on the margin, *scz. junior*—" to wit, the younger." Heraldus, however, changed his opinion, because Clement, too, says, " Dionysius the younger." The words mean more than this, however, referring probably to the fact that Cicero (*de Nat. Deor.* iii. 33, 34, 35) tells these and other stories of the elder Dionysius. To this Arnobius calls attention as an error, by adding to Clement's phrase " but."

[3] Only rustics, old-fashioned people, and philosophers wore the beard untrimmed; the last class wearing it as a kind of distinctive mark, just as Juvenal (iii. 15) speaks of a thick woollen cloak as marking a philosopher.

[4] *Impuberi.*   [5] Lit., " one."

mockery, if the deity was concealed in the statue consecrated to his name and majesty, why did he not punish with just and merited vengeance the affront of stripping his face of its beard and disfiguring his countenance, and show by this, both that he was himself present, and that he kept watch over his temples and images without ceasing?

22. But you will perhaps say that the gods do not trouble themselves about these losses, and do not think that there is sufficient cause for them to come forth and inflict punishment upon the offenders for their impious sacrilege.[1] Neither, then, if this is the case, do they wish to have these images, which they allow to be plucked up and torn away with impunity; nay, on the contrary, they tell [us] plainly that they despise these [statues], in which they do not care to show that they were contemned, by taking any revenge. Philostephanus relates in his *Cypriaca*, that Pygmalion, king[2] of Cyprus, loved as a woman an image of Venus, which was held by the Cyprians holy and venerable from ancient times,[3] his mind, spirit, the light of his reason, and his judgment being darkened; and that he was wont in his madness, just as if he were dealing with his wife, having raised the deity to his couch, to be joined with it in embraces and [face to] face, and to do other vain things, [carried away] by a foolishly lustful imagination.[4] Similarly, Posidippus,[5] in the book which he mentions [to have been] written about Gnidus and about its affairs,[6] relates that a young man, of noble birth (but he conceals his name), carried away with love of the Venus because of which Gnidus is famous, joined himself also in amorous lewdness to the image of the same deity, stretched on the genial couch, and enjoying[7] the pleasures which ensue. To ask, again, in like manner: If the powers of the gods above lurk in copper and the other sub-

---

[1] Lit., "punishment of violated religion."
[2] Clemens says merely "the Cyprian Pygmalion."
[3] Lit., "of ancient sanctity and religion."
[4] Lit., "imagination of empty lust."   [5] Cf. ch. 13.
[6] So Gelenius, reading *rebus* for the MS. and first ed. *re u* (MS. *ab*) *sc*.
[7] Lit., "in the limits of."

stances of which images have been formed, where in the world was the one Venus and the other to drive far away from them the lewd wantonness of the youths, and punish their impious touch with terrible suffering?[1] Or, as the goddesses are gentle and of calmer dispositions, what would it have been for them to assuage the furious joys of[2] the wretched men, and to bring back their insane minds again to their senses?

23. But perhaps, as you say, the goddesses took the greatest pleasure in these lewd and lustful insults, and did not think that an action requiring vengeance to be taken, which soothed their minds, and which they knew was suggested to human desires by themselves. But if the goddesses, the Venuses, being endowed with rather calm dispositions, considered that favour should be shown to the misfortunes of the blinded [youths]; when the greedy flames so often consumed the Capitol, and had destroyed the Capitoline Jupiter himself with his wife and his daughter,[3] where was the Thunderer at that time to avert that calamitous fire, and preserve from destruction his property, and himself, and all his family? Where was the queenly Juno when a violent fire destroyed her famous shrine, and her priestess[4] Chrysis in Argos? Where the Egyptian Serapis, when by a similar disaster [his temple] fell, burned to ashes, with all the mysteries, and Isis? Where Liber Eleutherius, when [his temple fell] at Athens? Where Diana, when [hers fell] at Ephesus? Where Jupiter of Dodona, when [his fell] at Dodona? Where, finally, the prophetic Apollo, when by pirates and sea robbers he was both plundered and set on fire,[5] so that out of so many pounds

---

[1] Lit., "agonizing restraint."   [2] Lit., "to."
[3] Cf. p. 198, n. 3.
[4] So Clemens narrates; but Thucydides (iv. 133) says that "straightway Chrysis flees by night for refuge to Phlious, fearing the Argives;" while Pausanius (ii. 59) says that she fled to Tegea, taking refuge there at the altar of Minerva Alea.
[5] From Varro's being mentioned, Oehler thinks that Arnobius must refer to various marauding expeditions against the temples of Apollo on the coasts and islands of the Ægean, made at the time of the piratical war. Clemens, however, speaks distinctly of the destruction of the

of gold, which ages without number had heaped up, he did not have one scruple even to show to the swallows which built under his eaves,[1] as Varro says in his *Saturæ Menippeæ*?[2] It would be an endless task to write down what shrines have been destroyed throughout the whole world by earthquakes and tempests—what have been set on fire by enemies, and by kings and tyrants—what have been stript bare by the overseers and priests themselves, even though they have turned suspicion away from them[3]—finally, what [have been robbed] by thieves and Canacheni,[4] opening [them] up, though barred by unknown means;[5] which, indeed, would remain safe and exposed to no mischances, if the gods were present to defend them, or had any care for their temples, as is said. But now because they are empty, and protected by no indwellers, Fortune has power over them, and they are exposed to all accidents just as much as are all other things which have not life.[6]

24. Here also the advocates of images are wont to say this also, that the ancients knew well that images have no divine nature, and that there is no sense in them, but that they formed them profitably and wisely, for the sake of the unmanageable and ignorant mob, which is the majority in nations and in states, in order that a kind of appearance, as it were, of deities being presented to them, from fear they might shake off their rude natures, and, supposing that they

---

temple at Delphi (p. 46), and it is therefore probable that this is referred to, if not solely, at least along with those which Varro mentions.

[1] Lit., "his visitors," *hospitis*.

[2] *Varro Menippeus*, an emendation of Carrio, adopted in LB. and Orelli for the MS. *se thenipeus*.

[3] Lit., "suspicion being averted."

[4] It has been generally supposed that reference is thus made to some kind of thieves, which is probable enough, as Arnobius (end of next chapter) classes all these plunderers as "tyrants, kings, robbers, and nocturnal thieves;" but it is impossible to say precisely what is meant. Heraldus would read *Saraceni*—"Saracens."

[5] Lit., "with obscurity of means." The phrase may refer either to the defence or to the assault of temples by means of magic arts.

[6] Lit., "interior motion."

were acting in the presence of the gods, put[1] away their impious deeds, and, changing their manners, learn to act as men;[2] and that august forms of gold and silver were sought for them, for no other reason than that some power was believed to reside in their splendour, such as not only to dazzle the eyes, but even to strike terror into the mind itself at the majestic beaming lustre. Now this might perhaps seem to be said with some reason, if, after the temples of the gods were founded, and their images set up, there were no wicked man in the world, no villany at all, [if] justice, peace, good faith, possessed the hearts of men, and no one on earth were called guilty and guiltless, all being ignorant of wicked deeds. But now when, on the contrary, all things are full of wicked [men], the name of innocence has almost perished, [and] every moment, every second, evil deeds, till now unheard of, spring to light in myriads from the wickedness of wrongdoers, how is it right to say that images have been set up for the purpose of striking terror into the mob, while, besides innumerable forms of crime and wickedness,[3] we see that even the temples themselves are attacked by tyrants, by kings, by robbers, and by nocturnal thieves, and that these very gods whom antiquity fashioned and consecrated to cause terror, are carried away[4] into the caves of robbers, in spite even of the terrible splendour of the gold?[5]

25. For what grandeur—if you look at the truth without any prejudice[6]—is there in these images[7] of which they speak, that the men of old should have had reason to hope and think that, by beholding them, the vices of men could be subdued, and their morals and wicked ways brought under restraint?[8] The reaping-hook, for example, which was

---

[1] Lit., "lop away," *deputarent*, the reading of the MS., Hild., and Oehler; the rest reading *deponerent*—"lay aside."
[2] Lit., "pass to human offices."
[3] Lit., "crimes and wickednesses." [4] Lit., "go," *vadere*.
[5] Lit., "with their golden and to-be-feared splendours themselves."
[6] Lit., "and without any favour," *gratificatione*.
[7] Lit., "what great [thing] have these images in them."
[8] So the MS., first four edd., Elm., Hild., and Oehler, reading *mores et*

assigned to Saturn,[1] was it to inspire mortals with fear, that they should be willing to live peacefully, and to abandon their malicious inclinations? Janus, with double face, or that spiked key by which he has been distinguished; Jupiter, cloaked and bearded, and holding in his right hand a piece of wood shaped like a thunderbolt; the cestus of Juno,[2] or the maiden lurking under a soldier's helmet; the mother of the gods, with her timbrel; the Muses, with their pipes and psalteries; Mercury, the winged slayer of Argus; Æsculapius, with his staff; Ceres, with huge breasts, or the drinking cup swinging in Liber's right hand; Mulciber, with his workman's dress; or Fortune, with her horn full of apples, figs, or autumnal fruits; Diana, with half-covered thighs, or Venus [perfectly] naked, exciting to lustful desire; Anubis, with his dog's face; or Priapus, of less importance[3] than his own genitals—[were these expected to make men afraid]?

26. O dreadful forms of terror and[4] frightful bugbears[5] on account of which the human race was to be benumbed for ever, to attempt nothing in its utter amazement, and to restrain itself from every wicked and shameful act—little sickles, keys, caps, pieces of wood, winged sandals, staves, little timbrels, pipes, psalteries, breasts protruding and of great size, little drinking cups, pincers, and horns filled with fruit, the naked bodies of women, and huge *veretra* openly exposed! Would it not have been better to dance [and] to sing, than calling it gravity and pretending to be serious, to relate what is so insipid and so silly, that images[6] were formed by the ancients to check wrongdoing, and to [arouse] the fears of the wicked and impious? Were the men of that age and time, in understanding, so void of reason and good sense, that they were kept back from wicked actions,

maleficia, corrected in the others *a maleficio*—" morals withheld from wickedness."

[1] Cf. ch. xii.
[2] The reference is probably to some statue or picture of Juno represented as girt with the girdle of Venus (*Il.* xiv. 214).
[3] Lit., "inferior."   [4] *Formidinum*.   [5] *Terrores*.
[6] Or, perhaps, "relate that images so frigid and so awkward."

just as if they were little boys, by the preternatural[1] savageness of masks, by grimaces also, and bugbears?[2] And how has this been so entirely changed, that though there are so many temples in your states filled with images of all the gods, the multitude of criminals cannot be resisted [even] with so many laws and so terrible punishments, and their audacity cannot be overcome[3] by any means, and wicked deeds, repeated again and again, multiply the more it is striven by laws and [severe] judgments to lessen the number of cruel deeds, and to quell them by the check [given by means] of punishments? But if images caused any fear to men, the passing of laws would cease, nor would so many kinds of tortures be established against the daring of the guilty: now, however, because it has been proved and established that the supposed[4] terror which is said to flow out from the images is in reality vain, recourse has been had to the ordinances of laws, by which there might be a dread [of punishment which should be] most certain fixed in men's minds also, and a condemnation settled; to which these very images also owe it that they yet stand safe, and secured by some respect being yielded to them.

27. Since it has been sufficiently shown, as far as there has been opportunity, how vain it is to form images, the course of our argument requires that we should next speak as briefly as possible, and without any periphrasis, about sacrifices, about the slaughter and immolation of victims, about pure wine, about incense, and about all the other things which are provided on such occasions.[5] For with respect to this you have been in the habit of exciting against us the most

---

[1] The MS. and both Roman edd. read *monstruosissima-s torvitate-s annis;* corrected by Gelenius and later edd. *monstruosissimâ torvitate animos,* and by Salmasius, Orelli, Hild., and Oehler, as above, *m. t. sannis.*

[2] The MS., first four edd., Elm., and Oberthür read *manus,* which, with *animos* read in most (cf. preceding note), would run, "that they were even kept back, as to (*i.e.* in) minds and hands, from wicked actions by the preternatural savageness of masks." The other edd. read with Salmasius, as above, *maniis.*

[3] Lit., "cut away."   [4] Lit., "opinion of."

[5] Lit., "in that part of years."

violent ill-will, of calling us atheists, and inflicting upon us the punishment of death, even by savagely tearing us to pieces with wild beasts, on the ground that we pay very little respect[1] to the gods; which, indeed, we admit that we do, not from contempt or scorn of the divine,[2] but because we think that such powers require nothing of the kind, and are not possessed by desires for such things.

[1] Lit., "attribute least."   [2] Lit., "divine spurning."

BOOK VII.

ARGUMENT.

To vindicate the Christians from any charge of impiety because they offered no sacrifices, Arnobius quotes Varro's opinion, that the true gods could not wish for these, whilst the images could care for nothing (1). The true gods, though unknown because unseen, must be, so far as their divinity is concerned, exactly alike, so as never to have been begotten, or be dependent on anything external to themselves (2). But if this is the case, on what ground ought sacrifices to be offered—as food for the gods? but whatever needs help from without, must be liable to perish if this is withheld. Moreover, unless the gods feed on the steam and vapour of the sacrifices, it is plain that they receive nothing, as the fire on the altar destroys what is placed on it; whilst, finally, if the gods are incorporeal, it is difficult to see how they can be supported by corporeal substances (3). It might indeed be supposed that the gods took some pleasure in having victims slain to them; but this is exposed to two objections,—that to feel pleasure necessitates the capacity of feeling pain, whilst these two states are becoming only in the weakness of mortals, and require the possession of the senses, which can only accompany a bodily form, from which the gods are supposed to be free; and that, secondly, to feel pleasure in the sufferings of animals, is hardly consistent with the divine character (4). It was commonly held that sacrifices propitiated the deities, and appeased their wrath. Against this Arnobius protests as utterly inconsistent with the view of the divine nature, which he conceives it necessary to maintain so persistently (5). But conceding this point, for the sake of argument, two alternatives are proposed: such sacrifices should be offered either before or after the divine wrath is excited. If the former is chosen, this is to represent the gods as wild beasts to be won from their savageness by throwing to them sops, or that on which to vent their rage; if the latter, without waiting to discuss whether the divine greatness would be offended by a creature so ignorant and unimportant as man (6), or what laws the gods have established on earth by the violation of which they might be enraged (7), it is asked why the death of a pig, a chicken, or an ox should change the disposition of a god, and whether the gods can be bribed into a gracious mood. Moreover, if the divine pardon is not given freely, it would be better to withhold it, as men sin more readily when they believe that they can purchase pardon for themselves (8). A protest is put into the mouth of an ox against the injustice of compelling cattle to pay the penalty of men's offences (9). Arnobius then points out that the doctrine of fate, that all things proceed from causes, and that therefore the course of events cannot be changed, does away with all need to appeal to the gods to render services which are not in their power (10). Finally, the miseries of men are a conclusive proof that the gods cannot avert evil (11), otherwise they are ungrateful in allowing misfortunes to overwhelm their worshippers. A brief *résumé* is given of the preceding arguments, illustrated by the cases of two men, of whom one has but little to give, whilst the other loads the altars with his offerings; and of two nations at war with each other whose gifts are equal,—which show how untenable the hypothesis is, that sacrifices purchase the favour of the gods (12).

Another pretext urged was, that the gods were honoured by the offering of sacrifices. How could this be? Honour consists in something yielded and something received (13). But what could the gods receive from men? how could their greatness be increased by men's actions (14)? The true deities should indeed be honoured by entertaining thoughts worthy of them; but what kind of honour is it to slay animals before them, to offer them blood, and send up wreaths of smoke into the air (15)? Still, if such horrid sights and smells were thought pleasing to the gods, why were certain animals and certain things chosen to be sacrificed, and not others (16)? The absurdity of offering to the gods the food used by us, is shown by supposing that pigs, dogs, asses, swallows, and other birds and beasts, were to sacrifice to men, in like manner, flies, ants, hay, bones, and the filth even which some of them eat (17). It is then asked why to one god bulls were sacrificed, to another kids, to a third sheep; to some white, to others black, to some male, to others female animals (18). The usual answer was, that to the gods male victims, to the goddesses females, were sacrificed, which brings up again the question as to sex amongst the deities. But passing this by, what is there in difference of colour to make the gods pleased or displeased as the victim might be white or black? The gods of heaven, it might be said, delight in cheerful colours, those of Hades in gloomy ones. In the time of Arnobius, however, few believed that there was any such place as Hades; and if this were so, there could be no gods there (19). But conceding this point also, and admitting that to their savage dispositions gloomy colours might be pleasing, Arnobius suggests that only the skins of animals are black, and that therefore the flesh, bones, etc. should not be offered, nor the wine, milk, oil, and other things used in sacrifices which are not black (20). It is next asked why certain animals were sacrificed to certain gods, and not to others; to which the only answer is, that it had been so determined by the men of former times (21). Or if it be suggested that a reason is seen in the sacrificing of fruitful and barren victims to mother earth and the virgin Minerva, such reasoning requires that musicians should be sacrificed to Apollo, physicians to Æsculapius, and orators to Mercury (22). Returning to the argument, that sacrifices should be offered to the gods to win favours from the good, to avert the malice of the bad, Arnobius points out, first, that it is impossible that there should be evil deities; and, secondly, that to suppose that the sacrifices were effectual, is to suppose that by them an evil deity could be changed into a good, and that, through their being withheld, a beneficent deity might become malevolent; which is as absurd as if one were to expect, on caressing a viper or scorpion, that he would escape being stung (23). He proceeds to call attention to various kinds of puddings, cakes, pottages, and other delicacies used in ceremonies, asking with scorn for what end they were employed (24, 25). It is next pointed out, that no reason can be offered for the use of incense, which was certainly unknown in the heroic ages, and unused even in Etruria, the mother of superstition, and could not have been burned on the altar until after the time of Numa. If, therefore, the ancients were not guilty in neglecting to burn incense, it could not be necessary to do so (26). Moreover, of what service was incense to the gods? If they were honoured by its being burned, why should not any gum be so used (27)? If incense is preferred because of its sweet smell, the gods must have noses, and share man's nature. Further, they may not be affected as we are by odours, and what is pleasant to us may be disagreeable to them; and *vice versa*. But such considerations are inadmissible with regard to the gods, for reason demands that they should be immaterial, and that therefore they should not be affected by odours (28). Arnobius next shows that the use of wine in ceremonies was as little based on reason as that of incense, for deities cannot be affected by thirst (29); and how could they be honoured with that which excites to vice and impairs man's reason (30)? The formula with which libations were made is ridiculed as niggardly and stingy (31); and the wreaths and garlands worn by the celebrants, and the noise and clangour of their musical instruments, are also turned into mockery (32); whilst it is shown that, to speak of the gods being honoured by the games dedicated to them, is to say that they were honoured by being publicly insulted in the ribald plays which were acted at these times, and by licentious and lustful conduct (33). All these detestable opinions originated in man's inability to understand what the deity really is, and in his therefore attributing to the divine nature what belongs to himself alone (34). In the three chapters which follow, he contrasts the opinions of heathen and Christians as to the divine nature, showing that to the former nothing seemed too bad to be attributed to their gods; while the latter, not professing to worship the gods, insulted them less by not holding such opinions (35-37).

The pestilences and other calamities are next discussed, which were supposed to have been sent by the gods as punishments for sacrifices or other honours withheld from them (38). Thus it was related that, the *ludi Circenses* having been violated, a pestilence ensued until they were once more celebrated in due form (39). Other pestilences also were got rid of, and enemies overcome, when gods had been brought across the seas and established at Rome; while, on the Capitol's being struck by lightning, evil was averted only by rearing towards the east an image of Jupiter in a higher place (40). But how can the story of the *ludi Circenses* be believed, which represents Jupiter as delighting in childish amusements, angry without cause, and punishing those who had done no wrong (41, 42), and going so far astray in making choice of a man to declare the cause of his anger (43)? In like manner Arnobius discusses the transportation of Æsculapius, in the form of a serpent, from Epidaurus to the island in the Tiber, after which it was said the people were restored to health (44–46). In reply to the question how it was that the plague ceased if the god did not really come to Rome, Arnobius asks how it was that, if the god did come to Rome, he did not preserve the city from all disease and pestilence thereafter (47); and as to the argument, that this did not happen because in later ages wickedness and impiety prevailed, reminds his opponent that at no epoch was Rome a city of the good and pious (48). So, too, the Great Mother was said to have been brought from Phrygia to enable the Romans to overcome Hannibal. But all that was brought was a stone (49); and are we to suppose that Hannibal was overcome by a stone, and not by the energy, resolution, and courage of the Romans? But if the Great Mother really drove Hannibal from Italy, why did she delay doing so until carried over the seas to Rome (50)? But without insisting on these objections, who will call her a goddess who is perfectly capricious, abandons her worshippers to settle amongst those who are more powerful, and loves to be in the midst of slaughter and bloodshed, whilst the true gods must be perfectly just and equally well disposed to all men (51)?

1. WHAT, then,[1] some one will say, do you think that no sacrifices at all should be offered? To answer you not with our own, but with your Varro's opinion—none. Why so? Because, he says, the true gods neither wish nor demand these;

---

[1] If this seems rather an abrupt beginning, it must be remembered that by some accident the introduction to the seventh book has been tacked on as a last chapter to the sixth, where it is just as out of place as here it would be in keeping.

while those[1] which are made of copper, earthenware, gypsum, or marble, care much less for these things, for they have no feeling; and you are not blamed[2] if you do not offer them, nor do you win favour if you do. No sounder opinion can be found, [none] truer, and [one] which any one may adopt, although he may be stupid and very hard [to convince]. For who is so obtuse as either to slay victims in sacrifice to those who have no sense, or to think that they should be given to those who are removed far from them in their nature and blessed state?

2. Who are the true gods? you say. To answer you in common and simple language, we do not know;[3] for how can we know who those are whom we have never seen? We have been accustomed to hear from you that an infinite number[4] are gods, and are reckoned among[5] the deities; but if these exist[6] anywhere, and [are] true gods, as Terentius[7] believes, it follows as a consequence, that they correspond to their name; that is, that they are such as we all see that they should be, [and that they are] worthy to be called by this name; nay, more (to make an end without many words), [that they are such] as is the Lord of the universe, and [the King] omnipotent Himself, whom we have knowledge and understanding [enough] to speak of as the true God when we are led to mention His name. For one

---

[1] Lit., "those, moreover."

[2] Lit., "nor is any blame contracted."

[3] On this Heraldus remarks, that it shows conclusively how slight was the acquaintance with Christianity possessed by Arnobius, when he could not say who were the true gods. This, however, is to forget that Arnobius is not declaring his own opinions here, but meeting his adversaries on their own ground. He knows who the true God is—the source and fountain of all being, and framer of the universe (ii. 2), and if there are any lesser powers called gods, what their relation to Him must be (iii. 2, 3); but he does not know any such gods himself (cf. the next sentence even), and is continually reminding the heathen that they know these gods just as little.

[4] Lit., "as many as possible."

[5] Lit., "in the series of."

[6] Lit., "are."

[7] i.e. M. Terentius Varro, mentioned in the last chapter.

god differs from another in nothing as respects his divinity;[1] nor can that which is one in kind be less or more in its parts while its own qualities remain unchanged.[2] Now, as this is certain, it follows that they should never have been begotten, but should be immortal, seeking nothing from without, and not drawing any earthly pleasures from the resources of matter.

3. So, then, if these things are so, we desire to learn this, first, from you—what is the cause, what the reason, that you offer them sacrifices; [and] then, what gain comes to the gods themselves from this, and remains to their advantage. For whatever is done should have a cause, and should not be disjoined from reason, so as to be lost[3] among useless works, and tossed about among vain and idle uncertainties.[4] Do the gods of heaven[5] live on these sacrifices, and must materials be supplied to maintain the union of their parts? And what man is there so ignorant of what a god is, certainly, as to think that they are maintained by any kind of nourishment, and that it is the food given to them[6] which causes them to live and endure throughout their endless immortality? For whatever is upheld by causes and things external to itself, must be mortal and on the way to destruction, when anything on which it lives begins to be wanting. Again, [it is impossible to suppose that any one believes this], because we see that of these things which are brought to their altars, nothing is added to and reaches the substance of the deities; for either incense is given, and is lost melting on the coals, or the life only of the victim is offered to the gods,[7]

---

[1] Lit., "in that in which he is a god."

[2] Lit., "uniformity of quality being preserved."

[3] The MS. and edd. read *ut in operibus feratur cassis*—"so as to be borne among," emended by Hild. and Oehler *teratur*—"worn away among."

[4] Lit., "in vain errors of inanity."

[5] The MS. and edd. have here *forte*—"perchance."

[6] Lit., "gift of food."

[7] Or perhaps, simply, "the sacrifice is a living one," *animalis est hostia*. Macrobius, however (*Sat.* iii. 5), quotes Trebatius as saying that there were two kinds of sacrifices, in one of which the entrails were

and its blood is licked up by dogs; or if any flesh is placed upon the altars, it is set on fire in like manner, and [is] destroyed, [and] falls into ashes,—unless perchance the god seizes upon the souls of the victims, or snuffs up eagerly the fumes and smoke [which rise] from the blazing altars, and feeds upon the odours which the burning flesh gives forth, still wet with blood, and damp with its former juices.[1] But if a god, as is said, has no body, and cannot be touched at all, how is it possible that that which has no body should be nourished by things pertaining to the body,—that what is mortal should support what is immortal, and assist and give vitality to that which it cannot touch? This reason for sacrifices is not valid, therefore, as it seems; nor can it be said by any one that sacrifices are kept up for this reason, that the deities are nourished by them, and supported by feeding on them.

4. If perchance it is not this,[2] are victims not slain in sacrifice to the gods, and cast upon their flaming altars to give them[3] some pleasure and delight? And can any man persuade himself that the gods become mild as they are exhilarated by pleasures, that they long for sensual enjoyment, and, like some base creatures, are affected by agreeable sensations, and charmed and tickled for the moment by[4] a pleasantness which soon passes away? For that which is overcome by pleasure must be harassed by its opposite, sorrow; nor [can that be] free from the anxiety of grief, which trembles

examined that they might disclose the divine will, while in the other the life only was consecrated to the deity. This is more precisely stated by Servius (*Æn.* iii. 231), who says that the *hostia animalis* was only slain, that in other cases the blood was poured on the altars, that in others part of the victim, and in others the whole animal, was burned. It is probable, therefore, that Arnobius uses the words here in their technical meaning, as the next clause shows that none of the flesh was offered, while the blood was allowed to fall to the ground.

[1] *i.e.* the juices which formerly flowed through the living body.

[2] The heathen opponent is supposed to give up his first reason, that the sacrifices provided food for the gods, and to advance this new suggestion, that they were intended for their gratification merely.

[3] Lit., "for the sake of."

[4] Lit., "with the fleeting tickling of."

with joy, and is elated capriciously with gladness.[1] But the gods should be free from both passions, if we would have them to be everlasting, and freed from the weakness of mortals. Moreover, every pleasure is, as it were, a kind of flattery of the body, and is addressed to the five well-known senses; but if the gods above feel it,[2] they must partake also of those bodies through which there is a way to the senses, and a door [by which] to receive pleasures. Lastly, what pleasure is it to take delight in the slaughter of harmless creatures, to have the ears ringing often with their piteous bellowings, to see rivers of blood, the life fleeing away with the blood, and the secret parts having been laid open, not only the intestines to protrude with the excrements, but also the heart still bounding with the life left in it, and the trembling, palpitating veins in the viscera? We half-savage men, nay rather (to say with more candour what it is truer and more candid to say), we savages, whom unhappy necessity and bad habit have trained to take these as food, are sometimes moved with pity for them; we ourselves accuse and condemn ourselves when the thing is seen and looked into thoroughly, because, neglecting the law which is binding on men, we have broken through the bonds which naturally united us at the beginning.[3] Will[4] any one believe that the gods, [who are] kind, beneficent, gentle, are delighted and filled with joy by the slaughter of cattle, if ever they fall and expire pitiably before their altars?[5] And there is no cause, then, for pleasure in sacrifices, as we see, nor is there a reason why they should be offered, since there is no pleasure [afforded by them]; and if perchance there is some,[6] it has been shown that it cannot in any way belong to the gods.

5. We have next to examine the argument which we hear

---

[1] Lit., "with the levities of gladnesses."   [2] *i.e.* pleasure.

[3] *Naturalis initii consortia.*

[4] So the MS. and first ed., according to Oehler, reading *cred-e-t*, the others *-i-* — "does."

[5] Lit., "these."

[6] Arnobius says that the sacrifices give no pleasure to any being, or at least, if that is not strictly true, that they give none to the gods.

continually coming from the lips of the common people, and [find] embedded in popular conviction, that sacrifices are offered to the gods of heaven for this purpose, that they may lay aside their anger and passions, and may be restored to a calm and placid tranquillity, the indignation of their fiery spirits being assuaged. And if we remember the definition which we should always bear steadily in mind, that all agitating feelings are unknown to the gods, the consequence is, a belief[1] that the gods are never angry; nay, rather, that no passion is further from them than that which, approaching most nearly to [the spirit of] wild beasts and savage creatures, agitates those who suffer it with tempestuous feelings, and brings them into danger of destruction. For whatever is harassed by any kind of disturbance,[2] is, it is clear, capable of suffering, and frail; that which has been subjected to suffering and frailty must be mortal; but anger harasses and destroys[3] those who are subject to it: therefore that should be called mortal which has been made subject to the emotions of anger. But yet we know that the gods should be never-dying, and should possess an immortal nature; and if this is clear and certain, anger has been separated far from them and from their state. On no ground, then, is it fitting to wish to appease that in the gods above which you see cannot suit their blessed state.

6. But let us allow, as you wish, that the gods are accustomed to such disturbance, and that sacrifices are offered and sacred solemnities performed to calm it, when, then, is it fitting that these offices should be made use of, or at what time should they be given? — before they are angry and roused, or when they have been moved and displeased even?[4] If we must meet them [with sacrifices] before [their anger is roused], lest they become enraged, you are bringing forward wild beasts to us, not gods, to which it is

---

[1] So the MS., LB., Oberthür, Orelli, Hild., and Oehler, reading *consec-*, for which the rest read *consen-taneum est credere*—"it is fitting to believe."

[2] Lit., "motion of anything."   [3] Cf. i. 18.

[4] Lit., "set in indignations."

customary to toss food, upon which they may rage madly, and turn their desire to do harm, lest, having been roused, they should rage and burst the barriers of their dens. But if these sacrifices are offered to satisfy[1] the gods when already fired and burning with rage, I do not inquire, I do not consider, whether that happy[2] and sublime greatness of spirit which belongs to the deities is disturbed by the offences of little men, and wounded if a creature, blind and ever treading among clouds of ignorance, has committed any blunder,—said [anything] by which their dignity is impaired.

7. But neither do I demand that this should be said, or that I should be told what causes the gods have for their anger against men, that having taken offence they must be soothed. [I do ask, however,] Did they ever ordain any laws for mortals? and was it ever settled by them what it was fitting for them to do, or what it was not? what they should pursue, what avoid; or even by what means they wished themselves to be worshipped, so that they might pursue with the vengeance of their wrath what was done otherwise than they had commanded, and might be disposed, if treated contemptuously, to avenge themselves on the presumptuous and transgressors? As I think, nothing was ever either settled or ordained by them, since neither have they been seen, nor has it been possible for it to be discerned very clearly whether there are any.[3] What justice is there, then, in the gods of heaven being angry for any reason with those to whom they have neither deigned at any time to show that they existed, nor given nor imposed any laws which they wished to be honoured by them and perfectly observed?[4]

8. But this, as I said, I do not mention, but allow it to pass

---

[1] Lit., "if this satisfaction of sacrifices is offered to."

[2] So the MS. and most edd., reading *laeta*, for which Ursinus suggested *lauta*—"splendid," and Heraldus *elata*—"exalted."

[3] It is perhaps possible so to translate the MS. *neque si sunt ulli apertissima potuit cognitione dignosci*, retained by Orelli, Hild., and Oehler, in which case *si sunt ulli* must be taken as the subject of the clause. The other edd., from regard to the construction, read *visi*—"nor, if they have been seen, has it been possible."

[4] Lit., "kept with inviolable observance."

away in silence. This one thing I ask, above all, What reason is there if I kill a pig, that a god changes his state of mind, and lays aside his angry feelings and frenzy; that if I consume a pullet, a calf under his eyes and on his altars, he forgets the wrong [which I did to him], and abandons completely all sense of displeasure? What passes from this act[1] to [modify] his resentment? Or of what service[2] is a goose, a goat, or a peacock, that from its blood relief is brought to the angry [god]? Do the gods, then, make insulting them a matter of payment? and as little boys, to [induce them to] give up their fits of passion[3] and desist from their wailings, get little sparrows, dolls, ponies, puppets,[3] with which they may be able to divert themselves, do the immortal gods in such wise receive these gifts from you, that for them they may lay aside their resentment, and be reconciled to those who offended them? And yet I thought that the gods—if only it is right to believe that they are really moved by anger—lay aside their anger and resentment, and forgive the sins of the guilty, without any price or reward. For this belongs specially to deities, to be generous in forgiving, and to seek no return for their gifts.[4] But if this cannot be, it would be much wiser that they should continue obstinately offended, than that they should be softened by being corrupted with bribes. For the multitude increases of those who sin, when there is hope given of paying for their sin; and there is little hesitation to do wrong, when the favour of those who pardon [offences] may be bought.

9. So, if some ox, or any animal you please, which is slain to mitigate and appease the fury of the deities, were to take a man's voice and speak these[5] words: Is this, then, O Jupiter, or whatever god thou art, humane or right, or should it be considered at all just, that when another has

---

[1] Lit., "work."   [2] Lit., "remedy."

[3] So *Panes* seems to be generally understood, *i.e.* images of Pan used as playthings by boys, and very much the same thing as the puppets—*pupuli*—already mentioned.

[4] Lit., "to have liberal pardons and free concessions."

[5] Lit., "in these."

sinned I should be killed, and that you should allow satisfaction to be made to you with my blood, although I never did you wrong, never wittingly or unwittingly did violence to your divinity and majesty, being, as thou knowest, a dumb creature, not departing from[1] the simplicity of my nature, nor inclined to be fickle in my[2] manners? Did I ever celebrate your games with too little reverence and care? did I drag forward a dancer so that thy deity was offended? did I swear falsely by thee? did I sacrilegiously steal your property and plunder your temples? did I uproot the most sacred groves, or pollute and profane some hallowed places by founding private houses? What, then, is the reason that the crime of another is atoned for with my blood, and that my life and innocence are made to pay for wickedness with which I have nothing to do? Is it because I am a base creature, and am not possessed of reason and wisdom, as these declare who call themselves men, and by their ferocity make themselves beasts?[3] Did not the same nature both beget and form me from the same beginnings? Is it not one breath of life which sways both them and me? Do I not respire and see, and am I not affected by the other senses just as they are? They have livers, lungs, hearts, intestines, bellies; and do not I have as many members? They love their young, and come together to beget children; and do not I both take care to procure offspring, and delight in it when it has been begotten? But they have reason, and utter articulate sounds; and how do they know whether I do what I do for my own reasons, and whether that sound which I give forth is my kind of words, and is understood by us alone? Ask piety whether it is more just that I should be slain, that I should be killed, or that man should be pardoned and be safe from punishment for what he has done? Who formed iron into a sword? was it not man? Who [brought] disaster upon races; who imposed slavery upon nations? was it not man? Who mixed deadly draughts, and gave them to his parents, brothers, wives, friends? was

[1] Lit., "following."   [2] Lit., "to varieties of manifold."
[3] Lit., "leap into."

it not man? Who found out or devised so many forms of wickedness, that they can hardly be related in ten thousand chronicles of years, or [even] of days? was it not man? Is not this, then, cruel, monstrous, and savage? Does it not seem to you, O Jupiter, unjust and barbarous that I should be killed, that I should be slain, that you may be soothed, and the guilty find impunity?

It has been established that sacrifices are offered in vain for this purpose then, viz. that the angry deities may be soothed; since reason has taught us that the gods are not angry at any time, and that they do not wish one thing to be destroyed, to be slain for another, or offences against themselves to be annulled by the blood of an innocent creature.

10. But perhaps some one will say, We give to the gods sacrifices and other gifts, that, being made willing in a measure to grant our prayers, they may give us prosperity and avert from us evil, cause us to live always happily, drive away grief truly, [and any evils] which threaten us from accidental circumstances. This point demands great care; nor is it usual either to hear or to believe what is so easily said. For the whole company of the learned will straightway swoop upon [us], who, asserting and proving that whatever happens, happens according to [the decrees of] fate, snatch out of our[1] hands that opinion, and assert that we are putting our trust in vain beliefs. Whatever, they will say, has been done in the world, is being done, and shall be done, has been settled and fixed in time past, and has causes which cannot be moved, by means of which events have been linked together, and form an unassailable chain of unalterable necessity between the past and the future. If it has been determined and fixed what evil or good should befall each person, it is already certain; but if this is certain and fixed, there is no room for all the help given by the gods, their hatred, [and] favours. For they are just as unable to do for you that which cannot be done, as to prevent that from

---

[1] Lit., "from the hands to us," *nobis*, the reading of the MS., both Roman edd., Gelenius, LB., and Oehler; for which the rest give *vobis*—"out of your hands."

being done which must happen, except that they will be able, if they choose, to depreciate somewhat powerfully that belief which you entertain, so that they[1] say that even the gods themselves are worshipped by you in vain, and that the supplications with which you address them are superfluous. For as they are unable to turn aside the course [of events], and change what has been appointed by fate, what reason, what cause, is there to wish to weary and deafen the ears of those in whose help you cannot trust at your utmost need?

11. Lastly, if the gods drive away sorrow and grief, if they bestow joy and pleasure, how[2] are there in the world so many[3] and so wretched men, whence [come] so many unhappy ones, who lead a life of tears in the meanest condition? Why are not those free from calamity who every moment, every instant, load and heap up the altars with sacrifices? Do we not see that some of them (say [the learned]) are the seats of diseases, the light of their eyes quenched, and their ears stopped, that they cannot move with their feet, that they live [mere] trunks without [the use of] their hands, that they are swallowed up, overwhelmed, [and] destroyed by conflagrations, shipwrecks, and disasters;[4] that, having been stripped of immense fortunes, they support themselves by labouring for hire, [and] beg for alms at last; that they are exiled, proscribed, always in the midst of sorrow, overcome by the loss of children, [and] harassed by other misfortunes, the kinds and forms of which no enumeration can comprehend? But assuredly this would not occur if the gods, who had been laid under obligation, were able to ward off, to turn aside, those evils from those who merited [this favour]. But now, because in these mishaps there is no room [for the interference of the gods], but all things are brought about[5] by inevitable necessity, the appointed course of events goes on and accomplishes that which has been once determined.

12. Or the gods of heaven should be said to be ungrate-

---

[1] *i.e.* the learned men referred to above.   [2] Lit., "whence."
[3] Lit., "so innumerable."   [4] Lit., "ruins."
[5] So Canterus suggests *conf-iunt* for the MS. *confic-* —"bring about."

ful if, while they have power to prevent it, they suffer an unhappy race to be involved in so many hardships and disasters. But perhaps they may say something of importance [in answer to this], and not such as should be received by deceitful, fickle, and scornful ears. This point, however, because it would require too tedious and prolix discussion,[1] we hurry past unexplained and untouched, content to have stated this alone, that you give to your gods dishonourable reputations if you assert that on no other condition do they bestow blessings and turn away what is injurious, except they have been first bought over with the blood of she-goats and sheep, and with the other things which are put upon their altars. For it is not fitting, in the first place, that the power of the deities and the surpassing eminence of the celestials should be believed to keep their favours on sale, first to receive [a price], and then to bestow [them]; [and] then, which is much more unseemly, that they aid no one unless they receive [their demands], and that they suffer the most wretched to undergo whatever perils may befall them,[2] while they could ward [these] off, and come to their aid. If of two who are sacrificing, one is a scoundrel,[3] and rich, the other of small fortune, but worthy of praise for his integrity and goodness,—if the former should slay a hundred oxen, and as many ewes with their lambkins, the poor man burn a little incense, and a small piece of some odorous substance,— will it not follow that it should be believed that, if only the deities bestow nothing except when rewards are first offered, they will give their favour[4] to the rich man, turn their eyes away from the poor, whose gifts were restricted not by his

---

[1] Lit., "it is a thing of long and much speech."

[2] Lit., "the fortunes of perils."

[3] The MS. reading is *hoc est unus*, corrected *honestus*—" honourable " (which makes the comparison pointless, because there is no reason why a rich man, if good, should not be succoured as well as a poor), in all edd., except Oehler, who reads *sceletus*, which departs too far from the MS. Perhaps we should read, as above, *inhonestus*.

[4] So the MS., LB., Hild., and Oehler, and the other edd., adding *et auxilium*—" and help."

spirit, but by the scantiness of his means?[1] For where the giver is venal and mercenary, there it must needs be that favour is granted according to the greatness of the gift [by which it is purchased], and that a favourable decision is given to him from whom[2] far the greater reward and bribe, [though this be] shameful, flows to him who gives it.[3] What if two nations, on the other hand, arrayed against each other in war, enriched the altars of the gods with equal sacrifices, and were to demand that their power and help should be given to them, the one against the other: must it not, again, be believed that, if they are persuaded to be of service by rewards, they are at a loss between both sides, are struck motionless, and do not perceive what to do, since they understand that their favour has been pledged by the acceptance of the sacrifices? For either they will give assistance to this side and to that, which is impossible, for [in that case] they will fight themselves against themselves, strive against their own favour and wishes; or they will do nothing to aid either nation[4] after the price [of their aid] has been paid and received, which is very wicked. All this infamy, therefore, should be removed far from the gods; nor should it be said at all that they are won over by rewards and payments to confer blessings, and remove what is disagreeable, if only they are true gods, and worthy to be ranked under this name. For either whatever happens, happens inevitably, and there is no place in the gods for ambition and favour; or if fate is excluded and got rid of, it does not belong to the celestial dignity to sell the boon of its services,[5] and the conferring of its bounties.

13. We have shown sufficiently, as I suppose, that victims, and the things which go along with them, are offered in vain

---

[1] Lit., "whom not his mind, but the necessity of his property, made restricted."

[2] Lit., "inclines thither whence."   [3] *i.e.* the decision.

[4] Lit., "both nations."

[5] Lit., "the favours of good work," *boni operis favor-es et*, the reading of Hild. and Oehler (other edd. *-em*—"the favour of its service") for MS. *jabore sed*.

to the immortal gods, because they are neither nourished by them, nor feel any pleasure, nor lay aside their anger and resentment, so as either to give good fortune, or to drive away and avert the opposite. We have now to examine that point also which has been usually asserted by some, and applied to forms of ceremony. For they say that these sacred rites were instituted to do honour to the gods of heaven, and that these things which they do, they do to show [them] honour, and to magnify the powers of the deities by them. What if they were to say, in like manner, that they keep awake and sleep, walk about, stand still, write something, and read, to give honour to the gods, and make them more glorious in majesty? For what substance is there added to them from the blood of cattle, and from the other things which are prepared in sacrificing? what power is given and added to them? For all honour, which is said to be offered by any one, and to be yielded to reverence for a greater being, is of a kind having reference to the other; and consists of two parts, of the concession of the giver, and the increase of honour of the receiver. As, if any one, on seeing a man famed for his very great power[1] and authority, were to make way for him, to stand up, to uncover his head, and leap down from his carriage, then, bending forward to salute him with slavish servility and[2] trembling agitation, I see what is aimed at in showing such respect: by the bowing down of the one, very great [honour] is given to the other, and he is made to appear great whom the respect of an inferior exalts and places above his own rank.[3]

14. But all this conceding and ascribing of honour about which we are speaking are met with among men alone, whom their natural weakness and love of standing above their fellows[4] teach to delight in arrogance, and in being preferred above others. But, I ask, where is there room

---

[1] Lit., "of most powerful name."

[2] Lit., "imitating a slave's servility"—*ancillatum*, the emendation of Hemsterhuis, adopted by Orelli, Hild., and Oehler for the unintelligible MS. *ancillarum*.

[3] Lit., "things."   [4] Lit., "in higher [places]."

for honour among the gods, or what greater exaltation is found to be given[1] to them by piling up[2] sacrifices? Do they become more venerable, more powerful, when cattle are sacrificed [to them]? is there anything added to them from this? or do they begin to be more [truly] gods, their divinity being increased? And yet I consider it almost an insult, nay, an insult altogether, when it is said that a god is honoured by a man, and exalted by the offering of some gift. For if honour increases and augments the grandeur of him to whom it is given, it follows that a deity becomes greater by means of the man from whom he has received the gift, and the honour conferred on him; and thus the matter is brought to this issue, that the god who is exalted by human honours is the inferior, while, on the other hand, the man who increases the power of a deity [is] his superior.[3]

15. What then! some one will say, do you think that no honour should be given to the gods at all? If you propose to us gods such as they should be if they do exist, and such as[4] we feel that we all mean when we mention[5] that name, how can we but give them even the greatest honour, since we have been taught by the commands which have especial power over us,[6] to pay honour to all men even, of whatever rank, of whatever condition they may be? What, pray, [you ask], is this very great honour? One much more in

---

[1] Lit., "what eminences is it found to be added," *addier*. So Hild. and Oehler for the reading of MS., first four edd., and Oberthür *addere* —"to add," emended in rest from margin of Ursinus *accedere*, much as above.

[2] So the MS., reading *conjectionibus*, which is retained in no edd., although its primary meaning is exactly what the sense here requires.

[3] The last clause was omitted in first four edd. and Elm., and was inserted from the MS. by Meursius.

[4] Lit., "whom."

[5] Lit., "say in the proclamation of."

[6] Lit., "more powerful commands," *i.e.* by Christ's injunctions. It seems hardly possible that any one should suppose that there is here any reference to Christ's command to his disciples not to exercise lordship over each other, yet Orelli thinks that there is perhaps a reference to Mark x. 42, 43. If a particular reference were intended, we might with more reason find it in 1 Pet. ii. 17, "Honour all men."

accordance with duty than is paid by you, and directed to[1] a more powerful race, [we reply]. Tell us, you say, in the first place, what is an opinion worthy of the gods, right and honourable, and not blameworthy from its being made unseemly by something infamous? [We reply, one such], that you believe that they neither have any likeness to man, nor look for anything which is outside of them and comes from without; then—and this has been said pretty frequently—that they do not burn with the fires of anger, that they do not give themselves up passionately to sensual pleasure, that they are not bribed to be of service, that they are not tempted to injure [our enemies], that they do not sell their kindness and favour, that they do not rejoice in having honour heaped on them, that they are not indignant and vexed if it is not given; but—and this belongs to the divine—that by their own power they know themselves, and that they do not rate themselves by the obsequiousness of others. And yet, that we may see the nature of what is said, what kind of honour is this, to bind a wether, a ram, a bull before the face of a god, and slay them in his sight? What kind of honour is it to invite a god to [a banquet of] blood, which you see him take and share in with dogs? What kind of honour is it, having set on fire piles of wood, to hide the heavens with smoke, and darken with gloomy blackness the images of the gods? But if it seems good to you that these actions should be considered in themselves,[2] not judged of according to your prejudices, [you will find that] those altars of which you speak, and even those beautiful ones which you dedicate to the superior gods,[3] are places for burning the unhappy race of animals, funeral pyres, and mounds built for a most unseemly office, and formed to be filled with corruption.

16. What say you, O you——! is that foul smell, then, which is given forth and emitted by burning hides, by bones, by bristles, by the fleeces of lambs, and the feathers of fowls, —[is that] a favour and an honour to the deity? and are

[1] Lit., "established in."
[2] Lit., "weighed by their own force," *vi.*
[3] *i.e. altariaque hæc pulchra.*

the deities honoured by this, to whose temples, when you arrange to go, you come[1] cleansed from all pollution, washed, and perfectly[2] pure? And what can be more polluted than these, more unhappy,[3] more debased, than if their senses are naturally such that they are fond of what is so cruel, and take delight in foul smells which, when inhaled with the breath, even those who sacrifice cannot bear, and [certainly] not a delicate[4] nose? But if you think that the gods of heaven are honoured by the blood of living creatures [being offered to them], why do you not[5] sacrifice to them both mules, and elephants, and asses? why not dogs also, bears, and foxes, camels, and hyænas, and lions? And as birds also are counted victims by you, why do you not [sacrifice] vultures, eagles, storks, falcons, hawks, ravens, sparrow-hawks, owls, and, along with them, salamanders, water-snakes, vipers, tarantulæ? For indeed there is both blood in these, and they are in like manner moved by the breath of life. What is there more artistic in the former kind [of sacrifices], or less ingenious in the latter, that these do not add to and increase the grandeur of the gods? Because, says my opponent, it is right to honour the gods of heaven with those things by which we are ourselves nourished and sustained, and live; which also they have, in their divine benevolence, deigned to give to us for food. But the same gods have given to you both cumin, cress, turnips, onions, parsley, esculent thistles, radishes, gourds, rue, mint, basil, flea-bane,

---

[1] Lit., "you show yourselves," *præstatis*.

[2] Lit., "most." So Tibullus (*Eleg.* ii. 1, 13): "Pure things please the gods. Come (*i.e.* to the sacrifice) with clean garments, and with clean hands take water from the fountain,"—perfect cleanliness being scrupulously insisted on.

[3] This Heraldus explains as "of worse omen," and Oehler as "more unclean."

[4] *Ingenuæ*, *i.e.* such as any respectable person has.

[5] To this the commentators have replied, that mules, asses, and dogs were sacrificed to certain deities. We must either admit that Arnobius has here fallen into error, or suppose that he refers merely to the animals which were usually slain, or find a reason for his neglecting it in the circumstances of each sacrifice.

and chives, and commanded them to be used by you as part of your food; why, then, do you not put these too upon the altars, and scatter wild-marjoram, with which oxen are fed, over them all, and mix amongst [them] onions with their pungent flavour?

17. Lo, if dogs—for a case must be imagined, in order that things may be seen more clearly—if dogs, I say, and asses, and along with them water-wagtails, if the twittering swallows, and pigs also, having acquired some of the feelings of men, were to think and suppose that you were gods, and to propose to offer sacrifices in your honour, not of other things and substances, but [of those] with which they are wont to be nourished and supported, according to their natural inclination,—we ask you to say whether you would consider this an honour, or rather a most outrageous affront, when the swallows slew and consecrated flies to you, the water-wagtails ants; when the asses put hay upon your altars, and poured out libations of chaff; when the dogs placed bones, and burned human excrements [at your shrines]; when, lastly, the pigs poured out before you a horrid mess, taken from their frightful hog-pools and filthy maws? Would you not in this case, then, be inflamed with rage that your greatness was treated with contumely, and account it an atrocious wrong that you were greeted with filth? But, [you reply], you honour the gods with the carcasses of bulls, and by slaying[1] other living creatures. And in what respect does this differ from that, since these [sacrifices], also, if they are not yet, will nevertheless soon be, dung, and will become rotten after a very short time has passed? Finally, cease to place fire upon[2] your altars, then indeed you will[3] see that consecrated flesh of bulls, with which you magnify the honour of the gods, swelling and heaving with worms, tainting and corrupting the atmosphere, and infecting the neighbouring districts with unwholesome smells. Now, if the gods were

---

[1] Lit., "by slaughters of," *cædibus*.

[2] Lit., "under," *i.e.* under the sacrifices on your altars.

[3] So all edd., reading *cerne-*, except both Roman edd., Hild., and Oehler, who retain the MS. *cerni-tis*—"you see."

to enjoin you to turn these things[1] to your own account, to make your meals from them[2] in the usual way, you would flee to a distance, and, execrating the smell, would beg pardon from the gods, and bind yourselves by oath never [again] to offer such sacrifices to them. Is not this conduct of yours mockery, then? is it not to confess, to make known that you do not know what a deity is, nor to what power the meaning and title of this name should be given and applied? Do you give new dignity to the gods by new kinds of food? do you honour them with savours and juices, and because those things which nourish you are pleasing and grateful to you? do you believe that the gods also flock up to [enjoy] their pleasant taste, and, just as barking dogs, lay aside their fierceness for mouthfuls, and pretty often fawn upon those who hold [these] out?

18. And as we are now speaking of the animals sacrificed, what cause, what reason is there, that while the immortal gods (for, so far as we are concerned, they may all be [gods] who are believed to be so) are of one mind, or should be of one nature, kind, and character, all are not appeased with all the victims, but certain [deities] with certain [animals], according to the sacrificial laws? For what cause is there (to repeat the same question) that that deity should be honoured with bulls, another with kids or sheep, this one with sucking pigs, the other with unshorn lambs, this one with virgin heifers, that one with horned goats, this with barren cows, but that with teeming[3] swine, this with white, that with dusky[4] [victims], one with female,

---

[1] In translating thus, it has been attempted to adhere as closely as possible to the MS. reading (according to Crusius) *qua si*—corrected, as above, *quæ* in LB.; but it is by no means certain that further changes should not be made.

[2] Lit., "prepare luncheons and dinners thence," *i.e.* from the putrefying carcasses.

[3] The MS. and first four edd. read *ingentibus scrofis*—"with huge breeding swine," changed by rest, as above, *incient-*, from the margin of Ursinus.

[4] Or "gloomy," *tetris*, the reading of MS. and all edd. since LB., for which earlier edd. give *atris*—"black."

the other, on the contrary, with male animals? For if victims are slain in sacrifice to the gods, to do them honour and show reverence for them, what does it matter, or what difference is there with the life of what animal this debt is paid, their anger and resentment put away? Or is the blood of one victim less grateful and pleasing to one god, while the other's fills him with pleasure and joy? or, as is usually done, does that [deity] abstain from the flesh of goats because of some reverential and religious scruple, another turn with disgust from pork, while to this mutton stinks? and does this one avoid tough ox-beef that he may not overtax his weak stomach, and choose tender[1] sucklings that he may digest them more speedily?

19. But you err, says [my opponent], and fall into mistakes; for in sacrificing female victims to the female deities, males to the male [deities], there is a hidden and very[2] secret reason, and one beyond the reach of the mass. I do not inquire, I do not demand, what the sacrificial laws teach or contain; but if reason has demonstrated,[3] and truth declared, that among the gods there is no difference of species, and that they are not distinguished by any sexes, must not all these reasonings be set at naught, and be proved, be found to have been believed under the most foolish hallucinations? I will not bring forward the opinions of wise men, who cannot restrain their laughter when they hear distinctions of sex attributed to the immortal gods: I ask of each man whether he himself believes in his own mind, and persuades himself that the race of the gods is [so] distinguished that they are male and female, and have been formed with members arranged suitably for the begetting of young?

But if the laws of the sacrifices enjoin that like sexes should be sacrificed to like, that is, female [victims] to the female [gods], male victims, on the contrary, to the male gods, what relation is there in the colours, so that it is right

---

[1] Lit., "the tenderness of." [2] Lit., "more."
[3] So the MS., Elm., LB., Orelli, Hild., and Oehler, reading *vicerit*, for which the others read *jusserit*—"has bidden."

and fitting that to these white, to those dark, even the blackest victims are slain? Because, says [my opponent], to the gods above, and [those] who have power to give favourable omens,[1] the cheerful colour is acceptable and propitious from the pleasant appearance of pure white; while, on the contrary, to the sinister deities, and those who inhabit the infernal seats, a dusky colour is more pleasing, and [one] tinged with gloomy hues. But if, again, the reasoning holds good, that the infernal regions are an utterly vain and empty name,[2] and that underneath the earth there are no Plutonian realms and abodes, this, too, must nullify your ideas about black cattle and gods under the ground. Because, if there are no infernal regions, of necessity there are no *dii Manium* also. For how is it possible that, while there are no regions, there should be said to be any who inhabit them?

20. But let us agree, as you wish, that there are both infernal regions and *Manes*, and that some gods or other dwell in these by no means favourable to men, and presiding over misfortunes; and what cause, what reason is there, that black victims, even[3] of the darkest hue, should be brought to their altars? Because dark things suit dark, and gloomy things are pleasing to similar beings. What then? Do you not see (that we, too, may joke with you stupidly, and just as you do yourselves[4]) that the flesh of the victims is not black,[5] [nor] their bones, teeth, fat, the bowels, with[6] the brains, and the soft marrow in the bones? But the fleeces are jet-black, and the bristles of the creatures

---

[1] Lit., "prevailing with favourableness of omens," *ominum*, for which the MS. and first four edd. read *h-* —"of men."

[2] That Arnobius had good reason to appeal to this scepticism as a fact, is evident from the lines of Juvenal (ii. 149-152): "Not even children believe that there are any Manes and subterranean realms."

[3] Lit., "and." Immediately after, the MS. is corrected in later writing *color-es* (for *-is*)—"and the darkest colours."

[4] *Similiter.* This is certainly a suspicious reading, but Arnobius indulges occasionally in similar vague expressions.

[5] Lit., "is white."

[6] Or, very probably, "the membranes with (*i.e.* enclosing) the brains," *omenta cum cerebris*.

are jet-black. Do you, then, sacrifice to the gods only wool and little bristles torn from the victims? Do you leave the wretched creatures, despoiled it may be, and shorn, to draw the breath of heaven, and rest in perfect innocence upon their feeding-grounds? But if you think that those things are pleasing to the infernal gods which are black and of a gloomy colour, why do you not take care that all the other things which it is customary to place upon their sacrifices should be black, and smoked, and horrible in colour? Dye the incense if it is offered, the salted grits, and all the libations without exception. Into the milk, oil, blood, pour soot and ashes, that this may lose its purple hue, that the others may become ghastly. But if you have no scruple in introducing some things which are white and retain their brightness, you yourselves do away with your own religious scruples and reasonings, while you do not maintain any single and universal rule in performing the sacred rites.

21. But this, too, it is fitting that we should here learn from you: If a goat be slain to Jupiter, which is usually sacrificed to father Liber and Mercury,[1] or if the barren heifer be sacrificed to Unxia, which you give to Proserpine, by what usage and rule is it determined what crime there is in this, what wickedness or guilt has been contracted, since it makes no difference to the worship [offered to the deity] what animal it is with whose head the honour is paid which you owe? It is not lawful, says [my opponent], that these things should be confounded, and it is no small crime to throw the ceremonies of the rites and the mode of expiation into confusion. Explain the reason, I beg. Because it is right to consecrate victims of a certain kind to certain deities, and that certain forms of supplication should be also adopted. And what, again, is the reason that it is right to consecrate victims of a certain kind to certain deities, and that certain forms of supplication should be also adopted, for this very rightfulness should have its own cause, and spring, be derived from certain reasons? Are you going

---

[1] Goats were sacrificed to Bacchus, but not, so far as is known, to Mercury. Cf. c. 16, p. 323, n. 5.

to speak about antiquity and custom? [If so], you relate to me merely the opinions of men, and the inventions of a blind creature: but I, when I request a reason to be brought forward to me, wish to hear either that something has fallen from heaven, or (which the subject rather requires) what relation Jupiter has to a bull's blood that it should be offered in sacrifice to him, not to Mercury [or] Liber. Or what are the natural properties of a goat, that they again should be suited to these gods, should not be adapted to the sacrifices of Jupiter? Has a partition of the animals been made amongst the gods? Has some contract been made and agreed to, so that[1] it is fitting that this one should hold himself back from the victim which belongs to that, that the other should cease[2] to claim as his own the blood which belongs to another? Or, as envious boys, are they unwilling to allow others to have a share in enjoying the cattle presented to them? or, as is reported to be done by races which differ greatly in manners, are the same things which by one party are considered fit for eating, rejected as food by others?

22. If, then, these things are vain, and are not supported by any reason, the very offering[3] of sacrifices also is idle. For how can that which follows have a suitable cause, when that very first [statement] from which the second flows is found to be utterly idle and vain, and established on no solid basis? To mother Earth, they say, is sacrificed a teeming[4] and pregnant sow; but to the virgin Minerva is slain a virgin calf, never forced[5] by the goad to attempt any labour. But yet we think that neither should a virgin have been sacrificed to a virgin, that the virginity might not be violated in the brute, for which the goddess is especially

[1] Lit., "by the paction of some transaction is it," etc.
[2] So all except both Roman edd., which retain the MS. reading *desi-d-eret* (corrected *-n-* by Gelenius)—"wish."
[3] So the MS., Hild., and Oehler, reading *d-atio*, approved of by Stewechius also. The others read *r-* —"reasoning on behalf."
[4] *Inci-ens*, so corrected in the margin of Ursinus for MS. *ing-* — "huge." Cf. ch. 18, p. 325, n. 3.
[5] The MS. reads *excitata conatus* (according to Hild.); corrected, as above, by the insertion of *ad*.

esteemed; nor [should] gravid and pregnant [victims have been sacrificed] to the Earth from respect for its fruitfulness, which[1] we all desire and wish to go on always in irrepressible fertility.[2] For if because the Tritonian [goddess] is a virgin it is therefore fitting that virgin victims be sacrificed to her, and [if] because the Earth is a mother she is in like manner to be entertained with gravid swine, then also Apollo [should be honoured] by the sacrifice of musicians because he is a musician; Æsculapius, because he is a physician, by the sacrifice of physicians; and because he is an artificer, Vulcan by the sacrifice of artificers; and because Mercury is eloquent, sacrifice should be made to him with the eloquent and most fluent. But if it is madness to say this, or, to speak with moderation, nonsense, that shows much greater madness to slaughter pregnant [swine] to the Earth because she is even more prolific; pure and virgin [heifers] to Minerva because she is pure, of unviolated virginity.

23. For as to that which we hear said by you, that some of the gods are good, that others, on the contrary, are bad, and rather inclined to indulge in wanton mischief,[3] and that the usual rites are paid to the one party that they may show favour, but to the others that they may not do you harm,— with what reason this is said, we confess that we cannot understand. For to say that the gods are most benevolent, and have gentle dispositions, is not only pious and religious, but also true; but that they are evil and sinister, should by no means be listened to, inasmuch as that divine power has been far removed and separated from the disposition which does harm.[4] But whatever can occasion calamity, it must first be seen what it is, and [then] it should be removed very far from the name of deity.

---

[1] *Quam*, i.e. the earth.

[2] Singularly enough, for *fecunditate* Oberthür reads *virginitate*—"inextinguishable virginity," which is by no means universally desired in the earth. Orelli, as usual, copies without remark the mistake of his predecessor.

[3] Lit., "more prompt to lust of hurting."

[4] Lit., "nature of hurting."

Then, [supposing] that we should agree with you that the gods promote good fortune and calamity, not even in this case is there any reason why you should allure some of them to grant you prosperity, and, on the other hand, coax others with sacrifices and rewards not to do you harm. First, because the good gods cannot act badly, even if they have been worshipped with no honour,—for whatever is mild and placid by nature, is separated widely from the practice and devising of mischief; while the bad knows not to restrain his ferocity, although he should be enticed [to do so] with a thousand flocks and a thousand altars. For neither can bitterness change itself into sweetness, dryness into moisture, the heat of fire into cold, or what is contrary to anything take and change into its own nature that which is its opposite. So that, if you should stroke a viper with your hand, or caress a poisonous scorpion, the former will attack you with its fangs, the latter, drawing itself together, will fix its sting [in you]; and your caressing will be of no avail, since both creatures are excited to do mischief, not by the stings of rage, but by a certain peculiarity of their nature. It is thus of no avail to wish to deserve well of the sinister deities by means of sacrifices, since, whether you do this, or on the contrary do not, they follow their own nature, and by inborn laws and a kind of necessity are led to those things, [to do] which[1] they were made. Moreover, in this way[2] both [kinds of] gods cease to possess their own powers, and to retain their own characters. For if the good are worshipped that they may be favourable, and supplication is made in the same way to the others, on the contrary, that they may not be injurious, it follows that it should be understood that the propitious [deities] will show no favour if they receive no gifts, and become bad instead of

---

[1] The MS. reads *ad ea quæ facti sunt*, understood seemingly as above by the edd., by supplying *ad* before *quæ*. Oehler, however, proposes *quia* —" because they were made [for them]." The reading must be regarded as doubtful.

[2] *i.e.* if sacrifices avail to counteract the malevolent dispositions of the gods.

good;[1] while, on the contrary, the bad, if they receive [offerings], will lay aside their mischievous disposition, and become thereafter good: and thus it is brought to this issue, that neither are these propitious, nor are those sinister; or, which is impossible, both are propitious, and both again sinister.

24. Be it so; let it be conceded that [these] most unfortunate cattle are not sacrificed in the temples of the gods without some religious obligation, and that what has been done in accordance with usage and custom possesses some rational ground: but if it seems a great and grand thing to slay bulls to the gods, and to burn in [sacrifice] the flesh of animals whole and entire, what is the meaning of these relics connected with the arts of the *Magi* which the pontifical mysteries have restored to a place among the secret laws of the sacred rites, and have mixed up with religious affairs? What, I say, is the meaning of these things, *apexaones, hirciæ, silicernia, longavi*, which are names and kinds of sausages,[2] some stuffed with goats' blood,[3] others with minced liver? What [is the meaning of] *tædæ, næniæ, offæ*, not those used by the common people, but those named and called *offæ penitæ*?—of which the first[4] is fat cut into very small pieces, as dainties[5] are; that which has been placed second is the extension of the gut by which the excrements are given off after being drained of all their nourishing juices; while the *offa penita* is a beast's tail cut off with a morsel of flesh. What [is the meaning of] *polimina, omenta, palasea*, or, as some call it, *plasea*?—of which that named *omentum* is a certain part enclosed by which the reservoirs of the belly are

---

[1] Lit., "these." This clause, omitted by Oberthür, is also omitted without remark by Orelli.

[2] So the edd., reading *farciminum* for the MS. *facinorum*, corrected by Hild. *fartorum*—"of stuffings." Throughout this passage hardly one of the names of these sacrificial dainties is generally agreed upon; as many are met with nowhere else, the MS. has been adhered to strictly.

[3] *i.e.* probably the *hirciæ*: of the others, *silicernia* seem to have been put on the table at funerals.

[4] *i.e.* tæda.

[5] So Salmasius and Meursius corrected the MS. *catillaminu-a-m* by omitting *a*.

kept within bounds; the *plasea* is an ox's tail[1] besmeared with flour and blood; the *polimina*, again, are those parts which we with more decency call *proles*,—by the vulgar, however, they are usually termed *testes*. What [is the meaning of] *fililla, frumen, africia, gratilla, catumeum, cumspolium, cubula?*—of which the first two are names of species of pottage, but differing in kind and quality; while the series [of names] which follows denotes consecrated cakes, for they are not shaped in one and the same way. For we do not choose to mention the *caro strebula* which is taken from the haunches of bulls, the roasted pieces of meat which are spitted, the intestines first heated, and baked on glowing coals, nor, finally, the pickles,[2] which are made by mixing four kinds of fruit. In like manner, [we do not choose to mention] the *fendicæ*, which also are the *hiræ*,[3] which the language of the mob, when it speaks, usually terms *ilia*;[4] nor, in the same way, the *ærumnæ*,[5] which are the first part of the gullet,[6] where ruminating animals are accustomed to send down their food and bring it back again; nor the *magmenta*,[7] *augmina*, and thousand other kinds of sausages or pottages which you have given unintelligible names to, and have caused to be more revered by common people.

25. For if whatever is done by men, and especially in religion, should have its causes,—and nothing should be done without a reason in all that men do and perform,—tell us and say what is the cause, what the reason, that these things

---

[1] *i.e.* tail-piece.
[2] *Salsamina*, by which is perhaps meant the grits and salt cast on the victim; but if so, Arnobius is at variance with Servius (Virgil, *Ecl.* viii. 81), who expressly states that these were of spelt mixed only with salt; while there is no trace elsewhere of a different usage.
[3] The first four edd. retain the unintelligible MS. *diræ*.
[4] *i.e.* the entrails. The MS., first four edd., and Elm. read *illa*.
[5] So the MS., LB., Oberthür, Orelli, Hild., and Oehler; but *ærumnæ* is found in no other passage with this meaning.
[6] Lit., "first heads in gullets."
[7] By this, and the word which follows, we know from the etymology that "offerings" to the gods must be meant, but we know nothing more.

also are given to the gods and burned upon their sacred altars? For here we delay, [constrained] most urgently [to wait] for this cause, we pause, we stand fast, desiring to learn what a god has to do with pottage, with cakes, with different [kinds of] stuffing prepared in manifold ways, and with different ingredients? Are the deities affected by splendid dinners or luncheons, so that it is fitting to devise for them feasts without number? Are they troubled by the loathings of their stomachs, and is variety of flavours sought for to get rid of their aversion, so that there is set before them meat at one time roasted, at another raw, and at another half cooked and half raw? But if the gods like to receive all these parts which you term *præsiciæ*,[1] and if these gratify them with any sense of pleasure or delight, what prevents, what hinders you from laying all these upon [their altars] at once with the whole animals? What cause, what reason is there that the haunch-piece[2] by itself, the gullet, the tail, and the tail-piece[3] separately, the entrails only, and the membrane[4] alone, should be brought to do them honour? Are the gods of heaven moved by various condiments? After stuffing themselves with sumptuous and ample dinners, do they, as is usually done, take these little bits as sweet dainties, not to appease their hunger, but to rouse their wearied palates,[5] and excite in themselves a perfectly voracious appetite? O wonderful greatness of the gods, comprehended by no men, understood by no creatures! if indeed their favours are bought with the testicles and gullets of beasts, and if they do not lay aside their anger and resentment, unless they see the entrails[6] prepared and *offæ* bought and burned upon their altars.

26. We have now to say a few words about incense and wine, for these, too, are connected and mixed up with your

---

[1] *i.e.* cut off for sacrifice.   [2] *Caro strebula.*   [3] *Plasea.*
[4] The MS. reads unintelligibly *nomen quæ*, corrected by Gelenius *omentum*, as above.
[5] Lit., "admonish the case of the palate;" a correction of Salmasius, by omitting *a* from the MS. *palati-a admoneant.*
[6] *Næniæ.*

ceremonies,[1] and are used largely in your religious acts. And, first, with respect to that very incense which you use, we ask this of you particularly, whence or at what time you have been able to become acquainted with it, and to know it, so that you have just reason to think that it is either worthy to be given to the gods, or most agreeable to their desires. For it is almost a novelty; and there is no endless succession of years since it began to be known in these parts, and won its way into the shrines of the gods. For neither in the heroic ages, as it is believed and declared, was it known what incense was, as is proved by the ancient writers, in whose books is found no mention[2] of it; nor was Etruria, the parent and mother of superstition, acquainted with its fame and renown, as the rites of the chapels prove; nor was it used by any one in offering sacrifice during the four hundred years in which Alba flourished; nor did even Romulus or Numa, [who was] skilful in devising new ceremonies, know either of its existence or growth, as the sacred grits[3] show with which it was customary that the usual sacrifices should be performed. Whence, therefore, did its use begin to be adopted? or what [desire of] novelty assailed the old and ancient custom, so that that which was not needed for so many ages took the first place in the ceremonies? For if without incense the performance of a religious service is imperfect, and if a quantity of it is necessary to make the celestials gentle and propitious to men, the ancients fell into sin, nay rather, their whole life was full of guilt, for they carelessly neglected to offer that which was most fitted to give pleasure to the gods. But if in ancient times neither men nor gods sought for this incense, it is proved that to-day also that is offered uselessly and in vain which antiquity did not believe necessary, but modern times desired without any reason.

[1] Lit., "these kinds of ceremonies, too, were coupled and mixed," etc.
[2] On this Oehler remarks, that the books of Moses show that it was certainly used in the East in the most ancient times. But Arnobius has expressly restricted his statement to the use of incense "in these parts."
[3] *Pium far.*

27. Finally, that we may always abide by the rule and definition by which it has been shown and determined that whatever is done by man must have its causes, we will hold it fast here also, so as to demand of you what is the cause, what the reason, that incense is put on the altars before the very images of the deities, and that, from its being burned, they are supposed to become friendly and gentle. What do they acquire from this being done, or what reaches their minds, so that we should be right in judging that these things are well expended, and are not consumed uselessly and in vain? For as you should show why you give incense to the gods, so, too, it follows that you should manifest that the gods have some reason for not rejecting it with disdain, nay more, for desiring it so fondly. We honour the gods with this, some one will perhaps say. But we are not inquiring what your feeling is, but the gods'; nor do we ask what is done by you, but how much they value what is done to purchase their favour. But yet, O piety, what or how great is this honour which is caused by the odour of a fire, and produced from the gum of a tree? For, lest you should happen not to know what this incense is, or what is its origin, it is a gum flowing from the bark of trees, [just] as from the almond-tree, the cherry-tree, solidifying as it exudes in drops. Does this, then, honour and magnify the celestial dignities? or, if their displeasure has been at any time excited, is it melted away before the smoke of incense and lulled to sleep, their anger being moderated? Why, then, do you not burn indiscriminately the juice of any tree whatever, without making any distinction? For if the deities are honoured by this, and are not displeased that Panchæan gums are burned to them, what does it matter from what the smoke proceeds on your sacred altars, or from what kind of gum the clouds of fumigation arise?

28. Will any one say that incense is given to the celestials, for this reason, that it has a sweet smell, and imparts a pleasant sensation to the nose, while the rest are disagreeable, and have been set aside because of their offensiveness? Do the gods, then, have nostrils with which to breathe? do

they inhale and respire currents of air so that the qualities of different smells can penetrate them? But if we allow that this is the case, we make them subject to the conditions of humanity, and shut them out from the limits of deity; for whatever breathes and draws in draughts of air, to be sent back in the same way, must be mortal, because it is sustained by feeding on the atmosphere. But whatever is sustained by feeding on the atmosphere, if you take away the means by which communication is kept up,[1] its life must be crushed out, and its vital principle must be destroyed and lost. So then, if the gods also breathe and inhale odours enwrapt in the air that accompanies them, it is not untrue to say that they live upon what is received from others,[2] and that they might perish if their air-holes were blocked up. And whence, lastly, do you know whether, if they are charmed by the sweetness of smells, the same things are pleasant to them which [are pleasant] to you, and charm and affect your [different] natures with a similar feeling? May it not be possible that the things which give pleasure to you, seem, on the contrary, harsh and disagreeable to them? For since the opinions of the gods are not the same, and their substance not one, by what methods can it be brought about that that which is unlike in quality should have the same feeling and perception as to that which touches it?[3] Do we not every day see that, even among the creatures sprung from the earth, the same things are either bitter or sweet to different species, that to some things are fatal which are not pernicious to others, so that the same things which charm some with their delightful odours, give forth exhalations deadly to the bodies of others? But the cause of this is not in the things which cannot be at one and the same time deadly and wholesome, sweet and bitter; but just as each one has been formed to receive impressions from what is ex-

---

[1] Lit., "the returns by which the vital alternation is restored and withdrawn."

[2] So the MS., Hild., and Oehler, reading *suffec-tionibus alienis*, for which the rest read *suffi* - —"the fumigations of others."

[3] Lit., "feel and receive one contact."

ternal,[1] so he is affected:[2] his condition is not caused by the influences of the things, but springs from the nature of his own senses, and connection with the external. But all this is set far from the gods, and is separated from them by no small interval. For if it is true, as is believed by the wise, that they are incorporeal, and not supported by any excellence of [bodily] strength, an odour is of no effect upon them, nor can recking fumes move them by their senses, not [even] if you were to set on fire a thousand pounds of the finest incense, and the whole sky were clouded with the darkness of the abundant vapours. For that which does not have [bodily] strength and corporeal substance, cannot be touched by corporeal substance; but an odour is corporeal, as is shown by the nose when touched [by one]: therefore it cannot, according to reason, be felt by a deity, who has no body, and is without any feeling and thought.[3]

29. Wine is used along with incense; and of this, in like manner, we ask an explanation why it is poured upon it when burning. For if a reason is not[4] shown for doing this, and its cause is not[5] set forth, this action of yours must not now be attributed to a ridiculous error, but, to speak more plainly, to madness, foolishness, blindness. For, as has been already said pretty frequently, everything which is done should have its cause manifest, and not involved in any dark obscurity. If, therefore, you have confidence in what is done, disclose, point out why that liquor is offered; that is, [why] wine is poured on the altars. For do the bodies of

---

[1] Lit., "as each has been made for the touching of a thing coming from without."

[2] So Gelenius and later edd., reading *afficitur* for the unintelligible reading of MS. and Roman edd., *efficit*—"effects."

[3] So all edd., without remark, reading *cog-it-atione*, although "meditation" has nothing to do with the sense of smell, and has not been previously mentioned. We should probably read *cog-n-atione*—"relation," *i.e.* to such objects.

[4] So LB. and Oehler, reading *ni-si* (MS. *si*), and other edd. inserting *non*, the negative being absolutely necessary to the sense, and supplied in the next clause.

[5] Lit., "nor will it have its cause."

the deities feel parching thirst, and is it necessary that their dryness be tempered by some moisture? Are they accustomed, as men are, to combine eating and drinking? In like manner, also, after the solid[1] food of cakes and pottages, and victims slain [in honour of them], do they drench themselves, and make themselves merry with very frequent [cups of] wine, that their food may be more easily softened, and thoroughly digested? Give, I beg, to the immortal gods to drink; bring forth goblets, bowls,[2] ladles, and cups; and as they stuff themselves with bulls, and luxurious feasts, and rich food, — lest some piece of flesh hastily[3] gulped down should stick in passing through the stomach, run up, hasten, give pure wine to Jupiter, the most excellent, the supreme, lest he be choked. He desires to break wind, and is unable; and unless that hindrance passes away and is dissolved, there is very great danger that his breathing will be stopped and[4] interrupted, and heaven be left desolate without its rulers.

30. But, says [my opponent], you are insulting us without reason, for we do not pour forth wine to the gods of heaven for these reasons, as if we supposed that they either thirsted, or drank, or were made glad by tasting its sweetness. It is given to them to do them honour; that their eminence may become more exalted, more illustrious, we pour libations on their altars, and with the [half] extinguished embers we raise sweet smells,[5] which show our reverence. And what greater insult can be inflicted upon the gods than if you believe that they become propitious on receiving wine, or, if you suppose that great honour is done to them, if you only throw and drop on the live coals a few drops of wine? We are not speaking to men void of reason, or not possessed of common under-

---

[1] Although this is clearly the meaning, Stewechius explained *solidos* by referring to the ancient belief that such offerings should be wholly consumed, and no fragment left.

[2] *Briæ*, drinking-cups, but of their peculiar shape or purpose we know nothing.

[3] Lit., "badly."   [4] Lit., "being strangled, may be."

[5] So LB., Orelli, and Oehler, reading with Salmasius *m-u-scos* (MS. -*i*-). Gelenius proposed *cnissas*, which would refer to the steam of the sacrifices.

standing: in you, too, there is wisdom, there is perception, and in your hearts you know, by your own[1] judgment, that we are speaking truly. But what can we do with those who are utterly unwilling to consider things as they are, to converse themselves with themselves? For you do what you see to be done, not that which you are assured should be done, inasmuch[2] as with you a custom without reason prevails, more than a perception of the nature of circumstances based on a careful examination of the truth. For what has a god to do with wine? or what or how great is the power in it, that, on its being poured out, his eminence becomes greater, and his dignity is supposed [to be] honoured? What, I say, has a god to do with wine, which is most closely connected with the pursuits of Venus, which weakens the strength of all virtues, [and] is hostile to the decency of modesty and chastity,—which has often excited [men's] minds, and urged them to madness and frenzy, and compelled the gods to destroy their own authority by raving [and] foul language? Is not this, then, impious, and perfectly sacrilegious, to give that as an honour which, if you take too eagerly, you know not what you are doing, you are ignorant of what you are saying, [and] at last are reviled, and become infamous as a drunkard, a luxurious and abandoned fellow?

31. It is worth while to bring forward the words themselves also, which, when wine is offered, it is customary to use and make supplication with : *Let [the deity] be worshipped with this wine which we bring.*[3] The words *which we bring*, says Trebatius, are added for this purpose, and put forth for this reason, that all the wine whatever which has been laid up in closets and storerooms, from which was taken that which is poured out, may not begin to be sacred, and be reft

---

[1] Lit., "interior."
[2] So most edd., reading *nimirum quia plus valet*, for which the MS., followed by both Roman edd., Hild., and Oehler, read *primum q. v.*, which Hild. would explain, "because it prevails above all [rather] than;" but this is at least very doubtful.
[3] *Vino inferio.*

from the use of men. This word, then, being added, that alone will be sacred which is brought to [the place], and the rest will not be consecrated.¹ What kind of honour, then, is this, in which there is imposed on the deity a condition,² as it were, not to ask more than has been given? or what is the greed of the god, who, if he were not verbally interdicted, would extend his desires too far, and rob his suppliant of his stores? *Let* [*the deity*] *be worshipped with this wine which we bring:* this is a wrong, not an honour. For what if the deity shall wish for more, and shall not be content with what is brought! Must he not be said to be signally wronged who is compelled to receive honour conditionally? For if all wine in cellars whatever must become consecrated were a limitation not added, it is manifest both that the god is insulted to whom a limit is prescribed against his wishes, and that in sacrificing you yourselves violate the obligations of the sacred rites, who do not give as much wine as you see the god wishes to be given to himself. *Let* [*the deity*] *be worshipped with this wine which we bring:* what is this but saying, *Be worshipped as much as I choose; receive as much dignity as I prescribe, as much honour as I decide and determine by a strict engagement*³ *that you should have?* O sublimity of the gods, excelling in power, which thou shouldst venerate and worship with all ceremonial observances, but on which the worshipper imposes conditions, which he adores with stipulations and contracts, which, through fear of one word, is kept from excessive desire of wine!

32. But let there be, as you wish, honour in wine and in incense, let the anger and displeasure of the deities be appeased by the immolation and slaughter of victims: are the gods moved by garlands also, wreaths and flowers, by the jingling of brass also, and the shaking of cymbals, by timbrels

---

[1] Lit., "bound by religion."

[2] This is admirably illustrated in an inscription quoted by Heraldus: "Jupiter most excellent, supreme, when this day I give and dedicate to thee this altar, I give and dedicate it with these conditions and limits which I say openly to-day."

[3] *Circumscriptione verborum.*

also, [and] also by *symphoniæ*?[1] What effect has the clattering of castanets, that when the deities have heard them, they think that honour has been shown to them, and lay aside their fiery spirit of resentment in forgetfulness? Or, as little boys are frightened into giving over their silly wailings by hearing [the sound of] rattles, are the almighty deities also soothed in the same way by the whistling of pipes? and do they become mild, [is] their indignation softened, at the musical sound of cymbals? What is the meaning of those calls[2] which you sing in the morning, joining [your] voices to the [music of the] pipe? Do the gods of heaven fall asleep, so that they should return to their posts? What [is the meaning of] those slumbers[2] to which you commend them with auspicious salutations that they may be in good health? Are they awakened from sleep; and that they may be able to be overcome by it, must soothing lullabies be heard? The purification, says [my opponent], of the mother of the gods is to-day.[3] Do the gods, then, become dirty; and to get rid of the filth, do those who wash [them] need water, and even some cinders to rub them with?[4] The feast of Jupiter is to-morrow. Jupiter, I suppose, dines, and must be satiated with great banquets, and long filled with eager cravings [for food] by fasting, and hungry after the usual[5] interval. The vintage festival of Æsculapius is being celebrated. The gods, then, cultivate vineyards, and, having collected gatherers, press the wine for their own uses.[6] The

[1] Evidently musical instruments; but while Isidore speaks of them as a kind of drum, other writers call them trumpets and pipes.

[2] At daybreak on opening, and at night on closing the temple, the priests of Isis sang hymns in praise of the goddess (cf. Jos. Scaliger, *Castigationes ad Cat.*, etc., p. 132); and to these Arnobius refers sarcastically, as though they had been calls to awake, and lullabies to sing her asleep.

[3] *i.e.* March 27th, marked *Lavatio* in a calendar prepared during the reign of Constantius.

[4] Lit., " and some rubbing of cinders added," *aliqua frictione cineris*; an emendation of Ursinus for the possibly correct MS. *antiqua f. c.*—" the ancient rubbing," *i.e.* that practised in early times.

[5] Lit., " anniversary."

[6] So the later edd., adopting the emendation of *ad suas usiones* for the corrupt MS. *ad* (or *ab*) *suasionibus*.

lectisternium of Ceres[1] will be on the next Ides, for the gods have couches; and that they may be able to lie on softer cushions, the pillows are shaken up when they have been pressed down.[2] It is the birthday of *Tellus*;[3] for the gods are born, and have festal days on which it has been settled that they began to breathe.

33. But the games which you celebrate, called *Floralia* and *Megalensia*,[4] and all the rest which you wish to be sacred, and to be considered religious duties, what reason have they, what cause, that it was necessary that they should be instituted and founded and designated by the names[5] of deities? The gods are honoured by these, says [my opponent]; and if they have any recollection of offences committed[6] by men, they lay it aside, get rid of it, and show themselves gracious to us again, their friendship being renewed. And what is the cause, again, that they are made quite calm and gentle, if absurd things are done, and idle fellows sport before the eyes of the multitude? Does Jupiter lay aside his resentment if the *Amphitryon* of Plautus is acted and declaimed? or if Europa, Leda, Ganymede, or Danæ is represented by dancing, does he restrain his passionate impulses? Is the Great Mother rendered more calm, more gentle, if she beholds the old story of Attis furbished up by the players? Will Venus forget her displeasure if she sees mimics act the part of Adonis also in a ballet?[7] Does the anger of Alcides die away if the

---

[1] *i.e.* feast at which the image of Ceres was placed on a couch, probably the *Cerealia*, celebrated in April. This passage flatly contradicts Prof. Ramsay's assertion (*Ant.* p. 345) that *lectisternium* is not applied to a banquet offered to a goddess; while it corroborates his statement that such feasts were ordinary events, not extraordinary solemnities, as Mr. Yates says (Smith's *Ant.* s. v.).

[2] Lit., "the impression of the cushions is lifted up and raised," *i.e.* smoothed.

[3] Thus the 25th of January is marked as the birthday of the Graces, the 1st of February as that of Hercules, the 1st of March as that of Mars, in the calendar already mentioned.

[4] The former dedicated to Flora (cf. iii. 25), the latter to Cybele.

[5] Singular.

[6] So the margin of Ursinus, Elm., LB., Orelli, Hild., and Oehler: the MS. reading not being known.   [7] Lit., "in dancing motions."

tragedy of Sophocles named *Trachiniæ*, or the *Hercules* of Euripides, is acted? or does Flora think[1] that honour is shown to her if at her games she sees that shameful actions are done, and the stews abandoned for the theatres? Is not this, then, to lessen the dignity of the gods, to dedicate and consecrate to them the basest things which a rigidly virtuous mind will turn from with disgust, the performers of which your law has decided to be dishonoured and to be considered infamous? The gods, forsooth, delight in mimics; and that surpassing excellence which has not been comprehended by any human faculty, opens[2] its ears most willingly to hear these [plays], with most of which they know they are mixed up to be turned to derision; they are delighted, as it is, with the shaved heads of the fools, by the sound of flaps, and by the [noise of] applause, by shameful actions and words, by huge red *fascina*. But further, if they see men weakening themselves to the effeminacy of women, some vociferating uselessly, others running about without cause,[3] others, while their friendship is unbroken, bruising and maiming each with the bloody *cestus*, these contending in [speaking without drawing] breath,[4] swelling out their cheeks with wind, and shouting out noisily empty vows, do they lift up their hands to heaven [in their admiration], start up moved by [such] wonders, burst into exclamations, again become gracious to men? If these things cause the gods to forget their resentment, if they derive the highest pleasure from comedies, Atellane farces, [and] pantomimes, why do you delay, why do you hesitate, to say that the gods themselves also play, act lasciviously, dance, compose obscene songs, and undulate with trembling haunches? For what difference is there, or what does it matter, whether they do these things them-

---

[1] So Meursius, Orelli, and Oehler, reading *existimat-ve*, all the others retaining the MS. *-ur-* —"Is Flora thought to be treated," etc.

[2] Lit., "adapts."

[3] Here also there is doubt as to what the reading of the MS. is. The 1st ed. reads *sine culpa*—"without blame," which is hardly in keeping with the context, emended *causa*, as above, by Gelenius.

[4] So Orelli explains *certare hos spiritu* as referring to a contest in which each strove to speak or sing with one breath longer than the rest.

selves, or are pleased and delighted to see them done by others?

34. Whence, therefore, have these vicious opinions flowed, or from what causes have they sprung? From this it is clear, in great measure, that men [are] unable to know what God is, what is His essence, nature, substance, quality; whether He has a form, or is limited by no bodily outline, does anything or not, is ever watchful, or is at times sunk in slumbers, runs, sits, walks, or is free from such motions and inactivity. Being, as I have said, unable to know all these things, or to discern them by any power of reason, they fell into these fanciful beliefs, so that they fashioned gods after themselves, and gave to these such a nature as they have themselves, in actions, circumstances, and desires. But if they were to perceive that they are worthless creatures,[1] and that there is no great difference between themselves and a little ant, they would cease, indeed, to think that they have anything in common with the gods of heaven, and would confine their unassuming insignificance[2] within its proper limits. But now, because they see that they themselves have faces, eyes, heads, cheeks, ears, noses, and all the other parts of [our] limbs and muscles, they think that the gods also have been formed in the same way, that the divine nature is embodied in a human frame;[3] and because they perceive that they themselves rejoice [and] are glad, and [again] are made sad by what is too disagreeable, they think that the deities also on joyous occasions are glad, and on less pleasant ones become dejected. [They see] that they are affected by the games, and think that the minds of the celestials are soothed by enjoying games; and because they have pleasure in refreshing themselves with warm baths, they think that the cleanness produced by[4] bathing is pleasing to the gods above. We men gather our vintages, and they think and believe that the gods gather and bring in their grapes; we

---

[1] Lit., "an animal of no value."
[2] Lit., "the modesty of their humility."
[3] Lit., "they contain their nature in a corporeal form."
[4] Lit., "of."

have birthdays, and they affirm that the powers of heaven have birthdays.[1] But if they could ascribe to the gods ill-health, sickness, and bodily disease, they would not hesitate to say that they were splenetic, blear-eyed, and ruptured, because they are themselves both splenetic, and often blear-eyed, and weighed down by huge *herniæ*.

35. Come now: as the discussion has been prolonged and led to these points, let us, bringing forward what each has to say,[2] decide by a brief comparison whether your ideas of the gods above are the better, or our thoughts preferable, and much more honourable and just, and such as to give and assign its own dignity to the divine nature. And, first, you declare that the gods, whom you either think or believe to exist, of whom you have set up images and statues in all the temples, were born and produced from the germs of males and females, under the necessary condition of sexual embraces. But we, on the contrary, if they are indeed true gods, and have the authority, power, dignity of this name, consider that they must either be unbegotten (for it is pious to believe this), or, if they have a beginning in[3] birth, it belongs to the supreme God to know by what methods He made them, or how many ages there are since He granted to them to enter upon the eternal being of His own divine nature. You consider that the deities have sexes, and that some of them are male, others female; we utterly deny that the powers of heaven have been distinguished by sexes, since this distinction has been given to the creatures of earth which the Author of the universe willed should embrace and generate, to provide, by their carnal desires, one generation of offspring after an-

---

[1] Cf. p. 343, n. 3.

[2] Lit., "by opposition of the parts of each." Considerable difficulty has been felt as to the abrupt way in which the book ends as it is arranged in the MS. Orelli has therefore adopted the suggestion of an anonymous critic, and transposed cc. 35, 36, 37 to the end. This does not, however, meet the difficulty; for the same objection still holds good, that there is a want of connection and harmony in these concluding chapters, and that, even when thus arranged, they do not form a fitting conclusion to the whole work.

[3] Lit., "of."

other. You think that they are like men, and have been fashioned with the countenances of mortals; we think that the images of them are wide of the mark,[1] as form belongs to a mortal body; and if they have any, we swear with the utmost earnestness and confidence that no man can comprehend it. By you they are said to have each his trade, like artisans; we laugh when we hear you say such things, as we hold and think that professions are not necessary to gods, and it is certain and evident that these have been provided to assist poverty.

36.[2] You say that some of them [cause] dissensions, that there are others who inflict pestilences, others who [excite] love [and] madness, others, even, who preside over wars, and are delighted by the shedding of blood; but we, indeed, on the contrary, judge that [these things] are remote[3] from the dispositions of the deities; or if there are any who inflict and bring these ills on miserable mortals, we maintain that they are far from the nature of the gods, and should not be spoken of under this name. You judge that the deities are angry and perturbed, and given over and subject to the other mental affections; we think that such emotions are alien from them, for [these] suit savage beings, and those who die as mortals.[4] You think that they rejoice, are made glad,

---

[1] Lit., "that effigies have been far removed from them." This may be understood, either as meaning that the gods had not visible form at all, or, as above, that their likenesses made by men showed no resemblance.

[2] 50 in Orelli.

[3] It is important to notice the evidence in this one sentence of haste and want of revision. In the first line we find a genitive (*discordiarum*—"dissensions"), but not the noun on which it depends; and in the apodosis a verb (*disjunctas esse*—" have been removed," *i.e.* "are remote") has no subject, although its gender imperatively requires that *has res*, or some such words, be supplied. One omission might have been easily ascribed to a slip on the part of the copyist; but two omissions such as these occurring so closely, must, it would seem, be assigned to the impetuous disregard of *minutiæ* with which Arnobius blocked out a conclusion which was never carefully revised. (Cf. Appendix, note 1, and p. 364, n. 3.) The importance of such indications is manifest in forming an opinion on the controversy as to this part of the work.

[4] Lit., "are of ... those meeting the functions of mortality," *obe-*

and are reconciled to men, their offended feelings being soothed by the blood of beasts and the slaughter of victims; we hold that there is in the celestials no love of blood, and that they are not so stern as to lay aside their resentment only when glutted with the slaughter of animals. You think that, by wine and incense, honour is given to the gods, and their dignity increased; we judge it marvellous and monstrous that any man thinks that the deity either becomes more venerable by reason of smoke, or thinks himself supplicated by men with sufficient awe and respect when they offer[1] a few drops of wine. You are persuaded that, by the crash of cymbals and the sound of pipes, by horse-races and theatrical plays, the gods are both delighted and affected, and that their resentful feelings conceived before[2] are mollified by the satisfaction which these things give; we hold it [to be] out of place, nay more, we judge it incredible, that those who have surpassed by a thousand degrees every kind of excellence in the height of their perfection, should be pleased and delighted with those things which a wise man laughs at, and which do not seem to have any charm except to little children, coarsely and vulgarly educated.

37. Since these things are so, and since there is so great difference between[1] our opinions and yours, where are we, on the one hand, impious, or you pious, since the decision as to[1] piety and impiety must be founded on the opinions of the [two] parties? For he who makes himself an image which he may worship for a god, or slaughters an innocent beast, and burns it on consecrated altars, must not be held to be devoted to religion.[3] Opinion constitutes religion, and a right way of thinking about the gods, so that you do not think that they desire anything contrary to what becomes their exalted position, [which is] manifest.[4] For since we

unti-um, corrected by Gelenius (according to Orelli) for the MS. *-bus,* retained, though unintelligible, by Canterus, Oberth., and Hild.

[1] Lit., "of."   [2] Lit., "some time."
[3] Lit., "divine things."
[4] So the MS., both Roman edd., Hild., and Oehler, reading *promptæ;* corrected *præsumptæ*—"taken for granted," in the rest.

see all the things which are offered to them consumed here under our eyes, what else can be said to reach them from us than opinions worthy of the gods, and most appropriate to their name? These are the surest gifts, these true sacrifices; for gruel, incense, and flesh feed the devouring flames, and agree very well with the *parentalia*[1] of the dead.

38.[2] If the immortal gods cannot be angry, says [my opponent], and their nature is not agitated or troubled by any passions, what do the histories, the annals mean, in which we find it written[3] that the gods, moved by some annoyances, occasioned pestilences, sterility,[4] failure of crops, and other dangers, to states and nations; and that they again, being appeased and satisfied by means of[5] sacrifices, laid aside their burning anger, and changed the state of the atmosphere and times into a happier one? What [is the meaning of] the earth's roarings, the earthquakes, which we have been told occurred because the games had been celebrated carelessly, and their nature and circumstances [had] not been attended to, and yet, on their being celebrated afresh, and repeated with assiduous care, the terrors of the gods were stilled, and [they] were recalled to care and friendship for men? How often, after that—in obedience to the commands of the seers and the responses of the diviners—sacrifice has been offered, and certain gods have been summoned from nations dwelling beyond the sea, and shrines erected to them, and certain images and statues set on loftier pillars, have fears of impending dangers been diverted, and the most troublesome enemies beaten, and the republic extended both by repeated joyous victories, and by gaining possession of several provinces! Now, certainly this would not happen if the gods despised sacrifices, games, and other acts of worship, and did not consider themselves honoured by expiatory offerings. If, then, all the rage and indignation of the deities are cooled when these things are offered, and

---

[1] *i.e.* offerings to parents, as the name implies, and other relatives who were dead.
[2] 35 in Orelli.
[3] Lit., "in the writings of which we read."
[4] Pl.
[5] Lit., "by satisfaction of."

[if] those things become favourable which seemed fraught with terrors, it is clear that all these things are not done without the gods wishing them, and that it is vain, and shows utter ignorance, to blame us for giving them.

39.[1] We have come, then, in speaking, to the very point of the case, to that on which the question hinges, to the real and most intimate [part of the] discussion, which it is fitting that, laying aside superstitious dread, and putting away partiality, we should examine whether these are gods whom you assert to be furious when offended, and to be rendered mild by sacrifices; or whether they are something far different, and should be separated from the notion of this name and power. For we do not deny that all these things are to be found in the writings of the annalists which have been brought forward by you in opposition; for we ourselves also, according to the measure and capacity of our abilities, have read, and know, that it has been recorded that once at the *ludi circenses*, celebrated in honour of Jupiter the supreme, a master dragged across the middle of the arena, and afterwards, according to custom, punished with the cross, a very worthless slave [whom he had] beaten with rods. Then, when the games were ended, and the races not long finished, a pestilence began to distress the state; and when each day brought fresh ill worse than what was before,[2] and the people were perishing in crowds, in a dream Jupiter said to a certain rustic, obscure from the lowliness of his lot, that he should go[3] to the consuls, point out that the dancer[4] had displeased him, that it might be better for the state if the respect due to the games were paid to them, and they were again celebrated afresh with assiduous care. And when he had utterly neglected to do this, either because he supposed it was an empty dream, and would find no credence with those to whom he should tell it, or because, remembering his natural insignificance, he avoided and dreaded approaching those who

[1] 36 in Orelli. [2] Lit., "added evil heavier than evil."
[3] So later edd., reading *vaderet* from the margin of Ursinus, while the first three retain the MS. reading *suaderet*—" persuade."
[4] *i.e.* the slave writhing under the scourge.

were so powerful,[1] Jupiter was rendered hostile to the lingerer, and imposed as punishment [on him] the death of his sons. Afterwards, when he[2] threatened the man himself with death unless he went to announce his disapproval of the dancer,—overcome by fear of dying, since he was already himself also burning with the fever of the plague, having been infected, he was carried to the senate-house, as his neighbours wished, and, when his vision had been declared, the contagious fever passed away. The repetition of the games being then decreed, great care was, on the one hand, given to the shows, and its former good health was restored to the people.

40.[3] But neither shall we deny that we know this as well, that once on a time, when the state and republic were in difficulties, caused either by[4] a terrible plague continually infecting the people and carrying them off, or by enemies powerful, and at that time almost threatening to rob it of its liberty[5] because of their success in battle,—by order and advice of the seers, certain gods[6] were summoned from among nations dwelling beyond the sea, and honoured with magnificent temples; and that the violence of the plague abated, and very frequent triumphs were gained, the power of the enemy being broken, and the territory of the empire was increased, and provinces without number fell under your sway. But neither does this escape our knowledge, that we have seen it asserted that, when the Capitol was struck by a thunderbolt, and many other things in it, the image of Jupiter also, which stood on a lofty pillar, was hurled from its place. Thereafter a response was given by the soothsayers, that cruel and very sad mischances were portended from fire and slaughter, from the destruction of the laws, and the overthrow of justice, especially, however, from enemies themselves belonging to the nation, and from an impious band of conspirators; but that these things could not be averted, nay, that the accursed designs could not be revealed,

---

[1] Lit., "of so great power."   [2] *i.e.* Jupiter.   [3] 37 in Orelli.
[4] Lit., "which either a . . . made," etc.
[5] Lit., "very near to danger of carrying off liberty."
[6] Cf. ii. 73.

unless Jupiter were again set up firmly on a higher pillar, turned towards the east, and facing the rays of the [rising] sun. Their words were trustworthy, for, when the pillar was raised, and the statue turned towards the sun, the secrets were revealed, and the offences made known were punished.

41.[1] All these things which have been mentioned, have indeed a miraculous appearance (rather, they are believed to have it), if they come to men's ears just as they have been brought forward; and we do not deny that there is in them something which, being placed in the fore front, as the saying is, may stun the ears, and deceive by its resemblance to truth. But if you will look closely at what was done, the personages and their pleasures,[2] you will find that there is nothing worthy of the gods, and (as has already been said often) [nothing worthy] to be referred to the splendour and majesty of this race. For, first, who is there who will believe that he was a god who was pleased with horses running to no purpose,[3] and considered it most delightful that he should be summoned[4] by such sports? Rather, who is there who will agree that that was Jupiter (whom you call the supreme god, and the creator of all things which are) who set out from heaven to behold geldings vieing [with each other] in speed, and running[5] the seven rounds of the course; and that, although he had himself determined that they should not be equally nimble, he nevertheless rejoiced to see them pass each other, and be passed, some in their haste falling forward upon their heads, [and] overturned upon their backs along with their chariots, others dragged along and lamed, their legs being broken; and that he considered as the highest pleasures fooleries mixed with trifles and cruelties, which any

---

[1] 38 in Orelli.

[2] So the MS., LB., Hild., and Oehler, reading *volu-p-tates*, i.e. the games and feasts spoken of previously; the other edd. read *-n-* — "wishes."

[3] Oehler explains *frustra* by *otiose*—"who was leisurely delighted;" but there is no reason why it should not have its usual meaning, as above.

[4] i.e. from heaven. Instead of *e-vocari*, however, Heraldus has proposed *a-* —"be diverted."

[5] Lit., "unfolding."

man, [even though] fond of pleasure, and not trained to strive after seriousness and dignity, would consider childish, and spurn as ridiculous? Who is there, I say, who will believe (to repeat this word assiduously) that he was divine who, being irritated because [a slave] was led across the circus, about to suffer and be punished as he deserved, was inflamed with anger, and prepared himself to take vengeance? For if the slave was guilty, and deserved to be punished with that chastisement, why should Jupiter have been moved with any indignation when nothing was being done unjustly, nay, when a guilty fellow was being punished, as was right? But if he was free from guilt, and not worthy of punishment at all, [Jupiter] himself was the cause of the dancer's vitiating the games,[1] for when he might have helped him, he did him no service—nay, sought both to allow what he disapproved, and to exact from others the penalty for what he had permitted. And why, then, did he complain and declare that he was wronged in the case of that dancer because he was led through the midst of the circus to suffer the cross, with his back torn by rods and scourges?

42.[2] And what pollution or abomination could have flowed from this, either to make the circus less pure, or to defile Jupiter, seeing that in a few moments, in [a few] seconds, he beheld so many thousands throughout the world perish by different kinds of death, and with various forms of torture? He was led across, says [my opponent], before the games began to be celebrated. If from a sacrilegious spirit and contempt[3] for religion, we have reason to excuse Jupiter for being indignant that he was contemned, and that more anxious care was not given to his games. But if from mistake or accident that secret fault was not observed and known, would it not have been right and befitting Jupiter to pardon human failings, and grant forgiveness to the blindness of ignorance? But it was necessary that it should be punished. And after this, will any one believe that he was a god who avenged and punished neglect of a childish show

---

[1] Lit., "was in the cause of the vicious dancer."
[2] 39 in Orelli. [3] So all edd., rejecting *s* from MS. *contemptu-s*.

by the destruction of a state? that he had any seriousness and dignity, or any steady constancy, who, that he might speedily enjoy pleasure afresh, turned the air men breathed[1] into a baneful poison, and ordered the destruction of mortals by plague and pestilence? If the magistrate who presided over the games was too careless in learning who on that day had been led across the circus, and blame was therefore contracted, what had the unhappy people done that they should in their own persons suffer the penalty of another's offences, and should be forced to hurry out of life by contagious pestilences? Nay, what had the women, whose weakness did not allow them to take part in public business, the grown-up[2] maidens, the little boys, finally the young children, yet dependent for food on their nurses,—what had these done that they should be assailed with equal, with the same severity, and that before [they tasted] the joy of life[3] they should feel the bitterness of death?

43.[4] If Jupiter sought to have his games celebrated, and that afresh,[5] with greater care; if he honestly [sought] to restore[6] the people to health, and that the evil which he had caused should go no further and not be increased, would it not have been better that he should come to the consul himself, to some one of the public priests, the *pontifex maximus*, or to his own *flamen Dialis*, and in a vision reveal to him the defect [in the games] occasioned by the dancer, and the cause of the sadness of the times? What reason had there been that he should choose, to announce his wishes and procure the satisfaction desired, a man accustomed to [live in] the country, unknown from the obscurity of his name, not acquainted with city matters, [and] perhaps not knowing what a dancer is? And if he indeed knew, [as he must

---

[1] Lit., "draughts of air."

[2] So, by omitting two letters, all edd. except 1st and Ursinus, which retain MS. *adult-er-æ*—"adulterous."

[3] Lit., "light."

[4] 40 in Orelli. The MS., 1st edd., and Ursinus want *si*.

[5] Lit., "and restored."

[6] The MS. and Ursinus read *reddere-t*—"if he was to restore;" corrected, as above, by omission of *t*.

have known] if he was a diviner,[1] that this fellow would refuse to obey, would it not have been more natural and befitting a god, to change the man's mind, and constrain him to be willing to obey, than to try more cruel methods, and vent his rage indiscriminately, without any reason, as robbers do? For if the old rustic, not being quick in entering upon anything, delayed in [doing] what was commanded, being kept back by stronger motives, of what had his unhappy children been guilty, that [Jupiter's] anger and indignation should be turned upon them, and that they should pay for another's offences by being robbed of their lives? And can any man believe that he [is] a god [who is] so unjust, so impious, and who does not observe even the laws of men, among whom it would be held a great crime to punish one for another, and to avenge one man's offences upon others?[2] But, [I am told], he caused the man himself to be seized by the cruel pestilence. Would it not then have been better, nay rather, juster, if it seemed that this should be done, that dread of punishment should be first excited by the father, who[3] had been the cause of such passion by[4] his disobedient delay, than to do violence to the children, and to consume and destroy innocent persons to make him sorrowful?[5] What, pray, was [the meaning of] this fierceness, this cruelty, which [was] so great that, his offspring being dead, it afterwards terrified the father by his own danger! But if he had chosen to do this long before, that is, in the first place, not only would not the innocent brothers have been cut off, but the indignant purpose of the deity also would have been known. But certainly, [it will be said], when he had done his duty by announcing the vision, the disease immediately left him, and the man was forthwith restored to health. And what is there to admire in this if he removed[6] the evil which he had himself breathed [into the man], and

---

[1] *i.e.* if he is a god. Cf. iii. 20.   [2] Lit., "the necks of."
[3] Lit., "the terror of coercion should begin from the father with whom."
[4] Lit., "even," *et.*   [5] Lit., "to his grief."
[6] The MS. reads *rett-ulit*, emended *ret-* —" gave back," *i.e.* got rid of, by 1st ed. and Ursinius; and *rep-*, as above, by Gelenius and others.

vaunted himself with false pretence? But if you weigh the circumstances thoroughly, there was greater cruelty than kindness in his deliverance, for [Jupiter] did not preserve him to the joys of life [who was] miserable and wishing to perish after his children, but to learn his solitariness and the agonies of bereavement.

44.[1] In like manner we might go through the other narratives, and show that in these also, and in expositions of these, [something] far different from what the gods should be is said and declared about them, as in this very [story] which I shall next relate, one or two [only] being added to it, that disgust may not be produced by excess.[2] After certain gods were brought from among nations dwelling beyond the sea, you say, and after temples were built to them, after their altars were heaped with sacrifices, the plague-stricken people grew strong [and] recovered, and the pestilence fled before the soundness of health which arose. What gods, say, I beseech? Æsculapius, you say, the god of health, from Epidaurus, and [now] settled in the island in the middle of the Tiber. If we were disposed to be very scrupulous in dealing with your assertions, we might prove by your own authority that he was by no means divine who had been conceived and born from a woman's womb, who had by yearly stages reached that term of life at which, as is related in your books, a thunderbolt drove him at once from life and light. But we leave this question: let the son of Coronis be, as you wish, one of the immortals, and possessed of the everlasting blessedness[3] of heaven. From Epidaurus, however, what was brought except an enormous serpent? If we trust the annals, and ascribe to them well-ascertained truth, nothing else, as it has been recorded. What shall we say then? That Æsculapius, whom you extol, an excellent, a

---

[1] 41 in Orelli.

[2] In the MS. and both Roman edd. the section translated on p. 365 is inserted here. Ursinus, however (pp. 210-11), followed by Heraldus (312-13), enclosed it in brackets, and marked it with asterisks. In all other edd. it is either given as an appendix, or wholly rejected.

[3] Lit., "sublimity."

venerable god, the giver of health, the averter, preventer, destroyer of sickness, is contained within the form and outline of a serpent, crawling along the earth as worms are wont to do, which spring from mud; he rubs the ground with his chin and breast, dragging himself in sinuous coils; and that he may be able to go forward, he draws on the last part of his body by the efforts of the first.

45.[1] And as we read that he used food also, by which bodily existence is kept up, he has a large gullet, that he may gulp down the food sought for with gaping mouth; he has a belly to receive it, and[2] a place where he may digest the flesh which he has eaten and devoured, that blood may be given to his body, and his strength recruited;[3] he has also a draught, by which the filth is got rid of, freeing his body from a disagreeable burden. Whenever he changes his place, and prepares to pass from one region to another, he does not as a god fly secretly through the stars of heaven, and stand in a moment where something requires his presence, but, just as a dull animal [of earth], he seeks a conveyance on which he may be borne; he avoids the waves of the sea; and that he may be safe and sound, he goes on board ship along with men; and that god of the common safety trusts himself to weak planks and to sheets of wood joined together. We do not think that you can prove and show that that serpent was Æsculapius, unless you choose to bring forward this pretext, that you should say that the god changed himself into a snake, in order that he might be able[4] to deceive [men as to] himself, who he was, or to see what men were. But if you say this, the inconsistency of your own statements will show how weak and feeble such a defence is.[5] For if the god shunned being seen by men, he should not have chosen to be seen in the form of a serpent, since in any form whatever

---

[1] 42 in Orelli.
[2] So the edd., reading *et* for MS. *ut* (according to Crusius).
[3] Lit., "restoration be supplied to his strength."
[4] So Gelenius, merely adding *t* to the MS. *posse*. The passage is, however, very doubtful.
[5] Lit., "how weakly and feebly it is said."

he was not to be other than himself, but [always] himself. But if, on the other hand, he had been intent on allowing himself to be seen—he should not have refused to allow men's eyes to look on him[1]—why did he not show himself such as he knew that he was in his own divine power?[2] For this was preferable, and much better, and more befitting his august majesty, than to become a beast, and be changed into the likeness of a terrible animal, and afford room for objections, which cannot be decided,[3] as to whether he was a true god, or something different and far removed from the exalted nature of deity.

46.[4] But, says [my opponent], if he was not a god, why, after he left the ship, [and] crawled to the island in the Tiber, did he immediately become invisible, and cease to be seen as before? Can we indeed know whether there was anything in the way under cover of which he hid himself, or any opening [in the earth]? Do you declare, say yourselves, what that was, or to what race of beings it should be referred, if your service of certain personages is [in itself] certain.[5] Since the case is thus, and the discussion deals with your deity, and your religion also, it is your part to teach, and yours to show what that was, rather than to wish to hear our opinions and to await our decisions. For we, indeed, what else can we say than that which took place and was seen, which has been handed down in all the narratives, and has been observed by means of the eyes? This, however, undoubtedly we say [was] a *colubra*[6] of very powerful frame and immense length, or, if the name is despicable, [we say it was] a snake,[7] we call it a serpent,[8] or any other

---

[1] These words, *non debuit oculorum negare conspectui*, should, Orelli thinks, be omitted; and certainly their connection with the rest of the sentence is not very apparent.

[2] Lit., "he was, and such as he had learned that he was, contained in the power of his divinity."

[3] Lit., "to ambiguous contradictions."   [4] 43 in Orelli.

[5] Lit., "if your services of certain persons are certain," *i.e.* if these facts on which your worship is built are well ascertained.

[6] What species of snake this was, is not known; the Latin is therefore retained, as the sentence insists on the distinction.

[7] *Anguem.*   [8] *Serpentem.*

name which usage has afforded to us, or the development of language devised. For if it crawled as a serpent, not supporting itself and walking on feet,[1] but resting upon its belly and breast; if, being made of fleshly substance, it [lay] stretched out in [2] slippery length; if it had a head and tail, a back covered with scales, diversified by spots of various colours; if it had a mouth bristling with fangs, and ready to bite, what else can we say than that it was of earthly origin, although of immense and excessive size, although it exceeded in length of body and [greatness] of might that which was slain by Regulus by the assault of his army? But [if] we think otherwise, we subvert[3] and overthrow the truth. It is yours, then, to explain what that was, or what was its origin, its name, and nature. For how could it have been a god, seeing that it had those things which we have mentioned, which gods should not have if they intend to be gods, and to possess this exalted title? After it crawled to the island in the Tiber, forthwith it was nowhere to be seen, by which it is shown that it was a deity. Can we, then, know whether there was there anything in the way under cover of which it hid itself,[4] or some opening [in the earth], or some caverns and vaults, caused by huge masses being heaped up irregularly, into which it hurried, evading the gaze of the beholders? For what if it leaped across the river? what if it swam across it? what if it hid itself in the dense forests? It is weak reasoning from this,[5] to suppose that that serpent was a god because with all speed it withdrew itself from the eyes [of the beholders], since, by the same reasoning, it can be proved, on the other hand, that it was not a god.

47.[6] But if that snake was not a present deity, [says my

[1] Lit., "bearing himself on feet, nor unfolding below his own goings."
[2] Lit., "to a."
[3] So Hild. and Oehler, reading *labefac-t-amus* for the MS. *-i-*.
[4] This sentence alone is sufficient to prove that these chapters were never carefully revised by their author, as otherwise so glaring repetitions would certainly have been avoided.
[5] Here the MS. and both Roman edd. insert the last clause, "what ... forests."
[6] 44 in Orelli.

opponent], why, after its arrival, was the violence of the plague overcome, and health restored to the Roman people? We, too, on the other hand, bring forward [the question], If, according to the books of the fates and the responses of the seers, the god Æsculapius was ordered to be invited to the city, that he might cause it to be safe and sound from the contagion of the plague and of pestilential diseases, and came without spurning [the proposal] contemptuously, as you say, changed into the form of serpents,—why has the Roman state been so often afflicted with such disasters, so often at one time and another torn, harassed, and diminished by thousands, through the destruction of its citizens times without number? For since the god is said to have been summoned for this purpose, that he might drive away utterly all the causes by which pestilence was excited, it followed that the state should be safe, and should be always maintained free from pestilential blasts, and unharmed. But yet we see, as was said before, that it has over and over again had seasons made mournful by these diseases, and that the manly vigour of its people has been shattered and weakened by no slight losses. Where, then, was Æsculapius? where that [deliverer] promised by venerable oracles? Why, after temples were built, and shrines reared to him, did he allow a state deserving his favour to be any longer plague-stricken, when he had been summoned for this purpose, that he should cure the diseases which were raging, and not allow anything of the sort which might be dreaded to steal on [them afterwards]?

48.[1] But some one will perhaps say that the care of such a god has been denied[2] to later and following ages, because the ways in which men now live are impious and objectionable; that it brought help to our ancestors, on the contrary, because they were blameless and guiltless. Now this might perhaps have been listened to, and said with some reasonableness, either if in ancient times all were good without exception, or if later times produced[3] only wicked people,

---

[1] 45 in Orelli.   [2] Lit., "wanting."

[3] The MS., 1st ed., Hild., and Oehler read *gener-ent*, corrected in the rest, as above, *-arent*.

and no others.¹ But since this is the case that in great peoples, in nations, nay, in all cities even, men have been of mixed² natures, wishes, manners, and the good and bad have been able to exist at the same time in former ages, as well as in modern times, it is rather stupid to say that mortals of a later day have not obtained the aid of the deities on account of their wickedness. For if on account of the wicked of later generations the good men of modern times have not been protected, on account of the ancient evil-doers also the good of former times should in like manner not have gained the favour of the deities. But if on account of the good of ancient times the wicked of ancient times were preserved also, the following age, too, should have been protected, although it was faulty on account of the good of later times. So, then, either that snake gained the reputation of [being] a saviour while he had been of no service at all, through his being brought [to the city] when the violence of the disease³ was already weakened and impaired, or the hymns of the fates must be said to have been far from giving⁴ true indications, since the remedy given by them is found to have been useful, not to all in succession, but to one age only.

49.⁵ But the Great Mother, also, says [my opponent], being summoned from Phrygian Pessinus in precisely the same way by command of the seers, was a cause of safety and great joy to the people. For, on the one hand, a long-powerful enemy was thrust out from the position he had gained in⁶ Italy; and, on the other, its ancient glory was restored to the city by glorious and illustrious victories, and the boundaries of the empire were extended far and wide, and their rights as freemen were torn from races, states, peoples without number, and the yoke of slavery imposed on

¹ Lit., "all wicked and distinguished by no diversity."
² Lit., "the human race has been mixed in," etc.
³ So all edd., reading *vi morbi*, except Hild., who retains the MS. *vi urbi*, in which case the brackets should enclose " of the disease," instead of " to the city." The construction, however, seems to make it impossible to adhere to the MS.
⁴ Lit., " to have erred much from."
⁵ 46 in Orelli.   ⁶ Lit., " from the possession of Italy."

them, and many other things accomplished at home and abroad established the renown and dignity of the race with irresistible power. If the histories tell the truth, and do not insert what is false in their accounts of events, nothing else truly[1] is said to have been brought from Phrygia, sent by King Attalus, than a stone, not large, which could be carried in a man's hand without any pressure—of a dusky and black colour—not smooth, but having little corners standing out, and which to-day we all see put in that image instead of a face, rough and unhewn, giving to the figure a countenance by no means lifelike.[2]

50.[3] What shall we say then? Was Hannibal, that famous Carthaginian, an enemy strong and powerful, before whom the fortunes of Rome trembled in doubt and uncertainty, and its greatness shook—was he driven from Italy by a stone?[4] was he subdued by a stone? was he made fearful, and timid, and unlike himself by a stone? And with regard to Rome's again springing to the height of power and royal supremacy, was nothing done by wisdom, nothing by the strength of men; and, in returning to its former eminence, was no assistance given by so many and so great leaders by their military skill, or by their acquaintance with affairs? Did the stone give strength to some, feebleness to others? Did it hurl these down from success, raise the fortunes of others [which seemed] hopelessly overthrown? And what man will believe that a stone taken from the earth, having[5] no feeling, of sooty colour and dark[6] body, was the mother of the gods? or who, again, would listen to this (for this is the only alternative), that the power[7] of any deity dwelt in pieces of flint, within[8] its

[1] So all edd. to Orelli, adding -*cm* to the MS. *quid*.
[2] Lit., "a face too little expressed with imitation."
[3] 47 in Orelli.   [4] Lit., "did a stone drive," etc.
[5] Lit., "moved by."
[6] So the MS. and edd.; but, on account of the unnecessary repetition, Ursinus proposed to delete *atri*. Unger (*Anal. Propert.* p. 87) has suggested very happily *arti*—"of confined, *i.e.* small body."
[7] *Vim*, suggested by Orelli, and adopted by Hild. and Oehler.
[8] Lit., "subjected to."

mass,[1] and hidden in its veins? And how was the victory procured if there was no deity in the Pessinuntine stone? We may say, by the zeal and valour of the soldiers, by practice, time, wisdom, reason; we may [say], by fate also, and the alternating fickleness of fortune. But if the state of affairs was improved, and success and victory were regained, by the stone's assistance, where was the Phrygian mother at the time when the commonwealth was bowed down by the slaughter of so many and so great armies, and was in danger of utter ruin? Why did she not thrust herself before the threatening, the strong [enemy]? Why did she not crush and repel assaults[2] so terrible before these awful blows fell, by which all the blood was shed, and the life even failed, the vitals being almost exhausted? She had not been brought yet, [says my opponent], nor asked to show favour. Be it so;[3] but a kind helper never requires to be asked, always offering assistance of his own accord. She was not able, [you say], to expel the enemy and put him to flight, while still separated from Italy[4] by much sea and land. But to a deity, if really one,[5] nothing whatever is remote, to whom the earth is a point, and by whose nod all things have been established.

51.[6] But suppose that the deity was present in that very stone, as you demand should be believed: and what mortal is there, although he may be credulous and very ready to listen to any fictions you please, who would consider that she either was a goddess at that time, or should be now so spoken of and named, who at one time desires these things, at another requires those, abandons and despises her worshippers, leaves the humbler provinces, and allies herself with more

[1] So Hild. and Oehler, reading *moli* for the unintelligible MS. *more*.
[2] Lit., "so great assaults of war."
[3] So Oehler, adding -*o* to the MS. *est*. The word immediately preceding is in the MS. *pavorem*—" panic," which is of course utterly out of place, and is therefore corrected, as above, *f-* in all edd., except 1st, Ursinus, and Hild.
[4] So—*ab Italia*—Oehler has admirably emended the MS. *habitabilia*.
[5] Lit., "if he is."   [6] 48 in Orelli.

powerful and richer peoples, truly[1] loves warfare, and wishes to be in the midst of battles, slaughter, death, and blood? If it is characteristic of the gods (if only they are true gods, and those who it is fitting should be named according to the meaning of this word and the power of divinity) to do[2] nothing wickedly, nothing unjustly, to show[2] themselves equally gracious to all men without any partiality, [would] any man [believe] that she was of divine origin, or showed[3] kindness worthy of the gods, who, mixing herself up with the dissensions of men, destroyed the power of some, gave and showed favour to others, bereft some of their liberty, raised others to the height of power,—who, that one state might be pre-eminent, having been born to be the bane of the human race, subjugated the guiltless world?

[1] All edd., except Hild. and Oehler, begin a new sentence here, and change the construction, seemingly following the mistake of the 1st ed.

[2] "To do ... to show;" so the edd., dropping -nt from the MS. *facere-nt ... præbere-nt*.

[3] Lit., "showed." Ursinus and Heraldus supposed that some paragraphs are now wanting which were originally found here. It should be noticed that in the MS. the usual subscription is found denoting the end of a book. "The seventh book of Arnovius (*sic*) ends, the eighth (*i.e* Octavius of Minucius Felix) begins," so that the present arrangement is not due to the binder, nor clearly to the copyist who wrote these words. Nothing can be more certain than that we do not have these chapters as Arnobius intended to leave them; but there is not the slightest reason to suppose that he actually left them otherwise than they have come down to us. Remembering this, we may well suppose that we have only the first draught of them. If so, the difficulties vanish, for nothing would be more natural than that, when Arnobius was drawing near the close of his work, the ideas of the conclusion in which the discussion was to be fairly summed up should force themselves upon his attention, and that he should therefore turn aside at once to give them expression roughly, without seeking completeness and elaboration, and should then hastily resume his argument, of course with the intention of afterwards revising and rearranging the whole. We may infer that the rearrangement was never effected, as there are sufficient proofs that the revision was never accomplished, whatever may have been the reason.

APPENDIX.

[This section, which is found in the MS. after the first sentence of ch. 44, was retained in the text of both Roman editions, marked off, however, by asterisks in that of Ursinus, but was rejected by Gelenius and later editors as the useless addition of some copyist. Oehler alone has seen that it is not " a collection of words gathered carelessly and thoughtlessly " (Hildebrand), and maintained that we have in it the corrections of Arnobius himself. If the three paragraphs are read carefully, it will be observed that the first is a transposition and reconstruction of the first two sentences of ch. 39 ; the second a revision of the interrogations in ch. 41, but with the sentence which there precedes placed after them here, whilst the third is made up of the same sentences in a revised and enlarged form. Now this must be regarded as conclusive evidence against the hypothesis that these sentences were originally scribbled carelessly on the margin, and afterwards accidentally incorporated in the text. Cf. p. 347, n. 3.]

E do not deny that all these things which have been brought forward by you in opposition are contained in the writings of the annalists. For we have ourselves also, according to the measure and capacity of our powers, read these same things, and know that they have been alleged; but the whole discussion hinges upon this : whether these are gods who you assert are furious when displeased, and are soothed by games and sacrifices, or are something far different, and should be separated from the notion even of this, and from its power.

For who, in the first place, thinks or believes that those are gods who are lost in joyful pleasure at theatrical shows [1] and ballets, at horses running to no purpose; who set out from heaven to behold silly and insipid acting, and grieve that they are injured, and that the honours due to them are

[1] Lit., " motions."

withheld if the pantomimist halts for a little, or the player, being wearied, rests a little; who declare that the dancer has displeased them if some guilty [fellow] passes through the middle of the circus to suffer the penalty and punishment of his deeds? All which things, if they be sifted thoroughly and without any partiality, will be found to be alien not only to the gods, but to any man of refinement, even if he has not been trained to the utmost gravity and self-control.[1]

For, in the first place, who is there who would suppose that those had been, or believe that they are, gods, who have a nature which tends to[2] mischief and fury, and lay these[3] aside again, being moved by a cup of blood and fumigation with incense; who spend days of festivity, and [find] the liveliest pleasure in theatrical shows[4] and ballets; who set out from heaven to see geldings running in vain, and without any reason, and rejoice that some of them pass [the rest], that others are passed,[5] rush on, leaning forward, and, with their heads towards the ground, are overturned on their backs with the chariots [to which they are yoked], are dragged along crippled, and limp with broken legs; who declare that the dancer has displeased them if some wicked fellow passes through the middle of the circus to suffer the punishment and penalty of his deeds; who grieve that they are injured, and that the honours due to them are withheld if the pantomimist halts for a little, the player, being wearied, rests a little, that *puer matrimus* happens to fall, stumbling through some[6] unsteadiness? Now, if all these things are

---

[1] Lit., "to the heights (*apices*) of gravity and weight," *i.e.* of that constancy of mind which is not moved by trifles.

[2] Lit., "of hurting and raging."

[3] *i.e.* evil dispositions.

[4] Lit., "motions."

[5] So the MS., according to Crusius, inserting *transiri*, which is omitted by Hild., either because it is not in the MS., or because he neglected to notice that Orelli's text was deficient. If omitted, we should translate, "that some pass, leaning forward, and rush with their heads towards the ground."

[6] Lit., "of something."

considered thoroughly and without any partiality, they are found to be perfectly[1] alien not only to the [character of the] gods, but to that of any man of common sense, even although he has not been trained to zealous pursuit of truth by becoming acquainted with what is rational.

[1] Lit., "far and far."

INDICES.

I.—AUTHORS REFERRED TO BY ARNOBIUS.

	PAGE
Acherontic books,	131
Ælius,	176
Aethlius,	283
Antias,	222
Antiochus, *Histories*, ix.,	277
Apollodorus,	207
Aristotle,	171
Arrian,	147
Butas, *Causalia* of,	241
Cæsius,	178
Cicero, *de Nat. Deor.* i. 35,	162
iii.,	154, 195
iii. 21,	196
iii. 33 sqq.,	296
pro Rosc. Am. c. 32,	262
Tusc. i. 10,	72
Cincius,	177
Clemens Alexandrinus, Λόγος Προτρεπτ.,	154, 195
Clodius, Sextus, *de Diis*, lib. vi.,	241
Cornificius,	176
Crates,	175
Ctesias, *Hist.* i.,	43
Diagoras,	24, 211
Ennius,	162, 211
Ephorus,	175
Epicharmus,	207
Epictetus,	147
Euhemerus,	211
Euripides, *Hercules*,	344
Fabius,	279
Flaccus,	241
Granius,	171, 176, 279
Heraclitus,	124, 253
Hermippus,	43
Hesiod, *Theog.* 77-79,	176
Hieronymus,	208

	PAGE
Hippo,	211
Homer, *Il.* i. 423,	276
xiv. 312,	215
Od. 296 sqq.,	207
Leandrius,	278
Leo Pellacus,	211
Libri Acherontici,	131
,, Fatales,	360
Lucilius, the *Fornix* of,	68, 242
Lucretius, iv. 1160,	157
Manilius,	176
Mnaseas,	175
Myrtilus,	175, 206
Nicanor,	211
Nigidius,	172, 178, 179
Numa Pompilius, *Rituals* of,	143
Orpheus,	242, 250
Panyassis,	207
Patrocles,	208
Philostephanus, *Cypriaca* of,	297
Pindar, *Pyth.* iii. 102 sqq.,	206
Piso,	176
Plato, *Meno*, st. p. 81,	90
Phædo, 64,	97
,, 81,	83
,, 113,	80
Phædrus,	101
,, 230,	69
,, 246,	171
,, 274,	139
Politicus, 269-274,	79
Republic, 379,	133
,, 457,	54
Theætetus, 158,	70
,, 173,	78
Timæus, 21,	198
,, 22,	8, 11
,, 41 ; 91, 103, 119, 120	
Plautus,	343

370 INDEX OF SUBJECTS.

	PAGE		PAGE
Plutarch,	208	Timotheus,	227
Polemo,	208	Trebatius,	340
Pomponius, *Marsyas* of,	68		
Posidippus,	286, 297	Valerianus,	279
Ptolemæus, *History of Philopator*, lib. i.,	278	Valerius,	230
		Varro,	176, 178, 179, 186, 283, 307
		de populo Romano, i.,	232
Sammonicus,	279	*de Admirandis*,	274
Sophocles, *Trachiniæ*,	217, 344	*Polyandria*,	278
Sosibius,	208	*Saturæ Menippeæ*,	299
		Virgil, *Æn.* vi. 472,	91
Tarentine poet,	244		
Theodorus,	211	Zeno,	276

II.—INDEX OF SUBJECTS.

ABDERA, proverbial for stupidity, 236.
Abusive language, punished by law, 216.
Acantho, mother of the fourth Sun, 196.
Acdestis, birth of, 227; a hermaphrodite, 227; self-mutilated by the craft of Bacchus, 228; love of Attis, 229; fatal consequences of his fury, 230.
Achaia, Christianity attested by miracles in, 76.
Acheron, 80, 253.
Achilles, 209.
Acorns and chestnuts, the food of primitive men, 87, 136.
Acrisius, buried in temple of Minerva at Larissa, 277.
Actæon, the horned hunter, 174.
Actors, freed from taxes, 217.
Admetus, served by Apollo, 207.
Adonis, loved by Proserpine, 209.
Adulterers, punished with death, 205.
Æacus, son of Jupiter, first builder of temples, 274; loved by the Nereid, 209.
Ælius, held that the Novensiles were the Muses, 176, 177.
Æneas, son-in-law of Latinus, 141; son of Venus, 209; deified, 177.
Æsculapius, son of Coronis, 27; killed by lightning, 32, 206; deified because he discovered use of herbs, 29, 32, 177; giver of health, 135, 167; distinguished by his staff, 301; golden beard torn from a statue of, 296; three gods named,
197; vintage festival of, 342; brought to Rome in form of a serpent, 356.
Æther, father of Jupiter, 195; shown not to be a god, 174.
Æthusa, loved by Apollo, 208.
Ætna, torches of Ceres lit at, 248, 259.
Agdus, Mount, 227.
Agesarchus, 278.
Aii Locutii, 21.
Alba, founded by Ascanius, 141; flourished for 400 years, 335; incense unknown in, 335.
Alban Hill, white bulls sacrificed on, 138.
Alcibiades, the Hermæ modelled after, 286.
Alcmena, seduced by Jupiter, 140, 245; mother of the Theban Hercules, 203.
Alcyone, 208.
Alemanni, said to have been overcome because Christians were to be found amongst them, 14.
Alimontian mysteries, 252.
Allegorical explanation of myths, 150, 179; rejected by Arnobius, 180.
Alope, loved by Neptune, 208.
Ambiguity of words, Jupiter ensnared by, 222.
Amphitheatres places of bloodshed and wickedness, 72.
Amphitrite, loved by Neptune, 208.
Amymone, loved by Neptune, 208.
Anchises, loved by Venus, 27, 209.
Angels' names, used as incantations, 34.

INDEX OF SUBJECTS. 371

Animals, man closely allied to the other, 82, 83, 84, 92; man not morally superior to the other, 315; deified and worshipped, 21.
Ant, Jupiter's conversion into an, 267.
Antiochus of Cyzicum, sacrilege of, 295.
Antiquity, the most fertile source of errors, 47.
Ancient customs, not adhered to by heathens as well as by Christians, 137.
Anubis, dog-faced, 301.
Apis, born in the Peloponnese, 28; called Serapis by the Egyptians, 28; those punished who revealed the abode of, 278.
Apollo, son of Jupiter and Latona, 140, 204, 208; son of Minerva and Vulcan, 196, 198; accompanied his mother in her wanderings, 27; found refuge on a floating island, 27; called Clarian, Delian, Didymean, Philesian, Pythian, 20; bow-bearing, 27, 204; Sminthian, 173; deceived those who enriched his temples, 206; served Admetus and Laomedon, 207; pirates plundered and burned temples of, 298; identified with Bacchus and the sun, 173; Rituals of Numa did not contain name of, 143; four gods named, 197; human heads offered to Dis and Saturn by advice of, 138; and Neptune, the Penates, 181; Hyperoche and Laodice buried in temple of Delian, 277; Telmessus buried under the altar of, 278; god of music, 330; mistresses of, 208; represented with lyre and plectrum, 285.
Apollonius, the Magian, 43.
Aquilius, 32.
Arabia, Christianity tested by miracles in, 76.
Arabians, worshipped an unshaped stone, 283.
Arcadia, Mars born in, 207.
Archesilas, affirms that man knows nothing, 72.
Archytas, assigns all things to numbers, 72.
Aristotle, adds a fifth element to the primary causes, 72; affirmed that Minerva was the moon, 171.
Argos, destruction by fire of temple of Juno at, 298.

Argus, slain by Mercury, 196, 301.
Armenians, believed that one god was cause of all divine manifestations, 195.
Armenian, Zoroaster an, 43.
Arnobius, date of, 13, 141; zeal as a heathen, 31.
Arsinoe, loved by Apollo, 208.
Asia, afflicted with mice and locusts because of the Christians, 14; Christianity attested by miracles in, 76.
Asses, sacrificed to Mars by the Scythians, 207.
Assyrians, war of Bactrians with, 8.
Atellane farces, 344.
Athenians, made their Hermæ like Alcibiades, 286.
Athens, fall of temple of Bacchus at, 298; Cecrops buried in temple of Minerva at, 277.
Atlantis, the fabled island, 8.
Atlas, prop of the skies, 139; grandfather of Mercury, 165.
Attalus, sent from Phrygia to Rome a stone as the Great Mother, 362.
Attagi, Phrygian name of goats, 229.
Attica, visited by Ceres, 263.
Attis, worshipped in the temples of Cybele, 33; son of Nana, 229; loved by Cybele, 211, 229; self-mutilation and death of, 230; rites established in honour of, 231; explained as the sun, 265.
Aulus, Capitol named from, 279.
Aurora's love of Tithonus, 209.
Aventine, Jupiter drawn down to the, 223.

BACCHANALIA, two kinds of, 242.
Bacchus, son of Semele, 173, 204; dashed by lightning from his mother's womb, 27; born again from his father's thigh, 204; giver of a good vintage, 135; represented as effeminate, 284; and as bearing a drinking-cup, 301; *phalli* displayed at rites of, 252; identified with the sun, 173; goats sacrificed to, 328; called Evius, 253; Nysius, 252; Zagreus, 242; Bromius, 204; torn in pieces by Titans, 32, 242; destruction of temple at Athens of, 298.
Bacis, the soothsayer, 51.
Bactrian, Zoroaster a, 43.
Bactrians, war of Assyrians with, 8.
Bæbulus, the Magian, 43.

INDEX OF SUBJECTS.

Banquets of the gods, 342.
Bark, used in ancient times for clothing, 136.
Baubo, entertainer of Ceres at Eleusis, 248.
Beetles, temples erected to, 21.
Bellonæ, 21, 168.
Berecyntian goddess, 236.
Binding of Mars and Venus, explained allegorically, 265.
Birthdays of the gods, 343.
Bocchores, 27.
Bona Dea, story of, 241; original name, 27.
Branch, a, worshipped by the Thespians, 283.
Brides, hair of, arranged with *hasta cœlibaris*, 138.
Brimo, Ceres named, 243.
Bromius, name of Bacchus, 204.
Brunda, Simon Magus threw himself from house-top at, 77.
Burnus, god of lust, 191.

Cœlibaris hasta, used in arranging hair of brides, 138.
Cæselii, 54.
Cæsius' enumeration of the Penates, 178.
Calamities, common to all ages, not caused by Christians, 6.
Calliope's son, Orpheus, 250.
Canacheni, 299.
Canary Islands, 276.
Cannæ, proscription of Sulla compared to the battle of, 262.
Capitol, Tolus Vulcentanus buried in the, 278; named from Olus, 279; destroyed by fire, 298; struck by lightning, 351.
Capitoline Jupiter burned along with the temple, 298.
Capitoline Hill, taken by Titus Tatius, 186.
Caprotina, name of Juno, 171.
Carians, the, sacrificed dogs to Mars, 207.
Carneades, affirmed man's ignorance of all things, 72.
Castor and Pollux, called Tyndarian brothers, 139; Dioscori, 204; sons of Jupiter and Leda, 140, 204; sons of Tyndareus, 27; buried in Lacedæmonia, 208; three sets of gods named, 197.
Castor, famed for his skill in managing horses, 27.
Castus, a fasting, 240.
Catamitus, carried off to be a cup-bearer, 209; object of Jupiter's lust, 245.
Cato, 161.
Cats, temples built to, 21.
Caudine Forks, Romans sent under the yoke at, 187.
Cecrops, buried in the temple of Minerva at Athens, 277.
Celeus, daughters of, buried in temple at Eleusis, 277.
Cerberus, 253.
Ceres, born in Sicily, 27; deified because she discovered use of bread, 29; gives good crops, 135; lusted after Jasion, 209; mother of Jupiter, according to Phrygians, 242; violated by him, 243; wanderings of, 248; her sacred rites called *Græca*, 143; identified with Diana and Luna, 173; said by Cæsius to be one of the Penates, 178; represented with protruding breasts, 157, 301; her temple at Eleusis, 277; falling of rain upon the earth denoted by union of Jupiter and, 256, 266; bread denoted by, 268; feast in honour of, 343.
Cestus, Juno's, 301.
Chæronea, Plutarch of, 208.
Chaldeans, mysterious learning of, 8; believed that one God appeared in all divine manifestations, 195.
Childbirth, Juno set over, 166.
Charms, used to appease unknown powers, 79.
Christ, recalled men from their errors, 29; revealed God's nature, 29; and man's condition and prospects, 30; was sent as a Saviour, 44, 55; His authority established by His mighty works, 36, 37, 39, 40, 74; and by His transmitting this power to His followers, 41, 42; said to have been a sorcerer, 34; but in Him there was nothing magical, nothing delusive, 44; helped all who came to Him, 40; access to the light only by, 135; invites all alike, 133; did harm to no one, but declared even to His enemies the way of salvation, 57; divine, 33, 44; the universe thrown into confusion at crucifixion of, 44; did not die, but His human form, 51; became incarnate, that He might mix with men, 50; was crucified for reasons beyond human comprehension, 52;

INDEX OF SUBJECTS.

the reason for the time of His appearance with God, 144; but an explanation may be found, 144, 145; the divine compassion extended to those who died before, 132; demons put to flight by the name of, 37; the secret thoughts of men known to, 37.
Christians, worship the supreme God, 20; worship Christ as giver of eternal life, 31, 101; prefer Christ's friendship to all that is in the world, 67; laughed at for their faith, 71; had more reason to follow Christ than the heathen to trust the philosophers, 74; called atheists, 169; said to be stupid and senseless, 21, 78, 160; exiled, tortured, given to the beasts, burned, 19, 218; have learned not to requite evil with evil, 9; no hope of aid as to this life held out to, 146; death brings release to, 147; accused of being the cause of all calamities, 3, 6; built no temples, and offered no sacrifices, 271, 272.
Christianity, novelty of, no real objection, 136, 138, 140, 142; the way of salvation, 135.
Chrysippus, object of Jupiter's lust, 209.
Chrysippus, asserted that the world would be destroyed by fire, 72.
Chrysis, Juno's priestess, burned at Argos, 298.
Cicero, the most eloquent of the Romans, 154.
Cincian law against gifts to advocates, 137.
Cincius, regards the Novensiles as the gods of conquered states, deities brought from abroad, 177.
Cinxia, a name of Juno, 171; presides over the loosening of the zone, 168; the Thespians worship a branch as, 283.
Cinyras, king of Cyprus, 207; king of Paphos, 278; deified Venus, a courtezan, 207; was buried in temple of Venus, 278; founder of the mysteries of Cyprian Venus, 242.
Circe, mother of the fifth Sun, 196.
Circus, story of re-celebration of the games of the, 35.
Cleochus (or Clearchus), buried in the Didymæon at Miletus, 278.
Clitor, daughter of, seduced by Jupiter, 209.

Cnidian Venus, copied from a courtezan, 286.
Cocytus, river in Hades, 80.
Cœlus, father of Saturn and Ops by Hecate, 141, 171; of the second Jupiter, 195; of the first Mercury, 196; of the Muses, 175; of Janus by Hecate, 170; Venus produced from the genitals of, 206.
Complices and *Consentes*, said to be the Penates, 178.
Concord, temples built to, 184, 185.
Conserentes dii, parents of Servius Tullius, 241.
Consus, god of devices, 166.
Corniculum, Ocrisia brought to Rome from, 241.
Cornificius, maintains that Novensiles preside over renovation, 177.
Coronis, mother of Æsculapius, 27.
Corybantes, rites of the, 242.
Coryphasia, epithet of the fourth Minerva, 197, 199.
Crates, affirms that there are eight Muses, 175.
Crete, Jupiter born and buried in, 196, 208.
Cronius, 74.
Cupids, three sets of winged, 197.
Curetes, drowned the cries of Jupiter, 179; saved him from death, 206.
Cyceon, the draught offered to Ceres by Baubo, 249.
Cyllenian, bearer of the *caduceus*, 172.
Cyprian Venus, statue of, loved by Pygmalion, 297.
Cyrus, 43.
Cytherean, the, *i.e.* Venus, 286.
Cyzicum, sacrilege of Antiochus of, 295.

DACTYLI Idæi identified with the Digiti Samothracii, 179.
Dairas, buried in the enclosure at Eleusis, 277.
Damigero, a Magian, 43.
Danae, loved by Jupiter, 245.
Dancer stops, expiation required if the, 213.
Daphne, loved by Apollo, 208.
Dardanus, the Magian, 43; Dardanus first celebrated rites of the Phrygian Mother, 143.
Dead, prayers for the, 218.
Decemvirs, decrees of the, 216.
Deluge, Varro's computation of the time of the, 232; human race destroyed by, 8.

Democritus' atomic theory, 72.
Desires, Venus the mother of the, 168.
Deucalion and Pyrrha, re-peopled the earth, 227.
Diagoras of Melos, denies that there are gods, 25, 211.
Dialis, flamen, mitred, 42, 216.
Diana, daughter of Jupiter and Latona, 139, 204; daughter of the first Minerva, 198; bow-bearing, found refuge on floating islands, 27; mighty in hunting, 164, 204; wars of the virgin, 211; represented with thighs half covered, 301; an unhewn log worshipped by the Icarians for, 283; fall of temple at Ephesus of, 298; Leucophryne buried in temple of, 278; shrine in Delian Apollo's temple of, 277; theologians mention three goddesses named, 197; identified with Ceres and Luna, 173.
Didymæon, Cleochus buried in the Milesian, 278.
Diespiter, son of Saturn and Ops, 202; lusted after his mother Ceres, 243; names of some who bore children to, 140.
Digiti Samothracii, said to be the Lares, 179, 181.
Dindymene, Pessinuntic, i.e. Cybele worshipped at Pessinus, 217.
Diomede, plains of, i.e. Cannæ, 187.
Dione, bore Venus to Jupiter, 27, 140.
Dionysius, robbed Jupiter and Æsculapius of their beards, 296.
Dionysus (see Bacchus), five gods named, 197.
Dioscori, sons of Leda and Jupiter, 202.
Dis, identified with Summanus, 275; human heads offered to, 138; wounded by Hercules, 208; allegorical explanation of rape of Proserpine by, 266, 276; gate of, i.e. Hades, 253.
Discordiæ, 168.
Dodona, Jupiter of, 26, 298; fall of Jupiter's temple at, 298.
Dogs, employed to guard the capitols, 295.
Dysaules, a goatherd in Attica, 248.

EARTH, the, identified with the Great Mother, Ceres, and Vesta, 172; a pregnant sow sacrificed to, 329; birthday of, 343.

Egeria, Numa advised by, 223.
Egypt, Christianity attested by mighty works in, 76; Apis called Serapis in, 27; letters invented by the fifth Mercury in, 196.
Egyptians, dumb animals worshipped by, 160; Christ said to have stolen the secrets of His power and teaching from the, 34; punished those who revealed the dwelling-place of Apis, 278; called the second Minerva Neith, 198; were afraid to utter the fourth Mercury's name, 196; believed that one deity was manifested under the various divine manifestations, 195.
Electra, seduced by Jupiter, 245.
Elements, number of the primary, 124; mistake as to Aristotle's conception of the elements, 72.
Eleusinia, origin of the, 249, 250; signs used in the, 251.
Eleusis, Ceres' visit to, 248; Dairas and Immarnachus buried in the enclosure of, 277; temple of Ceres at, 277.
Eleutherius, temple at Athens of Liber, 298.
Endymion, loved by Luna, 209.
Ennius, translated works of Euhemerus, 211.
Ephesus, fall of Diana's temple at, 298.
Epicadi, 54.
Epicurus, atomic theory of, 72; teaches that the soul is mortal, 97.
Epidaurus, Æsculapius brought from, 355; he of, i.e. Æsculapius, 164.
Epirus, Christianity attested by mighty works in, 76.
Equity, deified, 185.
Erechthidæ, i.e. Athenians, 251.
Ericthonius, buried in shrine of Minerva, 277.
Ethiopian sun, Isis tanned by, 27.
Ethiopians, visited by the gods, 276.
Etruria, mother of superstition, 335; arts of, i.e. charms and sacred rites, 241.
Etruscans, the, identified Penates, and Consentes, and Complices, 179.
Eubuleus, a swineherd in Attica, 248.
Eumolpidæ, origin of, 248.
Eumolpus, keeper of sheep in Attica, 248.
Europa, seduced by Jupiter, 245; represented on the stage, 343.

INDEX OF SUBJECTS. 375

Evius, performance of his shameful promise by, 253.
FABIUS, a favourite of Jupiter, 209.
Fate, all things happen according to, 317.
Fatua Fauna, *i.e.* Bona Dea, wife of Faunus, 27, 241; unlawful to bring in myrtle twigs to the rites of, 241; account of her death and rites, 241.
Fatuæ, 21.
Fauni, 21.
Faunus, son of Picus, and father of Latinus, 71; ensnared and bound by Numa's craft, 223; made the Aventine his haunt, 223.
Fawn's skin, worn by the initiated, 263.
Februtis, a name of Juno, 171.
Fescennine verses, sung at marriages, 202.
Fetiales, the forms of the, neglected, 137.
Fillets, worn by suppliants, 246.
Fire, the origin of all things, 72.
Flint, people of Pessinus worship a, 283.
Flora, watches over the blossoming of plants, 166; a harlot, 166; shameful actions done openly at games of, 344.
Floralia, the, 343.
Fluonia (or Fluvionia), a name of Juna, 171.
Fons, son of Janus, 170.
Fortune, a deity, 135; one of the Penates, according to Cæsius, 178, 181; represented with a horn filled with fruit, 301.
Fortuna Virginalis, maidens' garments offered to, 138.
Frugifer, a god with lion's face called, 282.
Furies, the, 168, 253.
Forks, Caudine, overthrow of Romans at, 187.

GABINIUS, the consul, 142.
Gætuli, afflicted with droughts because of the Christians, 14.
Gain, gods of, 191.
Galatians, Christianity attested by mighty works among the, 76.
Gallus, mutilation of a daughter of, 230, 237.
Galli, priests of the Great Mother, 33; beat their breasts, wailing for Attis, 240, 241.

Ganymede, carried off to satisfy Jupiter's lust, 267; represented on the stage in ballets, 343.
Garamantes, the tawny, 276.
Gaul, innumerable Christians in, 14.
Geese, the guardians of the Capitol, 295.
Genii of husbands, invoked at marriages, 138.
Genii of states, 21.
Genius Jovialis, said to be one of the Penates, 178, 181.
Germans, irruptions of the, regarded as special calamities caused by the Christians, 8.
Ghosts, the Lares said to be, 180.
Gnidus, statue of Venus at, loved by a young man, 297.
Goats, sacrificed to Bacchus and Mercury, 328; torn in pieces by bacchanals, 242.
God, the Lord of all things, the highest existence, 19, 20, 24, 25, 63, 150; before all things, 22, 24, 142; without form, 24, 158, 346; devoid of sex, 155, 346; uncreated, immortal, everlasting, 24, 102, 142; all agree that there is one supreme, 102; cannot be known by men, 345; all-powerful, 101; the creator of all things, 24, 150; the preserver of all things, 113; and the only one who can preserve souls, 131; nothing hurtful or pernicious proceeds from, 123; all, without exception, have experienced the compassion of, 132; all men know, by nature, 64; and no one doubts the existence of, 25, 130; although some deny it, 125; is not Jupiter, 27.
Gods, the, corruptible by nature, according to Plato, 103; born at some time, 24, 139, 346; of both sexes, 154, 346; have mistresses, brides, wives, 202; are hushed to sleep and awakened by their worshippers' hymns, 214, 342; are parched with thirst, 339; eat and drink, delighting in splendid banquets, 214, 334; are exposed to attacks of disease, etc., 164; cannot defend themselves, 16, 296, 302; make war upon each other, and are wounded, 215; take pleasure in shameful sights, 343, 344; and still more shameful acts, 209, 214; accuse the cruel fates, 215; are ignorant of the future, 163;

are artificers like mortals, 163; even act the part of slaves, 207, 211; are washed to make them clean, 342; were supposed to be angry at the Christians, 3, 18, 347; but had greater reason to be enraged at their worshippers, 21, 157, 161, 212, 219; were immortal, not in themselves, but through God's gift, 103; each set over some one thing, 135, 166; the true, do not wish for sacrifices, 307, 348; and are not soothed by them, 316; are free from passions, 272, 311; were supposed to dwell in their images, 294; although these were made of vile materials, 288; lay aside their anger when they receive sacrifices, 314, 318; accuse and make defences, 165; sinister, 187, 330; lesser, 64; Syrian, sprung from eggs, 28; of conquered states introduced by Romans into their families, 177; suppliants to some veiled, to others uncovered the head, 181.

Græca, rites of Ceres, 143.

Gratina, loved by Praxiteles, and taken as model of Cnidian Venus, 286.

Grits mixed with salt, or sacrificial meal offered to the gods, 167, 225.

Grundules Lares, 21.

Guardian deities, favour of, withheld, 167.

Guilt, contracted if the dancer halted or musician was silent, 213.

HADES, punishment in, 96; existence of, denied, 327.

Hammon, represented with a ram's horns, 284.

Hannibal's invasion of Italy, Phrygian mother's worship introduced at the time of, 143, 361; driven out of Italy by the goddess, 362.

Happiness, deified and worshipped, 184, 185.

Hasta cælibaris, hair of brides arranged with, 138.

Hearths, presided over by the god Lateranus, 189.

Heathen, the, hatred of the Christians by, 26, 147, 218; reviled Christians as illiterate, 48; dishonoured their own gods, 153, 157, 255; dishonoured their gods in sacrificing to them, 324, 340.

Hecate, mother of Saturn and Ops, 141; mother of Janus, 170.

Helenus, the soothsayer, 51.

Hellespontian Priapus, 157.

Henna, grove of, whence Proserpine was carried off, 259.

Heraclitus, referred the origin of all things to fire, 72.

Hercules, burned alive after punishment, 27, 32; son of Jupiter and Alcmena, 140, 209; this the Theban defended by his club and hide, 204; worshipped as divine, 144, 153; a mortal, deified, 177; wounded by Hippocoon's children, 208; entangled in robe of Nessus, 217; violated the fifty daughters of Thestius, 209; wounded Dis and Juno, 208; put an end to human sacrifices in Italy, 138; was a slave at Sardis, 207; burned on Mount Œta after an attack of epilepsy, 208; the Theban, burned on Mount Œta, 27; the Phœnician, buried in Spain, 27; six gods named, 197; deified because he subdued robbers, wild beasts, and serpents, 29.

Hermæ at Athens like Alcibiades, 286.

Heroes, of immense and huge bodies, 145.

Heroic ages, incense unknown in the, 335.

Hesperides, golden apples of the, 242.

Hippo of Melos, 211.

Hippocoon's children, Hercules wounded by, 208.

Hippothoe, seduced by Neptune, 208.

Hirtius and Pansa, deluge not quite two thousand years before the consulship of, 232.

Honour, deified and worshipped, 184, 185.

Hosthanes, grandfather of the Armenian Zoroaster, 43.

Human sacrifices, offered to Dis and Saturn, 138.

Hyacinthus, 209.

Hylas, 209.

Hyperboreans, 278.

Hyperiona, mother by Jupiter of the second Sun, 196, 204.

Hyperoche, buried in the shrine of Diana, 277.

Hypsipyle, loved by Apollo, 208.

IA, bride of Attis, 230; her blood turned into violets, 230.

INDEX OF SUBJECTS. 377

Iachus nursed (or loved) by Ceres, 157.
Ialysus, son of the fourth Sun, 196.
Icarians, the, worship an unhewn log, 283.
Idaei Dactyli, Greek name of Digiti Samothracii, 179.
Ignorance the lot of man, 72.
Ilium, girt with walls by Apollo and Neptune, 178.
Immarnachus, buried in the enclosure at Eleusis, 277.
Incense, unknown in the heroic age, 335; not used by the Etruscans in their rites, 335; nor at Alba, 335; nor by Romulus and Numa, 335; termed Panchæan gum, 336.
India, Christianity attested by mighty works in, 76; Liber sought to make himself master of, 211.
Indians, the, believed that one god showed himself in all the manifestations of the divine, 195.
Indigetes, deified mortals, 54.
Indigetes, living in the Numicius, 27.
Inferium vinum, phrase used in libations, 340.
Inuus, guardian of flocks and herds, 166.
Iphigenia, stags spoken of instead of, 258.
Isis, Ethiopian, 27; Egyptian, 211; lamenting her lost child and husband torn in pieces, 27; worship of, introduced after consulship of Piso and Gabinius, 142; statue of, burned, 298.
Itali, Saturn concealed in the territories of the, 206.
Images, Christ raised men's thoughts from senseless, 31; formed of clay, 31, 150, 292; bones, stones, brass, silver, gold, wood, and other materials, 288; made like infamous men and women, 286, 287; the gods said to be worshipped through, 280; fanciful shape of some, 282; disregarded by birds and beasts, 291; the gods caused to dwell in, 292; must be defended by men, notwithstanding the indwelling divinity, 295; despoiled by Antiochus and Dionysius, 296; used lewdly, 297; and even utterly consumed by fire, 298; set up to strike evil-doers with terror, 300.

Italy, visit of Hercules to, 138.
JANICULUM, founded by Janus, 27, 170.
Janus, 153; son of Cœlus and Hecate, 170; husband of Juturna and father of Fons, 170; first king in Italy, 170; represented as double-faced, and carrying a spiked key, 301; said to be the world, the year, the sun, 170; supposed to procure a hearing for suppliants, 170; and therefore mentioned first in all prayers, 170.
Jasion, loved by Ceres, 209.
Jovialis, genius, one of the Penates, 178, 181.
Julian, a magian, 43.
Juno, 135, 153, 204, 140; daughter of Saturn and Ops, 139; queen of the gods, 204; wounded by Hercules, 208; named Lucina, and aiding women in childbirth, 157, 166; said to be the air, 171; destruction of the temple, and priestess of, 298; and in the Capitol of the statue of, 298; named Caprotina, Cinxia, Februtis, Fluonia, 171; Ossipagina, Pomona, Populonia, 171; the cestus of, 301; at Cinxia, a branch worshipped for, 283; Samians worship a plank instead of, 283; one of the Penates, 179.
Jupiter, the greatest and best, 26; is not God, 27; had father and mother, 26; the Saturnian king, 204; son of Æther, 195; son of Cœlus, 195; son of Saturn, 196; of Saturn and Ops, 139, 141, 171, 202; born in Crete, 196; concealed in Crete, 171; buried in Crete, 196, 208; his cries concealed, 179; and his life saved by the Curetes, 206; overthrew his father, 206; the acts of, 211; made a meal unwittingly on Lycaon's son, 206; married his sister, 206; attempted to violate the mother of the gods, 227; lusted after Alcmena, Danae, Electra, Europa, and matrons and maidens without number, 245, 140; even after the boys Catamitus, 209, 245, and Fabius, 209; ravished his daughter Proserpine, 244; for lustful purposes became an ant, a golden shower, a satyr, 267; a swan, 205, 27; and a bull, 205,

243; spoken of as recounting his amours to his wife, 215; said to be the sun, 171; and by others to be the ether, 171; three gods named, 195; father of Apollo, Diana, Castor and Pollux, Hercules, Liber, Mercury, 139, 204; of the Muses, 139, 175; of the Sun, 196; of Hercules, 209, 217; Diespiter, 140, 202; fall at Dodona of the temple of, 298; destruction of the statue of Capitoline, 298, 351; termed Capitoline, 42, 298; the Thunderer, 298; the Olympian, 286; the Supreme, 139; the Stygian, *i.e.* Pluto, 139; Verveceus, 244; of Dodona, 19, 298; bulls sacrificed to, 329; represented with a thunderbolt in his right hand, 301; and as driving in a winged chariot, 171; gave power to the Novensiles to wield his thunder, 177; Pales the steward of, 178; the counsellors of, 178, 179; one of the Penates, 179; represented as an adulterer, 217; and as easily overreached, 222, 224; forced to leave heaven by Numa, 223; statues of, dishonoured, 296; descent of rain signified by the embraces of Ceres, 256, 266; the feast of, 342; ludi circenses celebrated in honour of, 350.

Juturna, wife of Janus, 170.

KINGS, speaking against, considered treason, 216.
Kronos, explained as chronos, *i.e.* time, 170; son of Cœlus and progenitor of the *dii magni*, 171.
Knees of images touched by suppliants, 291.

LACEDÆMON, Castor and Pollux buried in, 208.
Laodamia, seduced by Jupiter, 245.
Laodice, buried in the shrine of Diana, 277.
Laomedon, served by Neptune, 207.
Lares, commonly said to be gods of streets and ways, from the supposed etymology, 179; guardians of houses, 179; identified sometimes with the Curetes, sometimes with the Digiti Samothracii, 179; identified with the Manes, 180; said to be gods of the air, and also to be ghosts, 180.

Lares Grundules, 21.
Larissa, Acrisius buried in Minerva's temple at, 277.
Lateranus, the genius of hearths, 189, 193.
Latinus, grandson of Picus, and son of Faunus, 141; father-in-law of Æneas, 141.
Latium, Saturn concealed in, 206.
Latona, seduced by Jupiter, 245; mother of Apollo and Diana, 27, 139, 164, 204; wanderings of, 27.
Laverna, goddess of thieves, 168.
Lauræ, Lares said to be derived from, 179.
Lectisternium of Ceres, 343.
Leda, seduced by Jupiter, 140, 245; mother of the Dioscori, 204; represented on the stage, 343.
Left and right, merely relative terms, 187, 188; lucky, 188.
Lemnos, Vulcan wrought as a smith at, 196, 206.
Leucophryne, buried in Diana's sanctuary, 278.
Libations, in honour of the gods, 338, 339; formula used in, 340.
Libels, severely punished, 216.
Libentina, goddess of lust, 191.
Libentini (?), 21.
Liber, a deified mortal, 143, 177; deified because he taught men to use wine, 29; son of Jupiter and Semele, 139, 204, 252; Indian campaign of, 211; torn in pieces by the Titans, 32, 242; called Eleutherius, 298; Nysius, 252; visit to Tartarus of, 252; filthy practices of, 253; allegorical explanation of the tearing in pieces of, 266.
Libera, *i.e.* Proserpine, daughter of Jupiter and Ceres, 244.
Lima, goddess of thresholds, 191.
Limentinus, god of thresholds, 191, 193; gives omens in entrails of the victims, 194.
Limi, preside over obliquities, 192.
Lion, images with face of, 282.
Locusts, destruction of crops by, said to be caused by Christians, 7, 14.
Locutii, Aii, 21.
Log, worshipped by the Icarians for Diana, 283.
Lucina, aiding women in childbirth, 164.
Lullabies, sung to the gods, 342.
Luna, lusted after Endymion, 209; identified with Diana and Ceres,

173; cannot be a deity if a part of the world, 174.
Luperca, a goddess named, because the she-wolf did not rend Romulus and Remus, 186.
Lust, unnatural, attributed to the gods, 209.
Lycaon, Jupiter ate part of the son of, 206.
Lydia, 229.
Lynceus, piercing gaze of, 205.

MACARUS, father of Megalcon, 206.
Macedonia, Christianity attested by mighty works in, 76; starting-point of Alexander the Great, 9.
Magi, in heathen ceremonials, relics of the arts of the, 332; arts of the, had no good purpose, 35; demons won over by the charms of the, 131; said to raise by their incantations other gods than those invoked, 194; enumeration of famous, 43; used herbs and muttered spells in their incantations, 44.
Magian, used as equivalent to sorcerer, 34.
Magistrate, insults to a, severely punished, 216.
Magnesia, Diana's sanctuary at, 278.
Magus, Simon, overthrown by Peter, 77.
Maia, the beautiful, 27; mother of the third Mercury, 27, 140, 196, 204, 284.
Man, ignorant of his own nature, 69; such as the lower creatures, 82; possessed of reason, 83; not immortal, 95; wretchedness of the life of, 107, 108, 109, 317; a microcosm, 91; not necessary in the universe, 105; utmost extent of life of, 141; depraved in coming into life, 82.
Manes, the Lares said to be the, 180; inhabitants of infernal regions, 327.
Mania, mother of the Lares, 180.
Manium, dii, 327.
Marcius, a soothsayer, 51.
Marcus Cicero, 161.
Marpesian rock, proverbial comparison, 90.
Marpessa, loved by Apollo, 208.
Mars, born in Arcadia (?), 207; born in Thrace, 207; said to be Spartanus, 207; set over war, 168;
held prisoner for thirteen months, 207; loved by Ceres, 209; ensnared by Vulcan, 207; wounded by men, 207; a spear worshipped by the Romans as, 283; dogs and asses sacrificed to, 207; otherwise Mavors, 285; fighting signified by, 268; allegorical explanation of the binding of Venus and, 265, 266; the Romans spoken of as the race of, 217.
Marriage, forms observed in, 137, 138; three modes of contracting, 202; advocacy of promiscuous, 54.
Marriages, Fescennine verses sung at, 202.
Marsi, sold charms against serpent bites, 99.
Martius Picus, entrapped by Numa's craft, 223.
Mavors, i.e. Mars, 285.
Medes, Christianity attested by mighty works amongst, 76.
Megalcon, daughter of Macarus, and mistress of the Muses, 206.
Megalensia, mode of celebration of, 343.
Meles, son of the river, i.e. Homer, 207.
Mellonia, goddess presiding over bees and honey, 190; supposed to introduce herself into the entrails of the victim to give omens, 194.
Memory, wife of Jupiter, 140; mother of the Muses, 175.
Men, sprung from the stones cast by Deucalion and Pyrrha, 227; in early times of immense size, 145; deified because of benefits conferred on the race, 28, 29; souls shut up in bodies, 79.
Menalippe, seduced by Neptune, 208.
Mens, wife of Jupiter, and mother of the Muses, 175; mother of Minerva, 172.
Mercury, of service to men, 135, 143; son of Jupiter, 139, 204, 196; son of Maia, 27, 140, 196, 204, 284; grandson of Atlas, 165; five gods named, 196; lusted after Proserpina, 196; eloquent in speech, 165, 204; bearer of the caduceus, 172; of the harmless snakes, 204; born on the cold mountain top, 172; presides over boxing and wrestling, 167; and commercial intercourse and markets, 172; contriver of words,

380   INDEX OF SUBJECTS.

and named from the interchange of speech, 172; represented with wings, 301; and wearing a broad-brimmed cap, 284, 285; beardless, 285; slayer of Argus, 196, 301; a thief, 206; termed Cyllenian, 172; the second, named Trophonius, under the earth, 196; the first, son of Cœlus, and the fourth, of the Nile, 196; the fifth, slayer of Argus, and inventor of letters, 196; goats sacrificed to, 328, 329.

Mercury, *i.e.* Hermes Trismegistus, 78.

Merops, the first builder of temples, 274.

Metrodorus, held the atomic theory, 72.

Midas, first to establish worship of the Phrygian mother, 143; king of Pessinus, 229; wished to give his daughter in marriage to Attis, 229, 230.

Milesian Didymæon, Cleochus buried in the, 278.

Militaris Venus, presiding over the debauchery of camps, 189.

Mind, the, affected by ailments of the body, 70.

Minerva, 153; sprung from Jupiter's head, 140, 172; daughter of Mens, 172; daughter of Victory, 172; five goddesses named, 196; the first, mother of Apollo by Vulcan, 196; the second, identified with Sais, daughter of the Nile, 196; the fourth, named Coryphasia by the Messenians, 197; the fifth, daughter and slayer of Pallas, 197; said by some to be one of the Penates, 179; the wars of, 211; worshipped because she discovered the olive, 29; gives light to secret lovers, 207; temples of, used as places of burial, 277; image of, burned, 298; a heifer sacrificed to, 329; termed Tritonian, 165, 330; represented with a helmet, 301; said by Aristotle to be the moon, 171; said to be depth of ether, and memory, 171; spins and weaves, 165; used to denote weaving, 268; citizens of, *i.e.* Athenians, 251; called Polias, 277.

Money, a goddess, 192.

Montinus, guardian of mountains, 192.

Moors, 14; worshipped the Titans and Bocchores, 27.

Morning, hymns sung to the deities in the, 342.

Mother of the gods, married to Saturn, 172; fed Nana with apples, 229; a pine brought into the sanctuary of, 239, 262; a flint worshipped by the people of Pessinus for, 283; represented as bearing a timbrel, 301.

Mother, Great, said to be the earth, 172; Attis worshipped in the temples of, 33; represented with fillets, 217; termed Pessinuntic Dindymene, 217; birth and origin of rites of, 227; did not exist more than two thousand years before Christ, 232; brought from Pessinus to repel Hannibal, 361; a black stone worshipped instead of, 362; why represented as crowned with towers, 229, 240.

Mother, the Phrygian, first set up as a goddess, 143.

Mulciber, dressed as a workman, 301.

Murcia, guardian of the slothful, 192.

Muses, the, daughters of Jupiter and Memory, 139, 175; of Cœlus and Tellus, 175; three sets of Muses, 197; nine in number, 164, 176; number of, stated differently as three, four, seven, 175; and eight, 176; said by some to be virgins, by others matrons, 175; identified with the Novensiles, 176; represented with pipes and psalteries, 301; handmaids of Megalcon, 206.

Musician, guilt contracted at the games by the silence of the, 213.

Mutunus, a deity, 193.

Myndus, Zeno of, 278.

Myrmidon, son of Clitor's daughter, 209.

Mysteries, the pontifical, 332; named *initia*, 241; of Venus, 242; Phrygian, 242, 244; of Ceres, 247; Alimontian, 252, 262.

NÆNIA, goddess of those near death, 190.

Nana, daughter of king Sangarius, 228; debauched by an apple, 228, 236; kept alive by the mother of the gods, 229; mother of Attis, 229, 236.

Nativities, art of calculating, 139.

Natrix, the deadly, 15.

INDEX OF SUBJECTS. 381

Nebridæ, family of the, 263.
Neith, name of the second Minerva in Egypt, 198.
Nemestrinus, god of groves, 190.
Neptune, believed to be serviceable to men, 135; king of the sea, 208, 172, 285; brother of Pluto and Jupiter, 172; mistresses of, 208; girt Ilium with walls, 178; served the Trojan Laomedon, 207; lord of the fish and shaker of the earth, 172; one kind of Penates said by the Etruscans to belong to, 178; the Atlantis of, 8; armed with the trident, 172, 285; said to have been one of the Penates, 178, 181; means the outspread water, 172, 268.
Nereid, loved Æacus, 209.
Nile, father of the second Minerva, 196, 198; father of the fourth Mercury and of Vulcan, 196.
Ninus, leader of the Assyrians against the Bactrians, 8.
Nisi, 54.
Noduterensis, a goddess presiding over the treading out of grain, 190, 193.
Nodutis, a god presiding over the shooting corn, 190.
Novensiles, nine Sabine gods, or the Muses, 176, 182; presiding over renovation, 176; the nine gods who can thunder, 177; foreign deities received by the Romans, 177; deified mortals, 177.
Nomads, 14.
Numa, established forms of worship and sacrifice, 76, 335; unacquainted with incense, 335; advised by Egeria how to learn the way to draw Jupiter to earth, 223; overreached Jupiter by his readiness, 223, 226.
Numa Pompilius, name of Apollo not found in the rituals of, 143.
Numenius, 74.
Numicius, frequented by the *indigetes*, 27.
Nysius, Liber, 252.

OCRISIA, brought as a captive from Corniculum, 241; mother of Servius, 242.
Œta, the Phœnician Hercules burned on mount, 27, 208.
Olive, Minerva the discoverer of the, 172.
Olus, Capitol named from, 279.

Olympian Jupiter, 290.
Omens derived from points of spears, 137; from the entrails of victims, 139, 194; no longer observed in public business, 137.
Omophagia, *i.e.* Bacchanalia, 242.
Onion, thunder-portents averted with an, 224, 226.
Ops, sprung from Cœlus and Hecate, 141; mother of Jupiter and his brothers, 27, 139, 141, 171, 202.
Orbona, guardian deity of bereaved parents, 190.
Orcus, union of Proserpine with, 257.
Origin of things, Christ commanded men not to inquire into, 129.
Ornytus, Pallas slain by, 208.
Orpheus, the Thracian bard, 242; the Thracian soothsayer, 250.
Osiris, husband of Isis, torn limb from limb, 27.
Ossilago, a deity giving firmness to the bones of children, 190.
Ossipagina, a name given to Juno, 171.

PALES, guardian of the flocks and herds, 166; not a female, but a male steward of Jupiter, 178; one of the Penates, 178, 181.
Palladium, the, formed from the remains of Pelops, 207.
Pallas, father of the fifth Minerva, and slain by her, 197, 198.
Pallas, surname of Minerva, 198; overcome and slain by Ornytus, 208.
Pamphilus, a magian and friend of Cyrus, 43.
Panætius, a Stoic philosopher, 72.
Panchæan gums burned to the gods, 336.
Panda, origin of the name, 186.
Pansa, consulship of, 232.
Pantarces, a name inscribed on the finger of the statue of Olympian Jupiter, 287.
Pantica, *i.e.* Panda, 186.
Paphos, Cinyras king of, 278.
Parthians, Christianity attested by mighty works amongst the, 76.
Patella, goddess of things to be brought to light, 190.
Patellana, goddess of things already brought to light, 190.
Patrimus, place in the ceremonies of the boy called, 213.
Pausi, 21.

INDEX OF SUBJECTS.

Peace deified, 185.
Peleus, father of Achilles, loved by Thetis, 209.
Pellonia, a goddess who repels enemies, 186, 187.
Peloponnese, Apis born in the, 28.
Pelops, 209; the Palladium formed from the remains of, 207.
Penates, said to be Neptune and Apollo, 178, 181; gods of the recesses of heaven, 178; said to be of four kinds, 178; said to be Fortune, Ceres, the genius Jovialis, and Pales, 178, 181; and by the Etruscans to be the Consentes and Complices, 178.
Perfica, goddess of filthy pleasures, 189.
Peripatetics, Aristotle the father of the, 72.
Persians, the, overcome because of the Christians, 14; Christianity attested by mighty works among, 76; worshipped rivers, 283; skilled in secret arts, 195.
Pertunda, a goddess presiding over the marriage couch, 189.
Pessinuntic Dindymene, 217.
Pessinus, people of, worshipped a flint for the mother of the gods, 283; Great Mother brought from, 361; Midas king of, 229.
Pestilence, sent to punish pollution of the circus, 350; abated when deities were brought from abroad, 351; put to flight by Æsculapius, 356.
Peta, presiding over prayers, 190.
Peter's victory over Simon Magus, 77.
Phaethon, the sun the father of, 266; loved by Ceres, 209.
Phalli displayed in honour of Bacchus, 252; given in the mysteries of Venus, 242.
Phidias, sculptor of the image of Olympian Jupiter, 286; carved on it the name of a boy loved by him, 287.
Philopator, i.e. Ptolemy IV., 278.
Philosophers, pride of, 117; by their disagreement show that nothing can be known, 74.
Phœnician Hercules, 27.
Phoroneus, the first builder of temples, 274.
Phorbas, Attis found and brought up by, 229.
Phrygia, the rock Agdus in, 227; mysteries celebrated in, 242.

Phrygian mother, the, i.e. Cybele, 143.
Phrygians, the, overcome with fear at the sight of the Great Mother and Acdestis, 230; Christianity attested by mighty works among, 76; call their goats *attagi*, 229.
Phryne, native of Thespia, used as model for the statues of Venus, 286.
Picus, son of Saturn, and father of Faunus, 141; drugged and made prisoner by Numa, 223; surnamed Martius, 223.
Piety, altars and temples built to, 184, 185.
Pindar, the Bœotian, 206.
Pine, Attis self-mutilated under a, 230; borne to her cave by the Great Mother, 231; carried into the sanctuary of the Great Mother on certain days, 239, 262; wreathed with flowers, 230, 240; bound with wool, 239.
Pipe, a (*tibia*), borne by Acdestis when he burst in upon the Phrygians, 230.
Piso, consulship of, 142.
Plank, a, worshipped by the Samians for Juno, 283.
Plato, head of philosophers, 11; the disciple of Socrates, 72; the divine, has many thoughts worthy of God, 103.
Plato's doctrine of reminiscence criticised, 90; bodiless forms, i.e. ideas, 72.
Plutarch of Chæronea, 208.
Pluto, brother of Jupiter and Neptune, 172; king of the shades, 248.
Plutonian realms, i.e. infernal regions, 327.
Polias, Erichthonius buried in the sanctuary of, 277.
Pollux, son of Tyndareus, distinguished as a boxer, 27; buried in Sparta, 208.
Pomegranate tree, a, springs from the severed members of Acdestis, 228.
Pomona, a name given to Juno, 171.
Pompilius, the revered, 161; sacrifices thoroughly cooked and consumed in time of, 138.
Pontifex Maximus, 42, 216, 354.
Populonia, a name given to Juno, 171.
Portents, thunder, how averted, 223.

INDEX OF SUBJECTS. 383

Portunus, gives safety to sailors, 166.
Potua, presiding over drinking, 168.
Præstana, named because Romulus excelled all with the javelin, 186.
Praxiteles, in the Cnidian Venus, copied the courtezan Gratina, 286.
Prayers for the dead, and for all men, 218.
Priapus, the Hellespontian god of lust, 157; represented with immense *pudenda*, 301.
Proserpine, daughter of Ceres and Jupiter, 244; violated by her father, 244; carried off by Pluto from Sicily, 248, 27; called Libera, 244; named because plants rise slowly, 173; lusted after by the first Mercury, 196; loved Adonis, 209; allegorical explanation of the rape of, 256, 257, 261; barren heifers sacrificed to, 329, 328.
Prosumnus, a vile lover of Bacchus, 253; the god's compliance with his request, 253.
Protagoras, doubts as to existence of a deity, 25.
Prothœ loved by Apollo, 208.
Psylli, sellers of charms against serpents, 99.
Purification of the mother of the gods, 342.
Puta, a goddess presiding over the pruning of trees, 190.
Pygmalion, king of Cyprus, 297; an image of Venus loved by, 297.
Pyriphlegethon, a river in Hades, 80.
Pyrrha, women formed from stones cast by, 227.
Pythagoras of Samos, 72, 78; placed the cause of things in numbers, 72; burned to death in a temple, 32.
Pythian god, the, identified with the sun and Bacchus, 173; served Laomedon, 207; soothsayers are taught by, 166.

QUINDECEMVIRI, the, wore wreaths of laurel, 216.
Quirinus, excelled all in throwing the javelin, 186.
Quirinus Martius, Romulus torn in pieces by the senators, called, 33.
Quirites, 187.

RACES, guilt contracted if the music stopped at the, 213; in the games of Jupiter, 352; seven rounds of the course in, 352.
Regulus, cruel death of, 32; a huge serpent killed by the army of, 359.
Religion, credibility of, not dependent on antiquity, 140, 142; opinion constitutes, not ceremony, 348.
Reminiscence, the Platonic doctrine of, 86, 90.
Renovation, the Novensiles gods of, 177.
Rhodes, the fourth Sun born at, 196.
Right and left merely relative terms, 187, 188.
Rites of the mother of the gods, 239, 240; of Bona Dea, 241; of Bacchus, Cyprian Venus, and the Corybantes, 242; of Ceres in Phrygia, 242, 243.
Rituals of Numa, Apollo's name not found in, 143.
Rivers, worshipped in ancient times by the Persians, 283.
Roman matrons, not allowed to drink wine, 138; kissed to test their sobriety, 138.
Romans, the race of Mars, the imperial people, 217; had changed their customs and ceremonies, 137; Pellonia goddess only of, 187; worshipped a spear for Mars, 283.
Rome, age in time of Arnobius of the city, 141; Christianity attested by miracles in, 76, 77.
Romulus, founder of Rome, 161; sacrifices consumed in time of, 138; and his brother, 186; a deified mortal, 177; torn in pieces by the senators, 33; unacquainted with incense, 335; called Quirinus Martius, 33.

SABINE gods, the Novensiles, nine, 176.
Sabre, worshipped by the Scythians, 283.
Sacrifices, Christians offered no, 273; Varro's denial of any occasion for, 308; cannot feed gods, 309; cannot give pleasure to the gods, 310, 311; can neither prevent their anger, 312; nor satisfy their rage, 313; no reason can be found for, 329; purity and cleanliness required at, 323.
Sadducees, attributing form to God, 158.

Salt-cellars, tables consecrated by placing, 137.
Safety, temples and altars erected to, 184.
Sais, the Egyptian, offspring of the Nile, 196, 199; identified with the second Minerva, 196.
Samians, the, worshipped a plank for Juno, 283.
Samothracii Digiti, named Idæi Dactyli, 179; said to be the Lares, 179, 181.
Sangarius, a king or river, father of Nana, 228; attempted to starve his daughter to death, 228; exposed her child, 229.
Sardis, Hercules a slave at, 207.
Satirical poems punished by law, 216.
Saturn, son of Cœlus and Hecate, 141; overthrew his father, 210; attempted to destroy his children, 210; was driven from power by Jupiter, 206, 210; hid himself in Latium, 206; was thrown into chains for parricide, 206; father by Ops of Jupiter, 139, 141, 171, 202; of the third Jupiter, 196; mother of the gods married to, 172; founder of the Saturnian state, 27; father of the third Minerva, 196; when aged, taken in adultery by his wife, 208; tomb and remains of, in Sicily, 208; identified with Kronos, and explained as chronos, 170; progenitor of the *dii magni*, 171; planter of the vine, 171; bearer of the pruning-knife, 171, 284, 300; presides over sown crops, 192; before Hercules' visit to Italy, human sacrifices offered to, 138.
Saturnian king, the, *i.e.* Jupiter, 204.
Satyr, Jupiter assumed the form of, 209, 267.
Scauri, 54.
Scythian king and Circe, the fifth Sun the son of a, 196.
Scythians, irruptions of the, laid to the charge of the Christians, 8; sacrificed asses to Mars, 207.
Sebadia, 244.
Semele, mother of Liber by Jupiter, 140, 202, 173, 252, 267.
Senators, Romulus torn in pieces by, 33; abuse of, punished by law, 216.

Serapis, Apis in Egypt called, 28; the Egyptian, 211; introduction of the worship of, 142; temple of, burned to ashes, 298.
Seres, the, 276; Christianity attested by miracles among, 76.
Serpent, Jupiter assumed the form of a, 209, 244.
Serpent-bites, charms against, 99.
Servius Tullus, birth of, 242.
Shrine of Juno at Argos, 298.
Shrines, the Christians built no, 273.
Sibyl, the, 51.
Sicily, tomb and remains of Saturn in, 208; Proserpine carried off from, 248.
Sickle, borne by Saturn, 284.
Simon Magus, fiery car of, 77; overthrow and death of, 77.
Sinister deities, presiding over the left, 187, 188.
Sleep, what produces, 70.
Slumber, is life anything but, 70.
Sminthian mice, Apollo the destroyer of, 173.
Socrates, condemnation of, spoken of as the Trojan war, 262; not made infamous by his condemnation, 32; Plato the disciple of, 72.
Solecisms and barbarisms objected to Christianity, 48.
Sophists, pretentious show of the, 49.
Soul, nature, origin, and condition of the, taught by Christ, 30; in an intermediate state, 80, 101, 98, 120; immortal, and holding the fourth place in the universe, 91, 81; corporeal and mortal, 93; may become immortal through Christ, 100; death is the ruin of the, 100; does not come into this world divinely taught, 86, 81; cast into rivers of fire, 80; should flee from earth, according to Plato, 78; not begotten by God, 112; man's, not formed from the same pure mixture as the world's, 120; cast into fire by fiercely cruel beings, 81.
Souls said to pass into cattle, 83.
Spain, 14; Hercules buried in, 27.
Sparta and Lacedæmon, Castor and Pollux buried in, 208.
Spartanus, Mars identified with, 207.
Spear, a, worshipped by the Romans for Mars, 283.
Stage, gods brought on, 216, 217.

INDEX OF SUBJECTS.

States, genii of, 21.
Stentors, 145.
Sterope, loved by Apollo, 208.
Stoic theory, of the world, 124; that souls survived death for a little, 125.
Stone, the Arabians worshipped an unhewn, 283.
Stones, after the deluge men sprung from, 227; anointed with oil, and worshipped, 31.
Stone, a, sent from Phrygia as the Great Mother, 362.
Stygian Jupiter, *i.e.* Pluto, 139.
Styx, a river in the infernal regions, 80, 253.
Sulla, the proscription of, spoken of as the battle of Cannæ, 262.
Summanus, *i.e.* Pluto, 182, 261.
Sumptuary laws, not observed in time of Arnobius, 137.
Supreme Jupiter, the, in opposition to the Stygian, 139.
Sun, the, all things vivified by the heat of, 5; said to be only a foot in breadth, 130; identified with Bacchus and Apollo, 173; and with Attis, 265; five gods said to be, 196; represented with rays of light, 285; father of Phaethon, 266.
Swan, Jupiter changed into a, 205, 267.
Syria, plagued with locusts because of the Christians, 14.

TAGES, the Etruscan, 139.
Tanaquil and the *dii conserentes*, 241.
Tarpeian rock, the, taken by Titus Tatius, 186.
Tartarus, the darkness of, has no terrors to the immortal, 96; visited by Liber, 252.
Tellene perplexities, proverbial phrase, 252.
Tellus, mother of the Muses, 175. See also under *Earth*.
Telmessus, city in Asia Minor, 278.
Telmessus, the prophet buried under Apollo's altar, 278.
Temples, in many cases tombs, 277, 278; destroyed with their images, and plundered, 298; built to cats, beetles, and heifers, 21; built that men might come near and invoke the gods, 275; not raised by the Christians, 273.
Thales, attributed all things to water, 72.

ARNOB.

Theatres, the gods exposed to insult and mockery in the, 217, 218.
Theban Hercules, the, 27, 204.
Themis, the oracle of, 227.
Theodorus of Cyrene, 211.
Thesmophoria, origin of the, 247.
Thespia, Phryne a native of, 286.
Thespians, the, worshipped a branch for Juno, 283.
Thessaly, home of the Myrmidons, 209.
Thestius' fifty daughters, and Hercules, 209.
Thetis, loved Peleus, 209.
Theutis, the Egyptian, founder of astrology, 139.
Thieves, Laverna the goddess of, 168.
Thrace, Mars born in, 207.
Thracian, the, bard, *i.e.* Orpheus, 242; soothsayer, son of Calliope, 250.
Thrasimene lake, Roman defeat at the, 187.
Thunderer, the, *i.e.* Jupiter, 298.
Thunder, evil portented by, how averted, 223, 224.
Thyle, remotest, 276.
Tiber, Æsculapius brought to the island in the, 356.
Tinguitani, the, afflicted with droughts because of the Christians, 14.
Titans, the, worshipped by the Moors, 27; Liber torn in pieces by, 32, 242.
Tithonus, loved by Aurora, 209.
Titus Tatius, the Capitoline taken by, 186.
Tolus Vulcentanus, Capitol named from, 278.
Transmigration of souls, 83.
Treason to speak evil of kings, 216.
Trebia, Novensiles worshipped at, 176.
Trebian gods, *i.e.* the Novensiles, 182.
Trebonius, cruelly put to death, 32.
Tree wreathed with flowers in memory of Attis, 230.
Triptolemus, deified because he invented the plough, 29; native of Attica, first to yoke oxen, 248.
Tritonian maid, the, 165, 330.
Trojan wars, the condemnation of Socrates spoken of as the, 262.
Trophonius, the second Mercury, 26, 196.

2 B

Tullius (M. Cicero), 262; the most eloquent of the Romans, 154.
Tullius (Servius), king, half-raw sacrifices offered under, 138.
Tutelary demons, the Lares, 180.
Tutunus, 189, 193.
Tyndareus, father of Castor and Pollux, 27.
Tyndarian brothers, the, 139.

UNXIA, presiding over anointing, 168.
Upibilia, keeps from wandering, 190.

VARRO, distinguished by the diversity of his learning, 232; denies that sacrifices are acceptable to the gods, 307.
Velus, a magian, 43.
Venus, the Cytherean, sprung from the sea-foam and the genitals of Cœlus, 206; daughter of Dione, 27; lusted after Anchises, 27, 209; a courtezan, 207, 211; deified by Cinyras, 207; mother of the Desires, 168; of the imperial people, 217; wounded by a mortal, 207; represented on the stage by lustful gestures, 217; in statues and paintings nude, 285, 301; used to denote lust, 268; allegorical explanation of the binding of, 265, 266; named because love comes to all, 173; four goddesses named, 137; Cinyras buried in the temple of, 278; the courtezan Gratina the model of the Cnidian, 286; Phryne of more than one, 286; Pygmalion's love for the Cyprian, 297; a youth's love for the Cnidian, 297; mysteries of Cyprian, 242.
Venus Militaris, presiding over the debauchery of camps, 189.
Vesta, the earth said to be, 172; ever-burning fire of, 137.
Vestals, guarding the sacred fire, 216.
Vermilion, the images of the gods smeared with, 282.
Verrii, 54.
Victa, presiding over eating, 168.
Victims, Christians slew no, 273.

Victory, Minerva the daughter of, 172.
Vigils in the Thesmophoria, 247.
Vintage festival of Æsculapius, 342.
Violets, sprung from blood of Attis, 230.
Virtue, altars and temples reared to, 184.
Virginalis, Fortuna, 138.
Vulcan, explained as fire, 173; lame, 206; wrought as a smith in Lemnos, 196, 206; son of the Nile, 196; loved by Ceres, 209; father of the third Sun, 196; and of Apollo, by the first Minerva, 196; four gods named, 197; lord of fire, 139, 166, 164; represented in workman's dress, 301; with cap and hammer, 285.
Vulturnus, the father-in-law of Janus, 170.

WHEAT, introduced into Attica by Ceres, 212.
Will, free, in salvation, 133.
Wicked, souls of, pass into beasts, 83.
World, the, uncreated and everlasting, 124; created, but everlasting, 124; created and perishable, 124; theories of, 25, 73, 125; destruction by fire of, 72.
Worship, true, in the heart, 212.
Winds, the, represented as blowing trumpets, 282.
Within, the Penates said to be those, 178.
Wine, in the rites of Bona Dea, 241; sanctuary of Attis not entered by those who had drunk, 229; Roman matrons not allowed to drink, 138.

XERXES, the bridge and canal made by, 9.

ZENO, the Stoic, 72; of Myndus, 278.
Zeuxippe, loved by Apollo, 208.
Zoroaster, Bactrians led against the Assyrians by, 8; assigned by tradition to different countries and ages, 43.

T. and T. Clark's Publications.

Just published, in One large 8vo Volume, price 12s.,

A HISTORY
OF
THE CHRISTIAN COUNCILS,
FROM THE ORIGINAL DOCUMENTS,
TO THE CLOSE OF THE COUNCIL OF NICÆA, A.D. 325.

By CHARLES JOSEPH HEFELE, D.D.,

Bishop of Rottenburg, formerly Professor of Theology in the University of Tübingen.

Translated from the German, and Edited by

WILLIAM R. CLARK, M.A. OXON.,

Prebendary of Wells and Vicar of Taunton.

Two Vols. 8vo, 21s.,

THE CHRISTIAN DOCTRINE OF SIN.

Translated from the Fifth German Edition of Dr. JULIUS MÜLLER,

BY REV. W. URWICK, M.A.

'This work, majestic in its conception and thorough in its execution, has long been very influential in German theology, and we welcome this new and admirable translation. Those who take the pains to master it, will find it a noble attempt to reconcile the highest effort of speculation in the pursuit of theological truth with the most reverent acceptance of the infallible determination of Scripture. In Germany it has been for many years a notable obstructive to the spread of vital error, and a refuge for distracted minds.'—*London Quarterly Review.*

Crown 8vo, 6s.,

THE REDEEMER:
DISCOURSES TRANSLATED FROM THE FRENCH OF
EDWARD DE PRESSENSE.

'The whole volume is marked by a rare richness of thought and illustration, and by a high and fervid eloquence.'—*Evangelical Magazine.*

WORKS PUBLISHED BY
J. T. HAYES,

LYALL PLACE, ETON SQUARE, S.W., & 4, HENRIETTA STREET, COVENT GARDEN

The Kiss of Peace; or, England and Rome at one on the Eucharist. By G. F Cobb, Trinity College, Cambridge. 7s. 6d.; by post 8s.

The Union Review: A Magazine advocating the Corporate Reunion of Christendom By Writers in the English, Roman, and Greek Churches. Bi-monthly Nos., 2s. postage 5d. The Volume for 1870, 13s. 6d.; postage 1s.

Sancta Clara on the Thirty-nine Articles. 7s.; by post 7s. 5d.
'It formed the basis of Tract 90.'—*British Magazine.*'

Walker's Ritual Reason Why: 450 Points Explained. 4s.; by post 4s. 3d.

Liturgy of the Church of Sarum. Translated by C. Walker. 7s.; postage 5d.

Essays on Reunion. By English, Roman, and Greek Contributors. Introductory Essay by Rev. Dr. Pusey. 6s.; by post 6s. 4d.

Sermons on Reunion. By English, Roman, and Greek Contributors. Two Series. Each 5s.; by post 5s. 4d.

St. Thomas Aquinas on the Incarnation: A Digest of his Doctrine thereon. 6s.; by post 6s. 4d.

The Sarum Directorium: The Services of the Church, with the Sarum Rubrics added. By C. Walker. 4s.; postage 3d,

The Evangelist Library Catechism. By the Evangelist Fathers, Cowley. 3s.; by post 3s. 3d.

Tracts by the Evangelist Fathers, Cowley. Packet 1s. 8d.; by post 1s. 10d.

Redemption: Some Aspects of the Work of Christ Considered. By Rev. R. M. Benson, Cowley. 5s.; by post 5s. 6d.

Bennett's Sermons at the 'Mission' in 1869 at St. Paul's, Knightsbridge. 7s. 6d.; by post 8s.

The Church's Broken Unity; showing the Differences between the main Bodies of Dissenters and the Church. Suitable for the Parish Lending Library or Private Reading. In Five Volumes. (1.) On Presbyterianism and Irvingism. (2.) On Anabaptists, Independents, and Quakers. (3.) On Methodists and Swedenborgians. These first three Volumes, each 3s. 6d.; by post 3s. 10d. (4.) and (5.) On Romanism. These last two each. 4s. 6d.; by post 4s. 10d. By Rev. W. J. E. Bennett, Froome.

A Plea for Toleration in the Church. By Rev. W. J. E. Bennett. 1s.; by post 1s. 1d.

Tales of Kirbeck. First and Second Series. Edited by Rev. W. J. E. Bennett. Each 3s. 6d.; by post 3s. 10d.

Our Doctor's Note-Book. Third Series of 'Tales of Kirbeck.' 2s. 6d.; by post 2s. 8d.

Cousin Eustace: Conversations with a Dissenter on the Prayer-Book. By Author of 'Tales of Kirbeck.'

Leighscombe: A new Tale for Children. 2s.; by post 2s. 2d.

Curiosities of Olden Times. (Fifteen Stories.) By Rev. S. Baring-Gould. 6s.; by post 6s. 6d.

J. T. HAYES' WORKS—*continued*.

Rhineland and its Legends. Preface by Rev. W. J. E. Bennett. 3s. 6d. ; by post 3s. 10d.

Oswald, the Young Artist; inculcating Reverence at Church. By C. Walker. 1s. 6d.; by post 1s. 8d.

Norwegian Tales; or, Evenings at Oakwood. Preface by Rev. S. Baring-Gould. 3s. 6d. ; by post 3s. 9d.

Sir Henry Appleton: A Tale of the Great Rebellion. By Rev. W. E. Heygate, Brighstone, Isle of Wight. 5s.; by post 5s. 6d.

The Validity of the Holy Orders of the Church of England Maintained and Vindicated. By Rev. Dr. F. G. LEE, All Saints', Lambeth. 8vo, 572 pages. 16s.; by post 17s.

The Liturgical Reason Why. By Rev. A. Williams. Being Papers on the Principles of the Book of Common Prayer. By Author of 'Home Sermons,' etc. 4s. ; by post 4s. 3d.

Plain Words on the Psalms, as translated in the Book of Common Prayer. By MARY E. SIMPSON, Author of 'Ploughing and Sowing,' etc. With Commendation by the Rev. WALSHAM HOW. 6s. ; by post 6s. 6d.

The Services of the Church, according to the Use of the Illustrious Church of Sarum. Edited by CHARLES WALKER. 4s.; by post 4s. 3d.

The Liturgy of the Church of Sarum. Translated from the Latin. By Charles WALKER. 7s.; by post 7s. 5d.

The Bible and its Interpreters: Its Miracles and Prophecies. By W. J. Irons, D.D., Prebendary of S. Paul's. 6s.; by post 6s. 6d.

Sermons on Doctrine and Practice. By Rev. Dr. Oldknow, Bordesley. 4s. ; by post 4s. 3d.

The Primitive Liturgies (in Greek) of S. Mark, S. Clement, S. James, S. Chrysostom, and S. Basil. Edited by Dr. NEALE. 6s.; by post 6s. 4d.

The Translations of the Above. By Dr. Neale. 4s. ; by post 4s. 4d.

The Hymns of the Eastern Church: Translated by Dr. Neale. 2s. 6d. ; by post 2s. 7d.

A Sermon Help: The Moral Concordances of S. Anthony of Padua. Translated, Verified, and Adapted to Modern Use. By Rev. Dr. NEALE. 3s.; by post 3s. 2d.

Short Daily Readings at Family or Private Prayer. By Rev. J. B. Wilkinson, S. Paul's, Knightsbridge. Vol. I. From Advent to Lent; Vol. II. Lent to Ascension; Vol. III. From Ascension to Sixteenth Sunday after Trinity. Vol. IV. Completing Trinity-tide, with Readings for all the Saints' Days. In Four Volumes. Each 5s. 6d.; by post 6s.

Household Prayers. Preface by Dr. Wilberforce, Bishop of Winchester. 1s.; by post 1s. 1d.

A Prayer-Book for the Young; or, A Complete Guide to Public and Private Devotion. Edited by CHARLES WALKER. 4s.; by post 4s. 3d. Cheap Edition, 3s.; by post 3s. 2d.

Hayes' Catalogue posted for One Stamp.

J. T. HAYES, LYALL PLACE ; AND (CENTRAL BRANCH) 4, HENRIETTA STREET, COVENT GARDEN.

T. and T. Clark's Publications.

WORKS OF JOHN CALVIN,
IN 51 VOLUMES, DEMY 8vo.

MESSRS. CLARK beg respectfully to announce that the whole STOCK and COPYRIGHT the WORKS OF CALVIN, published by the Calvin Translation Society, are now t property, and that this valuable Series will be issued by them on the following v favourable terms:—

1. Complete Sets in 51 Volumes, Nine Guineas. (Original Subscription price al £13.) The 'LETTERS,' edited by Dr. BONNET, 2 vols., 10s. 6d. additional.
2. Complete Sets of Commentaries, 45 vols., £7, 17s. 6d.
3. A *Selection* of Six Volumes (or more at the same proportion) for 21s., with exception of the INSTITUTES, 3 vols.; PSALMS, vol. 5; and HABAKKUK.
4. Any Separate Volume (except INSTITUTES), 6s.

The Contents of the Series are as follow:—

Institutes of the Christian Religion, 3 vols.
Tracts on the Reformation, 3 vols.
Commentary on Genesis, 2 vols.
Harmony of the last Four Books of the Pentateuch, 4 vols.
Commentary on Joshua, 1 vol.
- on the Psalms, 5 vols.
- on Isaiah, 4 vols.
- on Jeremiah and Lamentations, 5 vols.
- on Ezekiel, 2 vols.
- on Daniel, 2 vols.
- on Hosea, 1 vol.
- on Joel, Amos, and Obadiah, 1 vol.
- on Jonah, Micah, and Nahum, 1 vol.
- on Habakkuk, Zephaniah, and Haggai, 1 vol.

Commentary on Zechariah and Malacl vol.
Harmony of the Synoptical Evangel: 3 vols.
Commentary on John's Gospel, 2 vols.
- on Acts of the Apostles, 2 vols.
- on Romans, 1 vol.
- on Corinthians, 2 vols.
- on Galatians and Ephesians, 1 vol.
- on Philippians, Colossians, and Tl salonians, 1 vol.
- on Timothy, Titus, and Philemo vol.
- on Hebrews, 1 vol.
- on Peter, John, James, and Jude, 1

In Two Volumes, 8vo, price 14s. (1300 pages),

THE INSTITUTES OF THE CHRISTIAN RELIGION.
By JOHN CALVIN.
Translated by HENRY BEVERIDGE.

THIS translation of Calvin's Institutes was originally executed for the Calvin Tran tion Society, and is universally acknowledged to be the best English version of the w The Publishers have reprinted it in an elegant form, and have at the same time fix price so low as to bring it within the reach of all.

In One Volume, 8vo, price 8s. 6d.,

CALVIN:
HIS LIFE, LABOURS, AND WRITINGS.
By FELIX BUNGENER,
AUTHOR OF THE 'HISTORY OF THE COUNCIL OF TRENT,' ETC.

'M. Bungener's French vivacity has admirably combined with critical care and v admiring reverence, to furnish what we venture to think the best portrait of Ca hitherto drawn. He tells us all that we need to know; and instead of overlaying work with minute details and needless disquisitions, he simply presents the disencumb features, and preserves the true proportions of the great Reformer's character. heartily commend the work.'—*Patriot.*

'Few will sit down to this volume without resolving to read it to the close.'—*Cler Journal.*

T. and T. Clark's Publications.

JOHN ALBERT BENGEL'S
GNOMON OF THE NEW TESTAMENT.
Now First Translated into English.
WITH ORIGINAL NOTES, EXPLANATORY AND ILLUSTRATIVE.

The Translation is comprised in Five Large Volumes, demy 8vo, of (on an average) fully 550 pages each.

SUBSCRIPTION, 31s. 6d.; *or free by Post*, 35s.

The very large demand for Bengel's Gnomon enables the Publishers still to supply it at the Subscription Price.

The whole work is issued under the Editorship of the Rev. ANDREW R. FAUSSET, M.A., Rector of St. Cuthbert's, York, late University and Queen's Scholar, and Senior Classical and Gold Medalist, T.C.D.

'There are few devout students of the Bible who have not long held Bengel in the highest estimation,—nay, revered and loved him. It was not, however, without some apprehension for his reputation with English readers, that we saw the announcement of a translation of his work. We feared that his sentences, terse and condensed as they are, would necessarily lose much of their pointedness and force by being clothed in another garb. But we confess gladly to a surprise at the success the translators have achieved in preserving so much of the spirit of the original. We are bound to say that it is executed in the most scholarlike and able manner. The translation has the merit of being faithful and perspicuous. Its publication will, we are confident, do much to bring back readers to the *devout* study of the Bible, and at the same time prove one of the most valuable of exegetical aids. The "getting up" of those volumes, combined with their marvellous cheapness, cannot fail, we should hope, to command for them a large sale.'—*Eclectic Review.*

CHEAP RE-ISSUE

OF THE WHOLE

WORKS OF DR. JOHN OWEN.
Edited by Rev. W. H. GOOLD, D.D., Edinburgh.

WITH LIFE BY REV. ANDREW THOMSON, D.D.

In 24 Volumes, demy 8vo, handsomely bound in cloth, lettered.

With Two Portraits of Dr. Owen.

Several years have now elapsed since the first publication of this Edition of the Works of the greatest of Puritan Divines. Time has tested its merits; and it is now admitted on all hands to be the only correct and complete edition.

At the time of publication it was considered—as it really was—a miracle of cheapness, having been issued, by Subscription, for Five Guineas.

In consequence of the abolition of the Paper Duty, the Publishers now re-issue the Twenty-four Volumes for

FOUR GUINEAS.

As there are above Fourteen Thousand Pages in all, each Volume therefore averages *Five Hundred and Ninety Pages.*

'You will find that in John Owen the learning of Lightfoot, the strength of Charnock, the analysis of Howe, the savour of Leighton, the raciness of Heywood, the glow of Baxter, the copiousness of Barrow, the splendour of Bates, are all combined. We should quickly restore the race of great divines if our candidates were disciplined in such lore.' —*The late* DR. HAMILTON *of Leeds.*

COMMENTARIES

PUBLISHED BY

JAMES NISBET & COMPANY,

BERNERS STREET.

I.

ON THE HOLY BIBLE. By the late Rev. Thomas Scott. Six Volumes. Imperial 4to, 50s., cloth.

II.

ON THE GOSPEL ACCORDING TO ST. MATTHEW. By the Rev. J. A. Alexander. Post 8vo, 5s.

III.

ON THE GOSPEL ACCORDING TO ST. MARK. By the Same. Post 8vo, 5s.

IV.

ON THE ACTS OF THE APOSTLES. By the Same. Two Volumes. Post 8vo, 15s.

V.

ON THE EPISTLE TO THE GALATIANS. By the Rev. Emilius Bayley, B.D. Post 8vo, 7s. 6d., cloth.

VI.

ON LEVITICUS, EXPOSITORY AND PRACTICAL. By the Rev. Andrew A. Bonar. 8vo, 8s. 6d., cloth.

VII.

ON THE EPISTLE TO THE ROMANS. By the late Rev. William Marsh, D.D. Small crown 8vo, 2s. 6d., cloth.

VIII.

ON THE HOLY BIBLE. By Matthew Henry. Nine Volumes. Imperial 8vo, 63s., cloth.

IX.

ON THE LAW OF THE OFFERINGS IN LEVITICUS. By the Rev. Andrew Jukes. Crown 8vo, 3s., cloth.

X.

ON THE EPISTLE TO THE EPHESIANS. By the Rev. Charles Hodge, D.D. Crown 8vo, 3s. 6d., cloth.

XI.

ON THE FIRST EPISTLE TO THE CORINTHIANS. By the Same. Crown 8vo, 5s., cloth.

XII.

ON THE SECOND EPISTLE TO THE CORINTHIANS. By the Same. Crown 8vo, 5s., cloth.

XIII.

ON THE GOSPEL ACCORDING TO ST. JOHN. In simple and familiar language. By G. B. Small crown 8vo, 3s. 6d., cloth.

XIV.

ON THE SONG OF SOLOMON. By the Rev. A. Moody Stuart, M.A. 8vo, 12s., cloth.

XV.

THE BIBLE MANUAL. Translated from the German. By Dr. C. G. Barth, of Calw, Wurtemburg. 8vo, 12s., cloth.

LONDON: JAMES NISBET & CO., 21, BERNERS STREET, W.

NEW BOOKS AND NEW EDITIONS.

The Day Office of the Church, according to the Kalendar of the Church
of England,—consisting of Lauds, Vespers, Prime, Terce, Sext, None, and Compline throughout the Year. To which are added the Order for the Administration of the Reserved Eucharist, Penance, and Unction; together with the Office of the Dead, Commendation of a Soul, divers Benedictions and Offices, and full Rubrical Directions.
A complete Edition, especially for Sisterhoods and Religious Houses. By the Editor of 'The Little Hours of the Day.' Crown 8vo, 4s. 6d.; cloth, red edges, 5s. 6d.

Spiritual Instructions on the Holy Eucharist. By the Rev. T. T. Carter,
M.A., Rector of Clewer. Second Edition. Crown 8vo, cloth, 3s. 6d.

The Primer, set forth at large with many Godly and Devout Prayers.
Edited, from the Post-Reformation Recension, by the Rev. GERARD MOULTRIE, M.A., Vicar of South Leigh. Fourth Thousand, 18mo, cloth, 3s.

The Hours of the Primer. Published separately, for the use of
Individual Members of a Household in Family Prayer. 18mo, cloth, 1s.

Lessons on the Kingdom, for the Little Ones of the Church of England.
By the Rev. W. H. B. PROBY, M.A. 18mo, cloth, 1s. 6d.

The Priest's Prayer-Book, with a Brief Pontifical. Containing Private
Prayers and Intercessions; Offices, Readings, Prayers, Litanies, and Hymns, for the Visitation of the Sick; Offices for Bible and Confirmation Classes, Cottage Lectures, etc.; Bibliotheca Sacerdotalis, etc. etc. Edited by TWO CLERGYMEN. Fourth Edition, much Enlarged. Cloth, 6s. With Common Prayer, 2s. 6d. additional.

Catechisings on the Life of Our Lord. By William Lea, M.A., Vicar
of S. Peter's, Droitwich, and Hon. Canon of Worcester. 12mo, cloth, 3s. 6d.

The Hidden Life. Translated from Nepveu's Pensées Chrétiennes.
Second Edition, Enlarged. 18mo, cloth, 2s.

The Imitation of Our Lord: A Series of Lectures delivered at All
Saints', Margaret Street. By the Rev. T. T. CARTER, M.A., Rector of Clewer. Fifth Edition. 8vo, cloth, 2s. 6d.

The Churchman's Companion. Third Series, enlarged. Vols. I. and II.
1870. 8vo, cloth, 4s. each.

The Epistle to the Romans. With Short Notes, chiefly Critical and
Doctrinal. By the Rev. T. CHAMBERLAIN, M.A., Student of Christ Church, and Vicar of S. Thomas the Martyr, Oxford. Foolscap 8vo, cloth, 2s.

Resting-Places : A Manual of Christian Doctrine, Duty, and Devotion.
For Private and Family Use. By the Author of 'The Plain Guide.' 18mo, cloth, 1s. 6d.; wrapper, 9d.

Miserere : The Fifty-first Psalm. With Devotional Notes. Reprinted
from Neale's 'Commentary on the Psalms.' With Additions by the Rev. R. F. LITTLEDALE, LL.D. Price 6d.; cloth, 1s.

Selections from the Letters of S. Francis de Sales. Translated from
the French by Mrs. C. W. BAGOT. Revised by a Priest of the English Church. Fourth Edition, foolscap 8vo, cloth, 1s. 6d.

Are You being Converted ? A Course of Sermons on Serious Subjects.
By the BISHOP OF BRECHIN. Third and Cheaper Edition, foolscap 8vo, cloth, 2s.

Footsteps of the Holy Child ; or, Lessons on the Incarnation. Edited
by the Rev. T. T. CARTER, M.A., Rector of Clewer. Parts I. and II. in one Vol., foolscap 8vo, cloth, 4s. 6d.

LONDON: J. MASTERS, 78, NEW BOND STREET.

T. and T. Clark's Publications.

MESSRS. CLARK *beg to offer a Selection of Eight Volumes from the following List of Works (chiefly forming the* BIBLICAL CABINET, *the first series of translations published by them*),

For ONE GUINEA, remitted with Order.

The price affixed is that at which they can be had separately, which is also much reduced.

ERNESTI'S PRINCIPLES OF BIBLICAL INTERPRETATION OF NEW TESTAMENT. Translated by Bishop Terrot. 2 vols., 8s.

PHILOLOGICAL TRACTS. 3 vols., 4s. each.
   Vol. 1.—Rossi and Pfannkuche on the Language of Palestine in the Age of Christ; Planck on the Nature and Genius of the Diction of New Testament; Tholuck on the Importance of the Study of Old Testament; Beckhaus on the Interpretation of the Tropical Language of New Testament. Vol. II.—Storr on the Meaning of 'The Kingdom of Heaven;' Storr on the Parables; Storr on the word 'ΠΛΗΡΩΜΑ;' Hengstenberg on Isaiah liii. Vol. III.—Ullmann on Christ's Sinlessness; Rückert on the Resurrection of the Dead; Lange on the Resurrection of the Body; M. Stuart on Future Punishment.

THOLUCK'S COMMENTARY ON THE EPISTLE TO THE ROMANS. 2 vols., 8s.
PAREAU ON THE INTERPRETATION OF OLD TESTAMENT. 2 vols., 8s.
STUART'S SYNTAX OF THE NEW TESTAMENT. 4s.
UMBREIT'S EXPOSITION OF THE BOOK OF JOB. 2 vols., 8s.
STEIGER'S COMMENTARY ON FIRST PETER. 2 vols., 8s.
BILLROTH'S COMMENTARY ON THE CORINTHIANS. 2 vols., 8s.
KRUMMACHER'S CORNELIUS THE CENTURION. 3s.
WITSIUS' EXPOSITION OF THE LORD'S PRAYER. 4s.
ROSENMULLER'S BIBLICAL GEOGRAPHY OF CENTRAL ASIA. 2 vols., 8s.
ROSENMULLER'S BIBLICAL GEOGRAPHY OF ASIA MINOR, PHŒNICIA, & ARABIA. 4s.
ROSENMULLER'S BIBLICAL MINERALOGY AND BOTANY. 4s.
WEMYSS' CLAVIS SYMBOLICA; or, Key to Symbolical Language of Scripture. 4s.
CALVIN ON THE EPISTLES TO GALATIANS AND EPHESIANS. 4s.
GESS ON THE REVELATION OF GOD IN HIS WORD. 3s.
ROSENMULLER ON THE MESSIANIC PSALMS. 4s.
COVARD'S LIFE OF CHRISTIANS DURING FIRST THREE CENTURIES. 4s.
HOFFMANN'S CHRISTIANITY IN THE FIRST CENTURY. 4s. 6d.
THORNLEY'S SKELETON THEMES. 3s.
THORNLEY'S TRUE END OF EDUCATION, AND THE MEANS ADAPTED TO IT. 3s. 6d.
CALVIN AND STORR ON THE PHILIPPIANS AND COLOSSIANS. 4s.
SEMISCH'S LIFE, WRITINGS, AND OPINIONS OF JUSTIN MARTYR. 2 vols., 8s.
ROHR'S HISTORICO-GEOGRAPHICAL ACCOUNT OF PALESTINE IN THE TIME OF CHRIST. 4s.
TITTMANN'S EXEGETICAL, CRITICAL, AND DOCTRINAL COMMENTARY ON ST JOHN'S GOSPEL. 2 vols., 8s.
BARBACOVI'S LITERARY HISTORY OF MODERN ITALY. 2s. 6d.
MY OLD HOUSE; or, The Doctrine of Changes. 4s.
NEGRIS' EDITION OF HERODOTUS, with English Notes. 4s. 6d.
   ,,   ,,   PINDAR,   ,,   ,,   4s. 6d.
   ,,   ,,   XENOPHON,   ,,   ,,   2s.
WELSH'S ELEMENTS OF CHURCH HISTORY. 5s.
NEANDER ON THE EPISTLE TO THE PHILIPPIANS AND ON THE EPISTLE OF ST JAMES. 3s.
EDERSHEIM'S HISTORY OF THE JEWISH NATION AFTER THE DESTRUCTION OF JERUSALEM UNDER TITUS. 6s.

T. and T. Clark's Publications.

In one volume 8vo, price 10s. 6d.,
The Doctrine of Justification: An Outline of its History in the Church, and of its Exposition from Scripture, with Special Reference to Recent Attacks on the Theology of the Reformation. (The Second Series of the 'Cunningham Lectures.') By the late Professor BUCHANAN.

'We must bear witness to the very great ability as regards both thought and style in which the book is written: the language is clear, solid, and easy.'—*Church and State Review.*

In one volume royal 8vo, price 18s.,
Dictionary and Concordance of the Names of Persons and Places, and of some of the more remarkable Terms which occur in the Scriptures of the Old and New Testaments. Compiled by WILLIAM HENDERSON, M.D.

'Dr. Henderson has done his work with much care; and altogether the book is well planned and well executed.'—*Literary Churchman.*

In demy 8vo, price 10s. 6d.,
A Critical and Exegetical Commentary on the Book of Genesis, with a new Translation. By Professor MURPHY.

'A work of most massive scholarship, abounding in rich and noble thought, and remarkably fresh and suggestive.'—*Evangelical Magazine.*

BY THE SAME AUTHOR.
In one volume 8vo, price 9s.,
A Critical and Exegetical Commentary on the Book of Exodus.

'It is the fruit of sound scholarship, and a devout study of the Pentateuch.'—*Evangelical Magazine.*

In two volumes crown 8vo, price 10s. 6d.,
Manual of Modern Pantheism: Essay on Religious Philosophy. By M. EMILE SAISSET. Translated, with an Introductory Essay, Marginal Analysis, and Notes.

'As a handbook to the theological side of modern speculation, it is a most valuable addition to philosophical literature.'—*Saturday Review.*

In one volume post 8vo, price 6s. 6d.,
Lectures on the True, the Beautiful, and the Good. By Victor Cousin. Translated from the last French Edition, under the sanction of the Author.

'We cannot too highly recommend this work. It is very long since we had a volume in our hands that has afforded us so much gratification in the perusal.'—*Art Journal.*

In crown 8vo, price 4s.,
The Symbolical Numbers of Scripture.—Chapter 1. The Time of the End. 2. The Time and Times and Half a Time. 3. The Numbers Three and a Half. 4. The Number of Beast 666. 5. The Number Ten, and the Millennium. 6. The related Numbers, Seven, Three, Four, Twelve. 7. The Number Forty. 8. The Numbers in the Book of Job. 9. The Number One Hundred and Fifty-three. By Rev. MALCOLM WHITE.

'We bear willing testimony to the general excellence of his work, which is well deserving of a place in the library of every biblical student.'—*Wesleyan Methodist Magazine.*

In two volumes crown 8vo, price 12s.,
Biblical Studies on St. John's Gospel. Translated from the German of Dr. RUDOLPH BESSER by M. G. HUXTABLE.

'We recommend the book most warmly to all.'—*Literary Churchman.*

STANDARD WORKS

JUST PUBLISHED, OR IN PREPARATION, BY

WILLIAM OLIPHANT & CO., EDINBURGH.

Just published, in handsome imperial 8vo, price 14s.,
Commentary on Paul's Epistle to the Romans: With an Introduction on the Life, Times, Writings, and Character of Paul. By WILLIAM S. PLUMER, D.D., LL.D., Author of 'Studies on the Book of Psalms.'

In the press,
Lectures, Exegetical and Practical, on the Epistle of James: With a New Translation of the Epistle, and Notes on the Greek Text. By the Rev. ROBERT JOHNSTONE, LL.B., Arbroath.

Just published,
The Doctrine of the Trinity underlying the Revelation of Redemption. By the Rev. GEORGE PATTERSON, Greenhill, Nova Scotia. In a neat volume of 250 pp., crown 8vo, price 3s. 6d.

In the press,
Things to Come. By the Rev. William Reid, Lothian Road United Presbyterian Church, Edinburgh.

CONTENTS: The Millennium—The Intermediate State—The Resurrection—The Judgment—Future Punishments—Heaven.

Now ready, in crown 8vo, price 5s.,
The Wisdom of the King; or, Lessons from the Book of Ecclesiastes. By the Rev. JAMES BENNET, St. John, New Brunswick.

Just published, price 2s. 6d.,
The Lost Found and the Wanderer Welcomed. By the Rev. W. M. TAYLOR, Bootle.

Just published, Second Thousand,
The Life of Sir Walter Scott, Bart. By the Rev. George GILFILLAN, Dundee. In neat crown 8vo, with beautiful Steel Frontispiece and Vignette, price 5s.

'Extremely readable. . . . Its publication, in view of the approaching Centenary, is opportune.'—*Scotsman.*
'With Scott's Centenary so near us, we ought to be thankful that the people have such a capital biography as Mr. Gilfillan's to turn to.'—*Dundee Advertiser.*
'A Life of Scott, full without being voluminous, was a desideratum. The want is effectually supplied by the volume before us.'—*Dumfries Herald.*

Recently published, in crown 8vo, price 5s.,
Thomas Chalmers: A Biographical Study. By James Dodds, Esq., Author of 'The Fifty Years' Struggle of the Scottish Covenanters.'

'A well-written and affectionate biography. Mr. Dodds has shown commendable industry, loving his hero without making an idol of him.'—*Publishers' Circular.*
'It contains a graphic account of a very remarkable man, written in a manly style, and none the worse for being enthusiastic.'—*The Daily News.*

EDINBURGH: WILLIAM OLIPHANT & CO.; AND ALL BOOKSELLERS.

VALUABLE WORKS FOR CLERGYMEN, MINISTERS, AND STUDENTS.

Christus Consolator; or, The Pulpit in relation to Social Life. By ALEXANDER MACLEOD, D.D. 5s.

The Early Years of Christianity. By E. DE PRESSENSE, D.D. A Sequel to 'Jesus Christ: His Times, Life, and Work.' 12s.

Jesus Christ: His Times, Life, and Work. By the same Author. Third Edition. 9s.

The World of Moral and Religious Anecdote: Illustrations and Incidents gathered from Words, Thoughts, and Deeds in the Lives of Men, Women, and Books. By E. PAXTON HOOD, Author of 'Dark Sayings on a Harp,' etc. 10s. 6d.

The Jewish Temple and Christian Church: A Series of Discourses on the Epistles to the Hebrews. By R. W. DALE, M.A., Author of 'Week-day Sermons,' etc. Second Edition, 6s.

Secular Annotations on Scripture Texts. By the Rev. FRANCIS JACOX. 6s.

One Thousand Gems from the Rev. Henry Ward Beecher. Edited by the Rev. G. D. EVANS. With Portrait, 5s.

Remarkable Facts: Illustrative and Confirmatory of Different Portions of Holy Scripture. By the late Rev. Dr. LEIFCHILD. Cheap Edition. 3s. 6d.

The Theology of the New Testament: A Handbook for Bible Students. By J. J. VAN OOSTERZEE, D.D. 6s.

First Principles of Ecclesiastical Truth: Essays on the Church and Society. By J. BALDWIN BROWN, B.A. 8vo, 10s. 6d.

Misread Passages of Scripture. First and Second Series. By the same Author. 3s. 6d. each.

Symbols of Christ. By Rev. CHARLES STANFORD. New Edition. 3s. 6d.

Central Truths. By the same Author. Third Edition. 3s. 6d.

The City Temple: Sermons preached in the Poultry Chapel, 1869-70. By JOSEPH PARKER, D.D., Author of 'Ecce Deus,' etc. 6s., cloth.

Ad Clerum: Advices to a Young Preacher. By the same Author. 5s.

Masterpieces of Pulpit Eloquence, Ancient and Modern, with Historical Sketches of Preaching in the different Countries represented, and Biographical and Critical Notices of the several Preachers and their Discourses. By HENRY C. FISH, D.D. Two vols. 8vo, 21s.

Lamps, Pitchers, and Trumpets: Lectures on the Vocation of the Preacher. Illustrated by Anecdotes, Biographical, Historical, and Elucidatory, of every order of Pulpit Eloquence, from the great Preachers of all Ages. By E. PAXTON HOOD. Second Thousand. 8vo, 10s. 6d., handsomely bound.

LONDON: HODDER & STOUGHTON, 27, PATERNOSTER ROW.

THE NEW FAMILY MAGAZINE,
EDITED BY THE
REV. E. H. BICKERSTETH, M.A.,
Vicar of Christ Church, Hampstead, and Chaplain to the Bishop of Ripon. Author of "Yesterday, To-Day, and for Ever."

EVENING HOURS:
A CHURCH OF ENGLAND MONTHLY MAGAZINE.

PART I., PRICE SIXPENCE.

Will be published on the 29th of March, 64 pp., imp. 8vo, with Illustrat[ions]

MANY as are the magazines which cover our tables, it is acknowledged tha[t the] Church of England is not adequately represented by any one which claim[s to] be for the general reader. There is still required one which, while of ma[rked] literary ability, shall be characterized by fidelity to Church doctrines and p[rin]ciples, yet of catholic sympathies — whose pages shall be thoughtful, popular — whose range of subjects shall be extensive, yet of exact informati[on] — whose religious articles shall be carefully guarded from dulness — and w[hose] secular ones shall be pervaded by a religious spirit.

The following list of subjects will show that it is intended to blend ins[truc]tion with recreation; while the names of the eminent Contributors a[ffords] ample proof that 'EVENING HOURS' will be both an able and a sound 'Fa[mily] Magazine.'

The Magazine is intended to embrace:—

1. Life-like Sketches and Narratives founded on History.
2. Biblical Papers, such as—
   The Alphabet of Prophecy: A Study for all.
   The indissoluble Union of the Old and New Testaments.
   The distinctive Characteristics of the Gospels, etc.
3. Short Expositions of Difficult Texts.
4. Jottings from the Fathers, with Life Sketches.
5. The Witness of the Reformers, with Life Sketches.
6. Martyrology.
7. The Antiquary's Book Store.
8. The Poet's Portfolio.
9. Hymnology and Church Music.
10. The Standard-bearers of the Church Fifty Years Ago.
11. Doctrinal and Liturgical Papers, such as—
    Brief Expositions of the Creeds and Articles.
12. God's Controversy with Rome.
13. Discussion of Practical Questions of [daily] Life, such as—
    The Home Circle on Sunday.
    The Daily Domestic Altar.
    Social Recreation and Amusements, [etc.]
14. Popular Scientific Articles; for example[—] On the Structure of the Human Body.
    On the Microscope and Telescope.
    On Botany and Geology.
15. Physical Geography.
    Geography and Natural History of the [world.]
16. The Sufferer's Couch.
17. The Children's Gallery.
18. Missions to Israel.
19. Missions to the Heathen Abroad—thei[r] History and Present Position.
20. Missions at Home.
21. Popular Proverbs and their Teaching.
22. Short Notices of Books.

The first Numbers will contain original Contributions by

THE LORD BISHOP OF RIPON.
HUGH MACMILLAN, Author of 'Bible Teachings in Nature.'
The Author of 'The Memorials of Captain Hedley Vicars,' and 'English Hearts and Hands.'
The Author of 'The Home Life of Sir David Brewster.'
Miss E. J. WHATELY, Author of 'The Life, etc. of Archbishop Whately.'
The Author of 'Broad Shadows on Life's Pathway,' and 'Doing and Suffering.'
R. DUDLEY BAXTER, Esq., M.A.
T. R. BIRKS, M.A., Author of 'The Bible and Modern Thought.'
J. C. RYLE, B.A., Author of 'The Christian Leaders of the Last Century,' etc., etc.
H. A. STERN, M.A., late Missionary in Abyssinia.
A. W. THOROLD, M.A, Author of 'The Pr[esence] of Christ.'
GORDON CALTHROP, M.A., Vicar of St. A[ugus]tine's, Highbury New Park.
J. F. FENN, M.A., Vicar of Christ Church, [Ro]tenham.
J. T. COOPER, Esq., Organist of Christ C[hurch,] Newgate Street, E.C.
W. H. COOK, Esq., M.D.
H. C. CORY, M.A., Clerical Secretary of Church Missions.
J. E. B. MAYOR, Fellow of St. John's C[ollege,] Cambridge.
W. E. LIGHT, Vicar of St. James', Dover.
Miss J. THRELFALL, and H. L. L.
E. H. BICKERSTETH, M.A., Editor.

'Evening Hours' may be obtained from all Booksellers in town or country. In [case] of delay or difficulty, the Publishers will undertake to send it free to the end of the [year] on the receipt of 5s. 3d. in postage stamps. A single specimen copy direct fro[m the] Publishers, free for seven stamps.

All literary Correspondence and MSS. must be addressed to the Editor, care o[f the] Publishers.

Prospectuses in detail on application.

LONDON: WILLIAM HUNT AND COMPANY,
23, HOLLES STREET, CAVENDISH SQUARE.

Monthly, 80 pp., demy 8vo, 1s.,

The Christian Advocate and Review.

EDITED BY THE

REV. EDWARD GARBETT, M.A.,

Vicar of Christ Church, Surbiton.

THE New Series of the CHRISTIAN ADVOCATE AND REVIEW was undertaken in 1867, with a view to supply to the Evangelical clergy and laity of the Church of England a Magazine of sound scholarly character, and yet sufficiently cheap to be within the reach of all. Eighty pages of original matter are supplied, on the first day of every month, for one shilling.

The necessity for some cheap organ of communication among the Evangelical portion of the Church, for the interchange of thought, and the discussion of current questions of Christian policy, belief, and practice, has been made more imperative by the events of the last four years. The interests of truth, and of the Church of England, earnestly plead for that trivial pecuniary sacrifice on the part of individuals required to support the circulation of such a Magazine as the CHRISTIAN ADVOCATE AND REVIEW, and to cultivate, through its means, unanimity of sentiment and identity of action.

For this purpose, the Editor of the CHRISTIAN ADVOCATE has not confined himself to any exclusive circle of contributors, but has ever been ready to accept papers from any quarter which attained the necessary standard of literary merit. It has been his anxious object to encourage the frank ventilation of opinions, so long as they are consistent with the great outlines of Evangelical truth taught in the word of God, and embodied in the formularies of the Church of England.

The CHRISTIAN ADVOCATE AND REVIEW contains articles on subjects devotional, critical, expository, doctrinal, historical, scientific, and biographical. Every number contains also reviews of books, and notices of the current literature of the day.

During 1870 two sections of the Magazine have been devoted to short notices, under the respective titles of the 'Library Table' and the 'Library.' The latter contains rapid reviews of works of permanent value, in theology and other kindred branches of inquiry. Longer reviews will be given, as at present, of books of more than usual interest and value, as opportunity may permit.

It is the object of the Editor of the ADVOCATE to combine decision of principle and firmness in the maintenance of truth with courtesy towards individuals, and a generous construction of personal motives.

The support of all who love the Protestant and Evangelical principles of the Reformation is earnestly invited to secure for the CHRISTIAN ADVOCATE that extensive circulation which is necessary to its prosperity and usefulness.

Forwarded post free on the day of publication, by the Publishers.

LONDON: WILLIAM HUNT & CO., 23, HOLLES STREET, W.

Simple Readings on the Gospels. Arranged in Daily Portions for the use of Families and Schools. Compiled from the Works of the Rev. J. C. RYLE, B.A., Rev. ALBERT BARNES, and other Expository Writers. By A. S. F. Two vols., each 3s. 6d.; or in one vol., 6s. [Vol. i. ready.

The Consoler and the Sufferer: Sermons on the Raising of Lazarus and the Passion Sayings of Christ. By the Rev. CLAUDE BOSANQUET, M.A., Vicar of St. Nicholas, Rochester; Author of 'How shall I Pray?' etc. 4s. 6d.

Christian Chivalry; or, the Armour of God on the Soldier of the Cross. By the Rev. SAMUEL GARRATT, M.A., Vicar of St. Margaret's, Ipswich; Author of 'Commentary on the Revelation of St. John,' 'Midnight Cry,' etc. Small 8vo, extra cloth, 3s.

BY THE SAME AUTHOR.

A Second Edition of 'Signs of the Times;' showing that the Coming of the Lord draweth near. With the added Signs of the last few Months. Fcap. 8vo, extra cloth, 2s. 6d.

A Second Edition of 'Seed scattered Broadcast; or, Incidents in a Camp Hospital.' By S. M'BETH. With an Introduction, and edited by the Author of 'The Memorials of Captain Hedley Vicars,' and 'The Life of the Rev. William Marsh, D.D.' Post 8vo, 3s. 6d.

The Prodigal Son. Uniform with 'Ourselves.' By Brownlow North, B.A. Magdalen Hall, Oxon., and Registrar for the Diocese of Winchester and Surrey. Cloth boards, extra, antique binding, 2s.

BY THE SAME AUTHOR.

A Fifth and Cheaper Edition of 'Ourselves.' 18mo, cloth limp, 1s. 9d.

A Third and Cheaper Edition of 'Yes or No? or God's Offer of Salvation.' Uniform with the above. Cloth limp, 1s. 9d.

The large type editions of the above two works, in extra binding, red edges, 3s., may still be had.

A Second Edition of 'The Rich Man and Lazarus.' A Practical Exposition. Large type, cloth boards, 1s. 6d.; antique, 2s.

The Unseen Guide; or, Stories and Allegories to Illustrate the Fruits of the Spirit. By M. and E. B. With Twelve Illustrations by the Brothers Dalziel. Second Edition; with Introduction by Miss CHARLESWORTH, Author of 'Ministering Children.' Small 4to, emblematic cloth, 3s. 6d.

Ninth Edition of 'Hymns for the Church on Earth.' Being Three Hundred Hymns, for the most part of Modern Date. Selected and arranged by the Rev. J. C. RYLE, B.A.
    In small 8vo, black cloth, red edges, 4s.
    Violet, limp cloth, 4s.
    Black antique, 4s. 6d.
    Violet, and extra cloth antique, gilt edges, 5s.
    Turkey morocco, 10s. 6d., 12s., and antique 16s. 6d.

New Editions of 'Home Truths.' Being the Miscellaneous Writings of the Rev. J. C. RYLE, B.A., Revised. Fcap. 8vo, extra cloth, lettered. Seven Series, each complete, with Frontispiece and Vignette Title. 3s. 6d. each volume.

New Editions of 'Expository Thoughts on the Gospels.' Designed especially for Family and Private Reading; with the Text complete. By the Rev. J. C. RYLE, B.A.
    ST. MATTHEW. Complete in one volume. 6s., cloth.
    ST. MARK. Uniform with the above. 5s.
    ST. LUKE. Vol. I. 5s. 6d.
    ST. LUKE. Vol. II. 7s.
    ST. JOHN. Vol. I. 6s. 6d.
    ST. JOHN. Vol. II. 6s. 6d.
    ST. JOHN. Vol. III. In course of publication.

This work is also kept in half morocco, at an excess of 3s. per volume; in extra half morocco binding, at 5s. 6d.; or whole turkey morocco, 6s. 6d. per volume.

For Me, and My House: A Manual of Devotions for Family Use. With a short Series of Prayers in Scriptural Language, selected from the Book of the Psalms of David. By the Rev. A. R. LUDLOW, M.A., formerly of Oriel College. Cloth boards, 1s. 6d.

LONDON: WILLIAM HUNT & COMPANY,
23, HOLLES STREET, W.

T. and T. Clark's Publications.

Just published, in demy 8vo, price 10s. 6d.,

THE DOCTRINE OF THE ATONEMENT,

AS TAUGHT BY THE APOSTLES; OR, THE SAYINGS OF THE APOSTLES EXEGETICALLY EXPOUNDED.

By Rev. GEORGE SMEATON, D.D.,
Professor of Exegetical Theology, New College, Edinburgh.

BY THE SAME AUTHOR.

In demy 8vo, price 10s. 6d.,

THE DOCTRINE OF THE ATONEMENT,

AS TAUGHT BY CHRIST HIMSELF; OR, THE SAYINGS OF JESUS ON THE ATONEMENT EXEGETICALLY EXPOUNDED AND CLASSIFIED.

Just published, Third Edition, revised and enlarged, crown 8vo, price 6s.,

THE TRIPARTITE NATURE OF MAN:

SPIRIT, SOUL, AND BODY.

APPLIED TO ILLUSTRATE AND EXPLAIN THE DOCTRINES OF ORIGINAL SIN, THE NEW BIRTH, THE DISEMBODIED STATE, AND THE SPIRITUAL BODY.

By Rev. J. B. HEARD, M.A.

Just published, in demy 8vo, price 10s. 6d,,

BIBLICAL THEOLOGY OF THE NEW TESTAMENT.

By CHRISTIAN FRIEDRICH SCHMID, D.D.,
Late Professor of Theology, Tübingen.

TRANSLATED FROM THE FOURTH GERMAN EDITION, EDITED BY C. WEIZÄCKER, D.D., BY G. H. VENABLES.

Just published, in crown 8vo, price 4s. 6d.,

THE LEADING CHRISTIAN EVIDENCES,

AND THE PRINCIPLES ON WHICH TO ESTIMATE THEM.

By GILBERT WARDLAW, M.A.

In Three Volumes, royal 8vo, price 36s.,

PROFESSOR SCHAFF'S HISTORY OF THE CHRISTIAN CHURCH.

HISTORY OF THE CHRISTIAN CHURCH.

By PHILIP SCHAFF, D.D.,
Author of 'The History of the Apostolic Church.'

From the Birth of Christ to Gregory the Great, A.D. 1—600.

T. and T. Clark's Publications.

In crown 8vo, price 5s.,

ROME AND THE COUNCIL
IN THE NINETEENTH CENTURY.

Translated from the French of FELIX BUNGENER.

Third Edition, in crown 8vo, price 5s.,

LIGHT FROM THE CROSS:
SERMONS ON THE PASSION OF OUR LORD.

By Dr. A. THOLUCK.

I. THE CROSS A REVEALER OF THE HEARTS OF MEN. II. THE SUFFERINGS AND DEATH OF CHRIST.

'These sermons have already attained a third edition, and abound in passages calculated to stir up the deepest feelings of devotion, and to awaken the most careless of sinful souls.'—*Rock*.

Third Edition, in crown 8vo, price 6s.,

THE SINLESSNESS OF JESUS:
AN EVIDENCE FOR CHRISTIANITY.

By CARL ULLMANN, D.D.

'We welcome it in English as one of the most beautiful productions of Germany, as not only readable for an English public, but as possessing, along with not a few defects, many distinguished excellences. . . . We warmly recommend this beautiful work as eminently fitted to diffuse, among those who peruse it, a higher appreciation of the sinlessness and moral eminence of Christ. The work has been blessed already, and may have its use also to an English public.'—*British and Foreign Evangelical Review*.

In crown 8vo, price 4s. 6d.,

THE PROBLEM OF EVIL:
SEVEN LECTURES.

By ERNEST NAVILLE.

TRANSLATED FROM THE FRENCH BY EDWARD W. SHALDERS, B.A., NEWBURY, BERKS.

T. and T. Clark's Publications.

In One large 8vo Volume, price 15s.,

A Treatise on the Grammar of New Testament Greek, regarded as the Basis of New Testament Exegesis. By Dr. G. B. WINER, Translated from the German, with large additions and full Indices, by Rev. W. F. MOULTON, M.A., Classical Tutor, Wesleyan Theological College, Richmond, and Prizeman in Hebrew and New Testament Greek in the University of London.

The additions by the Editor are very large, and will tend to make this great work far more useful and available for *English* students than it has hitherto been. The Indices have been greatly enlarged; and, as all students will admit, this is of vast importance. Altogether, the Publishers do not doubt that this will be the Standard Grammar of New Testament Greek.

'We gladly welcome the appearance of Winer's great work in an English translation, and most strongly recommend it to all who wish to attain to a sound and accurate knowledge of the language of the New Testament. We need not say it is *the* Grammar of the New Testament. It is not only superior to all others, but *so* superior as to be by common consent the one work of reference on the subject. No other could be mentioned with it.'—*Literary Churchman.*

Just Published, in Two Volumes, 8vo, price 21s.,

A Critical and Exegetical Commentary on the Acts of the Apostles. By P. J. GLOAG, D.D., Minister of Blantyre.

'It is a concise, scholarly, and complete commentary, adapted pre-eminently for service in the ministerial study of that book which unites in itself almost all the elements of New Testament revelation.'—*London Quarterly Review.*

'We can speak very highly of this attempt. The learning of the author is fully competent for his self-imposed task,—his judgment independent; and his opinions are expressed with such self-respect and dignity, as to render them entirely free from the charge of dogmatism.'—*Wesleyan Methodist Magazine.*

'A remarkably good commentary. . . . . It is a sound, scholarly, and generally reliable work.'—*Literary Churchman.*

Two Volumes, 8vo, price 21s.,

The Church of Christ: A Treatise on the Nature, Powers, Ordinances, Discipline, and Government of the Christian Church. By Professor BANNERMAN.

'The general tone of the work is dignified, earnest, temperate, and devout. We heartily recommend it to the shelves of our universities and students of theology.'—*London Quarterly Review.*

BY THE SAME AUTHOR.

In One Volume, demy 8vo, price 10s. 6d.,

Inspiration: The Infallible Truth and Divine Authority of the Holy Scriptures.

In One Volume, 8vo, price 9s.,

An Exposition of the Epistle of James, with an Appendix of Dissertations. By Rev. J. ADAM, D.D.

'This is a thoroughly and carefully written work, and will be of much service to the earnest Christian reader, inasmuch as it throws light upon the meaning of many, at first sight, obscure passages, and points out what may reasonably be presumed to be the under current of thought and purpose which renders this Epistle at once so beautiful and so complete. We have much pleasure in commending this volume to the notice of our readers.'—*Christian Observer.*

In 8vo, price 10s. 6d.,

Commentary on the Greek Text of the Epistle of Paul to the Galatians. By Professor EADIE.

'A full and elaborate commentary on the Epistle to the Galatians. Dr. Eadie has had no common task before him, but he has done the work remarkably well.'—*Contemporary Review.*

Ante-Nicene Christian Library.

A COLLECTION OF ALL THE WORKS OF THE FATHERS OF THE CHRISTIAN CHURCH, PRIOR TO THE COUNCIL OF NICÆA,

EDITED BY THE

REV. ALEXANDER ROBERTS, D.D.,
Author of 'Discussions on the Gospels,' etc.,

AND

JAMES DONALDSON, LL.D.,
Rector of the Royal High School, Edinburgh, and Author of 'Early Christian Literature and Doctrine.'

MESSRS. CLARK are now happy to announce the near completion of this Series. It has been received with marked approval by all sections of the Christian Church in this country and in the United States, as supplying what has long been felt to be a want, and also on account of the impartiality, learning, and care with which Editors and Translators have executed a very difficult task.

The whole Series will be completed in Twenty-four Volumes, of which Eighteen are ready, and the remaining Six will be published in the course of this year.

Each Work is supplied with a good and full Index; but, to add to the value of the completed Series, an Index Volume is preparing for the whole Series, which will be sold separately to those who may desire it, at a moderate price; and the complete Series (exclusive of General Index), in Twenty-four Volumes, will cost Six Guineas.

The Subscription for 1st, 2d, 3d, 4th, and 5th Years is now due—£5, 5s.
The Subscription to the Series is at the rate of 21s. for Four Volumes when paid in advance (or 24s. when not so paid), and 10s. 6d. each Volume to Non-Subscribers.

The Publishers, however, do not bind themselves to *continue* to supply the complete Series at this rate.

Single Years cannot be had separately, with the exception of current year, unless to complete sets, but *any Volume* may be had separately, price 10s. 6d.

The Homilies of Origen are not included in the Series, as the Publishers have received no encouragement to have them translated.

T. and T. Clark's Publications.

ANTE-NICENE CHRISTIAN LIBRARY—*continued.*

The Works are arranged as follow:—

FIRST YEAR.

APOSTOLIC FATHERS, comprising Clement's Epistles to the Corinthians; Polycarp to the Ephesians; Martyrdom of Polycarp; Epistle of Barnabas; Epistles of Ignatius (longer and shorter, and also the Syriac version); Martyrdom of Ignatius; Epistle to Diognetus; Pastor of Hermas; Papias; Spurious Epistles of Ignatius. In One Volume.
JUSTIN MARTYR; ATHENAGORAS. In One Volume.
TATIAN; THEOPHILUS; THE CLEMENTINE RECOGNITIONS. In One Volume.
CLEMENT OF ALEXANDRIA, Volume First, comprising Exhortation to Heathen; The Instructor; and a portion of the Miscellanies.

SECOND YEAR.

HIPPOLYTUS, Volume First; Refutation of all Heresies and Fragments from his Commentaries.
IRENÆUS, Volume First.
TERTULLIAN AGAINST MARCION.
CYPRIAN, Volume First; the Epistles and some of the Treatises.

THIRD YEAR.

IRENÆUS (completion); HIPPOLYTUS (completion); Fragments of Third Century. In One Volume.
ORIGEN: De Principiis; Letters; and portion of Treatise against Celsus.
CLEMENT OF ALEXANDRIA, Volume Second; Completion of Miscellanies.
TERTULLIAN, Volume First; To the Martyrs; Apology; To the Nations, etc.

FOURTH YEAR.

CYPRIAN, Volume Second (completion); Novatian; Minucius Felix; Fragments.
METHODIUS; ALEXANDER OF LYCOPOLIS; PETER OF ALEXANDRIA; Anatolius; Clement on Virginity, and Fragments.
TERTULLIAN, Volume Second.
APOCRYPHAL GOSPELS; ACTS AND REVELATIONS, comprising all the very curious Apocryphal Writings of the first Three Centuries.

FIFTH YEAR.

TERTULLIAN, Volume Third (completion).
CLEMENTINE HOMILIES; APOSTOLICAL CONSTITUTIONS. In One Volume.
ARNOBIUS.
DIONYSIUS; GREGORY THAUMATURGUS; SYRIAN FRAGMENTS. In One Volume.
(ARNOBIUS and DIONYSIUS, etc., in April.)

SIXTH YEAR (to be ready in 1871).

LACTANTIUS. Two Volumes.
ORIGEN, Volume Second (completion).
EARLY LITURGIES AND REMAINING FRAGMENTS.

LANGE'S
Commentaries on the Old and New Testaments.

MESSRS. CLARK have now pleasure in intimating their arrangements, in conjunction with the well-known firm of SCRIBNER AND CO., of New York, and under the Editorship of Dr. PHILIP SCHAFF, for the Publication of Translations of the Commentaries of Dr. LANGE and his *Collaborateurs*, on the Old and New Testaments.

Of the OLD TESTAMENT, they have published the

COMMENTARY ON THE BOOK OF GENESIS, One Volume,
imperial 8vo, to which is prefixed a Theological and Homiletical Introduction to the Old Testament, and a Special Introduction to Genesis. By Professor TAYLER LEWIS, LL.D., comprising Excursus on all the chief subjects of Controversy.

COMMENTARY ON PROVERBS, ECCLESIASTES, AND THE SONG OF SOLOMON, in One Volume. By OTTO ZÖCKLER, D.D., Professor of Theology at Greisswald.

They will publish (about April),

COMMENTARY ON JEREMIAH AND LAMENTATIONS,
in One Volume. By Dr. C. W. E. NAGELSBACH.

Other Volumes on the Old Testament are in active preparation, and will be announced as soon as ready.

Messrs. CLARK have already published in the FOREIGN THEOLOGICAL LIBRARY the **Commentaries on St. Matthew, St. Mark, St. Luke,** and the **Acts of the Apostles.** They propose to issue in the same form the **Commentary on St. John's Gospel,** which will not, however, be ready for some time.

There are now ready (in imperial 8vo, double column),

COMMENTARY ON THE EPISTLE OF ST. PAUL TO THE ROMANS. By J. P. LANGE, D.D., and F. R. FAY. Revised, Enlarged, and Edited by Dr. SCHAFF.

COMMENTARY ON THE EPISTLE OF ST. PAUL TO THE CORINTHIANS. By C. F.KLING, D.D.

T. and T. Clark's Publications.

Lange's Commentaries on the Old and New Testaments
—*CONTINUED.*

COMMENTARY ON THE EPISTLE OF ST. PAUL TO THE
GALATIANS, by OTTO SCHMOLLER, P.D. EPHESIANS, PHILIPPIANS, and COLOSSIANS, by KARL BRAUNE, D.D. In One Volume.

COMMENTARY ON THE EPISTLES TO THE THESSA-
LONIANS, by Professor AUBERLEN and RIGGENBACH. On the Epistles to TIMOTHY, TITUS, and PHILEMON, by Professor VAN OOSTERZEE. On the Epistle to the HEBREWS, by C. M. MOLL, D.D. In One Volume.

COMMENTARY ON THE EPISTLE OF JAMES, by Prof.
VAN OOSTERZEE. On the Epistles of PETER, by C. F. FRONMULLER, Ph.D. On the Epistles of JOHN, by K. BRAUNE, D.D. On the Epistle of JUDE, by C. F. FRONMULLER, Ph.D. In One Volume.

The New Testament is thus complete, with the exception of the Commentary on St. John's Gospel and on the Book of Revelation, which are in progress.

The Commentaries on Matthew, in one volume; Mark and Luke, in one volume; and on Acts, in one volume, may be had uniform with the above if desired.

Each of the above volumes (three on Old Testament and five on Epistles) will be supplied to Subscribers to the FOREIGN THEOLOGICAL LIBRARY and ANTE-NICENE LIBRARY, or to Purchasers of complete sets of Old Testament (so far as published), and of Epistles, at 15s. The price to others will be 21s. each volume.

Dr. Lange's Commentary on the Old and New Testaments is the combined labour of a large number of the most able and distinguished scholars and divines of Europe, who have spared no pains to make it the standard commentary of Christendom. Dr. Schaff is being assisted by several of the most eminent scholars in the United States, among whom are Professors Shedd, Yeomans, Hackett, Kendrick, Day, Drs. Poor, Schaeffer, and Tayler Lewis, and has made large and valuable additions, comprising nearly one-third more matter than the original German. It thus combines the united evangelical scholarship of Europe and America, and is a commentary truly scholarly and learned, yet popular, orthodox, and sound in the evangelical sense, and yet unsectarian and liberal, and catholic in spirit and aim, combining with original research the most valuable results of the exegetical labours of the past and the present, and making them available for the practical use of the clergy and the general good of the Church. No minister's or layman's library will be complete without it.

'It is with no common feelings of gratification that we note the progress of this truly noble work of Dr. Lange's through the press. There is no commentary in our language at all to compare with it in fulness, availableness, and scholarly care. . . . Those who have been turned away from buying or using it by reason of its bulk, or its look as a compilation, have lost much thereby. The series combines in quite an unexampled way original scholarship of the first order, with doctrinal and homiletical matter of a very rich and varied character.'—*Presbyterian.*

The Works of St. Augustine.

MESSRS. CLARK beg to announce that they have in preparation Translations of a Selection from the WRITINGS of ST. AUGUSTINE, on the plan of their ANTE-NICENE LIBRARY, and under the editorship of the Rev. MARCUS DODS, A.M. They append a list of the works which they intend to include in the Series, each work being given entire, unless otherwise specified.

The First Issue will comprise an entirely New Translation of

THE CITY OF GOD,

in Two Volumes, and will be ready about May.

All the TREATISES in the PELAGIAN, and the four leading TREATISES in the DONATIST CONTROVERSY.

The TREATISES against FAUSTUS the Manichæan; on CHRISTIAN DOCTRINE; the TRINITY; the HARMONY OF THE EVANGELISTS; the SERMON ON THE MOUNT.

Also the LECTURES on the GOSPEL OF ST. JOHN, the CONFESSIONS, a SELECTION from the LETTERS, the RETRACTATIONS, the SOLILOQUIES, and SELECTIONS from the PRACTICAL TREATISES.

All these works are of first-rate importance, and only a small proportion of them have yet appeared in an English dress. The SERMONS and the COMMENTARIES ON THE PSALMS having been already given by the Oxford Translators, it is not intended, at least in the first instance, to publish them.

The Series will include a LIFE OF ST. AUGUSTINE, by ROBERT RAINY, D.D., Professor of Church History, New College, Edinburgh.

The Series will probably extend to Sixteen Volumes. The Publishers will be glad to receive the *Names* of Subscribers, as early as possible.

SUBSCRIPTION: Four Volumes for a Guinea, *payable in advance*, as in the case of the ANTE-NICENE SERIES.

It is understood that Subscribers are bound to take at least the books of the first two years. Each Volume will be sold separately at (on an average) 10s. 6d. each Volume.

www.ingramcontent.com/pod-product-compliance
Lightning Source LLC
Chambersburg PA
CBHW051734300426
44115CB00007B/562